Poet
of the Ghetto

Morris Rosenfeld מאָריס ראָזענפעלד
1862 ~ 1923

Poet
of the Ghetto
MORRIS ROSENFELD

———❖———

Edgar J. Goldenthal

Ktav Publishing House
Hoboken, New Jersey

Library of Congress Cataloging-in-Publication Data

Goldenthal, Edgar J.
    Poet of the ghetto : Morris Rosenfeld / Edgar J. Goldenthal.
        p. cm.
    Includes a selection of Rosenfeld's Yiddish poems with English
translation, of his poems written in English, and of his short stories and
other prose in translation.
    Includes bibliographical references.
    ISBN 0–88125–600–5
    1. Rosenfeld, Morris, 1862–1923—Criticism and interpretation.
2. Yiddish poetry—History and Criticism. 3. Rosenfeld, Morris,
1862–1923— Translations into English. 4. Rosenfeld, Morris, 1862–1923.
Poems. English & Yiddish. Selections. II. Rosenfeld, Morris, 1862–1923.
Selections. English. 1998 III. Title.
PJ5129.R6Z76 1998
839'.113–dc21   97-40778
                                                                      CIP

Manufactured in the United States of America
KTAV Publishing House, 900 Jefferson Street, Hoboken NJ, 07030

*This book is dedicated to the only love I have ever known,
my wife,
Dr. Janice B. Goldenthal.
She has long been a civilizing influence
on one too easily driven by challenge,
conflict and ambition.*

Contents

Preface   ix

Foreword   xi

Acknowledgements   xv

1   Rosenfeld's Biography as part of the Immigrant experience   1

2   Antecedents, and Contemporaries in Yiddish Poetry   34

3   Yiddish Poetry in America   40

4   Rosenfeld's Descendants in Yiddish Poetry   71

5   Yiddish, Where It Came From And Where It Has Gone   83

6   Poetry, Its Meaning, Origins And Relation to Life   93

7   Criticism, Linguistics, Standards   115

8   Rosenfeld's Yiddish Poetry, Selected, With Critiques, Translations, Transliterations   135

9   Rosenfeld's Poetry Written in English   303

10   Rosenfeld's Short Stories, Other Prose, In Translation   327

11   Songs written to Rosenfeld's poetry, Photographs, Letters, Illustrations, Artifacts, Map Of Poland   357

12   Epilogue   373

Appendix   381

Bibliography   409

Illustrations

Copies of Two of Rosenfeld's Songs   357

Copies of artifacts, awards, data about his Centennial   359

Map of Russian Poland   363

Copies of letters to and from the poet including those by Rabbi Stephen Wise, Jane Addams, Upton Sinclair, Edwin Markham, etc.   364

Family Photographs, Rosenfeld and wife, son, daughters, parents   369

Preface

This book is a work of love and dedication. Morris Rosenfeld, a noted Yiddish poet who wrote in the crucial years that saw nearly two million Jews leave their centuries-old homes in Eastern Europe to emigrate to America, was a powerful and beloved voice in that milieu. He was a gifted and temperamental artist who gave joy and emotional support to his transplanted, troubled, oppressed brethren. If this were all he was to us we might not have felt impelled to write this book. But he was more. Rosenfeld was the maternal grandfather of Ed Goldenthal, the author. His aura as a man of greatness has been passed down wherever there have been Jews for more than a century.

However, until this book was conceived and begun, we had no real appreciation of the magnitude of Rosenfeld's talents and his contribution to society. Hence, the first sentence of its preface tells the story of this work: the more we learned of the poet the deeper our love and dedication to his memory developed. We discovered his background, his life history, his contemporaries, his problems (which had no solution) and the intensity of his talent. It was revealed that for every good reason, which will be amply developed in this volume, Morris Rosenfeld was indeed a Bard for His Time.

Foreword

One might well ask what impels a newly-retired professional from another field to write about a poet of a by-gone era and a world we only recognize by hearsay. In the five years it has taken us to research and write this book we have been exposed to what used to be called a congeries of data about someone who would have seemed the unlikeliest candidate for "Poet Of The Ghetto", for social activist and a reputation for fearless dedication to his immigrant brethren. There is something compelling about his persona, about his intensity and his recognition of the requirements and demands of those who ran from a land of oppression to the expansive, exciting America that still attracts the brave and the lovers of freedom. Coming from a nowhere-land he somehow developed the idea of becoming a poet when he must have known he was doomed to a life of penury. There is a difficulty in considering Rosenfeld objectively as a poet because we have become immersed in his personal and ethnic history, which have so affected his works. It is not that one cannot study his writing objectively the way we might those of Poe or Coleridge. It is that by learning so much about his personality and struggles with life itself, perhaps more than the usual degree of subjectivity in discussing his life and motivations may have crept into our appreciation. If we had known Poe or Coleridge personally and studied their lives as scrupulously as we have this poet then we might have an added dimension to our understanding of their works as well. Every effort has been made, however, to strike a fair balance. It is possible also that we may have extracted and brought to light the almost secret ingredients that produce greatness in a poet.

In an effort to develop a holistic study, this book will be composed of many sections. In advance it must be admitted that one man's dedication may be another man's boredom. One man's love can be another's unconcern. The author has the considered opinion that the study of a significant individual requires a broad-ranging research of his biography. Who was he, where did he come from, who were his antecedents, his contemporaries and his descendants in literature. It had to be learned what kind of language Yiddish is (where did it come from and where has it gone?). It was necessary to pry into the mindset and culture of the Jews of Eastern Europe and follow them on their tortuous road to the New World and to explore the effects of their painful odyssey. It was essential to read about the lives and to read some of the works of those poets who wrote in Yiddish before, during and after the years in which Rosenfeld wrote. One could be appalled by the viciousness of some of his critics, but this was countered by the new-found information that so many men and women supported and admired the little tailor-become-poet who lived in a world that was "too much with him, late and soon."

In an unusual method for discussing the talents of our poet and placing the origins of his poetic impulses in a category of creativity comparable with other writers, chapters on "Poetry" and on "Criticism" are included here. Rather than being boring attempts at pedantry, these chapters dig into the psychological and historical proclivities of poets and place the art of criticism where it belongs. Much time has been spent on the subject of criticism as an art form in itself, studying various standards and discussing the true nature of criticism as a basically subjective modality. And after all of that is done, an attempt has been made to criticize Rosenfeld's poetry and some of his prose by the reasonable standards we set out for those of our readers who live in our time of history. Also, we make an effort to establish some psychological understanding of Rosenfeld's persona in an attempt to describe the parameters of normalcy and creativity and Rosenfeld's location within those parameters.

Janice Goldenthal is more than the wife of the author. She is a newly-retired professor of English literature at Fairleigh Dickinson University in New Jersey. She has devoted much of her time and intellectual energy reading and editing this manuscript. Janice has the training and disposition to be objective in her critiques. Ed Goldenthal has to admit that his passions run deep and afar, possibly as a genetic contribution of "his grandfather, the poet!" Hence, the editorial "we" includes the presence of the ubiquitous Dr.

Janice Goldenthal, who used her brakes on the emotional Ed, seeing to it that he does not get "carried away", just as she applies them in "real life."

The poetry and prose writings of Rosenfeld take up many volumes. In this volume we shall include many of his poems, (poems in Yiddish and in English) some prose, numerous photographs and even a map of Poland. There will be included songs and lyrics that he wrote, letters to and from people of note and other artifacts to help make this a definitive exposition on the life and works of Morris Rosenfeld. We suggest that if you find yourself interested enough to read all this it is because Rosenfeld and his story are a solid piece of Americana. You may not have any affinity for Jewish history, or poetry, or the immigrant experience. You may also have no familiarity with the Yiddish language, but . . . aaaah . . . there's the rub! Yiddish is the real connection here. That most expressive, intensely personal, variegated and almost hilarious language is the clue to Rosenfeld and his success. He was its master. He elevated it to poetic heights. He and his language are worth reading and writing about.

Acknowledgments

Anyone who writes about an earlier generation, of deeds and creations of notables of the past, owes them all a debt of gratitude for the joy of their works, for the accumulation of data and observation that has deepened our well of knowledge. In writing about the poet Morris Rosenfeld we owe, most of all, an immeasurable debt to Dr. Leon Goldenthal, author of the Rosenfeld biography, "Toil and Triumph". Leon Goldenthal was more than a mere "son-in-law" of the poet, having married Rose, the poet's youngest daughter and the mother of Ed Goldenthal, this book's author. Leon and his father, Prof. Isaac Goldenthal, had read and revered the poetry of Rosenfeld since their years in Rumania at the turn of the Century. Leon had read Rosenfeld in Yiddish, German and Rumanian before he ever came to America in 1909. He dedicated years of his time to research and to create an authentic biography of the poet in 1960.

Leon was appointed custodian of Rosenfeld's effects after the poet's demise and so had a wealth of material to work from. When he had completed his book he donated many books, photographs and written data to the YIVO, (The Jewish Research Institute in New York City). When Dr. Leon Goldenthal wrote Rosenfeld's biography he included a number of "imaginary conversations", to round out his story. When the publisher saw that he said, "Leon, how do you know what Rosenfeld said to his wife in bed after he had spoken with Theodore Herzl," Leon replied, "Well, I simply extrapolated!" "You'd better call this book a novel, instead of a biography!", said the publisher. And so Leon had to reshape his book into novel form, leaving out much material that would be utterly out of place in a novel but perfect for a biography. We have included much of that previously unpublished material here.

Rosenfeld had left a two-foot by four-foot galvanized metal trunk that stayed in our attic for years. It was crammed with writings that Leon spent years trying to analyze. To his kids they looked like hieroglyphics. Rosenfeld wrote on cheap yellow unlined paper which turned brown with the years and the trunk was full of poems, scribblings, uncompleted works and corrections of previous works. There seemed to be nothing but such paperwork in the trunk and Leon died with the secrets of what that trunk actually contained. Knowing that Dad's tastes in poetry were different from ours, we have never been certain whether he had not discarded unfinished poems, rewritten works that Rosenfeld might have planned to resubmit for publication or inferior poems that, even though not published, might have shed more light on the struggles of the great poet for a form of perfection. From Dr. Leon Goldenthal we also were left with a large number of family photographs that, surprisingly, we had never seen before, and some of them are included in this volume. Incidentally, many documents from that trunk were gathered together in some sort of order and donated to the YIVO for preservation.

We wonder if you can imagine the shock of seeing your own father's inimitable notes scribbled on documents lying in the recesses of the YIVO archives on visits there to collect data for this book. And how about finding a note written by your own mother when she was about seventeen years of age telling an important organization that her father had recovered from an illness and was able now to read his poetry on a stage again! There is *so much* deeply personal involvement in writing a book of this sort.

We acknowledge our pleasure with the charming book, "The Teardrop Millionaire", a brief biography that includes quite a few of Rosenfeld's best poems. It was written by Aaron Kramer, whose translations of Rosenfeld's poems are among the most creative that we have read.

There have been many translators of Rosenfeld's poems and we are indebted to them all. Among the very first were Professor Leo Wiener, Rose Pastor Stokes, Helena Frank, and then Abraham Reisin (who wrote delightful poetry himself), Oda Yudinston, Belle Robbins, Florence Halper, Henry Greenfield and many others. Much is owed to writers of "sourcebooks" about the history of Yiddish and about the history of the European Jews who emigrated to America. Among the most valuable books for us is Irving Howe's,

"World of our Fathers", which gave us a fully developed sequence of historical and literary events to draw upon. "Morris Rosenfeld", translated and edited by Itche Goldberg and Max Rosenfeld (no relation) was a sympathetic and valuable book for us to own. Much was learned about the notable Yiddish and Hebrew-writing poets of Eastern Europe from the books by Ruth Wisse. That lady seems indefatigable. We enjoyed books by her on Peretz, Bialik and Sholem Aleichem. However it was the modern translations by Aaron Kramer and Max Rosenfeld that are invaluable to us and some of them are included here.

The YIVO has made available to us the wealth of "Rosenfeldia" they possess from letters, music, books, photographs and other artifacts, to the use of their premises for studying and duplicating Rosenfeld's works of all sorts. In the appendix of this volume will be presented an abbreviation of the catalogue that YIVO sponsored on the centenary of Rosenfeld's birth, in 1962. This catalogue lists much data they had about the poet, his times, his critics and his supporters. One might spend a lifetime of delight in and among those old documents. We thank YIVO and those individuals within their organization for their care and respect for Rosenfeld and his Yiddish counterparts. And for those who feel, as they read through our book, that we are perhaps elevating Rosenfeld unduly, as though he were some sort of deity, they may rest assured that we have both feet on the ground and offer the YIVO summary as some vindication of our inspiration and interest in this subject. Certainly some of his earlier critics might have used a different tone had they had any inkling of the extent of his talents and achievements, especially in the face of the trials he was forced to undergo. For the aforementioned writers and for the host of other writers whose works will be listed in our bibliography there is a special feeling of gratitude and affection. They wrote objectively, as objectively as a Jew can write about his people. This means that the love and respect, the sense of peoplehood, the closeness of affiliation with Jewish creativity and the depth of understanding of the challenges and responses to historical and social pressures that the Jews have experienced—all these are possessed by the writers we mentioned. We do not merely use them to quote and note. We hold them close to our bosoms as "mishpoche" (family), and tears come to our eyes as we recognize our kinship with such responsible and loving writers about our people.

The translations by Rose Pastor Stokes and Helena Frank are from their book, "Rosenfeld's Songs of Labor and other Poems" and those by Dr. Leo Wiener from Rosenfeld's volume, "Songs From the Ghetto". Wiener was not a poet, so his book contains literal translations of the poems in non-poetic form. Even so, they are impressive. And now, after almost a century has elapsed, we must acknowledge an almost incalculable debt to Dr. Wiener, former Professor of Semitic Languages at Harvard University, who brought Rosenfeld to the world's attention, much as a miner might bring forth a diamond from the obscurity of a mountain of dross and hold it high to glisten in the sunlight. Proudly we thank Dr. Wiener for his recognition of Morris Rosenfeld as a great talent, for his urging and support of the down-and-out poet and for his efforts to publish and publicize Rosenfeld's works. As a special note, some of Wiener's descendants live in New England today and to them we offer our heartfelt words of respect and appreciation for their grandfather (and great-grandfather). He "discovered" our grandfather and for this we are deeply grateful, ex post facto. One of Dr. Wiener's immediate descendants is Professor Norbert Wiener, a pioneer in cybernetics.

If we were to attempt the penultimate linguistic study of Rosenfeld's poetry we would have to defer to Benjamin Harshav, whose brilliant tome, "The Meaning Of Yiddish" has no peer. Our intent has not been to create such a work of scholarship but to tap the fluid resources of men like Harshav, Hazard Adams and Irving Howe to broaden the view of Rosenfeld and the subject of poetry in general and thus increase appreciation of Rosenfeld and his works. We acknowledge our debt to those who have contributed letters, photographs and other data and even translations. We thank Dr. Paul Riebenfeld, noted international lawyer and Zionist activist who translated part of Rosenfeld's "Lieder Des Ghetto" from the German and brought out the brief autobiographical note which we include in its entirety. Paul also took time out from a busy schedule to read through and offer editorial advice for this book. Paul, an octogenarian, had received a copy of Lieder Des Ghetto, Rosenfeld's first great work, for his Bar Mitzvah in Europe.

Of course we love dearly and thank our aunt Frieda Iona Hurwitz, who died in January 1997 at the age of 104 and a half. She was the last remaining offspring of Morris and Bessie Rosenfeld. Just a few years ago, at about age 96, Aunt "Iona" spoke into a tape-recorder and answered a series of questions put to her by her daughter, Mrs. Shirley Paull and, on another occasion, to Leslie Paull Falk, who wanted to know what kind of a man her great-grandfather, Morris Rosenfeld, was to his family. There will be more on this topic in our chapter on Yiddish Poetry in America. We do thank Shirley and Leslie for those tapes and a few photographs. We also thank a cousin, Minnie Rosenfeld, for a collection of photographs and letters and even a copy of Rosenfeld's citizenship papers. We included all these papers in our original draft of this book until our publisher put his hand to his heart and turned a little gray.

It is only fitting to thank Rifka Levine for trying, with great humor and forbearance, to teach us Yiddish, and for transmitting, more than she realized at the time, the excitement and delight that comes with learning and speaking that fascinating language. In addition, Rifke also transliterated several of Rosenfeld's poems and supervised the author's transliterations (without laughing out loud even once!). We also appreciate Sandy Greenberg's translations of several of Rosenfeld's poems which we then re-worked into acceptable poetic form. Idiomatic expressions are the most difficult to translate sometimes. Dr. Neil Salzman, of Fairleigh Dickinson University, graciously read and gave valuable suggestions for the format and style of this volume, for which we owe him due thanks. And let us not forget the electronic wizardry and editing skills of our son, Dr. Michael Goldenthal, whose talents are a constant source of surprise to me.

We apologize if we have omitted credit for anyone who deserves it. Surely any omission is by error and not by intent. Permission has been granted to reprint by: Harcourt, Brace & Co., for quotes from Irving Howe's *World of Our Fathers*; YIVO for much of their catalog on Morris Rosenfeld's career; Aaron Kramer for a few translations of Rosenfeld's poems; Max Rosenfeld for translations of some of Rosenfeld's poems and short stories; Ruth Wisse for quotes from *The Best of Sholem Aleichem* and *I.L. Peretz and the Making of Jewish Culture*; and Benjamin Harshav for quotes from *The Meaning of Yiddish* and *American Yiddish Poetry*. Thanks are due for quotes from Edmund Reiss' *Elements of Literary Analysis*; Hazard Adams' *The Interests of Criticism*; Francis X. Connolly's *Poetry, Its Power and Wisdom* and Richardson and Shroyer's *Muse: Approaches to Poetry*.

1

The Biography of Morris Rosenfeld As Part Of The Immigrant Experience

This chapter will be much more than a biography of Morris Rosenfeld. It would be presumptuous for us to attempt a general biography of that poet here when that has already been done so effectively by Dr. Leon Goldenthal in his "Toil and Triumph." What will be written here is a biography of Morris Rosenfeld in relation to the Jews of Eastern Europe, in an effort to determine the personality of that people and how Rosenfeld fit into the Jewish history of his times. As with an individual, we want to trace where they came from, how they lived, what were the circumstances that impelled them to emigrate and the condition of the country in which they landed. We wish to discuss their mindset in such times and try to determine what place a poet, of all people, could have in such a world of turmoil.

Morris Rosenfeld was born, as were his parents, in the tiny town of Buksha, close to the small city of Suwalki, in North-Eastern Russian Poland. His grandparents hailed from a small town near Buksha but moved to Buksha later on. According to a map from the 1963 edition of the Encyclopedia Britannica[1] Suwalki is about 100 miles Southwest of Vilna (Vilnius) the capital of Lithuania and about the same distance Southeast of a small inlet of the Baltic Sea into Lithuania. Suwalki is situated about twenty-five miles from the borders of both Lithuania and Russia. It seems always to have been a fertile land but the physical location near the borders of eternally embattled countries must have been disquieting whenever the uniformed hoodlums who ruled these countries rattled their sabres.

Suwalki and adjoining areas, including Buksha, were the sites of numerous battles and pogroms. In fact, according to a word-of-mouth tale by Rosenfeld himself (to the family), on the day of his birth there was just such a battle in his hometown and the glass windows of his house were shattered while he was being born. What an entrance! Is this story true? Well, Rosenfeld was a master story-teller and a poet, so who knows where fact begins and fancy finishes. In Rosenfeld's first major work, "Lieder Des Ghetto", translated into German, there is a very brief autobiographical note inserted into the Foreword. This work of art was illustrated by the foremost European Jewish artist, Moses Lilien, and the book was edited and had a Foreword by Berthold Feivel, an eminent German Jewish writer. Our reason for including this brief autobiography is that, for many reasons, it is very revealing. The following, then, is Rosenfeld's autobiographical note:

"I was born on December 25, 1862, in the small townlet of Buksha in Russian Poland. My grandfather, my father and all who belonged to my family were fishermen. This small town is situated between the forest and the sea. I was still a child when my family had to move to Warsaw, where I was sent to the Cheder (Hebrew School . . . ed.) where I learned Talmud and a little bit of German and Polish. When I was eighteen I was married and went to Holland. There I learned and practiced, for six months, the trade of diamond cutting. From there I went to England. Here I worked for three years in the sweatshops of London. From there I went to America where I remain until today. It was in the damp, dark sweatshops of New York where I learned to sing of oppression, suffering and misery. During the day I worked and at night I wrote my poems. The workshop destroyed my health and I had to give up my work at the sewing machine. I then turned to journalism and was for three years a collaborator on the most important Jewish newspapers. My position only improved when the first collection of my songs was published under the title, "Songs of the Ghetto". This was in 1898. A second edition came out in 1899, published by Professor Leo Wiener of Harvard University. During the early times of my creativity I published, at my own expense, two small volumes of my poetry, in German, entitled, "Die Blumenkette", which means a chain of flowers, and, "Das Lieder Buch", a book of songs. Thirteen years earlier I had written a small book called, "Die Glocke", which was a failure. I was very young and inexperienced. At that time I was working in the sweatshops and I really had no time to review the poems.

Thus they were printed with many errors. Afterward I bought up most copies of the book and destroyed them. With this I have described my life in its most important lines."[2]

May we ask our readers, "Did you really read that whole autobiography? Doesn't it sound a little strange?" Here is an author who is presenting his chef d'oeuvre to the world, which grabbed up every copy it could get on three continents, and he writes an autobiography like a guilty little child. Just like a little boy who blurts out everything he has done wrong all day the minute his Daddy comes home from work, so Rosenfeld tells the world of readers about all his mistakes. And then some of his facts are wrong. He mentions that his home was between the forest and the sea but our map shows the sea over 100 miles from his home. Also, the book, "Die Glocke" was withdrawn from publication not because it was poorly edited but because he had entitled it "Die Glocke" unaware at the time that a famous German author had previously published a book of poems with the same title. He was mortally embarrassed.

His family moved to Warsaw for a very brief stay. Then they went to Suwalki. From Suwalki he was sent to Warsaw to live with an uncle for a while when a plague of some sort struck Suwalki and all thirteen of his siblings died. His parents sent him away until the pestilence ended to avoid his becoming infected. Incidentally, as representative of the superstitions of the time, his parents had given him a new name, "Alter" (the older one), so that the Angel of Death might not recognize him and thus he would be saved. He may have studied for a few months in Warsaw while staying with his uncle, but when he returned to his family in Suwalki he learned that he was now an only child. [Incidentally, as a special note, although it is difficult to prove, we think that the name of his uncle's family was Sukenik, which is also the name of a world-famous archeologist who later lived in Israel. The son of Sukenik was known in Israel as Yigal Yadin. Both the elder Sukenik and Yigal Yadin worked on the original Dead Sea Scrolls.]

Also, Rosenfeld was sixteen or seventeen years old when he first got married. When they removed the veil of his bride, whom he had never seen before, and he took one look at the "homeliest woman in all of Poland" he dashed headlong out of the synagogue and didn't stop running until he reached Amsterdam! Also worth mentioning is the fact that his mother secretly gave him some food and clothing when he ran away. She really loved that boy and we wonder whether she was in favor of that marriage in the first place.

Rosenfeld mentioned nothing exciting or creative in his life. Here he had already received a reputation as a fighter for the poor and the downtrodden. His poems and polemical articles had started to inflame the working class to action yet he writes this bland little note about his life. To quote Berthold Feivel, the editor, "It almost appears as though the poet, as a result of the overflow of suffering, could not speak in everyday language but only by the poems from which the tears overflow." When Rosenfeld or any other prospective emigrant desired to leave Eastern Europe the closest port of appropriate size to accommodate a large passenger ship would have been Danzig (Gdansk) the largest port in Poland, only 125 miles from Suwalki. However, few emigrants were allowed to leave from such a convenient port. They had to traverse the whole of Europe (Poland, Germany, France, the Low Countries) to get to a port that would accept them. For a near-penniless alien from a tiny rural town in Eastern Poland this trip had to have been the ultimate introduction to a nightmare. The trip by ship (steerage class, deep in the hot, sweaty, smelly, dank and dim bowels of the ship) had to have been Kafkaesque in its surrealism. Life in Eastern Europe had indeed to be unbearable for simple folk to be willing to undertake such a voyage into the unknown. The entire trip was a culture-shock to the sheltered folk whose traditions had bound them to a closeness they never even realized themselves. Every step of the way they were forced to endure changes in diet, sanitary conditions, impositions on their Sabbath observances and then embarrassments when being "examined" by officials at the ports of embarkation and debarkation. They saw sights they had never dreamed of before. There were railroads, mountains and the hurly-burly of massive old cities that were thriving with industry. And when they got to the ports of embarkation there came the fight to get on board ship. Besides the expected requirement of some sort of payment for the journey (the cost of a trans-Atlantic voyage in steerage was about $30) there were inevitable delays for available berths, occasional separation of families and, for some, the unfortunate news that they might never get to America because of mental or physical ailments.

They must have felt that they really *had* to leave the Old Country to be able to tolerate these inconveniences. They could not have been a weak people. They were stronger than they would have believed, mentally and physically. Their faith sustained them as it had for millennia of even worse conditions than these. Here, at least, there was hope. There was hope that here in America, here in the Goldene Medina (The Golden Land), they would be able to reestablish their traditional peaceful lifestyle. They hoped to renew themselves in peace and security in a friendly milieu.

By and large, their hopes were ultimately fulfilled, but under the duress of circumstances they did not expect. When they reached America there was overcrowding, a paucity of good-paying jobs, a shortage of decent housing with proper sanitary facilities and above all, there was a terrible confusion involved in the entry into a whole new way of life. Many people, totally unprepared for all this, felt as though they had leaped from the frying pan into the fire. There was a language problem, which, while it was not insurmountable, did delay the immigrants in their quest for acceptance, education and progress. Inability to speak English delayed them in getting better jobs, finding their way about the big cities, and worst of all, it gave them a sense of insufficiency, of "second-classness". As a matter of fact, the so-called native Americans (we are not referring to the American Indians here) did look down upon these immigrants with their strange manners, strange clothes and customs, strange language and strange faith. However, the Yiddish language, denigrated by German Jews as a "jargon", served a valuable function; it helped keep the Jews together, and this "togetherness" was more than just comforting and strengthening. It showed them all that they were not each alone in this "battle for survival." Their language was a unifying force that enabled them to educate themselves and maintain their morale. There was soon established a multitude of Yiddish publications to appeal to every type of Jew. Unlike other immigrant groups who came to America over the past 300 years these newcomers were a literate group. They could read and write Yiddish and Hebrew and most of them were at least partially literate in at least one other European language (Russian, Polish, Rumanian, Lithuanian, French, German or others).

But they simply had to learn English—in a hurry! So the newspapers and magazines that sprang up all over made it their business to inform people where they could learn to read, write and speak English. An abundance of schools was created, mostly by cities like New York, Philadelphia and Chicago. The German-Jewish community, which had arrived here fifty years earlier had assimilated greatly. They had thrived financially, which made it possible for them to help their brethren by setting up schools and settlement houses. They held their noses while they did it, but they did help.

There are so many ways of describing the sort of people who emigrate. Who leaves his homeland, his family, his employment (if he has any), his sweetheart, perhaps his wife and children? There are some who would criticize an emigre as a weakling, one who could not stand the gaff and just "ran away" to seek an easier life. One suggestion to such a critic would be to put himself in the place of the emigre, honestly to imagine how he would react to poverty, oppression, lack of civil rights, loss of employment, deterioration (or, at best, staticism) of cultural values, with lack of growth or excitement, paucity of secular educational opportunities, the clear likelihood that he might be drafted into the Czar's army (where Siberian-like rigors would be imposed for many years), the endless taunting by ignorant gentile peasants and military hoodlums, periodic pogroms with rapes, looting, destruction of businesses and, worst of all, absolutely no hope that things could get any better since they had been this bad for generations. That is quite a dismal picture.

Those who "ran away" also "ran to." They had a fair impression of the better life they could expect in America, with the distinct possibility that in a few years, once they settled into the new milieu, they could bring their families to this promising land. Many ultrareligious (and older folk) for reasons peculiar to their age or the static state of their culture, could not visualize the benefits of a change in their lives. They could not be blamed for having reservations about the new land. Two thousand years of Jewish history, which they knew only too well, testified to the unreliability of political promises. At least they knew what they had, and rotten though it was, they were willing to accept it. Some were also too weak physically or emotionally to take such a journey, or were just fearful. Many ultra-religious folk refused to make such a major move as a mass emigration unless the Messiah came and sanctioned it or improved their lot in Europe. With such an attitude, and knowing how often the Messiah comes around, you know they would actually never leave the homes they were doomed to inhabit.

It has been our contention that those who have the courage to emigrate are the strong in their society; that they will only strengthen and improve any society to which they move. Those who crossed the Bering peninsula to become the American Indians were indeed the strong. Similarly, one must admire the spirit of those those who came with the Atlantic currents on reed rafts from Africa! Unusually courageous and strong people were they, who founded the Incas as they mingled with the Indians from Asia. Thor Heyerdahl, in his own courageous experiments, proved that reed rafts, which he fabricated in Africa, were able to follow the natural Atlantic currents and reach the shores of South America. Bold and strong, too, were those who took ships and braved the oceans to come to America in the fifteenth and sixteenth centuries. The weak and the comfortable stayed home, offering every reason they could devise to avoid the dangerous sea-voyage and the hardships of colonization. The Korean, the Vietnamese and the Haitian boat-people, who arrived more recently, are the strong, the brave and the adventurous. They too deserve a better life.

When Rosenfeld himself made his exciting journey to America, he must have been perceptive enough to evaluate the strength of his fellow emigres. He could see the challenges here. He could estimate that for strong people the challenges were not insurmountable. For the most part, the Jews were healthy and determined. Dirt-poor they were, for a certainty, but poverty is not a genetic factor. Weakness, lack of ambition, mental defectiveness and insufficiencies of eyesight and hearing may be genetically transmitted. But Rosenfeld was young and one of a multitude of eager and determined people. This was one of the reasons that he never questioned their desire to work or live a full life. He never castigated the masses the way he did "the bosses" and certain politicians. He knew he was directing his messages of hope and incitement to political action to a people quite capable of taking their lives into their own hands.

This arousal by the fiery poet was responded to the way he had hoped. They loved his poetry and forensic skills. They read every polemical article he ever wrote and encouraged him to be bolder. Of course he overstated his sentiments many times, creating almost as many enemies as he did friends. But for his time, for that place, for those people, his was a voice that could not be denied.

In a further attempt to expand upon the "Biography of European Jewry" it is important to know that one of the precipitating causes of the mass migration in the late nineteenth century was the assassination of Czar Alexander II in 1881. This Czar, while by no means a lover of Jewry, was at least less hostile than other Czars and offered them a chance to spread out a little from the confines of the shtetl (small townlet) and farms to attempt a facsimile of the life led by others in Russia and Poland. His successor, Alexander III, however, eliminated the relative enlightenment of Alexander II and his reign was known for its pervasive repression and brutality. If the name "Czar" connotes violence and inhumanity it is in great part due to the type of ruler that Alexander III epitomizes. Jewish life became intolerable. Simply to recite the fact that Russia and Poland lost so many people due to emigration does not express the depth of the loss to Russia.

All those creative, honorable non-violent individuals, who might have become valuable citizens of Russia but instead were forced to leave, were a brain-drain and a creative loss that is incalculable. If one just thinks of some of the Russian-Polish Jews whose families came to America, this brief list would emphasize that fact: Woody Allen, the Gershwins, Abe Burroughs, Felix Rohatyn, Justice Goldberg, Irving Berlin, Benny Goodman, Artie Shaw, Bob Dylan, Milton Berle, Chaim Gross, Louise Nevelson, Mark Rothko, Saul Bellow, Henry Roth, Ben Shahn, The Soyers, Geo. S. Kaufman, Jascha Heifetz, Arthur Miller, Jacob Epstein, Abbie Hoffman, Lennie Bruce, Harry James, Lee J. Cobb, Senator Goldwater, George Burns, Mike Nichols, Mort Sahl, Martin Balsam, Goldwyn and Mayer, Alan King, Richard Rodgers, Kirk Douglas, Ed Asner, Mel Allen, Judy Holliday, Billy Crystal, Clifford Odets, Sidney Hook, Jan Peerce, David Sarnoff, Lionel Trilling, The Three Stooges, Simon & Garfunkle, Elliot Gould, Barbra Streisand, William Shatner, Dagobert Runes, Gloria Steinem, Betty Friedan, Peter Falk, Phil Silvers, Sylvia Sidney, John Garfield, Debra Winger, Smith & Dale, Red Buttons, Jo Davidson, Ed Koch, Senator Frank Lautenberg, Supreme Court Justices Ginsberg and Dreyer and millions of others have helped make America great and exciting. We are talking about artists and writers, businessmen and inventers, theatrical performers, composers, judges, publishers, tycoons, legislators and researchers. We haven't even mentioned your neighborhood physician and dentist, your lawyer and accountant and the man who owns your local market. They (and possibly you, too) might have done the same for the Russian empire.

From 1881 to about 1910, well over one and a half million Jews emigrated from Eastern Europe to the United States. They were unable to maintain their own Jewish culture in Europe in safety any longer. There were too many external pressures and their own desires created internal pressures that could not be denied any longer. They made their own way into American social life. We know from history that absolute rulers have absolute whims which lead to absolute repression and absolute prejudice. Jews had been herded into the "Pale of Settlement", concentrated areas outside of which which no Jew would be allowed to live. Not only were Jews economically harassed but they suffered legal and social humiliation. They were ostracised from public schools, libraries, colleges, courts, theatres, transportation and the arts and culture of their country so that men like Soyer, Shahn and other great artists were forced to seek a normal existence elsewhere.

Tightening and loosening of the bonds of repression allowed some Jews to accumulate a measure of wealth and success. Then the rulers encouraged their hoodlums to destroy the homes and businesses and steal the wealth the Jews had accumulated. Of course this is an old trick. It has been done everywhere Jews have lived since ancient times, most recently in Germany and in the Muslim countries. So what's new? The Czars also censored Yiddish and Hebrew books and took to drafting men into the Army as young as the ages of 8 or 10. Taking these youths led to their almost certain destruction. "Neither stability nor peace, well-being nor equity was possible for them."[3]

"Bound together by firm spiritual ties,by a common language and a sense of destiny that often meant sharing martyrdom they were a kind of nation without nationhood."[4]. The central trait of this culture was an orientation towards "other-worldly values". They combined the worldly and other-worldly in order to survive, knowing that there was scant justice to be expected. The Sabbath was supreme, a day dedicated to the Almighty. The life of people in this situation of poverty, oppression, humiliation, injustice and precariousness led to a form of sluggishness. A lack of worldly awareness developed because of their isolation. Theirs was almost a clotted life, with inbreeding and an almost animal desire to survive. The writings of the relatively few poets and story-tellers were a form of catharsis to the depressed millions. Scholarship and devotion to a life of goodness and gentleness, essential aspects of their entire culture, prevented them from deteriorating to the truly animal nature of so many other depressed cultures all over the globe.

Scholarship and mitzvot (good deeds) were honored above all,[5] since they led to Godliness and took their minds off the mundane to the glory of learning. Some of the extremists among the orthodox resisted outside learning and outside culture. The use of the term "outside" was carefully chosen. The confinement of a whole people to a limited area for all their human activities was much like a giant concentration camp. "Inside" was where they were herded. "Outside" was the rest of the world; not just secular reading and eating habits but a world of information, religious diversity, economic opportunities, relative freedom of thought and every temptation created by Man.

"Outside" secular books were not always allowed by some of the orthodox Jewry, as much a result of the ignorance and prejudice of the ultra-religious as a fear (possibly unspoken) that once the society becomes secularized the bonds of religion and community that have enabled the Jews to survive against all odds, against every persecution, would be loosened. And, of course, one has only to look at America's Jewish community now, where secularization is almost complete, to observe the beginning breakdown of Jewish culture and the near extinction of the Yiddish language. If infrequent attendance at synagogue services, infrequency of Yiddish or Hebrew scholarship, divorce, intermarriages, changing of names and loss of a real sense of identity had all been the goals of every persecutor, then here it is occurring as a result of total freedom of information and an almost total secularization of our society. If America is a melting pot one has to ponder whether the values and traditions that have been melted down are being replaced by equally strong, supportive values to gird a social entity, the Jewish population, which has always been proven vulnerable when times are tough and demagogues take power.

In fact, many second and third generation American Jews feel uncomfortable in the presence of some particularly observant Jews who wear the garb and have many of the "peculiarities" of some nineteenth and eighteenth century European Jews. We call them "peculiarities" because those Jews *were* peculiar, not to their own place of residence or their own time but to the outside world. It is true that anachronistic garb and customs can lead to prejudice and it is understandable that many nearly assimilated Jews feel uncomfortable in the presence of Chassidic garb and mannerisms. It is as though we were sayng, "Their behavior makes us self-conscious and draws invidious attention to us. We feel that perhaps it is not good for the Jews." There is something ironic about our feeling uncomfortable about the blatant self-consciousness of some of our co-religionists in a world that has been consistently mired in lack of understanding, greed, self-absorption and the guilt of violence and oppression.

When a writer discusses Jews of any era he must always have in back of his mind the nature of the milieu in which those Jews were living. In Rosenfeld's case the clouds of anti-semitism always hovered overhead, right next to the winds of adversity, which continually brushed against our ancestors. The absolute certainty that none but disciples of Christ deserve the favors of God led to the belief that none but Christians deserve the respect of man. This wrong-headedness has led to a persistent barbarism that Attila the Hun would have enjoyed. Whereas many orthodox Jews share a belief in a form of "God's chosen-ness" and would not allow themselves to come in contact with "goyim" (strangers) there are precious few instances where Jews were guilty of unprovoked violence or repression of others simply because of their beliefs. This quality of social responsibilty was brought to America and indeed to wherever Jews migrated. They knew full well that prejudice and inconsideration is a double-edged sword. Hence, Jews have always participated in socially constructive movements wherever they went. In Russia itself, when the Czars were overthrown, Jews were in the forefront of the Russian Revolution, not because they reveled in violence but because they thought the millennium had arrived. Excitedly, they thought that the beastly governments of the Czars would be destroyed forever, that Man would live to enjoy his life and the fruits of his labor in peace, equality and fairness; fairness to all religious and ethnic groups.

What they did not absorb at the time was the gruesome fact that it was not solely the Russian, Polish or other *leaders* who were vicious. There is an inhumane streak that permeates the entire Slavic ethos, from peasant to intellectual. We are not foolish enough to claim that this "streak" is genetically transmitted. It is simply that for thousands of years these people have been cruel and inhumane. Give it any origin you wish. What a dreadful disappointment it was for Russian and Polish Jews to see yet one more "millennium" evaporate in anti-Semitic violence and repression.

It took many American Jews of Russian and Polish background the better part of seventy years to have their eyes opened to the truth. Those in Russia, on the spot, saw it right away but were helpless to ameliorate it. In America and Western Europe, well into the forties and fifties of this century, there were Yiddish writers, poets, artists, proletarians, some of this century's most intellectually brilliant people, who had this myopic view of the land of their fathers. Unconsciously, under the warp of an almost messianic belief in the potentialities of communism, they often performed a disservice to broader-visioned American Jewish writers, such as Rosenfeld, who never fell for the totalitarian mold of the "millennium" and concentrated their efforts on the real "tachlis" (brass tacks) of making America a better, safer place to inhabit, with full equality, all the civil rights that they would never have in Russia, and an opportunity for economic success. "As it was, the shtetl (small town), nestled in the crevices of a backward, agrarian economy, was almost the only place in which the Jews could live. Prohibited from owning land they made a living by trading, artisanship and their wits".[6] Life in the shtetl was precarious for more than economic reasons. It provided an easy concentration of the hated Jews for the gentiles' persecution. Concentration for thousands of years (how easily the word 'thousands' pops out of the computer!) on the "unreality of life" and the "reality of God" and His awesome greatness as well as His personal involvement with them, led to a truly unreal situation. "Living in an almost timeless proximity with the mythical past and the redeeming future. . . ."[7] the Jews created a dichotomy of feelings. As the pressures of history bore down mercilessly on them they were even more determined to aver the goodness and generosity of their God. It was only when some of the outside world leaked into their almost hermetically sealed existence that ideals such as Zionism and Socialism assumed a new importance to these step-children of Fate. And there the first cracks in their faith developed. It was such a world that poured its millions into the large cities of the West. Strangely enough, it was from such a world that the greatest of Yiddish writers and poets arose, bearing with them the certainty of their beliefs and the vigor, the anger, the insistence that God helps those who help themselves. The Jews were exhorted, especially by the febrile Rosenfeld, to rise in their own defense and to assume their rightful place in the world. There were not really many such poets. A love-song is a love-song. A tree blooming in Spring is an eternally recurring phenomenon. Such were the topics of most poets, but not for Rosenfeld. However, to be on the spot when almost an entire people has been transplanted to a new land, carrying with them the cultural trappings of another time and another place, to be able to see the forest for the trees and to have the capacity to speak to these people in their own "mama-loshn" (mother-tongue), this was the crowning opportunity for Rosenfeld, and he worked at the challenge until it broke him.

It is an interesting fact that while God was prayed to in Hebrew, He was spoken to as a father in Yiddish.[7] These Jews put total faith in the Almighty until finally aroused to act on their own behalf. The Shtetl was essentially a lawful place to live in. The emphasis on religion led to a formalized way of leading one's life. There was a concentration on "mitzvot" (good deeds), and a respect for law and order and the rights of one's neighbor. The Hebrew Code of Laws attended to every aspect of life and death. This led to an essentially moral people living in an essentially immoral (and amoral) world. Of course some shrew would give her husband a hard time and of course there were people who would break laws (the word "goniff" is a Hebrew word for thief). Some men might not be reliable in business or in affairs of the heart. We are, after all, dealing with human beings. Some wag once remarked that Jews are human too, only more so. Yet when the Shtetl was destroyed as a way of life it was as though some force had killed a rare species of flower living in a hot-house. The "poisonous"air of the secular world really did what the orthodox feared it would do. It "infected" the community; but not all at once. Its effects became apparent over a few years. When the "Yidlach" (an affectionate term for Jewish people) came to our shores a whole new life was created. Most Jews placed themselves in self-created ghettos for security and from sheer loneliness. Not only individuals but the whole society had to master English, learn American mores, find out how to get about on trains and trolleys, get decent lodgings and a decent job and try to bring the whole family over from the Old Country. All this and much more filled the minds of the immigrants.

But how about their psyches? What was the emotional impact of this wrenching dislocation from an oppressive nightmare to a new world of confusion, poverty and disenchantment? We have not read much about nervous breakdowns, suicides, family violence and desertions but of a certainty there was all of that misery. There was also crime on the streets as there is in all over-crowded slums. But from what we have read there was minimal crime, generally confined to rowdy youngsters, but later on, gangs were developed by those who could not conform to social restrictions. There was surprisingly little mention ever made of vandalism, rape or murder, they must certainly have existed. However, we all know that soul-wrenching experiences such as the Holocaust (which came half a century later) as the mass migration of almost a whole people, which brought our grandparents here, had to leave permanent emotional scars which still show their effects in the last days of the twentieth century. The sort of personal post-traumatic shock that is visible in movies such as "Shine" and "Sophie's Choice" was visible to the tutored eye that gazed upon our families as they scurried about frantically trying to establish some degree of normalcy and security in their lives here in the "Goldene Medina" (Golden Land).

When Rosenfeld shrieked for fairer treatment for working people, when he grouched and grumbled about the abominable conditions the immigrants were subjected to he implied that they could rebel if they have to. They could try to get a handle on their own lives. And just the knowledge that a brave poet shouted that idea on the front page of a newspaper was exciting. That was supportive and instigatory in the creation of the labor movement which ultimately developed in his lifetime. Rosenfeld's writings often had a universal appeal, yet he would not have had the same results with a Black audience. He knew of and sympathized with their plight. But if he were to write a paean of arousal to the Blacks he would have had to know their mother-tongue, their colloquial expressions, their religion and their daily mores. He would have had to work as a field-hand or a day-laborer. He would have had to sense the intuitive responses of a people with a million-year history in the darkness of Africa. What did he know about Africa? He had enough problems just being a Jew! But with his fellow Jews he could play on the strings of their hearts like Ravi Shankar on his 12-stringed sitar. He knew which words and ideas, which aspect of their background in the shtetl, which aspect of their daily grubbing for a few cents would create the greatest effect. He knew because of what he was and his afficionados loved his attitude. He was a curmudgeon.

He never purred. He growled. He took on their oppressors for them and with them. Rosenfeld was a bard for his time.

At times the question of realism comes to mind when one considers Rosenfeld, his contemporaries and their forebears back in the now deceased Jewish settlements of Eastern Europe. How realistic were those Jews who gave their lives and souls into the invisible hands of an eternal Creator who was given anthropomorphic qualities by the downtrodden? They hungered for an all-powerful father-figure to control their lives in a world far out of control. All over the world people have resorted to similar devices in an attempt to cope with the imponderables of existence. So much of this sort of dependence upon a super-being verges on the purely superstitious that one can understand how peasants everywhere revert to violence against their "alien" neighbors when faced with the exigencies of life. Whenever there was a storm, a natural cataclysm or an infected well, they cast the onus for these events on the stranger living next door.

This is not an effort to excuse the ignorant for their ignorance or the violent for their brutality. It is simply that there are contributory factors for any form of human behavior, anywhere, and it would be healthier if we could understand them and possibly correct them. Of course we understand that human nature will certainly be corrected some day. ("Ven der Mashiach vet kommen" . . . when the Messiah comes, it will happen!).

We are led to wonder how valuable the sort of belief that sustained the Jews for so long elsewhere in the world can be here, in a different universe, where materialism, live-for-today morality and self-indulgence have been satisfactory for so many in this land of almost endless bounty. This is not really a foray into philosophy. The questions, however, should be asked, "Have the cultural values of the shtetl been rendered useless because of changes in a society and relocation of its former victims? Have, indeed, the problems of survival, personal and national, all been solved? Have the immense problems of greed, arrogance, violence and prejudice been eradicated for good? Are the values of the shtetl out of date ?"

When and if personal reversals and vicious social upheavals occur, as they do all the time, will those Jews who have shed the protective shield of their cultural heritage be able to cope as well as Rosenfeld's immigrants did? Rosenfeld and his fellow writers could reach into the psyches of their countrymen and sense which of the supportive and creative chords to pluck. One can not be certain that the cultural dilution that has occurred will leave enough of that "moxie" to respond adequately to the call for action should it be necessary again. Rosenfeld would have been furious at the number of Jews who act out their lives as though they were not a part of a "tolerated" minority. They do not realize that the Milkens, the Bugseys, the litany of brokers and lawyers and physicians and businessmen who practice over-indulgence on the fringes of indecency and criminality are placing the rest of the Jewish community in jeopardy.

Minorities must lead more exemplary lives, even as they did in the old shtetl. "But this is no longer shtetl living," you say. "This is big old America!" Sure it is, but how many of us are creating abundant "reasons" for the eternal anti-Semites to fear us and hate us? There is a madness current with the American far-right fringes. Have you been paying attention? There is a madness current with the Black activists lately. They are aiming straight at us. Those are real victims looking for someone to blame. Can you think of anyone who is handy? And weak? And, added to all those haters, the "skinheads" have gone international now. They look as nutty as Hitler did in his early days but that does not make them any less dangerous. These are not the best of times. It is great to be "assimilated" into the American prototype of everyone's dreams. But does that assimilation have to include loss of identity and disregard for those cultural attributes that were like the steel supporting beams in a skyscraper: invisible, yet there for any eventuality?

Rosenfeld wrote thousands of poems on every subject that could impact on the minds of his fellow immigrants. He wrote about love and death, marriage and family troubles, labor and problems of the workplace, loneliness and ego-trips, ambiton and laziness, religion and insecurity, nature and the creation of Man. What resounding chord of solidarity and moral correctness could a poet reach for now? Could he pluck the chords of religious unconcern? Of insider trading? Of over-charging patients? Of shady legal and real-estate dealing? Of crooked labor practices? Of political impropriety? Those Jews who wrote in the nineteenth century and early years of this century came from a simpler society, with simpler economics and simpler social problems. They seem to have had a far more moral society. They even had simpler goals in life. How could a poet, even of Rosenfeld's power and temper, reach the minds and hearts of today's American Jews? This question, this problem, is a natural evolutionary effect of the New World on Jewish History.

In the words of Ba'al Makhshoves, the pioneer Yiddish critic, "the Jew had an overly sharp intelligence which tended to laugh and jeer at the contradictions of the life he was leading. . . . In Jewish wit one can hear the voice of self-contempt, of a people who have lost touch with the ebb and flow of life" Rosenfeld did not share in this opinion because, however true it might have been for the inhabitants of the shtetl, where "in Jewish mockery one can hear the sick despair of a people whose existence has become an endless array of contradictions, a permanent witticism,"[8] in America the immigrants felt—no—they *knew* that once aroused to enlightened self-interest they could rise to the level of respected human beings, with all the opportunities and delight that this great country had to offer. Rosenfeld sensed this early on. As he travelled on lecture tours all over this country and to Europe he reaffirmed his positive attitude towards the future of Jewry in America. He did not discuss Judaism, the religion, but the ethnic salvation of his compatriots. As with most revolutionaries or social protagonists the intensity of his campaign took its toll on his disposition, his place in the community and ultimately, his life.

Rosenfeld, as has been described in the biography by Dr. Leon Goldenthal, never learned how to take criticism, however well-meant it was. He did learn to take advice on writing and on English when he requested it or when it was offered in the correct tone of voice by a long-standing friend. But harsh criticism, which every author, especially in the field of politics and social affairs must learn to deal with, was one of Rosenfeld's total inabilities. Rather than respond to one of Abe Cahan's challenges to one of his ideas or foibles or poems calmly and respectfully, Rosenfeld stormed about like a spoiled brat. And who was Abe Cahan? Merely the editor of the leading Yiddish newspaper in the world. Cahan was a prime-mover in the establishment of a socialistic approach to American society and he had selected Rosenfeld to be on his staff when his newspaper was in its infancy. He was an instigator of the labor movement without which most proletarians might still be working for "coolie wages" in the work-place today. Cahan was definitely not the man to alienate. Go tell that to Morris Rosenfeld!

An editor has a right to edit. A publisher has a right to publish. A critic has a right to criticize, even unfairly. This is a free society.

Rosenfeld could not abide even the mildest criticism, even from friends. Some might have said that his fame "went to his head". It did, but it need not have led to such self-destruction as Rosenfeld brought upon himself. How much the human psyche can take of the world's burdens is not measurable. He took up a heroic defense of the Jewish immigrants and the problems of the proletariat and these were almost too much to bear in the pioneer days of immigration.

The straws that broke him were the vicious, unwarranted attacks on him by "Die Yunge" (the Young Ones), a young group of Marxist immigrant poets. These writers felt, like true existentialists, that complete destruction of the past and the present is essential to the creation of the future. Well, they succeeded in destroying Rosenfeld, the Yiddish poet for his time. They "made nothing" of him. He fought back furiously, but he was intemperate, alone in his struggle, not at all judicious in his language or his manners, and he came out the loser in the battle. But can anyone (except students of earlier times) remember the names of "Die Yunge"? Can anyone quote even two lines of one of their poems or sing one of their songs? Does anyone look back at the mention of their names with the same open eyes of delight and reminiscence that we see when we mention the name of Morris Rosenfeld? With no exceptions none of Die Yunge graduated to a much higher level over the years. "Die Yunge" are a blip on the historical screen. But Rosenfeld is still known and quoted and some of his songs are, even today, sung and remembered affectionately worldwide, wherever Yiddish culture is maintained at all.

Jewish culture in Eastern Europe was, for centuries, a "hothouse" culture. Very little new thought came forth. Although theirs was not a totally ignorant society the Jews were limited, culturally, to the religious documents which regulated their lives, to the strong hands of their rabbis and to little else. There was little intercourse between the Jewish culture and the surrounding gentile culture except for those areas regarding trade, the exchange of goods and, of course, the legalisms involved in dealing with the emissaries of the ruling classes.

It was not until the mid-nineteenth century that a few brilliant writers burst upon the scene as harbingers of a new, creative cultural life for the Jews. Mendele Mokher Sforim, Sholem Aleichem, Chaim Nachman Bialik and I.L.Peretz led their people from a static, boring state to a more interesting, intellectually appealing condition.That is to say that these men had an effect on the intellectual life of their communities.They had absolutely no effect on the actual physical lives of their fellow Jews. However one wishes to express the idea, it was as though these men were an infusion of yeast into the dough that comprised the Jews of that area. Instead of being the flattened Matzo, "the bread of affliction" of the Hebrews in the ancient desert that Israel had become, this yeast had caused a rise in the creative spirit of the Jews and they "rose" to their destined height. The writings of just a few men created the ferment that was necessary and Israel in the Diaspora (dispersion) blossomed forth.

Once the "Bread of Affliction" became the "Bread of Intellectual Renaissance", a whole host of native writers, poets, musicians and artists appeared as if by magic. The effects of those writers plus the gradual seeping in of the influences of intellectual freedom from the outside world wrought wonders. How little Man really requires to arouse his subconscious intellectuality! This sort of intellectual "explosion" had a counterpart in Austria at about the same time. The Jews of Galicia, Austria and Hungary also lived in small townlets (shtetlach) and in rural areas, practically insulated from the outside world. However, when Franz Josef became Emperor of Austria in 1848 he took a liking to the Jews. "My Jews", he called them.

From that time forth until the fin-de-siecle, an astounding development of Jewish talent and creativity overwhelmed the nation of Austria-Hungary, concentrating principally in Vienna. By 1900 Jews were dominant in all the arts, in medicine and pure science, in politics and even in the military. Pages could be devoted to a mere listing of Jews who reached fame and success in Vienna, giving that city the reputation it so richly deserved as center of the arts and sciences of the Western World. To mention just a few who admitted to being Jewish there were Stefan Zweig, Herzl, Mahler, Gropius, Werfel, Kokoshka, Schoenberg, Webern, Freud, Roth, Martin Buber and Husserl, Siegfried Markus (who invented the automobile) and a host of "converted" but ethnic Jews; Johann Strauss and family, Max Reinhardt, Hofmannsthal, Wittgenstein, Felix Salten (author of Bambi), Scientist Wasserman, novelist Wasserman, Arthur Schnitzler, etcetera.[9] We are speaking here of intellectual giants who are world-renowned even today in philosophy, religion, inventiveness, music, literature and the arts, the stage and science, including psychiatry. How much hope this should provide for other repressed peoples all over the globe! Who knows what Einsteins, Da Vincis and Mozarts lurk in the untapped, unencouraged genes of the multitude of unappreciated people everywhere?

To list more would be informative but boring. Yet let us quote Benno Varon in his concluding lines of a charming article, "The Jews in Fin-de-Siecle Vienna",[10] "Once upon a time Vienna was the rendezvous of genius. It still is a very beautiful town and a baroque gem. But in the last fifty years it has produced only two names of international resonance, both politicians; Bruno Kreisky and Kurt Waldheim. The creative frenzy is gone. So are the Jews."

When Rosenfeld came on the scene the revolution of Jewish intellectuality was already stirring. He was writing songs and poetry and entertaining others with his rich singing voice in the 1870's. But at this stage of his life he was not professional in his talent, nor did he know exactly what he wanted to do with his life. When Morris, in his teens, went to Holland and thence to England and on to America he became exposed to Western literature and music. It is not certain who influenced him most in his style but it is a surety that he needed no prodding in his subject matter. A born revolutionary, with a fanciful, persistent manner, he knew he was destined to be of social importance. He was impatient (and probably inefficient) as a diamond cutter, a tailor, a clothes presser. His mind was like a bubbling soup, always cooking, creating a rich, deep concentrate to act as a source of exciting poems and songs.

How could such a mind be wasted on a pair of pants? How could he be confined to the imprisonment of common labor when he was soaring with eagles and singing with nightingales? By the time he had reached New York Rosenfeld had read many of the classics and been exposed to the music of the Masters. The music he wrote bore no resemblance to Mozart or Mendelssohn. He was not trained at all as a musician. But the intuitive desire to sing songs of love and adventure prompted him to create catchy melodies to which he wrote his own lyrics. Very few of his better poems were simple, frothy love-songs. Actually, he wrote so many hundreds—thousands—of poems that there were included many such "frothy" love-poems. But although scores of them have seen the light of day he is best remembered for his labor poems and his socially-oriented works. He sang to the beauty of May when Spring had fully blossomed, to the intensity of his love for his son and of his joy for life. He sang to the needs of Man and the deeds of men. He aroused their spirit with prolific paeans of praise for the possibilities of men if they would only seize the day.

Such a man, with such an ego and such a talent was Morris Rosenfeld. Once he saw that he was heard and appreciated he would not be denied. He fought that his voice should be heard. He took the newly erupted intellectual curiosity of the Jews and drove it even further from the shtetl. He also used his forceful voice to speak up in his poetry for the rebirth of the state of Israel.

Sooner or later we must get to the psychological aspects of Rosenfeld. Was he paranoid? Was his life an act of self-delusion? Was he as great as he thought? Was he a phony? Was he worthy of the adulation he received? Was he a "sick cat" living on the milk of human kindness and finally dying of his own internal poisons? Did the anxieties of his life produce an alienation that affected his perspective? These are tough questions and must be dealt with, since Morris had a reputation for being quite excitable when "crossed". Possible examples of answers are: What is normal and who makes the diagnosis? Is the diagnostician "normal" and who makes that diagnosis? (We must be Jewish: always answering a question with a question!)

The reasons for devoting this much time to the psyche of a dead writer are clear to us. During his lifetime and since, some writers, even a couple of his descendants, manufactured and even repeated stories about Rosenfeld's emotionally extravagant displays. These required some research and study. In addition, we realize that there definitely *were* instances in his behavior that begin to look like a pattern that had best be understood as rationally as possible. Was there something pathological in the way he would work for a period of months or years in the garment factories and then abruptly leave "because it was bad for my health." Of course we now know how bad it was for everyone's health—physical and emotional health. But did he start to cough and thus exhibit his fear of contracting tuberculosis, which had taken so many of his friends? We never found evidence of that. Did he experience inordinate tensions and leave before he had a nervous breakdown? That sounds sensible. Did he feel he was in the wrong field at the right time and wasting his life on irrelevant duties when he might be soaring with nightingales? Most probably this lay behind much of his dissatisfaction with menial labor. But how come he suddenly went blind (after the death of his son, "Mayn Yingele")? And then, when they brought and read to him copies of all the Jewish newspapers claiming that he had died and the whole Jewish community burst out in an effusion of sorrow, he suddenly laughed at the irony of the situation and made an almost immediate recovery from his blindness. Right after his vision returned he went off on a triumphal European tour. Was grandpa tricky or quite neurotic—or both?

While we are considering the question of normalcy we must take notice of the behavioral patterns of most of the world, where it takes very little arousal to get populations involved in diabolical riots, religious upheavals, inhuman prejudices and bigotry that denies normal access to the decent opportunities of life to billions of people. At this moment, in the waning days of the twentieth century there are savage impulses all over our planet including armed militiamen in our beloved United States. So when we discuss normal behavior we must ask who is really normal: you and I?

Which of the world's famous and talented were "normal"? Poe? Peretz? Thoreau? Whitman? Mendele Mokher Sforim? Sholem Aleichem? Teddy Roosevelt? Moses? Christ? Proust or Henry James? Crane or Dreiser? Strindberg, Ibsen, Tschaikowsky, Moussorgsky, Faulkner, E.E.Cummings, or Hemingway? Gertrude Stein, William Carlos Williams, F. Scott Fitzgerald, Kerouac, Baldwin, Updike, Roethke, Kafka, Schnitzler, Leroi Jones, Ginsberg, O'Hara, Sexton or Plath, the two Shelleys? Where are the normal ones among those creative minds? And why should a creative person be normal? Doesn't normal mean something akin to "average"? Can genius be average? Does an "average" person devote his life and his health (and risk that of his family) to writing as a profession? Does an "average" person risk everything to promote imagery, to create visible dreams, to fight for ideas and ideals which are the products of his own mind? (The Greek word for "idea" or "ideal" is, "a product of your own mind"). Let us put it another way: one has to be "unusual" to be a successful creative person and all those mentioned were indeed unusual, including Rosenfeld.

It is our contention that Jewish history, objectively considered, lends credence to a belief that it has been a neurosis-producing experience for a culture to be subjected for thousands of years to the opprobrium, even hatred, of most of the world. We cannot call it a civilized world yet. We have learned how to live as pariahs for thousands of years and not collapse under the weight of such a burden. Some warpage of our psyches must have occurred. In order to accommodate we must have bent somehow to support the burden of hatred and prejudice, of holocausts and external madness in our world. And we know that Rosenfeld had an ample share of personal problems in addition: enough to break many a stronger man. Was he paranoid or didn't he have his aged mother and father, a younger brother, a wife and anywhere from three to five children to feed and clothe and care for? All this on the earnings of a penny a line for his poetry! Were his enemies real or imaginary? Well, we know he was not fighting hobgoblins but entrenched economic entities who ultimately required federal legislation and long strikes to get them off the backs of labor. Were his historical enemies paranoia or is not Jewish history enough to convince anyone that the Almighty dispenses justice with an uneven hand? Did he not have a gang of existentialist youngsters taunt him mercilessly in public, denigrate everything he said or did, as mean and uncaring as only youngsters can be? Yes, his very survival and that of his family was challenged. So if we are reminded that Rosenfeld really had a terrible "temper", we agree that he did. He certainly needed it. In fact, a burst of temper is often considered more therapeutic than "keeping it all in!'

An interesting but important aspect to the question of emotional stability in creative people is the data provided in "The Abnormal Personality In Literature" by Drs. Alan and Sue Stone, and in a recent article in the "Discover" magazine. Here Jo Ann C.Gutin wrote a brief article entitled, "That Fine Madness". They were discussing, primarily, cases of genuine madness in relation to creativity. We did not find any evidence from Rosenfeld's writing, behavioral patterns or personal history to justify such a diagnosis as depression, manic-depression, multiple personality or other psychoses in him. And although we are not attempting to act as amateur psychiatrists, something tersely written in the book by the Drs. Stone may have struck the mark. In discussing the subject of "Neurosis: The Symptoms of Anxiety", they state,[11] "The neurotic classically suffers either from anxiety or some symptom which protects him from anxiety. He maintains contact with reality but has some handicap which both he and people around him recognize as unnecessary, unusual, or sick. He may be afraid of animals, of heights, of travel. Unexpectedly his heart may pound with terrifying fear of impending death; he may act weak and sickly or become blind or paralyzed without physical cause; he may wash his hands countless times, and so on." This is not the serious form of illness where one hears voices or claims communication with divine authorities, or claims royalty or divine honors for himself. That type of "loss of reality" is all too common and goes back in human history to all sorts of genuine madmen, to sorcerers, to prophets and mystics and "witches" and does not relate to any honorable Yiddish poets we can name, off-hand.

To conclude this foray into amateur psychological studies we can agree that one has to be stronger in mind and body than we comfortable folk might imagine to endure what our grandparents went through. And on top of all that misery Rosenfeld had to appoint himself as "mashgiach" (someone in charge of seeing that things are performed "properly") for the whole proletarian movement. He had to see to it that society behaved correctly for his fellow workingmen. That alone is quite a burden.

Perhaps we should thank the powers that be, if they are listening, for the creative folk who, regardless of the personal burdens they bear, color this grim vale of tears and who have decorated an otherwise frightening trail through this valley of broken dreams. Let us thank the "not-normal" for adding excitement and vision, design and liveliness to an otherwise repressive and depressing scene of hopelessness and of struggle against almost insurmountable odds. They have been trying to help us even out the playing field of life so we can all have a chance at some modicum of success and happiness.

Rosenfeld had his effect on his society. It grew the way he wanted it to. It responded to his goading. It learned to speak English, fought for its rights and won, and it became Americanized. It grew confident in the few generations after it left the shtetl and the humiliation of immigrant-hood became a dim memory. Rosenfeld stayed about the same; just older, more tired and more irritable because he was left behind. But he was the son and the father and the grandfather of Yiddish literature in America. He was as lost in the whirling-dervish-hood of America as this author is in the age of computers, lasers and interstellar electronics. His tragedy was that he lived on past his prime (at only 61!) and did not know how to handle it. Basically a simple man with a one-track mind, he was derailed and he crashed. But what a great ride he took us on for a while! He did not have a nervous breakdown. He simply had a stroke while resting in an overly hot, airless room after consuming two cans of salmon. (Do you see what can stay in someone's memory for seventy-four years?). Knowing what we have already learned about him the thought occurs that he was probably agreeable to a suggestion by the "moloch amovis" (the Angel of Death) that this would have been as good a time as any to leave for parts unknown. We would not worry about Rosenfeld's psyche or put him down because he was not "normal" the way you and we think we are. He was not a psychopath or a sociopath or violent or "loony". He was a creative personality with more than his share of tensions; with a drive and a dedication that one could envy. Some might say, "If he only knew when to call its quits." But then, he really wasn't a quitter. In a way, he was setting an example for his people: don't quit, regardless!

In the last third of the nineteenth century, as the fresh air of intellectual inquiry seeped into the formerly closed Jewish society, skepticism became a natural reaction to the blind faith that was the usual state of affairs. While it is true that for many centuries a certain degree of argumentative discussions took place with sometimes exciting variations on matters of religious interpretation, basically no one in the Jewish communities threatened the totality of Jewish religious belief. The essentiality of an unbroken belief was patent for all to see. Intellectual discussions centered on internal facets of the religion; divining hidden meanings, interpreting the intent of sages who wrote the disputed passages much as Constitutional scholars here in America debate the intent and scope of passages in the Constitution. There was no intent at all to discard the basic document or to allow some (possibly foreign) religious philosophy to replace the backbone of Judaism, just as there has been no desire to replace the backbone of our democracy with some foreign political system simply because there is intense debate over the nature of our beliefs. These internal interpretations have always been a part of Judaism—and American democracy.

But with the advent of true intellectual freedom for the Jews there ultimately became nothing sacred enough to be spared full inquisitive appraisal. Many aspects of social philosophies of the time and those of the early to mid-20th century were used as comparative measuring sticks for scholars, even laymen, to judge whether

Judaism "measured up" to the true needs of its devotees. Was the religion archaic? Did it respond to the longing for personal and intellectual freedom that was by then beginning to sweep the world? Was the use of a Deity simply an instrument to control the emotions and behavior of the Jewish people? Was it all a ploy for certain classes to remain in power in the community? And even deeper in question, was religion a device to hide from Man the true hopelessness and uselessness of his presence here on earth? Was Man's predicament so precarious that one dare not give him freedom to see it with uncovered eyes lest he bring destruction and chaos upon himself? Was that Biblical reference to the burning bush an allegory that Man had best not see what life really is? It may be left to us, if we wish the job, to sum up the total effects of such freedom. In the light of the past one hundred years we all know the devastation that has occurred worldwide, not to mention the even worse scenario that may lie in the wings. "What hath Man wrought" with his new-found freedom? Without question, the scientific, social and literary aspects of this freedom are nothing short of spectacular. But the ability of Man to control his own impulses, to regulate his own and his leaders' powers of self-aggrandizement, of self-indulgence and retrogressive acts of barbarity has not kept pace with his scientific accomplishments."Man's inhumanity to Man" and his destructiveness of the environment go on unabated.

Rosenfeld did not participate in the intellectual tension between the devotees of orthodoxy and the opposing impulses of skepticism. He remained the product of his youth, Jewish to the core. Although his religious observances were not known to be strict he never denigrated the right of others to employ any approach they deemed most fitting to get the attention of God and to impress Him with their love and fidelity. Rosenfeld was not a warrior on that battlefield. His arena was the political and social field where simple sparring and tentative formalized posturing were out. He was a gladiator, vulnerable as was Achilles, but he wielded a mighty sword: his pen!

Yiddishkeit was a way of life, a sharing by the whole community of the rituals, customs, all aspects of the mores and all the fears and the delights which in sum define the difference between one ethnic group and another. Yiddishkeit was taken for granted by Rosenfeld. When he wrote his expository poetry it mattered not whether the laborer or working-man was orthodox or a skeptic, whether he came from Eastern Europe—or elsewhere—he was the subject of Rosenfeld's attention. As far as he was concerned, religion is religion, but the brass tacks of the situation remained, for him, "Can I get a job?" "What are the conditions of my working place?" "Am I being taken advantage of by the Boss?" "Can I find a decent place to live, where I can bring my family, where are there healthful sanitation facilities, or must I live in this stinking hovel with an outhouse for forty people in the backyard?" *and*, naturally, "Will I be able to earn enough to bring my family over here from the 'other side'?"

These were Rosenfeld's concerns. The personal relationship of Jews with God was just that: personal, and did not really trouble him. He was Jewish enough to write poetry about every Jewish holiday, about the Holy Land, and about God in a cemetery, but even his love-poems, which on occasion contained Biblical references, would often also contain a "hook", a reference to his struggle as a working man, which endeared him to his public. How he would feel today, in what may be the twilight of Jewish identity here in America, might well be considered one of those key subjects that would have next absorbed his full interest and power. Certainly it has had that effect on at least one of his grandchildren, who rankles with that old curmudgeon's vigor at injustice and Man's lack of true self-interest. Grandpa Rosenfeld had a considerable influence on his descendants, which may be discussed a little later in the volume.

In regard to Zionism, that less than 125 year old political movement to establish a homeland for Jews in what was called (by the Romans) Palestine, Rosenfeld's relationship with that movement was not the usual one. Although begun in Poland by such writers as Moses Hess, Zionism did not "get off the ground" as a political movement until Theodore Herzl wrote and became active in the 1890's. The attitude of certain "educated" European Jews was not always favorable for such a political movement. In the 19th century a group of Jews arose known as the "Maskilim", the enlightened ones. They were a reflection of a general European movement, the enlightenment. These Jews had an unsympathetic view towards traditional Judaism and there was an impatience towards the almost apathetic view of Zionism held by the average Eastern European Jew. After all, the rate of "exposure" to enlightenment varied from area to area. There was opposition from certain deeply orthodox segments towards the scary new extension into world politics. The deference towards tradition was almost impossible to dent. Hence quite a few Jews, especially those who had become ardent socialists and many who had lived in Germany developed a hostility towards those who seemed "stuck" in traditional ways. Those who aimed to create a permanent Jewish culture within the Diaspora failed to explore a whole world of possibilities that existed on the soil of Eretz Yisroel, the Land of Israel, the Holy Land. And the Maskilim resented the apathy of so many of their co-religionists. Their attitude, while understandable, was unfair.

The inflexibility of Jewish tradition, the Yiddish language and folk-culture, the Jewish gift for accommodation and non-violent resistance, irritated the 'more enlightened' Jews who approached the Jewish future from a different point of view. Although Morris Rosenfeld took his Zionism seriously he came to it later in his life, by which time the Zionists had come to realize that if they were to "save" the Jewish people there must be an affection for those they wished to save, otherwise their efforts were to be an exercise of individual political prowess without regard to the historical connection with their own people. This sort of attitude has plagued Jews and their leaders, including in the present State of Israel, since time immemorial.

Rosenfeld suffered from none of these dichotomies in affiliation. His belief in Yiddishkeit (Jewishness) could never have been eradicated. His love, nay, lifetime dedication, to Yiddish as a language and to Jewish survival as a viable ethnic entity were paramount in the man's psyche. His love for his people was as the love of a parent, or a creator. He did not intellectualize his religion or his ethnicity. He did not find it necessary to choose which of his "children" should have his love and attention. His poetry was an extension of his heartfelt belief that Israel must survive. He knew that millennia of injustice and oppression were but the time spent in a crucible whose intense heat would serve to strengthen the temper of the Jewish people, enabling them better to persevere.

He never could have anticipated the degree to which the dilution of Yiddishkeit as a result of the commingling of Jews with all other types of people would weaken the identity of Jews here in America. It may be an unfortunate result of that wonderful freedom of inquiry and expression that personifies America. There is now an alienation from the Jewishness of the past, despite the sentimental procedures used at weddings and Bar and Bat Mitzvas. The loosening of religious and cultural ties has led to a breakdown of the fellowship that once was a solid, effective personal culture from which this minority could derive the strength to withstand any and every attempt to annihilate them. Rosenfeld unquestionably would have taken up his cudgels to fight yet one more losing battle. He would have enjoyed such a fight. As he did several times before, he would have made enemies among the good and the bad, the influential and the media, none of whom could have fought with more intensity to salvage what is left of Jewry. Perhaps his descendants could take up this fight. It isn't always the winning that counts. It is the effort, the sense of fulfillment that one feels in rushing to the battlements to hold off the foe—in this case the foe is annihilation by self-neglect. In spirit Rosenfeld is still alive in the hearts of many who share his impulses of justice and love for the Jewish people.

One result of the rise in socialist thinking in the late 19th century within the Jewish communities of Eastern Europe was an awareness of their condition, which became a key factor that stirred the masses of both city and shtetl to their consider possibilities, their unused powers. Socialism in those areas, at that time, was not really successful. Most revolts by paupered workers were against paupered capitalists; Jewish businesses and factory owners who themselves had dire limitations in their access to raw materials, capital, shipping facilities and modern technology. Revolts against Gentile firms were virtually unheard-of.

It was claimed by some that the dream of every proletarian was to someday become "a capitalist". This situation made it almost laughable to expect such people to work intensively in a labor movement. In many areas the socialists found that unionization was a puerile effort by people whose real intent was to some day be "A Boss" themselves. The labor movement there had virtually no success. The one thing that was undeniable, however, was that there would be no turning back to the deprivation that had existed for so many years. The move to leave the Russian and Polish shtetl received its greatest impetus from the excesses (the pogroms and brutality) of the regimes of Nicholas II and III. In a few years millions had left the East, mostly for America.

It was just such a sensitized audience that Rosenfeld was able to address when they arrived in America. He had already been here by the time most of them arrived. He observed all and absorbed every aspect of their problems and potentialities. He worked, when he could find work, as a tailor. No one ever said to him, "That's a nice piece of work, Morris." or, "That's a nice pair of pants, Morris." Never! His mind was not on that kind of labor. Like it or not, his employers and fellow workers had to agree that this man marched to a different drummer. His eyes, two deep-set orbs gazing with a fiery intensity from beneath two bushy eyebrows, his tousled hair extending almost electrically from his head and his urgent expression all gave the man the appearance of a prophet. He appeared to be a man who could call upon divine powers to propel his forceful words to all who could listen.

When the proletarian masses read, or heard, Rosenfeld's exciting calls to action, when they read his uncanny description of the very life they were leading at that moment, his words produced the exact results he had planned. Only a man who had experienced the fear, the insecurity, deprivation, love of their family and their people, the fear of a rabble who were virtually expelled from an alien land, only such a man could be effective in reading their hearts and their minds. When a poet virtually in tatters, whose wife had to seek extra employment to keep their family from starving, sounds a clarion call from the heart, he is listened to. The fact that his voice was rich with the sounds and inflections of a familiar language was an added bonus. Add to this the fact that his imagery was beautiful and colorful, loaded with the colloquialisms that actually are untranslatable. This lent his voice the undeniable imprimatur of a genius of his time. In the poetry and prose included in this volume a modern American should be able to experience some of the excitement that Rosenfeld was able to produce. His short stories were a light-hearted foray into the life of the Lower East Side of New York: thoroughly delightful.

Earlier in this chapter we tried to discuss something of the psychological problems that Rosenfeld underwent and the effects upon his personality and his work. In our own day we are well aware of the destructive effects that poverty and stress can produce in many persons—especially in children.Within the immigrants and their children what Howe called "psychic uncertainties" developed and there are many who still bear the scars of the mass immigration as though they were a badge of dishonor to be worn from generation to generation. However these scars were not badges of dishonor but an important aspect of the unfathomable cost of relocating an ancient culture and recreating a new form of it on alien grounds. Had the immigrants been Christians it would have been less difficult, especially if they were Protestants. Had they been English-speaking it might have been even less difficult. But the Jews not only spoke an alien tongue and practiced a despised religion from a backward region but worst of all they had a history of being the world's pariahs for thousands of years. What a psychological burden these people, our dearest of kin, had to suffer from so helplessly! This alone was enough to wring torment upon the psyches of the immigrants and their offspring. Yet with it all they managed to survive and by the second generation to thrive here in this burgeoning land. (And the psychiatrists who spawned in such a culture were able to build up thriving practices as well!)

Let no one put down the qualities of the American civilization that welcomed these bedraggled newcomers. Firstly, they were actually welcomed. They met minimal prejudice, compared with what they would have received elsewhere in the world. They had constitutionally guaranteed civil rights, they settled in a civilized country with an educational system and hospital facilities open to all. There was a police force and a judicial system that was essentially fair. The playing field was not exactly even, but level enough (with a few rocks here and there) for an industrious people to persist and set the foundation for a solid future as American citizens.

The Jews did not find a welfare state with medicaid, medicare and the host of "relief" agencies that exist today. They provided basic care for themselves. The German Jewish community, which had been established more than half a century before the Eastern Europeans "came over", had become fully Americanized and become quite well accepted here. They had also established themselves successfully in the financial and business worlds. These German Jews looked down their Semitic noses at their unkempt and down-trodden brethren. It was not just the smell of herring, the pervasive presence of the yarmulke (little round skull-cap that religious Jewish men wear): it was also the unshaven beards, the long coats and the primitive lack of sanitation. It was as though the German Jews were looking at an advanced stage of primates who by religious affiliation alone were their relatives. Even so, the Schiffs, Warburgs, Bloomingdales, Strausses, Guggenheims and others, however their senses were offended, did not fail their co-religionists. They established schools, hospitals, settlement houses, aid societies of all sorts so that starvation, disease, ignorance and the feeling of desolation could be kept from speading and debilitating the already wounded minds and bodies of the immigrants. This was done with a sense of superiority by the donors and an uncomfortable gratefulness by the recipients.

It is not certain how badly things might have deteriorated had not the German Jews extended their hands to their distant relatives. What is sure is that the people stood fast and developed increasing feelings of self-confidence. What is also certain is that many of the factories that employed (and brutally exploited) the Jewish immigrants in the large cities of New York, Chicago, Boston and Philadelphia were owned by these German Jews. The owners generally grew exceedingly wealthy on the suffering backs of that immigrant labor. It took years of impatient socialist urging to get the workers to rebel, to strike, to literally fight for better working conditions and acceptable salaries. The labor movement in America, the foundation of the ILGWU (International Ladies' Garment Workers Union) and the Amalgamated Clothing Workers Union started as a revolt against the near criminal abuse of labor by the factory owners, who now, of course, are looked upon as pillars of our society. They were pillars then too: hard, rigid, unyielding, cold. The labor movement pitted Jew against Jew, as contrasted with the rest of the labor movement that developed in America.

Strangely enough, when Rosenfeld wrote his poems and polemical essays and articles and shouted out his diatribes against "the Bosses", "the millionaires" and "the oppressors" he never played upon the concept of fratricide. He treated "the Boss" as the impersonal creature of the capitalist system, just as the Boss treated the workers as impersonal cogs in his machines. The individual and the corporation were what had to be fought, as though there were a flaw in the system and the flaw had to be eradicated. Rosenfeld might have accused the "bosses" of anti-semitism, since most of the workers were Jewish. But the bosses were Jewish too! He might have called them un-American for mistreating American citizens and workers so cruelly. But he did not. Neither did most of the writers of the time. It might have been a good idea for Cahan of "The Forwards" to have a first page headline screaming, "Shame! Shame! Shame! Jews are Killing Jews! Jews are exploiting Jews! For Money! For Power!" Rabbis might have spoken at their services with scorn about the Jewish factory owners. But this was usually not done. Perhaps they kept in mind the initial support given by the

German Jews. Perhaps they weighed the damage all Jews might have suffered if the fratricidal conflict were extended beyond the community.

The owners of small factories had the problem of staying in business long enough for "things to turn around". There was a deep financial depression around 1905–07 from which the nation did not really recover until the start of the First World War. Businesses had to cut costs, usually at the expense of labor, to stay viable. Strangely enough, when the labor movement finally took hold to wring higher wages and improved working conditions from the employers the businesses did not fail. They thrived because the higher wages led to greater purchasing power and improved working conditions led to improved productivity of the labor force. It has always been thus: business management is long-sighted in terms of goals but short-sighted in understanding that increased wages and increased purchasing power can increase the potential of any business. Yesterday, today and tomorrow we can be assured that the mind-set of the businessman will not alter. Rosenfeld's struggle was to try to force that "mind-set" to yield enough for a living wage for his fellow immigrants. This is one struggle he won.

References

1. Encyclopedia Brittanica, 1963, Map #26
2. Rosenfeld, Morris, "Lieder Des Ghetto", Foreword
3. Howe "World Of Our Fathers", p. 7
4. ibid, p. 7
5. ibid, p. 10
6. ibid, p. 11
7. ibid, p. 14
8. ibid, p. 14
9. Varon, Benno, Midstream Magazine
10. ibid
11. Drs. Stone, "That Fine Madness", Discover Magazine

2

Rosenfeld's Antecedents and Contemporaries in Yiddish Poetry

In our preface we stated that it would be our intent to discuss Rosenfeld's contemporary writers as well as those who preceded him and some of those who succeeded him on the stage of Yiddish poetics. After all, no one writes in a vacuum. It is important to elucidate where Rosenfeld stood in the brief history of Yiddish letters. Note, please, that we did not say "Jewish" letters. Jews wrote in many languages, long before Rosenfeld lived and especially now in the latter three-quarters of the twentieth century. Yiddish letters refers particularly to those who wrote (in this volume, essentially, poetry) almost exclusively in Yiddish. This phenomenon started in earnest in the mid-nineteenth century with the writings of Mendele Mokhe Sforim. There was a sparse history of writing in Yiddish going back over a thousand years but this language was not a highly developed literary medium until a mere hundred and fifty years ago.

Mendele (let's call him Mendele from now on, not only for the sake of brevity but also out of affection) was the first major Yiddish novelist. He wrote in a prose that has been described as "almost shockingly stark in its evaluations of shtetl life, showing its bleakness, hopelessness, pain and fear." Only his wit and humor, and of course his belief in God, were saving graces. Anyone with a sense of Yiddishkeit—and a sense of humor—could revel in Mendele's satires or Sholem Aleichem's stories. Although Mendele wrote in the "old country" he was up to date enough to have some of his stories reprinted in Jewish publications the world over in the 1890's and later. A genuine pioneer in developing and expanding the linguistic potential of the Yiddish language, Mendele was probably one of the top four or five most influential Yiddish writers of all. It was not merely his linguistic skill, it was his bravery and originality in bringing this "young" language to the fore and using it to explore in print the lives and natures of the poor, depressed multitudes.

There were relatively few notable Yiddish writers in Europe during the last century. Mendele Mokhe Sforim was born in 1836, Sholem Aleichem was born in 1859, I.L. Peretz was born in 1852, Chaim Nachman Bialik was born in 1855, Morris Rosenfeld was born in 1862. These were the "greats" and each one was as individual and different in his mode of thinking as in his mode of writing. They all came from the same milieu but each one had a different approach to the problems of Jewry and to his means of expression. Other well-known writers then profiting from their labors were Isaac Meir Dik and Shomer, a "sensationalist" actually named Sharkevich, Sholem Asch, Joseph Opotashu, and only a few more.

Sholem Aleichem wrote only prose. He created stories such as "The Travels of Benjamin" and "The Old Mare". And almost everyone is by now familiar with his stories of Tevye, in "Fiddler on The Roof". He also launched, in 1888, a Yiddish Annual in which he encouraged Yiddish writers of all kinds to contribute. It was a major event in Yiddish "Belles Lettres". Rosenfeld was still a young man at this time, as was Peretz, an attorney and a brilliant writer, who wrote mostly in Hebrew and Polish. Peretz later concentrated on Yiddish as his main language of expression. He needed an audience, which is a statement he would have denied. Rosenfeld was not at all known in Europe at that time. He was not even a professional writer yet, and was not at all sure of his interests. Rosenfeld wrote almost exclusively in Yiddish then, as did Sholem Aleichem. Early on both Peretz and Sholem Aleichem felt that it would go better for the Jews if they tried to integrate more in the life of their Gentile neighbors as others were doing in Germany. Linguistic integration was Peretz' first objective. He educated his children and spoke to them at home in Russian or Polish. He shared a perennial mistake of the Jews in thinking that they would then be more acceptable to the "majority" and life would be easier for the them. Of course in hindsight we can see his error. Can any of us detect our own errors today without benefit of hindsight? Peretz thought that broader linguistic capabilities would enable his children to succeed in the struggle for reforms. As a student of history, Jewish history, he should have known better.

Rosenfeld missed out on that "opportunity" to write in Europe, if the life of chance pogroms, near-certain poverty and backward living conditions can be called an opportunity. When he decided, in his teens, to take off for America he left the life of the shtetl forever. Although he never forgot his roots and never denied his Jewishness, his writing took on an entirely different flavor than that of those who remained in the old world. He became an "Americaner" and used the newfound hope and freedom of expression to create a new tradition of Yiddish writing. Whereas the other greats had plenty of material to draw upon for their appealing stories and intense poetry, Rosenfeld used the same sensitivity to universal problems but drew on the endless source of human data from a different milieu as a basis for his poetry and stories.

As to the quality of the Yiddish spoken and written in Russia and Russia-controlled Poland, that of the Russian Jews was more highly developed in inverse relationship to the degree of freedom and opportunity allowed to the Jews. In Poland there were fewer restrictions so the language languished. This situation was reversed in Russia. Peretz wrote to Sholem Aleichem, "Your wish and goal, as I understand it, is to write for the sake of the audience that speaks the jarghon of jarghon-land. I, for my part, write for my own pleasure and if I take any reader into consideration he is of the highest level of society, a person who has read and studied in a living tongue."[1] He intended his works for the elite, the highly educated. In this he differed greatly from Sholem Aleichem and Rosenfeld, who wrote for the masses but, as it developed, these writers were read by every literate level of Jewish society. Rosenfeld spoke their "jarghon" and he created a pulsing beauty and fervor with that "jarghon", reaching the hearts and minds of the common man whom Peretz had by-passed.

This is not to suggest that any of these men bore hostility towards each other. It is simply true that Peretz looked down upon the very language of Yiddish that the exigencies of life ultimately forced him to write in. "His use of Yiddish would not prohibit the investigation of modernity, including his struggle against Jewish tradition and the language itself."[2] He seems, to this writer, to have been uncomfortable in the presence of his mother-tongue, "wishing to be more like him", etc., from Shakespeare's sonnet. Yet his attitude of self-importance does not take a jot away from the beauty and sensitivity of his poetry and prose.

Sholem Aleichem and Rosenfeld were never troubled with an identity crisis. They knew precisely who they were, where they came from, to whom they wished to direct their creations. Rosenfeld never questioned his use of Yiddish although he did share some of Peretz' benign neglect of the ecclesiastical aspects of Jewish life. These men could not be confined once the fresh air that seeped in from outside the ghetto had flowed into their senses. Rosenfeld and Peretz referred to God and to Biblical stories because they were brought up as orthodox Jews and were inculcated with religiosity. But few writers with intellectual freedom can be contained by an orthodox religion which, by definition, requires abject conformity and restricts both the writer's vision and his opportunities of inquiry and expression. The shtetl was no place to stay for the broad view of anything creative. Peretz, who was both influenced by and rejected by the Gentile world, found his creativity deeply affected by his doubts. Anyone who sees everything from all sides of the querstion can become paralyzed in terms of decision-making and action. Ambivalence can affect one's reactions to critical events. In the matter of a dialectic approach one can bring up too many antitheses to counter all your theses so that creating a synthesis is virtually impossible. Such a man was Peretz. Neither Rosenfeld nor Sholem Aleichem had this problem. They had other problems, but not one of identity, of conflict between the old and the new. Neither of them was as philosophical in his approach to writing as Peretz was. Peretz soon discovered that in the world of bigotry and political deviousness facts were an ineffectual weapon. Maurice Samuel, in his "The Great Hatred", pointed out that no bigot is ever convinced of his error by facts. His thesis was that anti-semitism is indeed a disease that takes stronger medicine than reason to conquer.

To Peretz humor was a tool used more to dilute anxiety than to help Man adapt his creativity to his social needs. However he did have a wry and penetrating sense of humor which he used on occasion to point up his ideas. Rosenfeld and Sholem Aleichem used facts decorated with an artist's brush to fit any occasion. The latter used humor as a two-edged sword, the former with a pungency that would brook no contradiction. From Howe and Wisse's "The Best of Sholem Aleichem" comes this neat little quote, ". . . . as Hillel

Halkin, one of the translators of this volume has noted, laughter in Sholem Aleichem's work is 'the explosive with which he systematically mines all escape routes leading away from the truth.' "[3] Rosenfeld's mining of the exits was not so subtle. He was not a subtle writer. When he planted a land mine to explode in the face of "the Boss" or "the oppressor" there were signs all over his poetry (and prose) letting his antagonists know where they had best not tread.

Rosenfeld did not do what Sholem Aleichem did: to provide Eastern European Jewry with an artificial world where they could live out their problems vicariously. Rosenfeld let his people know that the arena was not a fictional territory but the here and now. *They* were the gladiators. The home, the street and the place of work was the arena; here in America or in whatever country the working man was located who read his poetry. The fight was a fight to the finish and it was up to each man to play his role in the jousting of the day. Sholem Aleichem, no less concerned for the masses than Peretz or Rosenfeld, proposed to lighten the burden of his fellow Jews through laughter. Peretz had other burdens to transmit than the problems of Jewry in a hostile world. He had the problems of his personality which was egotistical and demanded constant attention and "respect". He had the burden of his ideas which caused him to invest much concentration and emotional currency in the dichotomy between traditional and modern Jewishness and between religion and secular belief. Peretz was so demanding of himself that he wrote in every aspect of Jewish lettres, involving himself in social movements, tried to support his family, attempted to excite the interest of the "ordinary Jew" in literature and a broader culture than was available in a shtetl. Any one of these interests alone could occupy a man full-time.

Sholem Aleichem, on the other hand, was a story-teller par excellence. He was a "khokhem" (a really wise person) who used literary devices to divert, to interest, to inspire his fellow Jews. He seems to have had a more balanced personality than many of his contemporary writers. Although his task may seem simple to the average reader, one must recall that he was a prototype of the Yiddish writer; a first force, inspirational and broad in his influence. He must have had some influence upon Rosenfeld, although it has never been identified.

At first Rosenfeld was not really a "story-teller" the way Sholem Aleichem was. Neither did his "meises" (tales) have the intellectual cutting edge of Peretz. Rosenfeld shared much of the egotism that Peretz exhibited, which was not always well received for either of them. Yet we know that it is unusual for someone to be able to create or be original without a strong ego. No one can push his work beyond the impersonal restrictions of publishers, critics and the masses to get it published, promoted, advertised and finally appreciated without a strong sense of self. Without such an ego Rosenfeld and Peretz might have written forever and no one would have known or cared about them. In a sense the great European Yiddish writers were not only Rosenfeld's antecedents, but his contemporaries as well. The history of Yiddish literature, unfortunately, is so brief.

References

1. Harshav, Benjamin, "The Meaning of Yiddish", p. 122.
2. Howe, Irving, "World Of Our Fathers", p. 506.
3. Raskin, Phillip, "Anthology Mod, Jewish Poetry".

3

Yiddish Poetry in America

After the pogroms in Russia of 1881–82, a new self-consciousness developed concerning the character of Jewish culture and the nature of Jewish existence. Yiddish literature, its prose and its poetry, underwent a metamorphosis as well. Enlightenment (Haskalah, in Hebrew) developed among Jews of Germany and Eastern Europe centering around the towering figure of Moses Mendelsohn, the philosopher, who was also one of the founding fathers of modern German bourgeois culture.

As usual, with the Jews, they felt that they would only get equality if they changed themselves, as they did in Babylon and Turkey and Spain and again later on in modern Germany. We never learn. The Greeks had a word for it, as they had a word for everything: "Hamartia", the unfortunate and erroneous single-mindedness, the "fatal flaw." So many of the Jews beyond the shtetl and the small farms of Eastern Europe thought they could assimilate their problems away. Naturally, it did not succeed. First Hebrew, then Yiddish became the language of the "enlightenment" among them. They may have "enlightened" themselves, but they had no effect on their environment.

By 1890, with the dramatic changes that transpired all over Europe and the advent of industrialization, the first stirrings of a socialist movement arose in reaction to the effects on their lives of that industrial revolution. Many Jews left first not for America but for jobs in the big cities of Europe, for which they were totally unprepared. They looked strange and untidy and their religious observances did not fit into the schedule of a factory existence. They became despised by the more "highly developed" society they were trying to join. Thus the principles of the Enlightenment survived but ceased to be effective or socially relevant for those Jews. These principles were "learning, aesthetization and self-realization".[1] This meant: to learn new languages and modern ways, to shed their distinctive appearance as Jews, to discard their traditional communal structures and become active in any number of socially-oriented movements. It could be Socialism, Zionism, Communism, a trade, a union; do anything but be a helpless cipher, a country bumpkin from a primitive land. The waves of pogroms, of course, persisted all over Russia, Poland, Bulgaria and Rumania, wherever the "superior" Gentiles lived whom the Jews were supposed to emulate. If the Jews had indeed emulated the violence and cruelty of their neighbors those cowards might have been less willing to take advantage of the benighted Jewish "patsies". Mahatma Ghandi and Martin Luther King thought they had started something new with "non-violent resistance". The Jews were thousands of years ahead of them. Pogroms were nothing new; they had occurred so many times before. But the Jews themselves became different. There were finally more than rumblings of resentment. They began to create organizations that were practical in preparing Jews to flee or to emigrate to Palestine (which required agricultural training). Many Jews who had "made it" to the safety of large modern communities tried to take their places as responsible and creative citizens.

It was in the more cosmopolitan cities that Heine, Kafka, Szulc and many others wrote in languages other than Hebrew or Yiddish. And by the time the 1880's and 1890's came around there was a renaissance of Yiddish and then the birth of a modern Yiddish literature. After the pogrom in Kishinev in 1903 decimated the population, the poet Bialik wrote a scorching poem in Hebrew, and then translated it into Yiddish, criticising the Jews for tolerating their state of victimization. Self-defense groups developed as a result of this. The name "Haganah" arose and was later used in Israel as a name for their defense force. A sort of schizophrenia developed within a substantial part of the European Jewish community. Some, who had become greatly assimilated in the large modern cities, looked down with embarrassment and contempt at their less fortunate brethren from the "lower classes" A serious dichotomy developed in the Jewish personality. It is still here, today, in the good old USA. The same sense of superiority and discomfort that a Harvard grad (Jewish, but who can tell?) might feel when he walks the streets of a large city and sees Yeshiva Bochers (Hebrew school students) with their payess and tsitses (sidecurls and fringed undershirt) or observes Chassidim (ultra religious Jews) with their dark fedora hats and long black gabardine coats . . . this same discomfort existed in European cities then as well.

This hypercritical self-loathing of a major segment of our people still has its psychological sequelae that are several generations old by now. According to Harshav, one must understand that for a Jew to be writing poetry or prose anywhere in the Diaspora (exile) he is not creating in a milieu that is essentially Jewish in character. Except in Israel he is not in a normal national (Jewish) state with its own Jewish schools, Jewish government or the other appurtenances of a Jewish society. He is tolerated, at best, in most areas of the world. For such people, literature has been of supreme importance. In a way it has been a substitute for nationhood, embodying all the cultural aspects that Jews remember and embodying an independence that one only acquires with true statehood. For the Jew, his poet and his writer, be he story-teller or polemicist, was the connecting link to his whole culture. This is where the creation of the State of Israel will ultimately have a massive impact on the Jewish psyche in every aspect, it is hoped. In Europe most of the Jews who wrote poetry at this time (late nineteenth century) also wrote in other languages than Hebrew. Frug, Bialik and Peretz, who wrote in Hebrew, also wrote in Yiddish. Edelstadt wrote in a Yiddish with Russian overtones. Grinberg wrote in a Yiddish with German influences and later on Moishe Leyb Halpern (of 'Die Yunge') also wrote in a German-influenced Yiddish.

Rosenfeld seems at first to have succumbed to romantic, Victorian-style Russian verse of the late 1870's and '80's. However, by travelling across Europe by himself, by reading Goethe and Heine, by coming to America and reading Poe and Whitman, he elevated his techniques by a self-induced evolution. He never developed into one of the newer Impressionist poets who received their inspiration from the later German writers. That did not fit his personality. Neither did he cater to the poetry of those post-Symbolists who "plunged" into European Expressionism. Both groups passed Rosenfeld by in their collision course with Destiny. It was as though the newer poets were "high" on some all-consuming drug that caused them to charge ahead in their convoluted styles of writing, roughly elbowing aside any one writing in a more traditional vein. Naturally, vast segments of the public do not follow the Expressionists, Impressionists, Symbolists, Dadaists, Introspectivists or any writers to whose style and attitude they cannot relate. Yet, as the modern writers evolved, the writing of Glatshteyn, for example, was so expressive, so elevated in language, so deep and painful to read that one wonders why more of the public did not recognize the genius of this man. He was so sad but so perceptive. How can we be angry at him for being part of a group (the Introspectivists) that was so cruel to those who immediately preceded them, (Die Yunge)? And after reading the writings of "Die Yunge", (The Young Ones) how can we be angry at them for the cruel manner with which they abused the traditional writers who preceded them, Rosenfeld, Winchevsky and Edelstadt? As intimated above, they were wearing blinders. They were writing frenetically in hopes that they could leave their mark. Although most of them did not succeed they did their best to decorate this spinning ball of insecurity with their artistry.

There were very few notable, truly competent men of Yiddish "letters" in America prior to Rosenfeld's appearance. And there were very few poets of that calibre during the early years of his career here (or even in Europe). Three names, Winchevsky and Edelstadt and Jehoash do stand out. They were men of strong personality, utter commitment to their philosophies and with considerable talent for the writing of Yiddish poetry. They shared the same poverty-ridden background. The intense struggle merely for the basics of subsistence colored their view of life and society. It is very easy, and puerile, for someone generations later, living in these days of comfort, security and acceptance with all the conveniences of modern life and a world apart from the psychic shock of immigration to criticise the attitude of extremism that these earlier Americans shared.

Edelstadt had left home at a tender age, reached America, and with the experience of the Czars etched on his soul, assumed a socialist stance in the search for an equitable society. A gentle man, he died of tuberculosis at an early age. But he worried about the fate of his Jewish people and wrote poetry to the end of his days. His poetry was not great but was beautiful, with the ineradicable influences of Russian sentimentalism permeating all. Dovid Edelstadt was a friend of Morris Rosenfeld, as was Morris Winchevsky, who was more anarchist than socialist. Coming from a land of repression, as these men did, to a land of freedom does not lead to an automatic change of attitude. Knowing the history of the Jews, which they certainly did know, having lived through the terrors of pogroms, which Edelstadt and Winchevsky certainly did, we have to understand their reluctance to accept whole-hog this new American system as the end-all and be-all of social philosophy. No matter how secure the social systems seemed at first to the Jews who migrated to Babylonia, Turkey, Spain, France, Germany, England, Poland or Russia, in the end security and acceptance for Jewry was a transitory experience and the dream of universal freedom and acceptance remained just that, a dream. (As a point of information—an up-date—an aide to a man named Farrakhan gave a virulent anti-semitic speech at Keane College in New Jersey just recently. He referred to New York as "Jew York" and to "Jew York Jewniversity" and remarkably few officials at the college objected to his poisonous anti-Jewish remarks!")

And so the dedication of Morris Winchevsky, Dovid Edelstat, Jehoash and Rosenfeld to a new, humane social order is understandable. Edelstadt was a socialist, Winchevsky was an anarchist, Rosenfeld was a socialist who contributed funds to the anarchist movement. (He donated a few cents at an anarchist meeting. His wife Bessie gave a few cents. Their daughter, my aunt Dora, gave a nickel!) Let us state, categorically, that this was a sacrifice for a poet who sometimes was paid only a penny a line for his poems and sometimes only fifty cents for a whole volume!

There were other Yiddish poets about in those early days (the 1890's) in America but none with the vibrancy and brilliance of these men . Among the most intense was Hayim Zhitlovsky, a Russian Jew the same age as Rosenfeld who also wrote in Yiddish. He was basically not a poet but a writer and activist who ultimately became a Stalinist. He was dead serious. "He analyzed Judaism in relation to the experience of the Jewish people, trying to separate supernaturalist faith from the ethical substance that had been intertwined with it and recognizing the value of religious customs for both morality and discipline. He was an ardent advcate of socialism and internationalism, religious sentiment and modernist rationalism. Pull all these apart, give them the breath of life and you have

Yiddish culture. Paste them together in a synthesis abstract and dogmatic and you have Zhitlovsky!"[2]

The literati of Rosenfeld's period were self-consciously Jewish. No poets or writers, except those of the extreme left, denied their Jewishness or their tradition. While many socialists felt that the culture of the ghetto was destructive, should be forgotten and should be countered with a new, creative construction that would be fair and equitable to all, few if any writers had enough grasp of the realities of their predicament to be able to offer reasonable plans for the future. It was easy to criticise and complain. There was more than enough inequity and suffering to go around thrice, but no one saw their socialism for what it was, a first step in the transformation of the shtetl community to a form of capitalism, so far untested by any of them. The socialism of Europe which sparked the Jewish revolution was like many social movements, extreme and unmanageable. Every man who had an idea wrote about it and tried to capitalize on it. Perspective was entirely out of the question. There were Bunds and Social Democrats, and Democratic Socialists, Communists, Labor Parties, Workers Parties, Socialist Labor parties, and so on and on ad nauseum. At the extreme left, Jewish activists wanted to eliminate every aspect of their tradition, to start anew as existentialists with a program. But in order to get an audience they had to write and speak in Yiddish! Who else would listen to them? Who else had a shtetl mentality to shed? Who else had an understanding heart that could recognize the pain and the intensity of the socialist activists?

In the next portion of this chapter we shall name and very briefly describe some of the better-known poets who were American contemporaries of Rosenfeld who wrote in Yiddish. It must be stated at the outset that we hold all these writers in great respect. We honor their work and their intent. It is certainly not fair to the memory of anyone to pigeonhole him by quoting a few lines from one of his poems. That is not the mission of this book. However, if a few lines can express the essence of a man's beliefs and can demonstrate the level of his talents then it might be fair to quote him on those grounds. But each one of them deserves "the full treatment" of study, understanding and appreciation. From "The Anthology of Modern Jewish Poems"[3] by Philip Raskin we draw many of the images of these poets. Ed Goldenthal, as a little boy, was privileged (although he did not realize it at the time) to meet Raskin and Reisin, Dr. Adolph Held, Calman Marmor and many others of the literati and Jewish cultural world at his own home where Ed's mother, Rose, would frequently entertain such folk on behalf of Morris Rosenfeld, her father. It was here that Rose's considerable faculty was revealed for making blintzes, holishkes (stuffed cabbage), chicken salad, kreplach (Jewish won-ton) and a chicken soup that was not only delicious but certainly must have had some medicinal value. Whatever immense social problems were discussed, it was done over a glorious dinner table.

Among many, Arthur Guiterman was a fine poet who shared Rosenfeld's background of poverty. He mourned a "wasted life" in a poem called "Thanksgiving". He wrote, "I seek and I rebel", but unfortunately, as was often the case, his voice was dimly heard despite the beauty of his poetry. Philip Raskin was also a notable poet for his time. He did not share Rosenfeld's tempestuous nature but wrote with pathos about the Jewish predicament. He wrote about the poor in "The Song of The Peddler" and "The Dead Assembly'-'and about Torquemada. An impressive line somehow lingers from that song of the peddler, *"I have a heart of stone and cannot pray"*. You must sense how hurt these people were, how tortured their psyches. So many of those poets died very young, some from the "sweatshop disease", tuberculosis, and one has to wonder, knowing a little about psychosomatic illnesses, whether the stress and emotional depression of the times could have predisposed these sensitive people to serious physical diseases.

Some of the poets were quite defeatist in their tone. Israel Zangwill, a noted intellectul poet and writer, was so in his poem, "Our Own", which sent a powerful but sad message about Jewish history. The poet Afim wrote, "A Benediction", sad and defeatist, saying, *"Blessed be all that delivers us from reality, from the misfortune of living: It is easier to die ..."* etc. This might be contrasted with the poetry of Chaim Nachman Bialik, who was still alive and writing in Europe, where the problems of existence were certainly worse. But Bialik wrote powerful poetry, with flights of fancy difficult for the common man to understand. His imagery was beautiful, on a par with the finest English poets. He was most creative, exhibiting prolific ideas filled with fears and tears and hopes and hopes dashed and confusion. What else is a poet for?

Ezekiel Leavitt wrote "To a Nightingale", a sad, wailing piece that was well written but his poetry did not seem to carry the same social significance that other poets of his time included in their works. Leavitt seemed more self-concerned. David Frishman, who wrote in Yiddish, also wrote mostly in Hebrew. He was a very sensitive poet. One interesting idea he created was a poem where he makes items for the Messiah, but he ends in disappointment. Most Yiddish writers from the gaol atmosphere of their youth felt this same way.

It is surprising how few poets here in America wrote about Eretz Yisroel (The Land of Israel) as a physical entity the way Bialik did in Europe. Bialik wrote a powerful poem about the sands of the Holy Land where countless bodies lie beneath the desert but still have a potential for the future—an exciting idea. Subconsciously, it is possible that those who emigrated here already thought of America as a promised land and were deeply involved in trying to make their new life a success.

Abraham Liessin wrote in much the same vein as the other rather depressed poets of his time. In one joyless poem he wrote,

> *Naught have I, oh my soul*
> *Wherewith to serve thee*
> *In this gray, weary, joyless life we live,*
> *Only my soul is mine*
> *And see, my soul I give.*

And elsewhere he wrote, in a relatively depressed poem,

> *I am a rainworm buried deep*
> *among the oozing, slimy things, . . .*

Well-expressed depression was the norm for such people in an abnormal situation. I.L. Peretz, a "grandmaster" among Yiddish poets wrote, in Europe, in his poem, "In Alien Lands",

> *The fields I tread bloom not for me*
> *I pluck a rose in early morn—*
> *A stranger's rose is but a thorn.*

Abraham Reisen was a prolific poet who not only wrote his own poetry well but, as a friend of Morris Rosenfeld, delivered the eulogy at his friend's funeral. His poetry was rather undemanding of the reader, of the world or of God. It was deceptively simple, aimed at an audience that constantly needed a voice like their own to express their life's problems. Reisen did this very well. Many of Reisen's poems are rather defensive, when contrasted with Rosenfeld. He never gives God a calling-down. He never berates nature for her cruelty and he does not castigate Man for his own self-neglect. Who says he has to? There was always Rosenfeld and Winchevsky and Edelstadt for that job. Reisen was loved because he wrote many, many warm and sympathetic poems. Philip Raskin's poetry was more worldly than Reisin's and showed more adventurousness. He claims that the instrument to use is courage and bravery, when from "The Two Thrones" he says

> *"Nay, it must be forged of courage*
> *in the bravest Jewish soul,*
> *and 'til then, child, we shall never*
> *ever reach our destined goal"*

This Zionistically oriented poem, one of several such, demonstrates a far-sighted quality in Raskin. His "Song of The Peddler", however, offers only the mildest reproaches to Fate for the tribulations of a peddler in the city and his recommendation is, *"I will go back to the fields and the wood."* Rosenfeld's prescription was to stand your ground and fight. The woods are fine for the flowers and the animals and to visit, but not to retreat to. In real life, though, Rosenfeld's prescription for the working man was not the one he took for himself. When he was ill and defeated by the harassment of some critics, he bought, with the family's help, a small bungalow "in the field and the wood" as Raskin had prescribed. Those who knew Rosenfeld best, his family, knew that he enjoyed a pastoral setting and wrote about its beauties endlessly. But he really preferred the city with its excitement, tumult, conflicts and social ferment. He had long ago left the shtetl and was now a "big-city boy."

In his poem, "On the Day of Atonement" Raskin wrote, *"I shall ask of heaven no gift"*, which philosophy was Rosenfeld's as well. However, Morris turned his inflamed eyes to the skies and did not ask—he *demanded* a better deal for Man and for Jewry. He never requested. His curmudgeonly passionate nature could only demand and thus he lived his life in poetry.

Jean Starr Untermeyer wrote strong, vital poetry. She deserved greater acceptance than she received as a poet with verve and determination. She wrote as she saw things; clear-eyed and outspoken. She had some of Rosenfeld's irreverence for the cold, inhumane powers-that-be. In "Tolerance and Truth" she speaks,

> *"Sometimes when I hear people mouth the word toleration*
> *I am moved by a fury and a kind of pity too*
> *Because I know they have run too long with Compromise,*
> *That girl of easy virtue*
> *Who yields to all with a slack smile . . ."*

For a moment we must interrupt this discourse to remind the reader that all the above poems were written in Yiddish and we are dealing here with translations. Even so, some of those poems had considerable power and effect. Each poet had his own "special" audience which waited impatiently for the next poem to be published.

Yehoash was a major poet for his time, one of the few whose impulses and foresightedness allowed him to be acceptable even to the Modernist poets of the teens and twenties of this century. Yehoash, whose real. name was Solomon Bloomgarten, was an exceedingly interesting poet, a lyricist and an intellectual, continually opposing "folk-like song" and modern colloquialisms. He and Rosenfeld were perhaps the first to create poetry in Yiddish with nature as the primary theme. He composed exotic poems far from the normal purvue of the usual East Side tenement dweller. Among his many accomplishments his tour de force was the first complete translation of the Old Testament into Yiddish. No one in any book we have read has had an unkind word to say about Yehoash. Here are a few of his lines from "JOB":

> *Infinite night, thou tyrant of worlds !*
> *The earth and the suns,*
> *the stars and the planets,*
> *They are nothing but toys for thee—*
> *A means to kill time and only to shorten*
> *The long and tedious procession of years,*
> *Of which even thou cannot be freed.*
> *And though recklessly strewn o'er vast spaces*
> *Whose distances none but thou couldst measure*
> *Yet are they helplessly bound like slaves*
> *And chained to thy will, thy whims and thy fancies*

He let God know that he was displeased with the way,

"thou playest with him now and smilest with joy
While the poor moth (man) down, suffers and struggles."

It is unknown what God replied to Yehoash, but we think He respected the poet's bravery and honesty. Also He was instrumental in seeing to it that everyone would love Yehoash.

All the proletarian poets of the time wrote their Yiddish poetry in the meters of Russian poetry, "the language of their ideological inspiration". But none of these men had the tremendous education and intellectual versatility of Avrum Leyeles. This man was a walking encyclopedia who was able to translate into several languages. He even translated Poe into Yiddish! As though Poe did not have enough "tsores" (trouble) already! Leyeles wrote a few years after Rosenfeld had passed his prime and was one of "The Insich Group", but we mention him here in order to compare the poets' backgrounds. His years overlapped Rosenfeld's and his ideas were expressed in a more "modernist" manner. His style of writing elevated Yiddish poetry several notches above the works of anyone who had written before him. His choice of words, his educated expressions, his younger perspective were all something Yiddish poetry now needed. But he never had the audience that Rosenfeld, Edelstadt or Yehoash had. Genius though he was, Leyeles had to write for a waning public. The attitude and exotica of "Die Junge" had driven away an audience for Yiddish poetry.

Joseph Bovshover (1872–1915) was a creative poet and was the only Yiddish poet of the 80's and 90's who was primarily interested in aesthetic problems in literature. There were quite a few other Yiddish poets of quality but we cannot do much more than to name a few of those who created some sort of impact on the immigrant readership. There was David Goldstein, a subtle lyricist and a genuine, sensitive poet, and Jacob Cohen, David Einhorn, A. Almi, Isidore Ascher, Martin Feinstein, Babette Deutsch, Regina Bloch, Alter Brody, Saul Tsernichowski and ever so many others who deserve more than simply a listing of their names. (That computer that lies in my head has just been activated by the name of Babette Deutsch. Didn't she make an appearance in our home once, years and years ago when I was a little boy in short pants—with an insatiable curiosity?)

This list of Yiddish poets could extend much further but that is not the primary mission of this book. We wanted to name those Yiddish poets who had an impact on the immigrants. Other writers who created beautiful poetry may be referred to in the course of further describing the evolution of the immigrants from total alien status to "Americans" of Eastern European origin. Later on we shall discuss the followers of Rosenfeld, Winchevsky and Edelstadt and try to bring to you our understanding of the evolution of Yiddish poetry as it was related to the evolution of world poetry at the same time. It must be stated that some of the Yiddish poets also wrote in English, with varying degrees of competency and success. Among the most successful, in the "early days" of this century, were Louis Untermeyer and Israel Zangwill. They were quite competent and effective in demonstrating to the literary world that a Jew can write as well as anyone native-born here. Some of the works of these men were actually taught in the public schools with other native writers such as James Whitcomb Riley and Emily Dickenson. Untermeyer was better known than Zangwill, especially after he had published his compendium of American English poetry.

Rosenfeld tried writing in English, but he was really out of his purvue when he did so. One of his poems was actually very well received and was taught in some of the nation's schools. It also received Presidential favor. It was called, "I Know Not Why" and is included in the "Poetry" section of this book. Even so, after his death a book of English poems that he had prepared for publication was apparently not attractive enough when his widow tried to interest publishing concerns in it.

Just recently we discovered several volumes of his poetry written in English. There was a definite improvement in his competency in that language the more he worked at it. He ardently desired to have an influence there and wrote several poems expressing his wish to write well in the language of Shakespeare and Whitman. We include quite a few of his English poems in a special section of this book, noting what we thought of them. Had he lived long enough we feel that he might have left his mark in America in that language as well as in Yiddish, since his talent at versification never left him and he never ran out of "commercial" ideas.

It is true that practically all poetry sounds better and is more authentic in the language in which it was originally conceived and written. Especially in Yiddish poetry, the rhythm, the rhyme, the words or phrases coined by the poet, the idiomatic expressions and colloquialisms, the national references, the Yiddishized alien words from Russian, Polish, and Hebrew that permeate the Yiddish language may at times be only marginally translatable. How difficult is the task of the translator! Take, for instance, a few lines from Rosenfeld's poem "Mein Yingele". Even the title is usually translated incorrectly. They call it "My Son", but the correct Yiddish for "My Son" would be "Mayn Zohn", or "Mayn Zuhn." "My Little Son", which is closer, is "Mayn Kleyner Zuhn". So what is a "Yingele"? The correct translation would be more like "My Youngster", or "My Young One". No one ever used that in the many translations of this poem that we have seen because that does not sound very poetic. In the following transliteration of the first few lines of this poem you can get a feel of the lilt of the Yiddish

> Ikh hob ah kleynem Yingele,
> ah zunele gor fayn,
> venn ikh derzay im dakht zikh mir
> di gantze velt iz mayn.

The best English translation we could find was by Aaron Kramer, a talented poet:

> I have a son, a little son
> a youngster mighty fine !
> And when I look at him I feel
> that all the world is mine.

That's mighty close because Aaron is a master translator, but it lacks the nostalgic warmth of the original Yiddish. Another translation went:

> I have a little boy at home
> a pretty little son
> I think sometimes the world is mine
> In him my only one.

We are not sure where that translation came from but it would be difficult for an English-speaking reader to have any conception of Yiddish as an expressive language by reading such a translation. Even the finest translators, such as Rose Pastor Stokes, Helena

Frank and Aaron Kramer can fall short of the "mame-loshn" that was at the core of Rosenfeld's writing. "Mame-loshn" means "mother-tongue", the way your language was spoken to you by your mother; the way in your mind and your heart you will always remember your language. Your mother-tongue is the index by which you will always refer to love and spirit, to life and death and to enterprise.

Few of the Yiddish-writing poets mentioned earlier have been adequately served by even the finest translators, including poet-translators such as Philip Raskin, Maurice Samuels, Elias Lieberman, Jacob Robbins and others. It would be very unfair to cast blame upon the translators. Yiddish, that linguistic stew, would confound even the greatest literary "chefs". It also would not be fair to compare poets, any more than, once a year on television, they give first prize to an actor or a song-writer, a director or a set-designer for the movies, stage or television. Great performances involve all the other elements mentioned above. And great poetry involves not alone the use of language, the nature of translations, the color and intent of the poem and the language in which it was written, but most important could be the timing and impact of the poetry itself upon the audience for whom it was intended. The nature of the audience is a key factor in the impact of any written work. Most writers might be annoyed at this fact, but it exists.

Rosenfeld's poems about labor and the working class, about Zionist impulses and the suffering of immigrants were most appreciated by those involved in that time, that place, that pinnacle on the curve of history when the poet's words served as a reflection of those people's souls and a mirror of their own lives. Rosenfeld was truly a bard for his own time, having had the knack for turning the mirror of history to the face of his contemporaries, allowing them to see themselves as they were and where they were. Rosenfeld was the on-the-spot poet, playwright, muck-raker, spark and stimulant in a vibrant time in history. Although he is gone now for three-quarters of a century, his songs are still sung and he is still remembered affectionately by those remnants of his own proletarian times, by the literati who know his works well and by those who appreciate the value of music and poetry in the struggle for social causes. Like a comet he came across the firmament, with the swiftness of interstellar speed. His light and his heat illuminated the needs and troubles of a people and aroused them to rebel and force the creation of a better life. He encouraged them to look at themselves, as they were too involved to do so on their own. And then he burned out and disappeared. He left behind not ashes but volumes of work, success in his social efforts and the continuing love of his constituency. Most comets leave sterile ash as a residue. Rosenfeld's ideas and aspirations are still fertile ground where can be planted more seeds of rebellion against tyranny, as well as flowering hope for the multitudes. Wherever his restless soul lies now his ideas are not moldering but still active.

We have discussed, so far, considerable data about the Jewish life in Eastern Europe and the motivations for emigration to America. We have mentioned the literary scene in Eastern Europe and in the early days after the immigration of Jews to America. It seems important now to delve a little deeper into the changes that occurred among the Jews after they arrived here. This is done so that we can try to explain what effects this situation had upon the writers of that time as well as what effects the writers themselves had upon the populace. Under no circumstances should anyone get the mistaken notion that we are attempting a duplication of Irving Howe's incomparable tome, "World of Our Fathers" or Leon Goldenthal's, "Toil and Triumph". We are employing the tone and some of the data from those authors to express our understanding of the milieu of the immigrant Yiddish writers. If you the reader are Jewish, pay attention! We are talking about your parents and grandparents, your great-grandparents too. Actually, we are talking about *you*, because this is your heritage, where you come from, and that has a great deal to do with who you are and where you are destined to go.

And so we return to a consideration of the immigrant mentality and ultimately we can relate this material to the writings of Rosenfeld and his contemporaries. Arriving in America with inflated hopes many immigrants lost their perspective and sense of direction. Many of them suffered severe psychological damage. They were used to wretchedness in Europe, but here there was a confusion of values and the pillars of their culture were crumbling. The factors that had kept their society together, such as rabbinical authority and communal mores which previously had been taken for granted, were now dissolving under the pressures of long days at the shop or factory, long trips to the place of employment and the strangeness of new surroundings. In order to remain faithful to traditional Judaism, as they desired to be, they had to make special efforts, compromises, at home, at the shop, in their communal behavior. It was difficult to maintain their religious observances where the new work ethic demanded a sacrifice of the time at home with the family and even the devotion of the Sabbath to personal concerns. A man rarely saw his children awake, was frequently unable to exert a man's role in the home, either in bringing up the children or maintaining his accustomed position as leader of the family. Trying to retain fragments of the culture he had lived with all his life and combining that with the smattering of the new American culture he was slowly acquiring was a difficult balancing act for the common man. This pressure left him on an island of confusion in a hectic sea of excitement and alien mores. We are talking about your grandfather, you know, and mine. Think of this state of Jewish affairs and think of writing poetry, of all things, in circumstances like that.

At the time the Jews left for America, almost all of them intended to maintain continuity with their tradition and faith. There were ample reasons to thank God and to experience the kind of hope that did not exist for European Jews for thousands of years. The surrogate faiths of anarchy and socialism and the undisciplined egalitarianism of the American scene were additional challenges to the immigrants. The former were transitory, rooted chiefly in complaints about the inequities of the workplace, and the latter offered no guides or solace to the souls of the confused and displaced masses. They were not oppressed enough to rebel, not uniform in their thinking, not organized in their responses, not secure enough in their living to be good material even for unionization until the 20th century. But they did admire the poetics of Rosenfeld and the brilliant socialist writings of Abe Cahan. They were good soil for a socially-motivated mass movement but needed some further "fertilizer" and soil enrichment which they had to develop within themselves.

This state of affairs did arrive in the 20th century, twenty or so years after the first Eastern European immigration began, twenty years for America to get its grip on their hearts the way it did on their imagination earlier on. In those twenty years the cumulative activity of Abe Cahan and Rosenfeld, Dr. Felix Adler (Chairman of the Society of Ethical Culture) and Bernard Weinstein, Abraham Reisen and even Joseph Barondess (that charismatic labor-agitator) had sensitized the former shtetl-dwellers to a new appreciation of their status and potentialities here in America. All of those leaders, whether shrill or calm, caustic or soothing, held out hope. None ever advised a return to the 'old country'. None ever allowed the natural nostalgia for the quiet (and sterility) of shtetl life and Russia itself to becloud their minds. They were all in America to stay and had better make the most of their presence.

Yiddish publications expanded in number and diversity of subject-matter. Rosenfeld was a frequent contributor of prose and poetry. Abraham Cahan was the razor's edge. There was none of the sophistication in these immigrants that some of their great grand-children might attribute to them. That is why a poet of Rosenfeld's nature was able to be drawn to their hearts. He was not the sophisticated poet of the style of Wordsworth, Tennyson or Byron. Nor was his prose the measured, temperate stroking of the pens of Carlysle, Franklin or Paine. No, indeed. His pen dripped vitriol and did not simply write, it etched! Small wonder that it burned him as well as his targets.

It is questionable whether Rosenfeld had an overall view of his society. He did not possess the education in economics, history or corollary social sciences to be able to obtain a view of his times with any real perspective. Nor indeed did he have an accurate perspective of his own place in his own time. The foregoing evaluations may seem superficial if one is going to ask, "How many great prophets had an education in economics, history and corollary social sciences?". But we were not expecting Rosenfeld to be a prophet; merely hoping that he was a man who understood economic patterns, social patterns and was able to gauge the tides of history to achieve an overall view. After all, if one is going to devote his life to a social cause, would it not be a commendable thought to have some idea of where he is on the historical scale? Of course he could intuit his position and that of his society, and this is what poets and dreamers do.

Many very competent writers throughout the ages had an almost primal sense of location, the way a bird does when flying from continent to continent. Not enough is known about the subconscious or the "primordial impulses" that are supposed to offer us a valuable adjunct to the intellect with which we have fortunately been endowed. We may be demanding too much from our poets even when they get carried away, with their burning eyes, and incant their "statements of allness" about God and Destiny and the behavior demanded of men. Rosenfeld was a full-time socialist, but he never enrolled as a member of any "Party", either Socialist, "Anarchist" or "Communist". This was at a time when the entire lower East Side of New York City was stewing in a broth of social revolt, fed by the rapid breakdown of the cultural bonds to the 'old country'. There was stress on the ties of orthodox religiosity and a casting loose of millions of poor people from a relatively sterile but closely bound shtetl life into a turmoil of nearly endless excitement, hope, deprivation, fear and alienation.

Changes in language, work schedules and customs and exposure to an entirely different philosophy of life gave the harried immigrants precious little time to pause and reflect on the overall picture. The American milieu, with its self-indulgence and expansiveness, with its confidence and sense of future opportunities and greatness gradually rubbed off on the new members of our society. Whereas the first generation often shrank back from any effort at conflict into the escapism of their work and their homes, they did not ignore the real world—the New World. How could they not be affected by the hulking presence of the burgeoning new society? If the opportunity to move upwards within this new world did not present itself for them, surely their children would be able to develop into "real Americans". If the stress of all that cultural breakdown and exposure to the storms of change encouraged a few to rise to personal heights of accomplishment it led many more to internal suffering and depression.

Nervous breakdowns, marital breakdowns, violence and street crimes among teenagers and young adults took on new proportions. As in any violent upheaval there had to be painful adjustments. There were too many maladjustments in family life, the backbone of Jewish survival throughout the ages. Family life was not the old-time 'homey' retreat that it was in the slower-paced, less intense life of Eastern Europe The mother frequently became the stereotypical "Jewish Mother", tender and overprotective to the point of suffocation, demanding everything from her husband and offspring that a dominating matriarch could think of. She wanted them to be productive, educated, neat and clean; to do their Hebrew School studies and their Public School homework, to practice the piano (and practice and practice and practice), to pull up their socks and their knickers and hold them in place with a garter, to go to work after hours and bring home a few dollars.

As often happens, when you give someone control, the tendency is for one to over-use it. The mother was prosecuting attorney, judge and jury on all matters concerning the home. The father was too tired and numbed from his ill-paying job in ill-ventilated, ill-heated and unsanitary factory conditions. The father had to be of stern stuff to make his impact on a family guided by such a mother. Resentment against these women was not obvious. Everyone tried to please them because of their own sacrifices for the family which were undeniable. The kitchen became the "command center" from which the Jewish mother, hassled by as many concerns as an army General, tried to run the family the way that General ran his Division. She had to deal with the supply of food and logistics in terms of procuring that food. She had to deal with destructive tactics such as laziness and even problems like insect infestation. She had to train her "troops" in techniques to combat the ways of the world while, at the same time, dispensing an adequate supply of genuine love to keep the morale high enough for survival. The kitchen became the throne-room of the home. In the vacuum left by a father who was not at home enough to maintain a commanding figure for all occasions, the mother assumed a role of matriarch which, in too many cases, left wounded psyches among their sons and daughters. Years later their influences on their offspring were exposed by psychiatrists who themselves had probably undergone similar experiences, (which may be why they became psychiatrists?).

But in those days who knew about such things as "family tensions" and "family induced traumata"? Freud should have practiced on Eldridge Street instead of in Vienna, where he had a wealthy clientele to treat. He would have seen more submerged egos and tension headaches than in all of Austria. Rosenfeld wrote poetry to all these people. He tried to bring ambition and love and social awareness to this struggling horde. He cajoled them, he cursed their oppressors, who in many instances were first-generation Jewish entrepreneurs. He enlisted the Almighty and His Angels and the forces of Nature to excite his audience. His was a specific tonic for a specific syndrome of social ills. His was an elixir of love and hate, guaranteed to induce you to help yourself and raise your self-esteem. He wrote to the Jewish soul. There is one, you know; hard to find these days but once-upon-a-time it was a veritably palpable entity. When we come to think about it, so many years after the immigration experience, it is almost amazing that the Jews of that time were delighted to read poetry in their daily newspaper. *Poetry!* Did you realize that your grandmother actually enjoyed poetry about life and love, about nightingales and sunsets, about the trials and tribulations of an emotional fellow-immigrant who bared his soul to her as though he were lying on a psychiatrist's couch? You see, the fact that these poems were not fancy-shmancy, but were written in every-day Yiddish is the reason this poet was so beloved. He wrote songs you could understand and to which you could relate. It was just this common touch, this universality, that excited us to learn more about Rosenfeld and write this testimonial to him.

One of the things that led to Rosenfeld's downfall and early demise was his inability to accommodate to the changes in Jewish life and Jewish perspective that developed in so short a time, and which he himself had helped to bring about. In just a few years, from the 1880's to the 1920's over one and a half million people, in a cavalcade that has known few equals, left their homes and businesses voluntarily, literally uprooted themselves, and became transplanted in an entirely foreign milieu. How can anyone at this stage of our culture absorb the essence of such a transformation? The author of this text has become subsumed by overpowering sensations from reading and studying a great mass of material about those years. As much as we try to identify with and peer out at the world with immigrant's eyes it is just impossible. We are too far from it. And just as difficult as it is to relate entirely to another generation in another world, one can only hazard the fuzziest guesses at the emotional and intellectual shocks and conflicts that those immigrants sustained. When we say, "We studied history." we mean, "We studied *about* history". Can you tell your wife, "This is how combat was on Guadalcanal and Bougainville?" You can only tell her "about it". She cannot live it ex-post facto and 12,000 miles away.

And so when we try to bring to the reader the world of Morris Rosenfeld, even though he was in our family, and even though we tried to understand "where he came from", it will never be possible to be sure we are absolutely correct. Critics from his own time could have been more accurate. That is, they could have been more so if they had wanted to. Some of his best friends became his severest critics because he alienated them. His staunchest supporter, his publisher, the truly eminent socialist newspaper editor of the "Jewish Forwards," Abe Cahan, became hateful to Rosenfeld. There were arguments about the quantity of work Cahan demanded of Rosenfeld, criticisms of the content of some of the poems. Possibly Cahan wanted too much of a left-wing slant in their attitude. Morris just didn't like anyone else telling him what he should write, when he should write it, what his tone or language should be when he offered his work for publication. And, most probably, Morris preferred his work to be displayed in the most advantageous locations in the newspaper. When you get two vibrant egos like Morris and Abe in one room, something has to give. The explosions were audible all over the place and Morris finally left for another newspaper. Rosenfeld probably brought this unfortunate event upon himself. He simply was not a humble or subservient man.

But something else has to be considered here. When we think of a poet, we imagine him being someone who receives an inspiration, thinks about it all, writes down what he has created and then takes some time to polish it as a finished work of art. If he has to work on a newspaper that demands a certain daily output, a certain political slant to the writings and a certain humility on the part of the poet, then there arises a great similarity to the factory work that had become dehumanizing and disrespectful to the ego that demanded full individuality for the worker. Rosenfeld was emotional, but no fool. He knew what he could do and he knew how well he could do it. The editor did not have any regard for the employee. His concern was "the bottom line", which is the dividing line between a creative mind and a businessman.

However, the criticism he received from the leftwing "Die Junge" ("The Young Ones") was not mere literary criticism. It was not a fair, educated appreciation of his work. It was violent personal degradation of a beloved, established poet under the delusion that by destroying what people loved in a capitalist world, a new order could arise on the ashes. In the long run, all they created was ashes. They produced more noise and pain than product, and what they killed was Morris Rosenfeld, who knew not how to defend himself either wisely or well. He might have joyfully laughed at them and used his laughter to support his own pleasure in life and deride his critics. He was too hurt to laugh, too self-important to enjoy laughter, too excitable to see this rabble in perspective. They reveled in his destruction like the Turks who vandalized the Greek treasures, and left nothing but broken idols.

But, strangely enough, where greatness lies, Death is but a temporary defeat. In "World of Our Fathers" Howe mentions Morris Rosenfeld on more than eleven pages of that striking volume. Morris is mentioned with respect in every major Jewish Encyclopedia and almost every collection of American Jewish verse. In October of 1993 we received a news-clipping from the Jerusalem Post, sent by a friend who is active in Jewish affairs, Saul Schwartz, in which the anniversary of Rosenfeld's death was being "celebrated" in Israel.

We realize that with the decline of the use of Yiddish as a spoken language, we could expect a neglect of the older, "primary" poets of Rosenfeld's vintage. But we regret that not enough sympathetic understanding of these creative, brave people is apparent in recent publications. It seems that present-day writers are either stuck on the name of Sholem Aleichem or still involved with the former shtetl residents and their tragic fate. To this day, however, it is Rosenfeld's poems that are still admired and his songs sung with nostalgia. Who sings the songs of "Die Yunge"? Who revels in their imagery? Who was influenced to rise above the turmoil of the ghetto to achieve a better life, or sing a lullaby to his child written by those young hatchet-men of Yiddish lettres? And yet, cruel and puerile as these alienated and self-absorbed poets were, they did contribute to Yiddish poetry. They opened the door to a more modern appoach to Yiddish writing. They brought novelty and some of the advances that had already been thoroughly explored in European (not Yiddish) writing.

When the author took a course in Yiddish (the better to be able to write this book), he discovered that Rosenfeld's poetry was used in the text for students. When his sons Mark, a psychologist, and Michael, a molecular biologist, went to a gathering of folk singers in 1993, they were delighted to see their great-grandfather's poem, "Mayn Yingele", in the program sponsored by Pete Seeger. You must realize with what pride we react at each surprising revelation that old Grandpa is still read and sung and remembered. Several generations after his death, educated Jews look with admiration at his grandchildren when they learn who we are, as though we had done something to merit this admiration.

When our beloved aunt, Freda Iona Hurwitz, the 104-year-old

last surviving child of Morris Rosenfeld, was interviewed by both her daughter, Mrs. Shirley Paull, and subsequently by her granddaughter, Mrs. Leslie Falk, she answered all the questions put to her in a deliberate and concise manner. They wanted to know what kind of a man her father, Morris, was. Was he excitable around the house? Was he full of self-importance? Did he show much care and attention to his children? Did he get much support from his wife and did his children know how famous he was? We got the answers loud and clear on the tape from that old lady, who reflected carefully before answering about her recollections of the "not so good old days." He was a loving and caring father, sacrificed his all for the family and he was supported and encouraged by his wife Bessie. When Iona was asked, "Was Morris very excitable?" the answer came, "Only if you bothered him while he was writing a poem." (which was most of the time!) Of course his children knew he was a famous man and got to meet all the eminent folks he associated with. These tapes contain, in the measured tones of deep reflection, some valuable insights into Rosenfeld's family life. When we spoke to Aunt Iona of the alienation of the "Yunge" from the work of her father, this charming lady was bright enough to have acquired a long-term, philosophical view of the conflict that destroyed her father. Even the family, she implied, had intuited that squabbles between artists are not earth-shaking events and that history moves in imponderable, unchangeable ways, as do the currents beneath the seas and the winds that circle the globe. In a nursing facility in North Carolina, where she was frequently visited by her daughters and only son, Frieda Iona Hurwitz knew that her father's reputation remains secure.

As we continued with our appraisal of Rosenfeld and the "landsmen" (countrymen) who emigrated with him, we learned that Jewish workers were not like other workers who emigrated from Europe at the same time. From other areas came the sons of peasants and workers who had very limited horizons and training. The Jews were, for the most part, literate, educable, industrious. They had lived a life of discipline because of the strictures of their religion. They were also mighty cautious not to antagonize the real leaders of their country, as they well knew how cruelly an antagonized ruler can behave. The Jews, to a great extent, sensed that one does not live by bread alone. A full culture of religion and learning, hard work and an awareness of their responsibilities to the community were an integral part of their life in Europe and now in America. While the socialists encouraged expectations of a Paradise for the workers, no one in his right mind expected it to arrive right away. In the meantime the lyricism and almost personal communication of the poetry of Rosenfeld and Edelstadt kept their spirits alive. Romanticism went well with socialism—both involved faith, a dreamy disposition and a heavenly goal to attain.

For those who had to live in the ghetto, the whole immigrant scene was more than a little unreal. The poverty and struggling were real enough as were the discomfort and anxiety. The entire uprooting and replanting of the Eastern European Jewish culture were all too real. But the world of anticipation and expectation, the internalization of social problems and exaggerated intensity in their approach to every change in the winds of fortune, even the degree of accuracy in their memories of the lands they had left, created an aura of unreality over the whole scene. Of course they were unaware of this themselves. The point of view of a man in the middle of a stew is different from that of a man looking at the stew from a stool in the kitchen. It was not for years that a more objective approach to their position in the new medina (land) dawned on the immigrants and their offspring. The fervid activity of the socialists and the almost nihilistic communists, who thrived in such turmoil, has left its marks, even on some Jews of today. While the left-wingers only succeeded in electing a few individuals to Congress (more to local office in New York), they gradually petered-out. The arch-radicals developed into the Communist party. The confirmed Socialists led ultimately to the formation of a Socialist Party, of very limited influence. But the impulse towards socialism was greater than any of the left-wing parties. It represented the actual formalization of the deep desires of the proletarian and most other categories of the immigrants of that time.

The socialist movement is the "home" where the immigrant yearning for equality, fraternity and liberty was welcomed and encouraged. Too many uninformed or ill-willed people since then have treated this movement as something "Un-American" or subversive. This is a most unfair assault upon the loyal, honorable and sensible approach by a thinking segment of our ancestry who were simply attempting to solve the desperate problems that history had foisted upon them. Anarchists and Communists were not the Socialists we refer to. Extremists serve their purpose too, but what they ultimately create is merely the goad to progress, not the product. Strangely enough, this socially-oriented movement had extensive ramifications. Although the Socialists as a political party had a sparse membership, their philosophy ultimately had enormous influence, reaching its apex in the deep social commitments of the Rooseveltian Democracy that saved the nation from violence and cataclysmic conflict during the Great Depression.

At a time when national self-indulgence and a laissez-faire attitude by the government allowed the American economy and social order to collapse around our heads like a house of cards, a brave and patriotic group of socially-oriented planners gave the people a New Deal. By reshuffling the cards and seeing to it that as few industrialists as possible could play the game with aces up their sleeves, the common man got a chance once more to play the game and not lose his shirt. The Republican years of Coolidge and Hoover encouraged the same national self-indulgence and concentrations of wealth and poverty that we see today after the Reagan-Bush-Clinton years. The conservative thinkers did not know then, as they do not know now, how to bring the country back to stability or how to return security and confidence to the working man. Many Jewish socialists (with a small "s") produced plans and techniques that encouraged the nation back to normalcy, slowly but surely. The Jewish wealthy became conservatives (then and now) and resisted every effort that could help the nation recover.

This bent for socialism affected the Jewish population and the rest of America also. On the local level, the Jews developed to a high pitch their concern for society, above and beyond their own needs. Whether they remembered it or not, the words of Rosenfeld were still a part of their new tradition of being socially-oriented, to fight against inequity and for a better life for all. Those songs of Rosenfeld were more than mere labor poems; they were paeans to their own inner goodness and fairness. To this day there is hardly a movement for social welfare that is not either led or partially peopled by Jews of the second, third or fourth generation. Jewish members of Congress, even the Republicans, are normally in the forefront of social progress.

This is a part of their socialist heritage, whether they are aware of it or not. Of course, Jews were not the only socialists, nor were they the only leaders in that political movement. The socialist movement had its impetus originally in Europe. But in this country, especially in certain industries, such as the fur, garment and the hat industries, there were many Jewish leaders in the early days of unionization. There were so many proposals and programs from these communally-oriented people during the New Deal days that when Norman Thomas, the perennial Socialist candidate for President of the U.S., ran for office, he was reputed to have observed that, as time went by, he could find less and less to criticize in the programs of the Democratic party that ran the nation. We do not intend to imply that extremes of any kind are acceptable, nor that everything that the New Deal did was correct. What we mean to state is that the history of the working public and their heritage of poverty and oppression in their immigrant days stayed in their collective memories and those who urged them on to self-realization, such as Rosenfeld, Edelstadt and Winchevsky, had a distinct niche that is not forgotten. The labor union movement, the techniques and principles of collective bargaining, medicare, medicaid, welfare, regulations to protect investments, banking, railroads, labor of children, real estate, farming and shipping, equitable treatment of women and minorities, and ever so much more, were the subjects of those who wished to foster an equitable society.

As with all social revolutions, they may have gone too far too soon. But those who came across from Europe at the time of the great migration and had to live in the chaos and humiliation of the ghettos do not have to be reminded how far we have come since then. And those Jews who were literate, who read the "Der Tog" (The Day) or "Die Forwards" (The Forwards) and read Rosenfeld's poems and articles in those publications know how much he contributed to their lives. Among the leadership of the social revolution was Abe Cahan, editor of the Forwards, the major Yiddish-language newspaper. He was a capable, strong-willed "Front Page" editor. In the early days of the paper (from 1898 on) he had Rosenfeld, Edelstadt and Winchevsky and a few genuine rabble-rousers to write for him. Among those influenced by this core of creative spokesmen were Morris Hillquit, Meyer London, Eugene V. Debs, Sidney Hillman, B. Charney Vladek, (whose grandson we knew before his untimely death and whose descendants are still active in labor law), Zimmerman, Dubinsky and Rosenberg. They were among the founders, or inspirers, of the socialist movement. Many of these men had been in the home of Morris Rosenfeld, as had been Jack London, Upton Sinclair and other social activists. It would be impossible to say for sure who influenced whom. Most probably they acquired mutual support from like-minded friends. They all knew they had a nucleus of friends wherever they spoke or wrote. We know for sure that many famous people admired Rosenfeld and kept in touch with him. We have letters available (in the archives of the YIVO) from Edwin Markham, Upton Sinclair, Jane Addams, Stephen S Wise, the banker Seligman, and a host of others who recognized something of value in the ardent socially-oriented attitude of Rosenfeld. Incidentally, although this digression has no historical significance except to the author, Jack London, the noted writer, used to play tennis with Rose Rosenfeld, the author's mother, who had a terrific forehand and a backhand that would have intrigued Martina Navratilova. (We are suddenly aware that perhaps we tend to exaggerate a little bit!)

International socialism, as originally conceived in Europe and shared here in America, failed because of unrealistic goals. Although Jewish socialism increased an intellectual understanding of the world we live in, it was unable to create a totally new, equitable society anywhere. However, the increased social consciousness of much of the world became a new, potent force in the firmament of history. Knowing the root causes of social problems does not guarantee that the general populace will understand and accept the prescription for a new society. Humanity moves slowly and retrogressive forces, which have decisive powers everywhere, make progress tedious, even dangerous to attempt. Jews in America, newly aroused, became more spirited, more combative and socially creative as they became more deeply rooted here. Despite serious disappointments, great strides have been made in terms of creating more humane conditions in the workplace and in every stratum a generally more equitable society for all has developed. Those of you who would like to read an excellent work about the immigrant writers might find that *A History of Yiddish Literature*, by Sol Lipzin, is very complete and expressive. Mr. Lipzin treats his subject-matter with the same excitement and emotional fealty that this author expresses for his own work. The love and respect with which he treats the Yiddish poets is like that of a son who admires his creative parent. One quote from his book pertains to Rosenfeld as much as it does to Edelstadt, the socialist-activist poet. He said, "His muse must have been a proletarian muse." This means, in a way, that the writer must sense that a greater power than his own limited strength is involved in his work. For certain, Rosenfeld felt this way.

The immigrant workers were not alone all the time. They created all sorts of fraternal and labor organizations and all manner of classes were available for them. "Die Arbeiter Ring", (The Workman's Circle), which was formed in 1898, was created to provide classes in almost everything from English language and literature to free love and electricity! They also provided members with sick care and funeral services. Rosenfeld was a member and is buried in their cemetery near Sholem Aleichem. Members of the Workmen's Circle spent much time learning facts and terminology to use in discussions, arguments and debates—which were endless. The Workmen's Circle encouraged people to open their eyes to see the work around them, open their mouths to speak up and open their hearts to their fellow men."Visionaries", who also abounded in the Jewish community because almost everybody thought he knew "all the answers", could also join the Workman's Circle, even if they would all end up, eventually, in that cemetery in Brooklyn.

Visionaries are those who, in their mind's eyes, can see the future through the haze of historical debris; through the convolutions of human thought and behavior. They can visualize changes that nature herself does not dare predict of its own condition. Of all the elements in Jewish history, the only ones we know of whose admonitions and predictions were almost exactly replicated in real life, years later, were those of the Eastern European Jewish orthodoxy. They feared that exposure to secular life and the challenges of a world they had actually never experienced themselves would lead to a breakdown of the bonds of fealty to the Jewish religion, its codes and customs. Ultimately their fears were that even the untaught affection for the "mameloshn un Yiddishkeit" (mother-tongue and Jewishness) would become diluted and ultimately vanish. We would again see "Germans of the Mosaic persuasion" and American GI's whose only palpable link to their past is the "H" on their dog-tags which signifies their belonging to a Hebrew tribal remembrance.

How did they know? Did they sense the true frailty of the bonds of Judaism? If the invisible bonds of atom to atom are rent, an atomic explosion can occur. A similar, if less violent, explosion has occurred with the rending of the bonds of Jewishness. No one is to blame. No Jew with a knowledge of the world could have wanted the Jews to remain in the unbearable misery of Eastern European villages. There were no opportunities there for the cultural and intellectual explosion that occurred when the Jews came to the New World, the Free World. Perhaps "Free" is the code word. Perhaps "free" means not merely freedom from the serf-like deprivation of the shtetl and Russian-Polish dominion. Perhaps "free" means loosening the shackles of a primitive religion, a primitive culture, an arena of ignorance on a world scale, untidiness and subjection to the malodorous niche that was carved out for them by History.

Certainly Rosenfeld was no seer, but in a letter to his dear friend and sponsor, Professor Leo Wiener, in 1897, he wrote, "the Zhargon has no future in this country anyway: within twenty-five years even the best works written in this language will remain mere literary curiosities." Despite this rather depressed attitude that he expressed at the time, he fought with anyone who would denigrate the use of Yiddish. Still, he was no seer. He was too close to and too involved with the turbulence and insecurity of his own time.

To write about a man who is still remembered by some of his remaining grandchildren would seem like a relatively easy task. However, in order to try to place his life and works in perspective it has taken great effort and investigation to try to even imagine what his personality was actually like. We have tried to bring to the reader what we have learned about his milieu and his family background. Until the preparation for this book was nearly completed, we had never fully understood why he had chosen the field of poetry, that least remunerative and most poorly understood of all careers, as his means of applying for a niche in history. (More on this subject in a subsequent chapter.)

Among the writers who attempted to describe the stripped-to-the-bone level of existence in which the immigrants were forced to live until they could rise by themselves, there was none more objective, yet friendly and warm, than the non-Jewish essayist, Hutchins Hapgood. After spending many days in the ghetto of the Lower East Side of New York, Hapgood wrote many essays which he combined into a volume, in 1902, called "The Spirit of The Ghetto". This sympathetic description of what many might term an indescribable morass was illustrated by the young artist, Jacob Epstein, who was just starting his career and was met, almost casually, by Hapgood during his wandering about the ghetto. Hapgood noted that there was something about these immigrants that enabled them virtually to transmogrify themselves from denizens of an almost animal-like habitat, where they scurried about grubbing for existence, into new beings without any role-models to imitate. They kept what they could of the past and adapted as quickly as possible to what they imagined was the "real American" of their time, as demonstrated to them in big-city life. The weight of history was upon them. The stress of change was like a goad beneath their skin; the burden of survival was almost unbearable. But beneath it all pulsed a vitality, a sense of the importance of their being in the mosaic of the world. Indeed, if the word "mosaic" does not come from "Moses" it might well have. The tapestry of life and the tiles of a "mosaic pattern" require a weaving of the fibers and a juxtaposition of the inanimate, immutable colors and shapes that may have gotten their origins in the dim reaches of the creation of Earth and the first dawn of color and variety. With what seems like a haphazard selection of values and tones of achievement, the immigrant Jew became metathesized from deplorably unsophisticated small-townniks to big-city denizens; from unicultured pariahs of the world to artisans, artists, philosophers, physicians, dentists, teachers of every conceivable discipline, scientists, writers, actors, politicians, movers and doers. All this was done in an alien society, all with good will, all within two generations. How much more could anyone have expected of immigrants?

There must have been something explosive in the human psyche that could lie repressed for thousands of years by uncaring civilizations all over the world and then, almost suddenly, burgeon forth, flower, in the 19th and 20th centuries. How quickly did the Jews from the farms and small villages of Europe leap over the centuries to assume a position of parity (at least) with their fellow-residents of Europe and the New World! In a bare forty years, from 1880 to 1920, millions of repressed Jews came to an area where relative freedom of opportunity and relative freedom of expression encouraged them to assume a niche in the Western world, equivalent to the cultural founders of Western society. Not only was the Jewish religion the foundation of Christianity and Mohammedanism, but Jewish respect for the humane discipline of life is still the model by which civilized societies live.

This appreciation by the author is, of course, an overview. Those individual Jews living during that critical forty years were assuredly not aware that they were "chips in a mosaic"or "threads in a tapestry". Only a few were granted the pedestals of "visionaries", on observation posts that enabled them to view with historical, almost Biblical perspective, the frame that they and their people were occupying in the broad moving picture of history. Most artists and leaders were obsessed with the problems of the moment. Only a very few others were able to take "the long view". In a sense, most of "the greats" had, at times, the capacity to visualize their contemporary life in its historical context, the ability to distance themselves from the moment to see Jewish life in perspective. Such men were "Mendele" and Sholem Aleichem. Of course, almost anyone who could look at himself and laugh had to be able to stand back a few paces from the mirror and let out that guffaw that means, "Que face buffo!" ("What a funny face! What a quaint being I am in this strange, transient world!").

Rosenfeld, as trapped as he was in the struggle between his ego and his true place in the arts, was likewise a poet for the Ages. Coming, as he did, from such a background of relative hopelessness to a milieu that was such a hekdish (mad, chaotic situation) of poverty and confusion, of rootlessness and change, it is nothing less than amazing that he (and only a few others) chose poetry, of all things, to make his living from and to use as his lever to pry a little space for himself in the celestial Hall of Fame. For those "strangers in paradise" who came to this Golden Land, Rosenfeld brought beauty and excitement urging them to think of themselves in higher terms than just, "ich bin ah machine" (I am a machine); just a cog in a wheel. He gave them a raison d'etre and by inflaming their imagination aided them in suffering through the nightmare that was immigration and resettlement.

He was never depressed in his writing. He never suggested that they surrender to loneliness and rejection. He had the forceful voice of a prophet; the pounding pulse of the Jewish heart that did not yield for twenty centuries of dispersal. He was indeed a bard for his time, and, unfortunately, all too human in his response to criticism.

References

1. Harshav, Benjamin, "The Meaning of Yiddish", p. 122.
2. Howe, Irving, "World Of Our Fathers", p. 506.
3. Raskin, Phillip, "Anthology of Modern Jewish Poetry".

4

Descendants Of Rosenfeld In Yiddish Poetry

Sometime around 1909–10 a group of young Jewish poets used to hang around the coffee-shops of the lower East Side of New York's Manhattan. As happened in Europe's culture-conscious centers in Germany, France, Austria and Russia these neophytes fed on each other's excitement. They shared the same Jewish heritage of deprivation and transplantation to America. They shared the same dismay at the conditions of the poor Jews everywhere and were profoundly shaken in their confidence that capitalism could solve the problems of the common man. They all agreed amid feverish arguments and dire predictions that only a veritably nihilistic destruction of all that exists is essential before a new form of beneficent society could be created. As so often happens to Jews they figured that if "we" sacrifice our beliefs, our heritage, our customs and creativity to this, as yet nonexistent, new social order "they" will like us better, "they" will accept us."They" will let us lead a better life. Oh how sad that these bright youths (almost none of whom were truly educated in history, economics, sociology, psychology or other sciences) should fall into so deep a trap. Their goals were well meant but their technics impossible and unnecessary to effectuate.

Some of the earlier poets and writers in the Jewish community here felt the same way, years before. Yehoash, Edelstadt, Zhitlovsky also were "anarchists". Even Rosenfeld paid more than lip service to the newly formed organizations offering rebellion to the disenfranchised poor who seemed as lost in this heaving world as a chip of wood upon the seas. Rosenfeld was known to have paid sixpence for a publication about the eight Chicago anarchists whose plight created a world-wide stir.

As Americans living in a time of relative security and comfort we may find it almost impossible to relate to the lives of desperation that our grandparents underwent. Jewish history was adequate proof of the unreliability of every form of government they had ever experienced. Not since the days before the destruction of the Temple and their dispersal across the face of this globe had Jews experienced a government that accepted the Jews on an equal footing with everyone else with the promise of permanence and security. Coming to this country, with all its bounty and burgeoning power, the Jews were suspicious, despite their apparent acceptance, of the possibilities of final, ultimate disaster in case this capitalist system did not work out.

When you have lost everything or are suffering unremittingly, it is to be expected that you will seek some revolutionary avenue to travel to a different form of living. Thus anarchy, Socialism, Fascism and Communism arose. Almost all of the Earth's four-plus billion people live in poverty and oppression. Can anyone believe that revolutions and dictatorships will now end just because Russia has possibly disintegrated as a world power? The Blacks here in America today are on the same path that all people ultimately tread when they feel that their lives are unfulfilled and the future looks hopeless to them. Even though much of the responsibility for the problems they face could be dealt with by themselves and within themselves, their poverty and second-class citizenship and their attitude towards the whites are all obvious now. Social problems do not take much to bring them to a crisis stage and must be heeded by those interested in creating a just and balanced society. The same sort of despair in which it seems that no one is listening to their cries that the Jews went through for so long a time is a ticking time bomb for this ultra-complacent America. We urge, as Rosenfeld's grandchildren, that our fellow citizens pay heed to the problems of the underprivileged. We should also be aware that the "right wing" of the nation has been flapping threateningly lately in a revived divisiveness that even includes the use of firearms. Threats to liberty do not always come from the "left". Anyone who can relate sympathetically to the social impulses of our grandparents must share in our well-considered admonitions, since we are all aware that history does have a tendency to repeat itself. This historical tendecy towards repetition is due to the fact that two to three generations after some calamitous events have taken place there is no longer any true memory of the event extant and unless there is some organized effort to remind people by use of the media, by having plays performed, books written or songs sung about those past events they become a part of "history" and we all know how eager people are to read history and to learn from it.

Without any proof or evidence that socialism or communism or anarchy could or would provide the beneficence that they were looking for, many Jews fell into the same trap that almost all of the European working-class stumbled into. They looked for a panacea the way others look for the Messiah when all else seems to be hopeless. Russia fell deepest into the hole, and just as the hands on the clock of socialism went all the way around to the extreme of communism, there were working-class people all over the world who invested their lives and their hope in varying degrees of socialism, looking for "Mr. Goodbar", the dude who would make life all happiness and comfort. As we all know by now, ex post facto, "Mr. Goodbar" does not exist, yet.

This brief background should make it a little easier for some of us to understand how some of our not so distant ancestors could have developed into ardent socialists of varying degrees. It also should explain why so many Jewish poets were so concerned with the urgent social problems of the times they lived in that they felt impelled to join organizations and write about the hopefulness of a future that took the common man into account. As Rosenfeld approached the final years of his writing, partially burned-out by the unbanked fires of his nature and by the cruel winds of adversity, he was faced with a new development in the evolution of Jewish writing, the appearance of a group of young, newer immigrants who also wrote in Yiddish but in a different vein. These were "Modernists"; talented, sensitive, creative and just as dirt-poor as Rosenfeld ever was. These men, who called themselves "Di Yunge" (The Young Ones) "reflected all the modern tensions of a self-ironic society in the process of losing a traditional value-system; the throes of urban alienation gripping the scattered descendants of a close-knit near-feudal community; the tension between the demands of

Modernist art on the one hand and the repeated search for new forms of mimeses and expression on the other; . . ."[1].

These young writers wanted to elevate Yiddish poetry a few notches beyond the traditional forms of poetry that were employed by Rosenfeld, Winchevsky, Edelstatdt and Yehoash, the basic four of American Yiddish poetry until that time. Better read than those writers and under the influence of Russian, Polish, French and German Modernists they created an interesting form of Yiddish poetry, entirely new on this landscape. The works of Blok, Baudelaire, Rimbaud, Rilke, Sologub, Bryusov, Hofmannsthal and others gave new impetus to the almost revolutionary writing of these young men. At first their work was looked upon with contempt by some of the more traditional writers and the public did not accept them at all. These men wrote "art for art's sake" which would have been just fine if they could have interested the public in their esoteric poetry.

The best known of these poets were Mani Leib, Zisha Landoy (Landau), Reuben Iceland, Joseph Rolnick and Moshe Leib Halpern. Some Yiddish writers, like Halpern and H.Leivick, were less a force within Di Yunge. They shared, primarily, a distaste for earlier Yiddish poetry which they considered unaesthetic and tendentious, socially-activist in motif and too concerned with a journalistic mood. Of course in this they were partially correct. They felt, as Landau was known to state, that those poets of Rosenfeld and Edelstadt and Winchevsky's era were little more than "the rhyme department of the labor movement" which was also not entirely inaccurate. Di Junge were not only in revolt against the subject matter of their predecessors. They were devoted to changing the forms and meters of the writing and to eliminating references to traditional content, including Hebraisms, journalistic techniques, sentimentality and Germanisms. Their writing was melodious and "aesthetic" but the content was, if not vacuous, then like the product of someone whose head is in the clouds and his heart closed to the world about him. We all know what youth is. We all had that serious condition at least once in our lives. Another word for that condition is immaturity and with that phase often comes corollary inconsideration and self-adulation that temporarily blinds us to respect and due regard for our elders and our predecessors. In primitive man the trick was to kill your father and eat his heart. This was to give you strength and the superior ability to meet the problems of the day. In the Catholic Church every Sunday the parishioners "eat of the body of Christ and drink of his blood." Seriously speaking! You see, civilization hasn't gone very far at all, has it?

These young Jewish writers felt that they had to make their mark in the world of letters by demolishing their predecessors. They had to kill them off and eat their hearts, figuratively speaking. Nothing new about that. These men had no goals but chose to live by their senses, in their poetry, at least, and in their other publications. What permeated their work was an estrangement from the land of their origin, Russia, as well as a homesickness for the quiet and closeness of the shtetl. How sad it was that with all the newness to be gloried about in this country these men not only wallowed in a childish nostalgia for the land that rejected them but also treated the few poets who loved and supported the immigrant population as though they, these poets, were pariahs. "Di Yunge" castigated Rosenfeld, Winchevsky and Edelstadt with a viciousness that is usually reserved for a foe. It is difficult for a layman to understand why poetry cannot be written in a climate of good will, even if the form of the poetry is different from that of its predecessors. Just as Van Gogh painted only for himself, breaking with tradition, having no audience (did he ever sell a painting during his lifetime?) and saying to his brother, "I don't want to express society's point of view. I just want you to know what I feel," so these young men rejected the past, rejected the present, lived in a dream-world of beauty and art and were duly neglected by the public. In fact, the attention they are getting now, near the year 2000, from perceptive students such as the husband and wife Harshav team is more understanding and flattering than they received during their lifetimes. Despite their talents they were like actors who constantly play "to an empty house." They knew what *they* liked but did not regard the taste of the public as germane.

Mani Leib's notable poem, "Shtiller, Shtiller", has been described as causing "resignation to be raised to heroism", the antithesis of the activist poetry of Rosenfeld, Winchevsky, Jehoash and Edelstadt and others who tried to give poetry a social significance in addition to its astheticism. Young as these "Yunge" were, their pervasive mood of weariness and resignation might have been a psychological reaction to the awful plight of the Jews in transition. The outside world was of less consequence to them than what was going on within their heads. This did not prevent those young poets from devoting their entire creative lives to opening the world of Yiddish poetry to new vistas. Leib and Leivick were indeed talented men, leaders of their particular cult of beauty; sad, tortured souls, the very anomalies one would expect to see develop after millennia of oppression.

It may seem strange to ask this question here and now, but one has to wonder why Rosenfeld did not become that sort of writer. Possibly the advent of similar poetry in Europe took place after Rosenfeld's personality had been formed. He was not interested in the modernist modes of expression. "Di Yunge" themselves were subjected a few years later, in the 1920's to the same senseless, frenetic, emasculating viciousness of a group known as Introspectivists. "In Zich", meaning developing one's point of view and ability to appreciate the true status of all vital things from within one's self, was the source of their philosophy of expression. We have to wonder what happens to some people when they get an idea that they think is new and valuable. First, before their idea has matured and taken hold on the public imagination, they attack and destroy the name and reputation of all who precede them. "Di Yunge" were "too poetic"!, just as Rosenfeld wasn't "aesthetic"! And so it went with other splinter groups of poets whose need for attention and appreciation were greater than their discipline as writers, greater than their common decency as human beings. The fact that perhaps their new idea will really take hold some day (as some of it did, twenty years later) is no excuse for bad manners.

Rosenfeld fought back like a tiger, impetuously, insultingly, meeting his personal critics in a bitter struggle that demeaned them all and shortened Rosenfeld's life. Who ever said that Grandpa was always sensible and couth? We hardly knew him; certainly never saw him angry or rough. But now, after reading about that old curmudgeon, seeing how he refused to be put down by some self-infatuated youths, we only wish he had been more circumspect in his battle with them. After all, this was only about poetry, not national borders. Or was it only about poetry? Was it not a threat to take away from this man the raison d'etre of his entire life?

The "In Zich" group was also at least as "left wing" as was Di Yunge. They were more alienated than their predecessors, more involved with complete changes in the art form of their poetry, not at all aesthetic in their outlook or their forms. We came to their poetry by accident. It is entirely out of our usual range of reading.

Remember, we are "Americans of the Jewish persuasion," readers of almost everything under the sun, except Yiddish literature, until now. It was only when we started to read voluminously in researching material for this book, that we even heard, for the first time, the name of the Introspectivists. In fact, truly, we feel as though we have come upon a new planet that has been circling our heads in darkness and silence for all our lives.

Where have we been? We cannot "like" the "In Zichists" for their abuse of old Grandpa. But they were very interesting poets; serious, talented, innovative and more than a little weird. And since we are somewhat like comets ourselves, too soon to whisk out of sight, how grateful we are to have discovered this little Introspective planet that has been just around the bend all these years! Remember how we titled "Di Yunge" young and immature? We must do the same for the "In Zich" group, which included Jacob Glatshteyn, Jacob Stodolsky, Celia Dropkin, N. Minkov, B. Alquit, A.Leyeles, Mikhl Licht. Of the entire two groups of poets we have been discussing only one truly major poet has developed, Jacob Glatshteyn. This man's poetry is worthy of many studies and much more attention than it has been given until now. His relationship to the "In Zich" people gradually became more peripheral though it was he and Leyeles and Minkov who started the group. They were primarily interested in an entirely new concept of Yiddish poetry. They were influenced by recent Modernist movements in Europe: Futurism, Expressionism, Vorticism, Imagism, etc. Benjamin Harshav, in his "The Meaning of Yiddish" briefly describes Introspectivism as, "A literary trend launched in 1919, began a theoretic and practical revolt against the dominance and 'poeticalness' of the Young Generation. . . . for them a poem represented a kaleidoscope of broken pieces from the social world, as perceived in the psyche of a sophisticated urban individual and as expressed in a unique rhythmical fugue.

"Theirs was post-symbolist poetics, stressing free verse, open thematics and language and an end to the poetic ivory tower. . . . they developed a rather Anglo-American poetics of irony, dramatized and objectified poetic situations and intellectual understatement; they formed a much more mature, anti-sentimental, and honestly harsh view of the real world. They were the focal point of the best poetry written in Yiddish."[2] This long quote from Harshav informs you that he is a linguist par excellence and expresses this subject-matter far more authoritatively than we can. You simply have to know when to call in a specialist! It was unfortunate not only on a personal basis but also for the continuity of Yiddish letters that the "Introspectivists" treated "Die Yunge"as coldly and uncaringly as the latter had treated the conventional poets who preceded them.

Before we go much further we must explain that there is a valid reason for our including so much material here about the two most influential groups of Yiddish poets who wrote during the teens and twenties of this century. They impacted directly on the life and reputation of Morris Rosenfeld. Di Yunge and Rosenfeld were involved in a clash of personalities that wore down the core of Rosenfeld's resistance and led ultimately to his premature demise. The youngsters saw that Rosenfeld fell for their bait too easily and were involved in a feeding-frenzy at his expense. Had not Rosenfeld and the poets of his generation contributed to the appreciation of poetry by the immigrants, "Di Yunge" and "In Zich" might not have had an audience. The public was "sensitized" to reading poetry— Yiddish poetry. Had not the "hot-heads" of Rosenfeld's generation fought for workers' rights for years, at the expense of their own health, those later poets might not even have secured decent jobs to support themselves. It is strange how the esthetic and the practical can sometimes join hands this way.

The traditional poetry of Rosenfeld was anathema to the "modernists": His sentimentality, his meter and rhyme, his socially oriented verses and the traditional sentiments about Jewish life were aspects that some were too "modern" to be concerned about. Ultimately, as they "grew up", the Yiddishkeit that was in the bones of these young rebels became apparent in their poetry, despite their efforts to deny it and to change the world of poetry. The deep feeling that they denied became part of their work. Their sense of pathos, their inner writhing at the vagaries of Fate, erupted as it would with any feeling poet. They did change the outer forms of their poetry at the same time. In one of their publications the "Inzichists" stated categorically, "We have no tradition. We have very little that can serve as tradition for us. Tradition begins, perhaps, with us, strange as it may sound."[3] Sounds very existential, doesn't it? The world is destroyed, all values are gone. There is nothing left to cling to except our own essence, so we start tradition from today on. This is day ONE of the Universe!

However, is that existentialism or solipsism? Is it the first page of a new Bible or self-infatuation? They have no tradition, they say, yet they are held by the apron-string of the very mamaloshn (mother tongue) they use for every expression. They try desperately to escape the web, with new art forms, some of which are as involved and complex as a section from the Kabbala. There are some poems by these Modernists that truly require a cryptographer rather than a poetic analyst to decipher. And when it is understood, what did they say? What did they write that is of such great consequence? Despite a lifetime of sincere, heartfelt creativity they left a body of works that failed to impress the Jewish reading public and they themselves must have died in disappointment that they had "cast pearls before swine." It was patent that they were frustrated that their work had led to so little admiring recognition.

Unfortunately, the fact that both Die Yunge and the Inzichists were concerned, at first, only about themselves and their art left very little room in their hearts for their people, its tradition and its honored writers. Only they, the newcomers on the scene, deserved attention. By concentrating on "innovation" and "originality" in their works, by castigating traditional poets who had been standard fare for the working public, by refusing to write in a form that the public could understand and appreciate, they deprived the public for twenty five years of having a body of poetry that could have served to form an important and necessary part of any culture. All this in the name of "art". Yiddish was *such* a new language; Yiddish poetry was less than fifty years old; the people were trying to re-establish a new culture on the ashes of the old. This was indeed creating a disservice toward their fellow immigrants, to claim as they did that they had no tradition! The more subjectively they wrote the more alienated and confused with reality they proved to be. No tradition, indeed! No history? There was no Torah and no Talmud? There were no auto da fe's, no pogroms, no Tevye's all over Eastern Europe? No problems of survival for their fellow immigrants to weigh on their hearts? There was no glory that was Greece and Grandeur that was Rome? They tried to cast tradition aside, as does a true existentialist, but the world went on without them.

Even so, reading their poetry and knowing of their lives, who can criticize with anything but understanding? The indescribable struggle of alienated young minds attempting to establish a new identity on the rubbish heap of the old does warrant our consideration; especially after they themselves had tried to turn the past into a rubbish heap. We can understand, had they been our own sons, how they could be guilty of causing aggravation for the old-timers of Yiddish letters. Yet it is true that neither Shakespeare, Poe, Byron, Coleridge or Wordsworth would have felt it necessary to climb over the bodies of their predecessors in order to demonstrate their talent. They simply wrote and published in a decent respectful manner that did not take the mensch from the man. An unfortunate consequence of the modernist movements in Yiddish poetry was an acceleration of the disuse of Yiddish as a language. Who sang the songs of Landau or Mani Leib? Who recited the poetry of any of the Modern poets to their children or sang them lullaby's from Leivick or Leyeles? The shtetl sulked in the corridors of their hearts and they refused to listen to the foot-steps. By depriving the American Jewish public of a full body of poetry to bring into their homes for more than a generation the Modernists did contribute to the disuse of Yiddish as a language here. The very names "The Young" and "The Within One's-Self" tell the story. Narcissus was simply not a very socially oriented figure.

The answer to the problems discussed above is, of course, alienation. These men were by-products of a shattered culture. Like splinters from a fallen tree. they were sharp, they were fresh and bright in the sunlight, but they represented a fragmented mentality, unable to see the whole and unable to feel their own pulse which beat in a different syncopation than their fellow Jews. They had all the intellect one would need to write great poetry but only two or three reached maturity in their personalities and their work. Leyeles, Leivick and Glatshteyn bore the imprimatur of "Master Of His Art". One cannot look meanly at the point of view of one who has suffered so interminably that life and its complexities might indeed appear to be a kaleidoscope of broken pieces best viewed through a long tube with a light at the end. It was viewed not with the expectation that a newly reconstituted whole would appear but a magnification and brightening of the disconnected fragments, each particle left to dazzle as a shard of life. When you are alienated and fractured psychically you might view life in this way. When you are a poet you have a right to try to find meaning in the randomness of life and the nihilism of the defeated persona.

Except for the works of Leyeles, Leivick and Glatshteyn little remains of the efforts of either"Di Yunge" or the "Inzichists". Students and scholars, who refuse to let the dead lie still, are the only ones who still actively pursue the writing of those men. Perhaps a man with the brilliance and talent of Benjamin Harshav can bring their works back to life. He fanned their sparks in; "The Meaning of Yiddish" and "American Yiddish Poetry". But who can see the light of those sparks? Even we, the grandchildren of Morris Rosenfeld had to take a course in Yiddish to read his works. But to understand them, to gather in one's mind the references to a broken life or visualize the fragments of history and the tortured psyches from another era, that is asking too much of us. Oh how we would love to be able to read Glatshteyn and Rosenfeld in the original without stumbling and having to look up all the esoterica in the dictionaries of Harkavy and Weinreich. Rosenfeld was the bard for his time and Glatshteyn was the bard for his era. He, above all seems to be the giant that Yiddish required to evolve into the instrument for dealing with twentieth century Yiddishkeit. We wonder: do we still have time to learn? But Glatshteyn knew, after the Holocaust, that Yiddish was living on borrowed time and that he was doing what Arthur Miller once claimed for himself, "my writing is merely a fingerprint on the ice-cubes of time!"

We will not continue this discussion beyond the early years of the Modernist poets because it no longer relates directly to Rosenfeld's life or his poetry. It should suffice for us to claim that Yiddish as a language and its poetry became broadened and more sophisticated with the increased freedom and exposure to Western culture. Yiddish poetry took on the hues and the qualities of much Western poetry as the years went by, reacting chameleon-like to the changes in environment, as did all Western poetry. However, one major difference exists between the poetry of the modern Jewish writers and the modern poetry in France, England, Germany, Russia and Italy. Those other languages will live on, undisturbed by their poets, used and abused by a billion people who never even dream about their language vanishing. But the Yiddish poets are indeed writing on "ice-cubes." Their readership is vanishing, their works dripping downward into the oblivion of a forgotten world. What happens to a poet's heart when he knows this and is helpless to reverse his course? Was there something prophetic in the "Introspectives'" concentration on the disjointed fragments of chaos?

Was there not a holocaust a few years later? Were they not writing with a subconscious sense of foreboding? It is a 'puzzlement.'

The tension between traditionalists and modernists, between both and realism, is all a matter of point of view. Traditional Yiddish writers and artists created from the immediacy of their life experiences. They did not have the "luxury" of an expanded culture during their formative years. They drew from the only well in town, the lives of their fathers and the current source of their woes, both the same well of tears, a deep eternal flow that leaves the taste of salt upon the lips. Later poets had the advantage of seeing the light of hope beyond the horizon. They could draw courage from the multicolored prisms lit by the sun. They knew, subconsciously, that this new light was coming to the world, if only they could keep their souls under control and wait. Each man greets the dawn of a new day in his own way. The early Jewish writers greeted it with trepidation bordering on despair. "Di Yunge" and the "Introspectivists" greeted it with a new-found freedom and sense of encouragement so that they could try new forms of expression and seek fundamental truths previously hidden in the dark of night.

And then, when all seemed possible, came the darkest night of all, the Holocaust, bringing the hopes of the civilized world to its most shocking set-back in history. Atavism and barbarism caused shock-waves to permeate the arts and wrought severe damage to the hopefulness in Man. This was reflected in the post-holocaust poetry of all men, particularly Jewish writers and artists. Nor is the primitivism in Mankind over yet. This is not your Hollywood scenario, where we weather a terrible storm and then all go down to the beach together and play. Blackness, horror and mindlessness loom on every horizon. Chaos and anarchy have set in like the germs of a serious disease all over the world. The Atlantic Monthly recently devoted an entire issue to the infection of chaos worldwide, written by a man named Kaplan. What new forms of art and poetry can one foretell for such a forbidding future? The Jews will be there, as usual, to cry in pain. The world should listen, this time.

References

1. Harshav, Benjamin, "The Meaning of Yiddish", p. 162
2. ibid, p. 172
3. Harshav, Benjamin and Barbara, "American Yiddish Poetry", Appendix

5

Yiddish: Where It Came From And Where It Has Gone

One of the distinguishing attributes of Rosenfeld's poetry is the fact that he wrote principally in Yiddish. Had he written in modern German, French, English or Japanese, as examples of well-established conventional languages, it would have been relatively easy to translate his prose and less difficult to translate and understand his poetry. But Yiddish is not a 'conventional' language. It developed from a myriad of sources, from a Zhargon (Jargon) to language status relatively recently. It did not flourish as a language for scientific purposes or for literary value until the late nineteenth century.

According to Galvin and Tamarkin , *The Yiddish Dictionary and Sourcebook,* [1] Yiddish had its roots in a mixture of dialects used by Jews in the Rhine valley of western German states during the Middle Ages. During the ninth and tenth centuries Jews, who had been expelled from Northern France and Italy and settled north of the Pyrenees and Alps in a region Jews have long called Ashkenaz, were the first to use the language that came to be called Yiddish.

The Ashkenazim, as they were called, never stayed for long in any one area. Outside pressures forced them to move East or West, back to France or the Low Countries or East to Poland, Russia, Slovakia or Rumania, and so on. The language that came to be known as Yiddish acquired a different "complexion" in each country to which the Ashkenazim traveled. Characteristics that differed from the original basis of Rhineland German were acquired. Words, expressions, even inflections from each country the Jews went to were used.

These "accretions" to their language were nothing new to the Jews. From the days of their first dispersal to Babylonia there started to be added a multitude of languages upon the original Hebrew of the Jewish Kingdom. Hence developed the language called Aramaic, a synthesis of Hebrew and Babylonian, used by the Hebrews for centuries. Many Aramaic words and expressions survive to this day in Scriptures and in Yiddish. A crossword puzzle in the New York Times recently noted that Jesus spoke Aramaic! Hebrew has always been the "loshn-kodesh", the holy language of the scriptures and the prayers, and of the Commentaries on the Holy documents. Learned Jews spoke Hebrew especially in regard to the sacred functions of the religion, but in ordinary conversation they spoke whatever patois was normal for whatever country it was in which they lived.

As an example of Diaspora languages (those languages spoken by the Jews in whatever land they were dispersed to) there were : Aramaic, Judeo-Greek, Judeo-Arab, Judeo Latin, Judeo Italian, Judeo-Provencal, Judeo-French, Judeo-Persian, and from Judeo-Spanish came four varieties; Ladino, Romance, Judesmo and Spaniolit. Scholars have isolated such exotic languages as Bulchaic of Central Asia, Tartic of the Caucasus, the extinct Arphatic of Northern France, Crimchak of the Crimea, Catalania of Iberia and Shuadit of Provence.[2] It is quite apparent that we Jews really have been dispersed like no other people in history. We are reminded of certain feathery seed-clusters that are blown from the branches of their mother-tree and carried by the wind to land, one at a time, on alien soil far away in an effort by nature to propagate their kind everywhere. Sometimes the soil is rocky and inhospitable. Sometimes these seeds light on fertile, friendly soil. But they are eternal strangers, always the seeds of some foreign tree that lives only through these offspring. A simple re-reading of the exotic languages mentioned in this paragraph is enough to bring tears to our eyes.

Yiddish is written in Hebrew orthography (Hebrew letters written from right to left, with modifications). Yiddish was much different in Medieval times than current Yiddish is. One would be hard-put to understand it now even though it was the colloquial language of the Jews of Central Europe. However, Hebrew was never neglected for rituals and prayers. Also, most individuals who had to maintain some social intercourse with the surrounding communities learned to speak some of the languages of those areas.

Thus they were able to develop some use of the French, Spanish, German, Arabic, Persian, and other local languages of those lands.

In the eighteenth Century a moderate form of enlightenment reached the Jewish settlements in Europe. There the more enlightened individuals were called Maskilim, Jewish intellectuals and assimilationists, who were caught up in the European spirit of enlightenment. These Maskilim deprecated the use of Yiddish, calling it a Zhargon (Jargon). They felt (correctly, at the time) that the language was appropriate for the household, the farm, the nursery, the shop, but not for elevated literature or science. They thought of Yiddish as a "linguistic pastiche". In a way, that is just what it was: a multi-faceted tongue with a history and linguistic structure that was extraordinarily complex. "Yiddish is 12th Century Rhenish German. It contains elements of Hebrew in its vocabulary but it never adopted Hebraic syntactical form. Its morphology, syntax and accidence have remained purely Germanic and it is properly classified as a German tongue."[3]

There is so much more that can be said about the origin and use of this language that it would be overwhelming and far exceed the scope of this book. Our bibliography will mention some excellent volumes for anyone more deeply interested in Yiddish linguistics. We bow to the brilliance of such linguistic experts as the Weinreich family (bothUriel and Max), Benjamin Harshav, Alexander Harkavy and Solomon Birnbaum, among others. However, for our purposes, trying to discuss the Yiddish language and Morris Rosenfeld's place in its evolution, we must move on to discuss those writers who preceded Rosenfeld in writing (especially poetry) in Yiddish. There truly were not very many intellectuals who wrote literature in Yiddish in Europe and especially in America, but we must mention whose who had a distinct influence on the development of the Yiddish language.

In 1507 there appeared the earliest classic of Yiddish literature. It was the "Bovo Bukh", written by a Hebrew grammarian named Elijah Levita (1468–1549, known as "Bokher". This book was a collection of tales in verse based on the Bible and was followed by a series of Yiddish prayer-books designed for women. Then, in 1602, the most popular of all early Yiddish publications, the "Mayse-Bukh" appeared. This collection of folk-tales and Talmudic stories by Jacob ben Isaac Ashkenazi (1550–1620) was followed by his "Tseno-Ureno". This was a "Women's Bible". Sometime in the 1590's the first Yiddish rendition of the Pentateuch made its appearance. Some publications, written by Rabbi Nakhum of Bratislav and Rabbi Lev Yitchkhok of Berdichev were circulated in the eighteenth century.

Most Yiddish writings until the nineteenth century were not secular, although the language was the colloquial language of the time. Apparently the successful writers of those years felt that their public would be happiest with stories based upon Biblical motifs. Subsequently, though, after the public's appetite for Yiddish literature had been whetted, it became apparent to Jewish writers that they had better draw upon folk stories if they wanted to maintain the public's interest and expand the scope of Yiddish literature.

It was not until the mid-nineteenth century that Yiddish came into its own as a respected literary medium for poetry and quality prose writing. Alexander Zeyderboym (1816–1893) created a newspaper, Kol Mevaser, as an all-Yiddish medium. It was a first. Yiddish was scorned, not by the Gentiles, but by those who wrote in Hebrew. Some of them, although they spoke colloquial Yiddish in their everyday life, refused even to cooperate in the creation of a Yiddish dictionary. But we should be used to big egos and mistaken assumptions amongst our Jewish brethren by now. Y.L Gordon, a notable Hebrew Poet, and Isaak Meyer Dik, a famed story-teller, were among those who saw no future for Yiddish during the nineteenth century.

Finally Yiddish came alive as a language for poetry and prose with the advent of four brilliant writers, about whom we have spoken earlier. They were as different from each other as day is from night. First came Mendele Moykher Sforim (S.J.Ambramovich, (1836–1917), then Y.L.Peretz (1852–1915) and then the most popular Yiddish writer of all time, Sholem Aleichem, (Solomon Rabinowich, 1859–1916). These three men elevated the Yiddish language to the level of every other tongue that was used in poetry, folk tales and serious literature of all types. Add to this mix the writings of Chaim Nachman Bialik, who lived at the same time as these other men, and there develops a sudden explosion of quality writing in Yiddish.

If you have have been following these pages carefully you will have noticed how few quality Yiddish-writing poets had existed in the world until the middle of the nineteenth century. None! Morris Rosenfeld was born in 1862 and died in 1923. He was a contemporary of all the greats who created a Yiddish literature. He had few, if any predecessors in the writing of Yiddish poetry on the level at which he wrote. Mendele, Sholem Aleichem and Peretz were able to write in Polish and in Hebrew but chose Yiddish for their mature writing because they felt that utilizing the mother tongue was a most efficient means a means of reaching the widest possible audience. They also used the great storehouse of folk material of Jews in the Pale that was best expressed in the vernacular. Thus we became aware that Rosenfeld was in on the birth and development of true classical Yiddish literature. He made use of the same universal sources of material that touched the hearts of his fellow Jews as his contemporaries employed in their poems, songs and stories. But he was the only one of the "greats" to have moved to America when he was a young man and thus his motifs, although universal in nature, were the products of the new milieu in which the hordes of immigrants were living. Morris Rosenfeld became the poet of the ghetto in America. His language expanded to incorporate the thinking and the frenetic pace of this new homeland. The problems of the shtetl, of the pogrom-ridden country-side of backward countries and the second-class non-citizenship of vicious autocracies were not the subject-matter of his writings. He had left the stultifying atmosphere of the Pale of Settlement and his writing and his language reflected the hope that America provided him and his fellow immigrants. As a contemporary of those other "greats" he received enthusiastic acceptance by the Jewish residents of Eastern Europe and the immigrants who came to England and America.

Yiddish turned out to be a liberating medium, not only for folk tales and household stories, but for serious studies elucidating the bases for psychological problems in individuals and describing truths in the commonalty of all people. It is able to reach the most simple and ordinary individuals. Using their "mama-loshn" the writer could probe their lives and bring forth the human material that develops into universal stories with universal themes. The girl who worked at a sewing machine, the man who pressed clothes, and every hungry proletarian knew that someone existed who understood his pain. Mendele, Sholem Aleichem and especially Rosenfeld shared in their life of trepidation and deprivation. But none shared in the feeling of abandonment by the Almighty the way Rosenfeld did. He strummed his music to the beat of their hearts and sang his songs in the language that their mothers had spoken to them when they were young and most impressionable. We are all aware that language is more than a means of communication. Even when one is talking to himself—silently—he uses his native language to express his innermost feelings, and he tries to transmit his insecurities and hopes to some indefinable deity using his mother-tongue, because that is the only language God understands.

Yiddish is gradually fading out of existence. What a shame! This author had to study it to learn the beauty of the poetry and prose of Rosenfeld and his contemporaries. We had to learn the language, the inflections, the mood and the temper of another time to try to appreciate the bard of that time. We hope you will forgive a brief digression while we express our dismay that while we write about a socially conscious poet of a hundred years ago millions of people this very day are still suffering the way the Jewish immigrants did at that time. Where is the Bard for *this* time? Wherever he is he had better sing the mother-tongue of the masses; the jargon of the needy. He had better gear up his courage, steel up his heart and prepare for a fight for the rest of his days. There are now, as always, millions of selfish and uncaring people, many in positions of great power, who will resist to the death any attempts to benefit the week and the needy. There are some who may feel that these remarks are not necessary in a biography, but one cannot have spent so many hundreds of hours studying the impulses and motivations of the Ghetto Bard without deepening his empathy with the underprivileged. If Rosenfeld can have such an effect on someone seventy-five years after his demise, imagine how potent his voice was during the immigrant experience.

As we have learned from our studies, in all languages the colloquial, the spoken language, was the start of all literature. Folk stories and folk-songs were orally transmitted for centuries. Yiddish folk-stories must also have been orally transmitted this way for untold centuries but were not written down in this language until the sixteenth century, when the Yiddish language is assumed to have become distinctive enough to be described as a language rather than a patois. And we learned another interesting shard of information from our studies; it appears that the first written literature in almost all languages was not prose but poetry! This may be because cadence and rhyme make poetry (song) easier to remember and repeat and to join in recitation with other members of the family (tribe or extended family).

In addition, poetry is generally more succinct, more easily listened to and more easily directed to a given conclusion than prose. Hence the itinerant songster who carried news and gossip, history and folk-stories from town to town was the precursor of the prose writer. So much of the Bible is poetic in form, in cadence and tone, that it bears out this contention in part. Rosenfeld himself stated that his first contacts with Yiddish literature were poetry and that it was his father and grandfather who "made-up" the verses while in a boat, fishing. He had to have been intrigued by his personal experience with this creation of poetry right on-the-spot in order for him to acquire an affinity for it at an early age. His biography testifies to his experience at singing his own poems and songs at the age of ten, or younger, at family functions.

There are several languages which form the backbone of Yiddish: German, Hebrew, Polish and Russian. Much of the vocabulary and grammar is derived from German. Mutation and permutation have made the two languages distinctly different by now. Yiddish still employs some archaic German words which have not been used by the Germans for centuries. The German words ein (one), schon (pretty), wo (where), wir (we), Donnerstag (Thursday), konnen (to be able), fertig (ready), aus (out), become in Yiddish, "ane, shoyn, voo (or voe, or vee), mir, Deenstuk, kennen, fartik and oys." Any words with the German "aus", like haus (house), maus (mouse) become oys: "hoys, moys etc ." Words ending in "ig" are, in Yiddish, as "ik". However many German words remain virtually unchanged. Krank (ill), lachen (to laugh), land (land), jeder (other), kalt (cold), oder (or), noch (yet), singen (to sing), unter (under) and a host of other words are identical in German and Yiddish.

Below is a partial list of words that are Hebrew in origin, but are not always pronounced in the same Hebrew intonation that might be spoken in Spain, Turkey or North Africa. The Mediteranean inflection went through its own metamorphosis over the milennia. Hebrew words such as Torah and Rosh Hashanah have become Toyreh and Rush Hahshooneh in some Ashkenazi dialects. Many dialects twist these "holy" words and each twist makes some Jew in the next town laugh. The following words are Hebrew words incorporated into the Yiddish language: in addition to all the letters of the alphabet, the Holidays, the names attributed to the Almighty, the Holy land and places in it are all, of course, Hebrew. A few examples of words derived from Hebrew are: Aleph, bet, emess, aphilu, efsher, eretz, Yisroel, Bar Mitzvah, galut, matzos, mishpokhe, melamed, khokhem, yom, tov, mogen dovid, medina, seykhl, shalom, aleykhem, tsores, makhitunem, mazel, goniff, and many hundreds more. These have not been translated just to test how assimilated you are!

The poems of Rosenfeld that we include in this book will be written in the original Yiddish, in Yiddish transliteration and in English. If you wish to read the transliteration with an authentic sound you might receive help from the following guide to pronunciation. The chart demonstrates the letter that has been transliterated, what it sounds like in English and an example of the use of that sound in Yiddish words. Authorities differ as to many of these pronunciations, which is proof that it is Jewish. If there were three Jews in a room they would certainly differ on almost anything, so why should the language be different? We use, essentially, the pronunciation guide of the YIVO, the Jewish Research Institute, which has established an almost universally accepted "standard" guide. Galitsianers (Jews from Galicia) will not pronounce words the same way as Litvaks (Jews from Lithuania and Latvia). But the herring tastes the same to both.

Despite numerous schools and programs for teaching Yiddish, use of the language is dying out. It is being replaced rapidly everywhere by the colloquial languages of all of the countries that Jews live in. Jews no longer live in ghettos, in enclosed areas called a "Pale of Settlement", or in a "shteltl" of Eastern Europe. Certainly they like to congregate in whatever city they reside in, but they do not speak Yiddish as their main tongue. In another twenty years the first two generations of immigrants and their children will have almost entirely passed on and with them their mother-tongue. Their grandchildren will study it, here and there, as an effort not to let the old culture die. But the very problem we, as serious students, struggled with in trying to write this book will be doubly confounding to our children and grandchildren. A language is a dead language when it is no longer used daily for the expressions and needs of life. To learn Yiddish just to read Rosenfeld's or Glatshtayn's poetry is asking a lot of someone. This is a serious loss as is any important segment of our past that fragments away and is dissolved in the tears of oblivion. What is more important is the dilution of the ethnicity, of the Yiddishkeit (Jewishness) of which the language was only a part.

Our love for Yiddish persists for so many valid reasons. It is warm, expressive, flexible, and embodies our history and the nature of our people. It is all-inclusive. It brings us closer at once to anyone who demonstrates that he uses even a few words of Yiddish. When a movie star tells a reporter that she hates to "shlep" all that luggage from coast to coast we are not impressed. But when a new-found golfing partner, who looks like a member of the Royal Family, says he needed that new set of golf-clubs "vih a toyten bankes!", (like a dead man needs a certain medical treatment), he has kindled the flames of a new friendship. We have something in common. We "speak the same language", even if only in part.

The poems that we include in this book will be in the original Yiddish, in transliteration and in translation into English. If you wish to read the transliteration with an authentic sound you might receive help from the following guide to pronunciation. The chart demonstrates the letter that has been transliterated, what it sounds like in English and an example of that sound in Yiddish words.

We use, essentially, the pronunciation guide of the YIVO, which has established an almost universally accepted guide for pronunciation. Galitzianers (Jews from Galicia) will not pronounce words the same way as Litvaks (Jews from Lithuania). But the herring tastes the same to both.

GUIDE TO YIDDISH PRONUNCIATION

This is a guide to pronouncing Yiddish usiong the YIVO technique rather than the "sounds-like" or the Germanic method.

Letters	Sound in English
kh	for the gutteral sound frequently spelled with a "ch", as in Germanic words like macht, nacht
oh	for the sound of "aw", as in straw, or the short "o" as in done, won
ey	for the sound oy "ay", as in play
ay	for the sound of "aye", as in mine, cry
uh	for the sound of the long "u", as in dune, rune
uf	or the sound of the short "u" as in put
af	or the sound of "ah", as ion calm, balm, mom
ih	for the sound of the long "e" as in feel
i	sometimes used for the short "e", as in mitt but often used for the long "e", as in thee
e	for the sound of "eh", as in met, get and at the end of a word. As in German, the final "e" is pronounced. There are no silent letters.
o	for the sound of "uh", as in gutt, mutt
kn	sometimes an "e" is omitted before an "n", after a consonant, as in blikn, shikn, but the sound is almost identical with blikken, shikken
dt	sometimes a "dt" is placed at the end of Germanic words, such as handt, vandt, but the sound is identical with hant, vant

References

1. Galvin, Tamarkin "Yiddish Dictionary Sourcebook"
2. ibid
3. Cohen, Mortimer, "Rosenfeld's Transliterations"

6

Poetry: Its Meanings, Its Origins, Its Relationship to Life

Those of you who have read this far in our book have become aware that this is an unusual series of expositions and intrusions into various disciplines, such as linguistics, criticism, language, history, poetry, sociology and biography. So now you get the idea. This is a holistic approach to the life and times of a single man, who used the immigrant experience as his chief arena. It is important to assess the impact of all the above corollary disciplines upon the art form that Morris Rosenfeld chose. We might have added psychology and even anthropology as adjunctive disciplines since they, too, are of interest when we are discussing a man and his times, his personality and the forces that lie within him and those which press upon him.

In our bibliography, which is extensive, you will note the lengths to which we have gone to become "authoritative" in our study. You may wish to read some of the wondrous works we have been referring to and others which are simply in our bibliography because they form an intellectual foundation for our thesis. Come along with us, then, and discover what we have learned about poetry and language and the minds that make them, and how they apply to our study of Morris Rosenfeld.

Only an English teacher or a "critic" can enjoy plucking a poem apart to see what is beautiful in it and why the poem has its effects on the reader. This procedure is very much like pulling a daisy apart to find out if "she loves me, she loves me not," or like crushing a rose to savor its heavenly breath. But there are disciplines that must be followed to aid in an objective analysis of a poet's technique and to help determine why his poetry has such impact. Notice the use of the word "objective", a cold word indeed. In a way it is like saying, "The lover looked objectively at his bride to fathom how she managed to steal his heart." We authors, then, are the lovers who are trying to determine how the poet, Morris Rosenfeld, managed to steal our hearts. Once we admit our love for the poetry and once we confess to our familial relationship to the poet our claim to objectivity will be suspect. Suspect or not, the effort has been made to study Rosenfeld's poetry objectively but with love. We will not be pulling the leaves off the daisy nor is this an autopsy. It is a study based upon what we consider the only honest means of appraising another person's works efficiently. Our standards will be revealed as we write, probably with too many digressions. Just as we used various historical texts and other sources to learn about the immigrant experience and the place of this one exciting poet in that experience, so we shall now discuss the art of poetry, and in the next chapter, the discipline of Criticism, to expand further on the techniques used by Rosenfeld and how we may best appreciate his works.

If Nature is, as the German philosopher Friedrich von Schelling (1775–1854) says, "to one, nothing more than the lifeless aggregate of an indeterminable crowd of objects, or the space in which, as in a vessel, he imagines things placed; or to another one the soil from which he draws his nourishment and support; or to the inspired seeker alone, the holy, ever-creative original energy of the world, which generates and busily evolves all things out of itself,"[1] then it takes someone of Rosenfeld's nature to sense the freshness of the forest's breath, as he felt the pulse of the exciting time of history during which he lived and he palpated the yearning of his people for justice, recognition and love. Rosenfeld was not a philosopher nor did he have the mind of a cleric or an accountant. He looked at Nature as Schelling did. You will note, when you read his poetry, how frequently Nature or her manifestations are mentioned in his works.

When students describe Joan of Arc or the Hebrew Prophets as "possessed" by their missions, as transformed into other than human representations of their arts, they might well have included Morris Rosenfeld as such an example. Except for his attention to his family, Morris was consumed by his single-minded goal of describing the world of his fellow proletarians in the most powerful and poignant tones in an attempt to jostle their apathy to inspire them to fight for their own self-interests. No prophet, no cleric, no exponent of the occult could have transported his personality so single-mindedly in that one direction more than Rosenfeld did. So it is small wonder that he alienated so many who would have been his friends. He lacked the oily ingredients that lend themselves to compromise.

We promised you earlier in this book to attempt to solve one of the "mysteries" of Rosenfeld's life and finally, after much study and thought, the answers came to us as in an epiphany. The "mystery" is, "Why, of all the professions in the world, did Morris Rosenfeld decide to become a poet?" It was an ill-paying profession, usually unsuccessful in terms of general acceptance and might subject the writer to all sorts of criticism and "second-guessing" as to the form and timeliness of his creations. If we reason this out together, the reader and the author, using the data we have accumulated, we should be able to provide the answers which have not been elucidated by any previous studies of Rosenfeld's life.

Remember we are talking about a man born in 1862 in a tiny town in Russian-occupied Poland where the fields of opportunity were already limited either by fiat or by the customary prejudices that existed against Jews in most of Europe since the ascendancy of Eastern Christendom in the 9th Century, A.D. At that time Jews were reduced to second-class citizenry and informed in various ways just how far they could go in personal and communal development. It is obvious, then, that the educational and employment opportunities did not exist for Rosenfeld to aspire to become a lawyer, a physician, a dentist, an accountant, an engineer, an explorer, a stock-broker, even a student of the Western (or Eastern) classics. In short, he was a product of a static, near sterile, society where his opportunities had to be limited to work on a small farm, or to have a small business in the shtetl, or to become a Hebrew-School teacher. He might have thought of taking up one of the minor occupations that were indigenous to the ghetto: a "moyl" (one who performs circumcisions), a "maschgiach" (A man who certifies the kosher quality of foods), a "shatchun" (one who arranges marriages) and so on. There was nothing there to tax his imagination. After reading what we have written about Morris, can anyone imagine him in any of those "professions"? Not a chance! He fit nowhere.

What did that leave for him? Teaching, music and the arts and philosophy. Hardly a choice that could make a substantial living for him. We all know he would never become a farmer, a lawyer or a shopkeeper. There was nothing for him in the shtetl, nothing for someone who possessed an indefinable niggling in his soul to be of importance to his people. He, himself, was unable for years to find an outlet for his pent-up emotions. Nothing but poetry gave him the sense of fulfillment and attention that he simply needed. When you read his poetry you will notice that his expressions had an almost messianic fervor in his self-designated role of spokesman for the underprivileged workmen. He was almost rabbinical in his desire to see the world work out correctly and fairly. Also he gazed upon nature, until his dying days, with the eye of an artist and the soul that only a poet could bring to bear. He had to go away from that tiny townlet in Eastern Poland to find himself, to discover a niche for his temperament and his persona. Our sons did the same thing in the twentieth century after graduating from high school. Teenagers are teenagers regardless of the century. They traveled to California, to Europe, to Israel and played the guitar all over the place.

Rosenfeld did not play the guitar but he wrote poems and created songs which gradually attracted notice to his talents. He sang his songs and his poems to his family, his fellow workmen and to clusters of young intellectuals he would meet. He was encouraged by the response. From Poland Rosenfeld wandered to Amsterdam, where the life of a diamond-cutter was definitely not for him. He claimed that it affected his health. Nonsense. He was bored and confined and probably very inefficient at that kind of work. He had to run away again, this time to the sweatshops of London's garment center. There he could only find menial labor and again he ran away. He was an escape-artist long before Houdini even went into show-business. He first ran away from the shtetl and from an abortive marriage to "Poland's homeliest woman". He ran and he ran and he ran. We know what he was running from; from oppression, boredom, ordinariness and lack of attention. But what was he running to? To fulfillment, creativity and for the first time in his life. . . . acceptance. He was like the seed of a plant dropped willy-nilly by the wind on distant soil. The shell of the seed opens and the plant sinks its roots, turns its green leaf to the sun and grows.

So Rosenfeld landed in the East Side of New York's Manhattan. He worked, to survive, in the garment industry, as a tailor, a presser; who knows what else. He was terrible at it, but he gradually discovered himself. He saw the myriad of problems that his fellow-immigrants faced and began to voice his opinions. He was beginning to sink his roots in the fertile immigrant milieu. If there was anything certain about Morris Rosenfeld (and this grandson) it is that whenever an opinion was to be expressed, "zey hubn zikh nit fahshemt!" (They were never ashamed to speak up!). Morris had discovered even in his youth in Poland and in the turmoil that was London's (and Leeds') Jewish Ghetto, that he had a knack for versi-fication (inherited from his mother and grandfather). People around him actually enjoyed hearing his poems (were they really poems at first, or jingles?), and even singing the simple melodies he created. We cannot say he "wrote" that music because he was untutored in that art. Note that we said, "hearing his poems", be-cause, as with the ancient troubadours, he recited and sang his own works. The quality of his voice and his emotive powers lent more credence to his subject matter and more enjoyment to his recita-tions. How was he to know that indeed he was following in the footsteps of all early poets, who used to wander from place to place singing to all who would listen? After all, poetry existed long before prose writing.

Little did he know that Richard the Lionhearted, (and Rich-ard's father) were troubadours first, before they became leaders of men. It was not until the 18th century that prose become the usual language of fiction. However the earliest fiction in verse dates from about the 8th century! In other words there was a span of almost eleven centuries before prose was widely used in fiction. One im-portant aspect to remember about poetry is that originally it was oral and was generally used for oracular and prophetic purposes. The structure of poetry, the patterns of its rhythm and its sound, gave it a particular attractiveness that made it easier to remember and recite. Whether it was a cleric or a troubadour, his words had broad impact because of the musicality in his expression. We all know how someone is admired for his ability to sing, especially if he creates rhymes on the spot. Hence poetry was most acceptable, whether it was for carrying the news of the times, bringing the words of a preacher or simply used for entertainment.

In the 1880's, then, Rosenfeld began to circulate his poetry. He created a couple of small collections of his poetry and had a few poems accepted for publication in various newspapers and journals. He was recognized from the start as a creative man. That was really all the encouragement he needed to start on a career of poetry and, later on, journalism. He was paid pitifully little for his writing all his life. But, as will become abundantly clear when we discuss the existence of "The Muse" who inhabits the psyche of a very few people in every generation, you will come to understand how he found his acceptance by his own personal "Muse". He was not able to do anything other than devote himself to satisfying Her. As you may gather from reading Leon Goldenthal's "Toil and Triumph" and this book, Rosenfeld was literally driven to create; forced by an inner compulsion to write his poetry and his stories.

But what did he have to say ? It is all very well and good to want to write, but for whom and for what? Obviously, only a man in a dungeon or on a desert island writes just for himself. Many artists claim that they create simply for themselves. Bialik was such a person. So why did he show his writing to everyone and keep trying to have it published? Shyness is fine. Candidness is finer. Rosenfeld wanted people to admire his work, and him. He craved attention and respect. He knew from the first that he had landed in a place that needed someone to express the nostalgia for the "old country" and yet offer a dream for the future in the "Golden Land". They called this the "Golden Land" but received little of the gold at first. The social and the labor poets, including Rosenfeld, were sounding boards for the immigrants and they wrote powerful messages that reverberated across the land.

And so, by deduction and by intuition we lay claim to a reasoning through which we can explain how Rosenfeld came to his chosen field of poetry as his life's work. This may have seemed obvious to most folks, but there is nothing "obvious" when we try to understand someone's motivations. Also, in truth, we cannot guarantee the existence of a Muse, but then perhaps someone has to be chosen for such a life as a poet's by a winking star in a constellation with a sense of humor.

Adams[2] quotes Baudelaire (1821–1867), "It is useless tedium to represent what exists, because nothing that exists satisfies me !" This was written in a piece of criticism. It is an example of the effete, self-satisfied smugness that represents much of European writing and criticism in the nineteenth century. "I prefer the monsters of my fancy," he continues, "to what is positively trivial." You would not find any proletarian writers of Rosenfeld's era debasing the arts or nature in this manner. The world was "too much with us" for the Jewish artists who struggled so to create an art and a literature that was expressive as well as faithful; dynamic and original. When the Yiddish writers described "monsters of my fancy" they were Dybbuks and the Angel of Death who hovered above all the time, the psychological by-products of millennia of repression and unfulfillment, as well as the Tsarist military behemoths and the pogromists who lived down the street. Merely to describe reality was in itself to picture an inhuman monster.

Expressionist art was not truly developed until years after Rosenfeld started in his career but had he read Baudelaire's remarks he would have laughed at the irony of a first-class writer decrying the existence of existence! Baudelaire's statements were made at a time when the question of "copying Nature" arose as a concern for artists of the physical arts. It could not have referred to music or prose literature since where in Nature does one see a novel or hear a quartet, even when the wind is whistling through the trees and the earth at times grumbles in its own unintelligible (but undeniable) language. Baudelaire was expressing an attitude that art critics were struggling with; whether representational art was truly art or merely copying Nature. As though one could indeed copy the flight of a bird or the crash of the waves! It does seem that a serious problem with some intellectuals is the remoteness to which their mental processes are removed from reality. What is also remarkable is that ego can act as an interplanetary vehicle, able to transport one to stellar residences unknown to rational Man.

Writers like Sholem Aleichem, Peretz and Rosenfeld had no dichotomy in their views of the world. When a character in a poem or story was brought to life by those men he had a direct connection, or was an allusory reference or an allegorical reference, to some down-to-earth situation that every Jew, in fact every common man could point to as something he can understand. The Yiddish artists of Rosenfeld's era did not draw upon fancy to escape from the tortures of their minds. There were no Van Goghs on the Jewish scene. Even when Kafka wrote, troubled as he was, one knew whence his characters derived their origins. It was not until the twentieth century that art and literature took off into spatial concepts that tried to avoid or escape from reality. Perhaps these artists' view of reality was so personal that one could only guess what that artist meant by what he said or did. In a sense, many Modernists deemed it a tour-de-force when they could create something that appeared (or sounded) totally unrecognizable and divorced from any concept of reality that a normal mind could conceive. Rosenfeld found enough excitement and variety, sufficient provocation and intensity to describe and expound upon. He did not need to fabricate a whole new world to work on. The Jews never run out of problems that demand their concern and the creativity of their writers and their artists.

Goethe could assert [3] "I am rather of the opinion that the more incommensurable and the more incomprehensible to the intellect a poetic product is, so much the better it is." Possibly so, but it would be interesting to discover what mind can comprehend the incomprehensible, and why must we expect an artist to be the one who has such powers? Why not a scientist, or a prophet, or even a clergyman who has felt himself touched by the hand of the Almighty?

There are many philosophical levels to poetry and prose. The Jewish writers from Eastern Europe were no intellectual slouches. They had a "direct line" to the Infinite One, if thousands of years of conversation with Him can be counted upon as a reference. Yet with all the imponderable problems with which they were faced they took a more practical route to dealing with the world of reality. Theirs was not a philosophy of ignorance or primitive simplicity. It was a natural way of dealing with the awesome powers of a divinity, a personal approach that was akin to a son speaking to his father, even though his "father" was a king, a giant, a frightful force with incalculable might. By endowing the Almighty with anthropomorphic attributes they could handle the almost inter-personal problems that God presented to them. This obscured, in a way, the cold, black, unimaginable chasm that lies beneath one's feet, a gap into the reaches of eternity, something that is unconsciously covered over with this "relationship" with the power that created it all.

One does not have to do what Baudelaire suggests, "create monsters of my fancy" to be a poet for the ages. One has to take what exists; it is terrifying enough. One has to use the clay of Man which is variegated and moldable enough for any artist. When Rosenfeld, or any other great poet expresses himself he is pinching a piece of that clay, sampling a snip of the inconceivable world that exists, and voila! a poem is created. How else explain Poe's "tintinnabulation of the bells", or the exquisite sonnets of Shakespeare or

Rosenfeld's "Die Yiddishe May" (The Jewish May). Who needs the "monsters of his fancy"?

Sigmund Freud (1856–1939) admitted freely that he did not discover the unconscious. It was the poets, he said, who made that discovery. In Freud's, "Creative Writers and Day Dreams", he says, "The unreality of the writer's imaginative world has very important consequences for the technique of his art. For many things which, if they were real, could give no enjoyment, can do so in the play of fantasy, and many excitements, which in themselves are actually distressing, can become a source for the hearers and spectators at the performance of the writer's work".[4] And Adams states in this same dissertation, "Freud's attitudes towards the poet . . . I think are as ambivalent as Plato's. On the one hand he speaks with great admiration for the poets and recognizes that his own psychological studies owe much to them On the other hand he thinks of art as a "narcotic", with the derogatory implications this word carries . . . . . . For Freud, art is ultimately harmless. Nevertheless it is illusory and there is something neurotic about creating illusions. They remind Freud, no doubt, of the fantasies of his patients."

The fact that a poet, even now, is depicted as someone "a little touched" (touched by a Muse?) is merely a continuation of many centuries of the same belief. Many great poets were fair to admit that they had been influenced by some esoteric power: Homer "gave himself" to his Muse and it is not unreasonable that Rosenfeld made the same admission. He even wrote poems to his Muse. "Who was she?" you may ask, seriously or not. Can you call her "Inspiration","Subliminal Influence", "A stepchild of the Gods?" Whether we take this "superstition" seriously or not, many fine creative minds felt that they were receiving "extraterrestrial aid." How else explain someone creating a life of sacrifice, intense struggle and humiliation except as a self-dedication to the Muse; for no real reward except the subconscious sense that he has given himself to the Goddess of Poetry. These lines from a poem, "Wild Music" written in 1935 by one of Rosenfeld's grandsons,[5] explain it exactly:

> *I was born to be crushed and torn*
> *by the force of poetry,*
> *by the sadness of beauty*
> *by the demons of duty*
> *a soul in coventry.*

O Beauty! O Love! O Art!
How you wear on the strings of my heart!
Like a heavenly child on a harp gone wild
You are tearing my soul apart!

Poetry is not an affectation for the poet. It is not a game or something "to do" in his spare time. It is everything in his life. Every mood, every experience, every observation is expressed either verbally or in writing or simply in musical tones, but it is felt deep inside as poetry. No one has to tell this to the poet. He knows it. Trust him. He will tell you this. Rosenfeld used every emotion and every experience in the forum of his poetry. He needed no philosopher or critic or professor of literature to tell him, "Write that down! That's material for a poem!" No way. He wrote it as soon as he could, even on wrappings from the grocery store, and the verse poured out of him like a hemorrhage of ideas and words. In fact, we actually have a piece of a brown paper grocery bag on which Rosenfeld jotted down a few lines of a poem. He couldn't wait until he got home to write his thoughts down. His own sensibilities are the essence of the art and science of the poet. They are a synthesis of emotion and intellect; and the ultimate result is a poem. Whether it is "good or bad" in the eyes of the beholder it is truly the catharsis of one captured by the Muse; let us call it the "spirit of creation." The poet is pleased. His "Muse" is delighted, and the reader has to make up his own mind whether he likes that poem or not. Actually, the poet may not care too much whether or not some individual likes his poem. Certainly he would like to feel that his art is recognized and appreciated. But once that poem has escaped from his mind he is already thinking about the next one he is going to write. He only sees the world in poetic terms.

This is why, when we criticize the works of a poet, we do it for ourselves. Anything good we say can please the poet. Anything contrary can only hurt the poet. But it cannot change anything. The poem is like a burst of temper. What can you change after it is past? There are considerable differences in the degree to which poets allow their intellects to influence their poetry. Some poets, such as Rosenfeld, Poe and even Allen Ginsberg use their intellect to shape, trim, control and guide the expression of a poetic idea. Rosenfeld's Muse was an excitable, emotional lady, but he used his intellect to reign her in a little. The more intellect there is, the less passion; the more measured response, the less effect of the Muse upon the poet. Almost anyone can use a rhyming dictionary and a thesaurus and count elements of a certain rhythm to create a rhyming, rhythmic piece of writing. But where is the passion, where are the filaments drawn from the heavens to weave into the fabric of a true poem? There have been very few poets whose works can be appreciated eternally. Among them are Tennyson and Wordsworth, whose words are well crafted, their rhymes and meters are precise; their ideas planned with an accountant's penchant for detail and exactitude. Their expressions are now part of our cultural heritage. However, as to our personal taste, we prefer the lyricism and wrenching expressiveness of more romantic poets.

Poe, Coleridge, Whitman and Rosenfeld and all the other impassioned lyric writers had the deepest sources of imagery and the most intense forces that drove their pens. Had Rosenfeld a different agenda, a different background, a different culture, he would still have written as he did. He might possibly have had a more highly educated verbiage in some regards but certainly not with a richer or more expressive language than Yiddish. The poet's art is genetically programmed. It is inheritable in one form or another, either in literature, art or music or some other muse-ridden form of expression. With the individual's nature goes his creativity. The concept that a poet is at least a little "possessed" by the Muse dates back at least to Aristotle and Plato and has not left the scene yet. John Keble, writing early in the nineteenth century, stated that "the Muse seems revived as a power working mysteriously below the level of consciousness." And Aristotle suggested that the poet's nature helped define tragedy. Is it possible that there are genes for the arts?

Yet the whole concept of a Muse may be superstition, a ploy to try to explain creativity by bringing in some God-like influence moving around in someone's psyche. Why not, in this modern day and age, when computers are almost able to think on their own— why not admit that the mind has facets that earlier Man did not understand: that reason and creativity are an upgraded application of the normal powers of the mind? We are discovering great things about the left and right sides of the brain. Why not admit that some "human software" is capable of creativity in many directions, even in the applications of business acumen, political sensitivity, humane responses and even the herd instinct that attracts human animals to their own kind without conscious effort? It has taken thousands of years for artists finally to establish their right to be considered the true creators of their own works, inspired, perhaps by extraordinary sensitivity, but still masters of their own selves. As one can understand then, from an historical view of the creative individual, he has long been considered as someone akin to a madman; perhaps not really demented but more than a little strange. No wonder the world is taking so long to become civilized. It is not there yet. If the poet is a little mad then what can we say about the rest of humanity which, judging by the daily newspapers and the history books, seems all too frequently to behave as though it has left the cave of the aborigine just yesterday.

We really do not need the Hollywood descriptions of a poet, artist, or musician as a wild-haired, funky-looking Romantic with very little self-control or worldliness. We can well do without the almost tongue-in-cheek portrayal of creative individuals as a little crazy, wild-eyed, unkempt; "seeing things" and "hearing voices." The writers of those Hollywood epics are often excellent talents. Nevertheless they usually write for the least common denominator, for the anti-intellectual attitude of the "masses", and so it is easy to titillate those "masses" by putting poets down as a little daft and unreliable. Then those "non-intellectuals" who see the movies will always think of a poet in those terms and laugh at him. As a matter of fact, they also think of college professors and intellectuals (and writers!) in the same boorish terms. This is no accident. For reasons of "making money," these Hollywood types prostitute their own talent .

There is, of course, a difference between "seeing things" and "hearing voices" like an individual with multiple personalities or other psychiatric conditions and the truly creative soul whose sensibilities towards the world of nature and the human condition are almost like extra-sensory perception. These men can draw inferences from their worldly experiences and describe them in crystalline forms so that their ideas virtually glow in the minds of their readers. The "Muse", you know, is not your ordinary leprechaun!

Wordsworth rejected those who decorated their *prose* with poetic devices and indulged in "gaudiness and inane phraseology." He objected to vain attempts at artistry with "arbitrary and capricious habits of expression." Poetry is poetry and prose is prose, yet quite often a masterful writer of prose comes close to poetry in a capsule of descriptiveness. When Thomas Mann, in "The Magic Mountain", describes the cough of a tubercular patient as heard by his hero, Hans Castorp, he phrases it as "a cough that has no conviction and gives no relief; it does not come out in paroxysms, but is the feeble, dreadful welling up of the juices of organic dissolution." Mann exceeds the norm for prose expressiveness, drawing not only upon observation and imagination but employing the sensitivity of the Muse herself.

It would be virtually impossible to write an entire novel in such poetic terms, although Thomas Mann almost succeeded. Poetry, even in such sagas as "The Ancient Mariner", is essentially a brief encounter with some aspect of life (or its antagonist, Death). Since the encounter is brief, the expression must be a crystallization of the poet's feelings on the subject. As such, there should be an economy of words and a directness of movement. Few poets, including Poe, Wordsworth and Coleridge troubled themselves to write really long poems. In prose, there are no such limitations for the author. If he wants to write four hundred pages in a novel, he may do so. Even Shakespeare would have been hard-pressed to write a four-hundred page poem without boring himself and his readers. It would have been a self-defeating effort. Hence, poetic imagery may well "decorate" or enhance prose creations but the novelist must know the difference between the two modalities of expression and not be pretentious with his writing.

With Rosenfeld we do not have to concern ourselves with affectation or imitation or mistaken expressiveness. While his poetry is drawn from a well, fed by the Muse, his prose is more down-to-earth and realistic. He writes with the same passion and directness that he employs in his poems but for some reason there is more of the "common man" in him than comes through in his poetry. He does not transcend the mundane in his prose, although his powers of observation and his facility with the Yiddish language still exist abundantly. Even his sense of humor seems much more expansive in his prose. But Rosenfeld is not the giant in Yiddish literature because of his prose, even though some of the "samples" we have included in this volume are pleasant, well-written examples of satiric writing. Then again, how many great writers were equally facile in both poetry and prose? Bialik and Peretz were exceptions in Yiddish. Poe was a master in English.

Questions are always asked about a poet, "What does he know of reality?" Is he aware of it? "Does he live in a dream world and if so, does he write of this subcontinent of the psyche and how are we supposed to relate to and understand his voice?" Of course, students of the mind and its projections, psychologists, philosophers, even neurologists, may call into question even the objectivity of the so-called balanced or nonpoetic mind. So many factors are involved in the processes of observation and assimilation of physical objects as well as the formulation by the mind of ideas and concepts that science has not yet devised a "table of elements" that can be considered permanent and applicable to all human mental processes. The factors involved in memory alone are still subjects of intense study, as though that subject were a poorly charted continent with unknown wildlife and hidden resources.

Thus the poet who lives on that mysterious continent, with its denizens of insight, intuition, hope, frustration, love and hatred, anxiety and happiness—such a myriad of poorly illuminated aborigines—this man must be treated with special care when we try to estimate his creations and their values. It is much like the marine biologist's task when he obtains a rare specimen of animal from the ocean depths. He knows that this specimen is the living embodiment of primeval urges and anatomy, as well as being, anachronistically, a member of the present. This creature may express the inchoate yearnings that tie together the continuous elements of the ages—the past, the present and the future. Whose estimation of Shakespeare, Poe, Whitman and yes, even Rosenfeld, can remove the universality and eternal grace of their thoughts and words? Do you see now the problems involved in honestly "analyzing" a man's poetry?

As Adams states, "The self is more complicated than most of us had thought. The poet probably does not know what he has unconsciously expressed" (Who does? ed). . . . "Unconscious material can hardly be amenable to a judgment of sincerity. It is almost as if the Muse had reappeared in the form of the Freudian Id and the poet were again as helpless as Plato insisted he was."[6] That quote bears re-reading. It demonstrates the brilliance of Plato and the continuum of thought over the ages on the origins of talent. Perhaps this will all be solved when we produce a computer that can create real poetry from its own chips and the synapses of its wiring.

Contrary to most critics we do not believe that a poem stands alone on its own merits. It has to be considered as an expression of the poet's ego and a part of the poet's being; his conscious and his unconscious. It has to be considered as a phenomenon of a certain time, a certain age. It has to be considered in the context of the sociological and psychological demands of the era in which it was written. It has to be considered as an extension of the poet's own life, his background, his intentions, his beliefs. A poem, in brief, is a substance extruded from a human mind at a certain time and place, under certain conditions and crystallized under certain pressures and forces. A poem is a complex of human, historical and sociological concerns. The more universal its subject and themes, the longer it may have social acceptance.

We agree with Coleridge that, in discussing a variety of sources, the poem is essentially an offspring of a verbal culture which it also helps to create. When extraneous artifacts somehow replace the poem in the critic's eyes then one must wonder why the critic is bothering with the poem at all. He may be more interested in exploring the life and the mind of the poet, who is the real object of his concern. *That is exactly what we are doing in this book.* It is strange to admit, however, that a poet's life may be a mess, yet his poetry can be "a thing of beauty and a joy forever".

Language and vocabulary frequently fail adequately to indicate the dimensions of feelings, of hope, mythic experiences, intimations of death, eternity, infinity—the unknowns of all human history. A poet is uniquely qualified to attempt a linguistic approach to any of these subjects. He may have to invent words, names and individual concepts to describe his visualization of such inescapable aspects of reality. When his works are blessed with success it means that he has been able to transmit his cerebrations to someone else where ordinary language might fail. To quote Cassirer, "The artist is just as much a discoverer of the forms of nature as the scientist is a discoverer of facts or natural laws," and so we understand what Archibald McLeish meant in his poem, Ars Poetica, that "a poem should not mean, but be." Ezra Pound used a Greek term, logopoiea, "the dance of intellect among words" to describe poetry. It is a great concept. But Pound abused the use of his Muse and his Muse was not amused and carried Pound over the brink of rationality to the feared shores of a psychiatric sub-continent, from which he never fully returned. This was sad, since Pound was a man of unquestioned talent, and unfortunately, an abominable anti-Semite.

We have written much about the poet and his unique characteristics, his special qualifications and even his aspect to the world for thousands of years. How about the reader of poetry; does the reader need certain qualifications as well? Connolly[7] states, "A reader's physical condition, his mental attitude, his previous education, his habits of behavior, his linguistic references, all these may interfere with, or qualify, his participation in the emotional excitement intrinsic to the poem." Also the age, the sex and experiences in life, the maturity and cultural background of the reader can qualify appreciation of the poetry. Indeed, as many variations as may exist in the psyche and background of the poet may exist in the reader. Small wonder, then, that true poetry enthusiasts are often as esoteric and interesting as the poets themselves.

To further describe poetry, Connolly says that "the imaginary world of a poem is not therefore an absurd world. It has its own kind of truth".[8] One of the reasons we are not impressed by the attitude of the INZICH group of poets (whom we discussed in our chapter on Descendants of Rosenfeld in Yiddish Poetry) is, quoting from their own journal,[9] ". . . we write deliberate discontinuous compositions and alogical devices of poetic language". Is that poetry? If we apply the foregoing concepts of poetry and their ramifications to the writings of Morris Rosenfeld, what do we discover? Did Rosenfeld have an "in" with the Muse? He said he did. He acted as though he did. It is not that he behaved like a "meshuggina" (lunatic). He didn't roll his eyes to the skies and claim that he heard the voice of God. He left that "mishigass" (madness) to some far-out preachers and to self-ordained Messiahs. He did not claim any supernatural or primeval forces were at work on him. But they were. His total dedication to his art, his inability to be happy in any other work, his intensity and absorption in his moods of creativity, his ability to draw references from every human experience in poetic form for a distinct purpose were all aspects of one subsumed by the influence of a Muse. As you know, the Greeks had a word for it and the word Muse, from "Musica," was the word that best applies to some overwhelming influence on Morris Rosenfeld.

We might also inquire,"What was Rosenfeld's vision? Did he express a clear, informed, rational idea of some future society; some future race of Man? Did he picture some attainable milieu for his own people and the outside world? Did Morris penetrate, in his own fashion, the central mysteries of human existence?" "Did he understand the intended order of the Universe?" Of course he didn't. That is asking too much of a poor tailor-poet from a shtetl in Poland who came here to press pants and found out that he was a mighty good poet! Rosenfeld was not a philosopher or a planner. He was not a sociologist or anthropologist or a leader of men. And incidentally, we do not know any of the above "specialists" who could reply "Yes" to the question, "Do you understand the intended order of the universe?" The Kabbalists come close, but poets can only intuit such matters.

Rosenfeld was an uncommon common man who deserved the Medal of Honor for a difficult lifetime of devotion to the cause of humanity. In the course of his career he was inexplicably endowed with the ability to draw upon hitherto unexpected sources of power and expressiveness to bring a world of love and hope and confidence to the downtrodden. We don't know if the Muse, Greek or Jewish, ever realized what she had gotten into when she penetrated the psyche of Morris Rosenfeld!

When we get to the discussion of Rosenfeld's poetry we intend to demonstrate, with the actual poetry at hand, those elements of universality, personal reference, and ethnic reference as well as those portions of his language that contain religious or historical references. This will demonstrate the scope of his writings.

Another interesting concept we have discovered is that all poets, however original and creative, are in a way disciples of their language, or languages. But the reader as well, to understand fully what his poet has written must also understand the language of that poet's time. Connolly has written, "The intelligent reader of poetry must remember that language changes throughout its development in vocabulary, syntax, spelling and pronunciation."[10] Like Dante and Chaucer, Rosenfeld "helped raise a rude provincial dialect to the level of a polished national language.", as Connolly states. Connolly's book on poetry was a joy to read, particularly in his references to "the music of words" ("Verbal music") as well as the rhythm and melody of language. When we tried to think of examples of musicality in the written word, we became impelled to remember that the Bible itself is virtually a musical masterpiece. The measured cadence and stresses, the dignity and legitimate sense of importance of the Biblical passages together create the aura of a document truly handed down from an almighty power through the hands of trusted minions. Part of the creation of poetry is the effort to establish the mood for which the poem was written so that the message of the poem is given cause for greater credence. Part of poetry is its "effect". Since poetry was originally an oracular and even prophetic device, its verbal potency still exists.

This is not merely a vestige remaining from the past. The "effect" is essential as an integral part of the poem. Without that, one might as well have put his phrases into a newspaper article. Without having to be an intellectual one has to know that the primary purpose of poetry is the direction of a complex of emotional and intellectual content toward some goal the poet has in mind. Whether it is derived from an escapism from worldly or personal traumata or an inability of the poet to feel a sense of security or fulfillment in his own world, the product of such an involved individual can offer someone else an interesting, even exciting avenue for escape. These criteria apply even if the poet is merely trying to "cure the world" of its ills by "teaching" or "preaching."

There is something of Whitman in a few of Rosenfeld's poems. That is, they were meant to be read aloud quietly to one's self. Read them aloud, with feeling, the way you would read Whitman's "Out Of The Cradle Endlessly Rocking". It is music and just reading it aloud is like singing. These poems are a threnody to the pains of life, a cry, a *geschrai* in the wilderness. Rosenfeld considered his life seriously and his poetry was his life. We may criticize his occasionally unreasonable behavior towards his critics: it really was unreasonable. But he was not a reasonable man. For some strange reason he understood that he, of all people, had to be the one who rebels against "the system". *He* had to speak out forcefully regardless of the cost to himself. For a person of great ego it is astounding that Morris did so little for himself, "far zikh aleyn". He did little to hold friends. That would have meant taking criticism calmly, or it might have meant compromise where his work was concerned. He had ego and great pride, but where his family was concerned he abjectly solicited funds from anyone who would help him out. Remember, he had a wife and four children, a mother and father, an uncle and a younger brother living with him, all in three or four rooms, and all on the income of a penny a line for his poetry! That responsibility alone would be enough to drive one "up the wall".

The Rosenfelds lost several of their children, the first three while they were youngsters themselves living in England. The most painful loss was that of his beloved son Joseph, at age fifteen. Joseph was the little boy for whom Rosenfeld had written his immensely popular poem, Mayn Yingele "(My Little Son) in the 1890's. Apparently some hateful Polish immigrant youngsters threw Joseph down a flight of stone steps in Yonkers. He died from a sarcoma of the shoulder blade, which had been damaged in the fall. The entire Jewish world learned about this tragedy through Rosenfeld's poetry.

It is very nice to support your parents in their old age, but Rosenfeld's father and his uncle lived to almost 106 years of age, his mother until age 96. This placed a seemingly endless burden on the young poet. Incidentally, the author of this book is named after Rosenfeld's father, Ephraim, and his middle name is that of Joseph, the "Yingele" immortalized in Rosenfeld's poems. Ed Goldenthal actually saw his great-grand-uncle at age 105 at the Montefiore Home for the Aged, in the Bronx, New York City. We as kids had barely heard of Santa Claus, but upon recollection, that is whom the great-grand-uncle looked like. He, too, had been a fisherman in Suwalki in Russian-occupied Poland before he came to New York. Rosenfeld's poetry was appreciated by the Yiddish-speaking public for several reasons. There were inherent tendencies to rhyme in both the culture and the religious documents of the Jews. Simple rhymes have been used "almost forever" by the denizens of the ghetto. Whatever literature we find about the Jews contains some simple rhymes about virtually every subject. Even in daily conversation there are rhyming patterns such as "ah leck un ah shmek", "ah sheyneh, reyneh kaporeh", "nit geshtoygen un nit gefloygen". Translations here would be of no avail.

These rhymes were a technique in their subconscious desire to block out the severity of their lives. Just to have a singsong or a rhyme in daily conversation was actually a charming device, even leading to a saving upbeat humor. There is musicality in the Hebrew prayers. Since earliest times the cadence of the prayers has been a distinctive feature of Jewish life. This feature has been emulated, by the way, in the prayers of both the Muslims and the Catholic Church. When one considers that prayers were an integral part of daily living then the frequency of a sing-song inflection in the language is quite understandable. To the best of our knowledge there were no great Jewish "song-writers" or composers or musicians before the eighteenth century. Although we cannot verify the assumption factually, there had to have been troubadour-type singers everywhere in early Jewish life. It is part of human development. The only problem with that concept is that these fellows never wrote their material down so it cannot be proven. Poetry exists in the Sacred writings of the Jews, some attributed to Solomon and other sages. The Jewish Holy Days are replete with songs and poems and even the prose tracts are sung with constant melodies. These factors all indicate a receptive soil upon which any young poet can demonstrate his talent. An additional reason why poetry should find a responsive audience among the Jews may lie in the repressed creativity with which they suffered for ages and which simply ached for expression.

Almost suddenly, in the nineteenth and early twentieth centuries, with the escape from the confines of ghetto life, the escape from orthodox repression of secular study (including scientific study) and with the newfound exposure to the music, literature, art, architecture and intellectual freedom of Western culture it was almost as though the Jews, who had been kept for thousands of years as though in an airless tunnel, in a trice were able to breathe huge sighs of fresh air. This fresh air cleared their minds. They desperately required a healthy milieu, a fertile soil for their collective and individual cultural growth. Their exposure to the West was the event that changed Jewish culture forever. Rosenfeld tried manfully to retain as much as was practical of the old way of life as he fought to bring an appreciation of the new opportunities in this changing environment. The Jews accepted him because he spoke their language and he reveled in the inspiration of their lives. They accepted him because he understood "today" and intuited what had to be done to provide for a better tomorrow. They adored him because of his rambunctious nature; his lack of fear before "the bosses" and the "powers that be" in the publishing world and because of the seductive lyricism in his words. He was indeed a bard for his time. Rosenfeld wrote, to quote Wordsworth, "the real language of men": not formal, not stilted, not abstract nor perverse.

Rosenfeld's love of nature was real. He was not a "big-city boy" by choice and as soon as got a chance he moved out of New York City to Yonkers. From there he went to a rural upstate New York hamlet called Spencertown. About two miles down the road was Blueberry Hill, which actually turned blue from the ripe wild

blue-berries in late summer and early fall. Around the bend from
that hill was another hill where Edna St. Vincent Millay made her
residence. We do not know if both poets ever met, but if they did it
was possibly on Blueberry Hill, where love of nature (and of blue-
berries) could be practiced shamelessly. When Rosenfeld writes of
nature and her manifestations he does so in remarkably simple fashion. There is no pretense, no lofty language, no search through the
thesaurus for a "fancier" word or "trickier" rhyme. We do not have
to worry about affectation or feigned love of nature from Rosenfeld.
He loved Nature as she exists and he went anywhere to meet her
and greet her. He could write such simple, pleasant poems, as any
youth might create who falls in love for the first time and tries to
explain it to himself. To quote Pascal, "The heart has reasons of
which reason has no knowledge"."The poet consciously shapes the
unconscious shadows which give energy and life to his cognition
and in writing out of the unconscious wellspring the poet trans-
mutes the archetypal sources into consciously communicated lyrical
forms or into characters in a poetic drama. T.S. Eliot says that the
pre-logical mentality persists in civilized man but becomes available
to them through the poet."[11]

But there is something that must exist in the reader, also, for
the poem to have its desired effect. If the poem expresses some cry
or expression of the "primordial image" or some "invisible order of
the unconscious psyche that is common to the race,"[12] then the poet
intuits his subconscious connection with that of his targeted reader.
He knows where his shafts will be most effective and aims them
well at the desired target. As we read Rosenfeld's poetry in Chapter
Eight, whether in the original Yiddish, in English translation or in
transliteration, the truth of some of the almost extravagant claims
we have made about his creativity will become apparent.

References

1. Adams, H., The The Interests of Criticism, p. 27
2. ibid, p. 22
3. ibid, p. 33
4. ibid, p. 35
5. Goldenthal, Edgar, Unpublished
6. Adams, H.,"In The Interests of Criticism," p. 64
7. Connolly, F., "Poetry, Its Power and Wisdom," Introduction
8. ibid, 109–110

9. Harshav and Harshav, "Amer. Yiddish Poetry," Appendix
10. Connolly, F., "Poetry, Power, Wisdom," 265
11. ibid, 265–266
12. ibid, 288

7

Criticism And Appreciation

If we are to criticize and appreciate a work of art (in painting, sculpture, poetry, prose or music) we must have some working manner of appraisal so that we do not criticize something unfairly or ignorantly (uninformedly). There is, of course, a whole career of criticism which takes much study and provides much more data than we shall provide you with in this volume. However, after reading this chapter the reader will have an enhanced ability to appraise and appreciate the poetry of Morris Rosenfeld or any other poet.

"Although there have been scores of different approaches to literature in the history of criticism many of them seem more concerned with other matters than the work of literature itself. For example, biographic criticism often tends to neglect the work in favor of the author, folk criticism is likely to be most interested in the folklore itself, psychological criticism is apt to use criticism as a means of promoting Freud or Jung or Adler and sociological criticism may turn out to be an apologia for Marx"[1] We can ask, if we are deeply interested in our own psychology, why we have responded the way we have to a particular poem, painting or piece of music. The relevant question is, "What in this work has caused me to respond the way I have?. When we are sufficiently interested in a work to ask this question then we have arrived at what may be termed the esthetic response . . . we should now be interested in the work on its own terms and separate ourselves, our own personal likes and dislikes, from the work. . . . this should enable us to see that work of art objectively". This is the view of Edmund Reiss and we shall present other viewpoints subsequently.

Generally, when we hear the term "criticism" the inference is that there is an adverse appreciation of the work at hand. However in the field of the creative arts—art, literature, music, architecture—criticism means an attempt at analysis of the work to try to determine the artist's meaning, his techniques and whether or not his work is effective. This procedure is supposed to exclude the reviewer's own personal likes or dislikes—if such a position is possible. The last thing anyone wants is for someone to tear a poem apart and examine each aspect of it coldly. This procedure would be suitable for analyzing a clock or an engine by testing each gear, spring and wheel and checking the electric current to see if all still works. We have a basement full of such items that this author could not put back together again. There is always one piece that is left out and the machine does not work. A poem would not work either if that were the way one has to analyze it. In analyzing poetry we have to try to determine what the poem is trying to say, what devices the poet uses, how well he fulfills the purpose of the poem, are his adjectives appropriate, do his allusions to Biblical or historical references contribute to the effect that the purpose demands? This does not "take the clock apart, leaving it in pieces". It is more like testing the components of a building to see if the structure serves its purpose and how well it will stand the test of time. In the arts the whole is often more than the sum of its parts. The work must be seen in parts and as a whole.

While this is only in part the point of view of the author of this book, Reiss is quite persuasive. He writes, "As existential philosophy has insisted, there is a great difference between knowing and being and to extend this idea we may say there is a great difference between knowing and doing. The literary artist is involved with his writing, he is creating it, but he is only the agent of its creation. Going into his writing are various themes, images and structures that may exist in or be significant to him or his subject, but he is most likely unaware of their presence, much less of their significance".[2] Do you see how Plato still has his grip on the minds of his disciples even after thousands of years? When you are asked, "What's new in Criticism?" you will not find it in Reiss, because he still subscribes to the notion of Plato who said that all poets are daft, firmly in the grip of their Muses. And even Freud shared that viewpoint. Whether or not we subscribe to Plato-Reiss, we must constantly caution ourselves not to attempt to see more in the writer's work than is actually there. Do not "read meanings" in his work that may only exist in your own mind. Do not look for the "ten faces in the cartoon". Do you remember, when you were a child, how the Sunday newspapers had a cartoon in which, we were informed, the cartoonist had hidden ten faces. We were sure they were in there and had fun finding them. A serious poet does not purposely obscure his subject, or his theme to make it seem more "arty" than it is. The poet is not creating "double-crostics" or "Murder She Wrote" mysteries. Of course, by his intensity and by his dedication to his subject a writer may, unbeknownst to himself, exhibit a rashness or an overstatement of purpose or even unpleasant redundancies which do subtract from the critical quality of his poem. And, as expressed in an excellent book by Herbert Leibowitz, (Fabricating Lives—Explorations in American Autobiograpy), ". . . . the poet (Walt Whitman) gave me my first inkling of autobiography's renegade power . . . and its multiple forms of self-disclosure and self-concealment".[3]

As we have maintained frequently in this book there are forces at work on the psyche of the poet of which he may or not not be aware, aiding and abetting his talent and his drive to create. But do not let any critic tell you that he can perform his little autopsy on that poet's work and hold up, with his little tweezers, the part of the poem that demonstrates just what affect the Muse has had on the poet and his work. Men who have to write for deadlines, or who, because of poverty, have to "pad" their work with excess baggage, do not have the time or inclination to edit carefully or to omit some of the "deathless" verbosity with which they have upholstered their chef d'oevres. Ericcson, Freud and others have written on the psychological background of poets. We are ill-equipped to enter that arena. However, we submit one note of caution: just as readers of poetry must understand that there is something in their psyches that makes them receptive to poetry, so the psychologist must know what there is in his own psychological make-up that leads to *his* ideas about poets and their psychological backgrounds. As stated earlier, none of us lives in a vacuum and our own past is one of the experiential factors in appraising creative personalities. One can see, then, that there are inherent difficulties in criticism of art and literature, with as many variables as there are individuals. Setting standards can be quite presumptuous. Today's' standards are to-morrow's scrapwood: except for that rascal, Plato, whose views fit comfortably into a really archaic pattern yet are still acceptable today! Usually, however, today's taste is yesterday's culture-shock. How unfair it is to the creative spirit who pours his art (and his heart) into his own mold and discovers that others can only view his work "dispassionately", with the cold eye of an appraiser esti-mating the value of an old farmhouse in a field of corn. When it comes to describing the "taste" of a writer or the "taste" of a critic, one is involved in a personal appraisal of a work of art. Very often we hear the expression, "The public's taste . . . .". Has the public's taste been manipulated by the personal taste of the critic? And how does one measure the taste of the public; simply by the "bottom line?"

We do not take lightly the task of applying our own sense of taste to the works of Morris Rosenfeld. We observe openly that there are differences in age, education, historical perspective, war experience and social background between Morris and the author of this text. In other cases, there might be differences in gender, financial success, social philosophy and religion. When all is consid-ered, we remember that Rosenfeld came from Eastern Europe over a century ago . . . a different world . . . from a home of poverty and oppression. His education after puberty was entirely self-taught and he went through that wrenching experience of flight from home and immigration to our land. None of these experiences have we had. Nevertheless, there are remarkably more aspects to our back-grounds than possibly in any other author that qualify us to offer a "critique" of Rosenfeld and his works. The author is more than just a grandson of Morris Rosenfeld, sharing much of the temperament and excitement with the world and society's problems that occupied Rosenfeld's mind. The interest in "the working man" and social justice that the author has exhibited all his adult life unquestionably received its impetus from "Grandpa" via his mother Raisela, (Rose), Morris' youngest daughter. The sheer delight in poetry and in po-lemical writing that he enjoys is, if not inherited, then certainly a trait that receives its justification in the works and style of Morris Rosenfeld. The author was only about six years of age when Morris died and could not have known his grandfather very well, nor did he do any serious reading of Rosenfeld's works until 1991, when he turned seventy-four. It is purely and simply that the excitability with life, the raw talent for poetry, the affinity with the down-trod-den, the hypercritical attitude towards the "guys at the top" and the impatience with the pace of social justice lend a surer sense of affiliation with Rosenfeld's emotions and a stronger basis for appreciation. On balance, this close sensitivity should prove a legitimate and effective aid in understanding Rosenfeld. One has to understand that Morris Rosenfeld was a poet of the ghetto. He wrote for a certain milieu: the everyman of the immigrant population. These people were none too critical, eager to be encouraged and appreciated. Rosenfeld filled that order better than any of his contemporaries.

From Janice Goldenthal, the author's wife, who helped edit this manuscript, and whose only relationship to Morris was membership in the family by marriage to his grandson, one can expect a more expert, cooler appraisal, since she is a Professor of English and can employ well the "tools of her trade". In addition, Janice experienced more than an outsider's view of the poet. She knew Rose, the poet's daughter, very well. They got along famously. Rose was as sensitive and perceptive of her father's nature and his motivations as any offspring could be. She loved poetry and could write her own poems quite well. Actually, she lived poetry. Her entire being was suffused with the poetry of Poe and Whitman, Tennyson, Wordsworth and James Whitcomb Riley. Her great love for music led her to spend ever so many waking hours at the piano, where she was expert at Chopin, Liszt, Mozart and Beethoven. Who but Raisele could have managed to fit Poe's "The Raven" to part of Beethoven's "Moonlight Sonata" (Sonata Quasi Una Fantasia)?

Incidentally, (and here is a charming digression), Rose Rosenfeld Goldenthal named her first two sons Edgar and Allan. She didn't have the courage to name the third son Poe, but named him after her father, Morris Rosenfeld He was better known to the world of attorneys as Maurice R. Goldenthal. Maurice passed away in November of 1995 without ever seeing this book. To associate with Rosenfeld's daughter Rose was to learn that poetry can indeed govern one's appreciation of the world. Like her Dad, but without his drive and ego, Rose could create a rhyme for any occasion in a trice and so modify the lyrics of any song that they best expressed the mood of the moment. Rose had a humorous glint in her eye, a sense of the ridiculous, that, to the best of our knowledge, her father did not possess in sufficient quantity. He did not exhibit a light, playful sense of humor that could take the edge off any serious situation. After all, he did have much more struggling and adversity in his life than did his children. Had he possessed a lighter side more often, like Sholem Aleichem, he might have lived longer and with less tension.

When we discuss the works of any poet, in this case Rosenfeld, what standards should be set to evaluate them? Do we have to consider whether he was really a poet because he was or was not committed to any brand of social or political activism? Must we wonder whether he was a good poet because his allegories and illusory effects were not according to pigeon-holes set out by Plato or Sidney, Richards or Mazzori or Oscar Wilde? Whose works could satisfy all of them? Or, indeed, whose works could satisfy any of them, except their own?

In offering our critiques of Rosenfeld's poetry, we shall use our own point of view but shall also mention, on occasion, the way that particular work was received by his public. Our agenda is to analyse Rosenfeld's works fairly and honestly. The fact that he was our "Grandpa" need not imply that we shall not use the standard bases for criticism. We had to know whether he used the proper tools of the poet, or his emotions took reason from his pen or whether he was so myopic that his view of the world was too foreshortened for proper perspective and universality to be possible in his poetry and prose. On those occasions where we found that a poem fell short of his own standards for style or content we mentioned that fact. One statement we are sure of, since it was made by the poet himself; "My pen is both a lyre and a sword!". It certainly was.

Anatole France says[4], in discussing the critic and the reader, "The critic should simply be one who relates the adventures of his soul among masterpieces. . . . (saying) 'Gentlemen, I am going to speak of myself on the subject of Racine, or Shakespeare, or Goethe or Pascal'". This indicates to us that *we must read the poet for what he means to us, as individuals, not to a list of formulations* that dictate what he should have written to conform to that list. How do his ideas, his crying, his laughing and jeering, his awe at the world relate to us nearly one hundred years after he wrote that material. Also, how did he relate to his contemporaries? The basis of criticism is the effect that the poet had upon his readers: what has he tried to say, how well did he say it and how well was it received by his targeted readers? Notice that we did not ask how well he was received by cold-nosed hypercritical snobs of the literary establishment who make a living out of criticising someone else's work and are often more interested in turning a phrase that will identify themselves as unusually sharp and perceptive. The poet is one small but strident voice in the wind. While the wind carries the confused sounds of a world in ferment the mere fact that his voice can be heard (and that someone else wishes to hear him) is a positive factor in his "rating". We may not want to hear noisy or shrill expositive sounds, but when they are directed to us, when they insinuate themselves into our consciousness, then that shrill poet has hit his mark. How many of us can claim with assurance that our voices have an impact? Indeed, will anyone at all care to hear what we have to say? Even our own kids? How potent one's voice must be to pierce the wind and vibrate in the mind of a troubled and hassled world!

Because Rosenfeld had the ear and the affection of the Jewish world of his time and for over two generations, we are studying him in an attempt to bring his name out of the shadows. We are aware of the impossibility of accurately appraising the impact of someone's creativity on the psyche of a bygone era. It is *so* difficult to attempt any identification with the life of Eastern European immigrants! Only in the printed words and actions of those who were able to express the sense of their own world can "alien" souls such as we are go back in time to appreciate Rosenfeld and his culture. We have spent a lifetime trying to assimilate with your everyday American; not to stand out as "different", or as "foreign". We have not been afraid of achieving, merely of "sticking out" like a sore thumb. But in a world of sore thumbs there has to be a special way of looking at one's self, and that is what we are trying to accomplish.

Ever since Plato's time it has been known that literary criticism has always had to deal with the relationship between the literary work and its audience. Horace said, in the Ars Poetica, "The aim of the poet is to inform or delight, or to combine together in what he says both pleasure and applicability to life. He who combines the pleasing and the useful wins out by both instructing and delighting the reader." A critic, however, is still only one individual; one who employs his own point of view. Does he view the poem from a tight, inflexible, even insensitive vantage point so that this poem seen from another angle would not meet his approval? And must the poem perform a "therapeutic function? Does it teach things unsuitable to the young or even to the middle-aged, as Plato concerned himself about? Is the poem too rational; is it irrational (and thereby subversive!)? How many critical points of view have to concern one on the value of a poem? What role does artistic technique play? One man's delight is another man's boredom. whether we are dealing with poetry, prose, art or even television productions. Plato objected strenuously that poetry "feeds and waters the passions instead of drying them up", (from Dialogues 70). That Plato was a spoil-sport! Must poems only be hymns to the gods, or serve utilitarian purposes?

Remember how the Communist hierarchies in Russia, China and Korea, Vietnam and Cuba perverted the writing of literature to be only "socially redeemable" expressions acceptable to them. Somehow we feel that Plato should have read a good book like Frazier's, "The Golden Bough" to see how much fun the Greeks could really be, and how humanly fallible and exciting all those gods really were. One can readily comprehend from reading all the conflicting standards of poetic criticism that a poet must indeed have an octopus-like capability to write in perhaps eight fashions, or ten fashions, or twenty fashions, in order for that poor, tired mind to create something that is able to satisfy the world.

Primarily in its early years, immigrant Yiddish culture was unpretentious, without avant-guard distortions, with a sense of reality that was evident in its behavior, its hopes and even its dreams. Perhaps there was a form of pretense in "Die Junge" and the "Inzichists", who, being in a way iconoclasts and existentialists, had to be "different". They had to be consciously different, consciously destructive of the past modes of literary culture, and in so being, they constructed, with few exceptions, a nearly sterile literature, only dimly related to the experiences of the large mass of immigrants from whom they originated. While it is true that some of Die Junge's poetry was more than competent as works of art, their work was quite divorced from the view of reality to which most usual forms of poetry could relate and which most audiences could appreciate.

The human ego is a product of the brain, one to a person. Each person's ego will only allow him to accept (or produce) that which it will allow him to see. If an ego is so great that reality is like one of those distorted figures one sees in a carnival mirror, then the creation of such an ego-driven individual will be similarly distorted. This means that only an exceedingly small number of individuals will view reality from the same point of view, or with the same sensibility as the man who created that work of art. When Rosenfeld wrote, his ego drove him to achieve, to be recognized, to make an impact on the consciousness of his readers (and listeners). But he did not distort his style or his ideas to conform to an artificially contrived shape. He did not try to force words and ideas into a mold that did not normally reflect the modes of human expression. There is something about the iambic pentameter, for example, that makes it more readily acceptable and pleasing to the usual listener than meters and forms that are especially contrived just to be "different". The meter and tone of emphasis that one finds in the Bible are, to the Semitic and Western ear, quite pleasing and effective for the expression of almost any normal human emotion. We wonder how that marvelous creation would have been received had it been written in an individualized, cryptic language that reflects solely the approach to literature that Di Yunge and the Inzichists employed.

While it is true that a poem need not exhibit meter, nor must it possess rhyme, it must have other qualities which describe it as poetry rather than merely stilted prose. Even if the poem is a forty-page ode (the Ancient Mariner, for example), or a sonnet, or Haiku, there is something in poetry that is different from any other form of writing. It must be the crystallization of an idea, or a series of ideas. It must not be an on-dragging complex of rambling words that seem to struggle towards the cover of the book because it knows that there it must end. A harangue is a harangue even if it is called a poem by an undisciplined, untaught or incompetent writer.

Those who took poetry and created new forms were not necessarily destructive. When the sonnet developed its ultimate shape it did not end the writing of poetry that did not conform to the sonnet's architecture. It is simply that if a poem has a variant structure it cannot be called a sonnet. And if a poem has eleven lines and ninety-four syllables it cannot be called Haiku. Call it anything else you wish. Rosenfeld was enough under the influence of conservative poets not to wander into the bogs of untried poetic rhyme and meter. Whereas his ideas were not limited, the structure of his poetry was. There were variations, of course, but he was not an innovator of poetic structure. He had enough room in the usual modes of versification to say all he had to say. Even so, one of his favorite poets was Walt Whitman, for whom he even wrote a poem of appreciation. As you will find in our next chapter, *Rosenfeld's*

Poetry, there are evidences of Whitman's influence on Rosenfeld in a few instances in both his Yiddish and English poems. Incidentally, Whitman did affect some of the poets who wrote in Yiddish later than Rosenfeld, particularly the "Inzichists". It seems to this writer, who has tried his hand at poetry, that free verse, or unrhymed verse are less demanding of the poet who otherwise might have to struggle to keep his words in a straight-jacket of counted syllables and conform to exacting standards of rhyme. This does not in any way denigrate free or unrhymed verse, because, in all honesty, the passion of versification is less restrained in free and unrhymed stanzas and the poet has to be less of a "mathematician of language". Possibly when the Muse learns how to use a computer and can tune in on the electronic reaches of the Internet, poetry will become less a concentration on form than an expression of content with coded concepts that we cannot even conceive of in these primitive days.

Peretz, Rosenfeld and Bialik were disciplined poets, regardless of the personal problems they experienced in their lives. With the near eclipse of Peretz recently and the almost total eclipse of Rosenfeld we find particular discomfort at the loss of such beauty to the world's attention. Eclipse does not mean that something has disappeared. It simply means that "out of sight is out of mind". Things are in the deep shadows created by the wave of newer times and newer interests. Like the planets in eclipse they may survive for an eternity, but if they are not here before our eyes they are like "full many a gem of purest ray serene that is doomed to shine unseen." Those aspects of their work that are now anachronistic remain of interest only to the scholars who probe the past. Those aspects that have universal applications and truths can always be of interest to future generations. Sometimes they may have to be rediscovered again and again for the newer generations to learn that they are indeed part of a continuum: that others, years before them, have lived through similar situations and experienced those same universal life crises and written about them feelingly and intelligently.

Writers like Peretz and Rosenfeld, of whom there were precious few, employed universal themes drawn from Jewish life. A depressed Frenchman, a subjugated Arab or Black, or a deprived Russian is in the same plight as many of the Jews we know about. The historical quirk of Fate that allowed the Jews to survive is one of the idiosyncrasies of destiny. But human problems are human problems, wherever they occur. Rosenfeld cried for the world. Peretz didn't cry or mourn. He commiserated and pointed up inequities, offering, occasionally, hope for the future. Like Tevye leaving Anatevka, "who tried to take his world with him wherever he went the Jews tried to take the world of the shtetl with them to the Western world, or wherever they went."[5] It did not work. They shed the traditions, the dress, the language and the customs like the leaves of an artichoke, one by one, until all that was left was the sweet, tender heart that was so defenseless and vulnerable. This was demonstrated by Sholem Aleichem in his stories; even in the Broadway play, "Conversations With My Father" and by Rosenfeld in his poems of love and beauty. Some of the tough prickly leaves of that artichoke remain here and there, but the core of the people who were able to persist through millennia of hardship remains. Rosenfeld knew that his role was to describe the beauties and the problems that the world showed to them.

Poets have probably existed since the earliest of times, wherever a language existed that could lend itself to eloquence and descriptiveness and whenever Man was developed enough in his senses to appreciate, to create and to express himself linguistically. Poetry is the crystallization of ideas in a specific format that is different than prose, where more time and space is devoted to the explanation of ideas and feelings, as well as to historical and personal expression. Poets can describe in a phrase or two, with or without rhyme or rhythm, the essence of an idea that a prose writer might expand upon for chapters or volumes. Both devices serve the purpose of their authors and can be equally appreciated. The ability that certain great poets have exhibited to write poetry with passion and clarity, with rhyme and meter, with elegance and precision and at the same time to have something of universal import to express— this ability is genius and we must be everlastingly grateful that these poets have existed. Poe and Shakespeare are but two of these geniuses in the English language. Goethe and Heine were masters in German. Bialik, Peretz and Rosenfeld were the masters in Yiddish, Some of Rosenfeld's poetry is indeed exquisite in the skill and care of its fabrication, the beauty of its images and language, the admirable quality of its concepts and the manner of so expressing them. Its sensitivity to pain and suffering is of the highest order. In fact, some of Rosenfeld's writing, poetry and prose, seems to demonstrate, by the book, the definition of exquisite pain. Certainly many of Rosenfeld's poems, such as "In The Shop", "Mein Yingele", "Die Yiddishe Mai", "Der Sturm", and others can be regarded as exquisite, as would rare gems, jungle flowers or the fur of the chinchilla.

As to elegance, that is a term probably never applied to Rosenfeld or his works. He was not an elegant man in terms of consistent propriety or refinement. His emotions, his ego, his concept of himself as a champion, a gut-fighter for the poor and down-trodden, none of these lend themselves to an image of Rosenfeld as an elegant man. But his poetry, by its sharply chiseled features, by its knowledge of its own import, and its ability to stand head and shoulders over its contemporary Yiddish poetry, looking with piercing eyes at the forces of Nature, at society, at the Deity itself, there we find an elegance in Rosenfeld's creations. Much as a leopard, crouched on a limb ready to pounce on its prey, is elegant in its lines, pure in its motives, and economical in its construction, so too is Rosenfeld's poetry.

Of course, not every poem of Rosenfeld reached the heights of elegance or exquisiteness. He wrote prolifically under a variety of pressures that affected the quality of his work at times. Whether these pressures were externally or internally induced it is not easy for us to determine. Certainly aggravation, illness, cruel criticism by unscrupulous "competitive" writers caused some of his work to suffer. His own ego to produce even when new ideas were not forthcoming led to some deficient poetry. We will not include any of those poems here. Even to include a great many of his better ones would take up an excessive number of pages. But so many of Rosenfeld's poems were indeed elegant in terms of their posture on the literary scene. They stood above the crowd the way a hero returning from battle, bloodied sword in hand, might stalk through the multitude. Yes, the uncommon common man, Morris Rosenfeld, born in Buksha, Russian-Poland, on the night of a battle between now-long-forgotten armies, was able to drive his intellectual powers to a ferocious form of elegance, if such a term ever existed before. If you want to read an exquisite poem, one that is crystalline in its clarity and capable of tearing your heart out, read "All Are Silent", ("Alle Shvaygn) which is included in this volume.

Bialik and Peretz wrote in a style that was grand, superbly competent, deeply felt and consciously representative of the inner feelings of the Jews of their generation: probably of the Jews of all time. The problems of love, greed, inhumanity and persecution have always been with us Jews. Someday we must figure out why we have survived. Perhaps it is like someone getting ill in a tightly-packed subway car, where he is too weak to stand up on his own two feet and the crowd is so tightly packed that the ill person cannot fall to the ground. Perhaps we have not died because the world won't let us die. They need to torture and abuse us for themselves; they won't let us fall to the ground. We also know that the Catholic Church and the Muslim hierarchy would suffer terribly if there were no Jews to accuse, as though we are the necessary "negative" for every "positive" in their Church's philosophy. If there were no Jews they would have to invent us, for their own purposes. These are indeed some painful truths that most writers are too careful to discuss. Not so with Rosenfeld or this grandson.

Among the first subjects to experience a writer's ego are the spouse and children, who probably often wished that they could escape the almost constant emoting, poetry readings, shouts against heaven and Man and history. Woe to the wife who says, "That's awful! It makes no sense at all! Who wants to hear such stuff?" Fortunately for Rosenfeld, his wife, relatively uneducated though she was at first, had a subconscious intellectuality which was truly able to guide the tempestuous genius of her husband with love and consideration. Remember that their marriage was a true love-match, which was quite rare in the Europe of their youth. She must have had an innate sense of which writing was good and which was banal. No writer can stand constant carping and criticism for long. It destroys his confidence and the inner peace of mind that is essential for the creative soil to remain fertile.

In discussing peace of mind let us consider for a moment Rosenfeld's purview of writing. His interest in the historical and social problems of the Jews took as much of his life and strength as would the interest of a physician whose entire career is devoted to cancer patients or the terminally ill. How the accumulative pain and frustration must weigh upon the psyche of such a man! How Fate and the inconsideration of God must tear at his religious beliefs and his natural optimism!. Rosenfeld's purview was depression, poverty, violence, hatred, frustration and loss of hope. His foes were also apathy, occasional jealousy, the contrary egos of publishers and other writers, and worst of all, his own self-image, which was ultimately to destroy him. We must confess, old Grampa spent much of his time and talent combating negatives. If it were not for his poems on love and nature, his works would simply be too painful to read for a protracted time for any degree of enjoyment.

As Wisse described Peretz so we can describe Rosenfeld. In part, "buried in him, but not far beneath the surface, was a solitary man with powerful feelings who yearned for things beyond the attainable".[6] The frustration had to be inconceivable for both writers. Our reader can only try to imagine how he (she) might feel under such circumstances. Deep feelings and deep committment can be sorely frustrated. How would such frustrations manifest themselves in the reader's own powers of concentration and creativity? How long before one would start getting angry, irritable, or even violent?

As noted before, there has long been abroad (and even in the family of this author) the idea that poets are all temperamental, difficult to get along with, frequently irrational and certainly like the apocryphal "absent-minded professor". No scientific studies to that conclusion are at hand concerning the verity of such concepts. However, many poets themselves were guilty of that assumption and possibly thought that they were entitled to be forgiven for what is not easily forgivable in "ordinary people": temper tantrums, sloppiness in dress and manners and forgetfulness in everyday responsibilities. What comes to mind here is a remark made by Dr. Leon Goldenthal, author of "Toil And Triumph". Speaking to his eldest son, who was guilty of all the above transgressions, he said, "Ed, you have all the social and temperamental attributes of a great poet; but can you demonstrate the talent to justify such a temperament!" The young man knew then that bouts of temper and lack of responsibility around the house were not readily accepted with grace or appreciation even by a loving family, unless he could demonstrate a form of genius that could outweigh other mundane behavioral characteristics.

In considering a written work of art there are many aspects of that work that must be taken into account. While we have no intention of expanding on this topic at all, we must explain that when we studied Rosenfeld's creations we kept in mind the standards for composition, such as: "What is the 'point of view' of the writer?, What is his 'style', and what are his 'subjects' and his 'themes'?. Does he use many of the accepted devices for literary composition, such as allusion, illusion, allegory, historical, Biblical or other extraneous references. Does he employ onomatopoeia, rhyme, meter,

musicality? What is his tone? Does he employ symbolism, meta-
phor, oxymorons, hyperbole, irony, paradox, imagery or simile?
What are the pattern formations of his poetry." Do not fret! Out
of mercy to those who did not choose to read this book as an English textbook we shall not discuss these elements any further or
even put their definitions in the appendix of our book. Occasionally,
"en passant", we may mention those elements of poetry that are of
prime significance to us at the time.

We have made several observations about Rosenfeld and his
works which deserve to be entered here. He spoke to a relatively
uncomplicated audience, some of whom were relatively uneducated
in the Classics of any nation. His audience was primarily of the
working classes; immigrants from a land alien to the United States.
This is not to assume that his audience was composed of unintelli-
gent ignorami. On the contrary; most Jews were learned in their
Holy Scriptures, in Yiddish writings of all manner and many of
them were indeed cultured in foreign lands and well versed in diverse literatures in diverse languages. To appreciate Rosenfeld did
not mean one had to be an ignorant pauper from the shtetl.
Strangely enough, some of his most appreciative readers were those
Jews who had "made it" in business and industry, or who had risen
through the ranks to positions of honor in universities and the professions. And many American Gentiles who were patrons of the
arts recognized the importance of Rosenfeld's contributions to our
culture. Hutchins Hapgood, Teddy Roosevelt, Upton Sinclair, Jack
London, Edwin Markham, Jane Addams, Rabbi Stephen S. Wise
and numerous others sensed the depth of Morris' feelings and the
fact that his artistry touched the chords that resonated to the sensibilities of the immigrant Jews

His writing was not without humor, but it was not "one-liners"
or funny stories of the Sholem Aleichem variety that brought him
fame. It was more of the bitter-sweet, sardonic wit that illuminated
his crusade for the proletarians. He was not the kind of left-winger
who was out to destroy Capitalism. He was a Socialist whose goal
was to improve the lot of the working man. He was not sitting in
his den in a posh suburban residence writing about the tribulations
of his people. He was "there", on the spot, while the whole immigrant experience was all going on. It was he, not someone else,
whose observations and experiences he was utilizing. He was a
"now" person, always excited, always dedicated, always pushing to

be heard. In a manner he was somewhat like Bob Dylan, (Robert Zimmerman) who sang songs that ignited a new self-consciousness in the youth of the 1960's.

Some of Morris' poems and prose writings are silly, pressing for attention when obviously inspiration was lacking at that moment and the need to earn a living was paramount. These do not deserve to be reprinted for a century or more and we do not include any of them here. Yet one wonders how this self-tutored man could often write such sophisticated work, how his cadence and rhyme could be of such high quality, even in translation. As to translations, he said it best, "You can imitate a diamond with its shape and its size, its glass-like appearance. But an imitation, like a translation, rarely has the fire, the sharp inimitable edge, the cold dignity of a diamond". Even so, some of Rosenfeld's poems have been so well translated that much of the original impact is retained. Just read the translations of Max Rosenfeld and Aaron Kramer included in this volume.

Many of Rosenfeld's poems are dedicated to Jewish religious Holy days and there are many Biblical references. Even when writing poems about philosophy or the manifestations of nature he would frequently exhibit a "Jewish" consciousness and bring the topic right back home to the Ghetto residents who read his poetry. We knew so little about our Grandfather that it was a revelation to discover how educated he was in the essences of Jewish religion, Jewish history and in "Yiddishkeit" (the mannerisms, the mores, the personal side of Jewishness).

When you read a few of his poems in the next chapter you will note how some of his poetry is truly autobiographical, such as "Why I Am I", "The Lion", and "My Youth", among many. With this poet you do not have to ask, "Is this poetry Jewish, or just poetry written by a Jew?". Rosenfeld was immersed in his Jewishness. Who was the wag who remarked, at seeing the art of a Jewish painter, that one could detect the aroma of chicken fat in the presence of that man's paintings? One could make the same remark in the presence of Morris Rosenfeld's poetry. And yet there is the universality of his themes that carries him a step beyond the parochial.

We have been unable to find many references to Messianic themes in his writing. This concept, that originated in the preachings of Isaiah and is peculiar only to the Jewish people (and its offspring, Christianity and Islam), was a clever ploy to offer hope to a people who had every reason to be hopeless: a nation in poverty, in bondage, helpless before the whims of destiny. The recurrent interest in an impending visit from a Messiah whenever conditions reached a new low was used and abused for millennia by the ruling clergy and individuals taken in by their fanaticism. Rosenfeld showed us no evidence that he counted on a Messiah to deliver the Jews from their problems. Rather, he made every effort to stimulate his fellow Jews to rouse themselves to achieve a decent life by their own hands. If the Messiah wants to come and sit at their table and break bread with them He is honored and welcome.

We hope that we have demonstrated that not only is "objective poetry" a paradox in terms but that "objective criticism" is equally as paradoxical in terms, perhaps not so much in prose criticism as in poetic criticism, since there is "The Muse" to contend with in poetry. That is the indescribable element that transcends logic and reason and which can dominate the romantic and the lyric poet and even some of those ultra-modern approaches to poetry which seem so involved and surreal that one wonders whether the Muse hasn't lately been smoking something stronger than tobacco. Rosenfeld did not borrow his subjects or his themes from Western literature in any significant amounts. And interestingly enough, he did not devote much time to describing life in the shtetl or the farms of Eastern Europe. He wrote about nature, about love, about the life of an immigrant worker and the struggles to survive under rough circumstances. He wrote practically nothing about the years he spent in London or even about the ships and the voyages he and his fellow immigrants made to come to this country. The longer Morris lived here in the United States the more he was taken by the beauty of the countryside. He wrote in hundreds of poems about every aspect of America's physical beauty. He also became unusually patriotic. Morris wrote in his poems about his love and respect for this great open-hearted land that offered him and his people a haven from the tribulations of the world.

Rosenfeld had no existential ideas. He was not philosophical about creating a new reality here in America. His reactions for the most part were "gut" reactions, in almost every purview of his life; in his dealings with the "bosses", in his family life, in his dealings with his publishers and combating his modernist critics. Among the many surprises we discovered at the YIVO archives was the existence of a book on "Philosophical Ideas", in Yiddish, by Rosenfeld. That alone might be a suitable project for one of his great-grandchildren. All they have to do is learn Yiddish, learn all about the old poet, take off some months from their patients and experiments and let the world know what Rosenfeld philosophied about in his latter years. We wonder what his contributions would be in that discipline.

There was no perceptible eroticism in any of his work However, from another point of view, in his latter years, not having even reached the age of sixty, he was prevailed upon to have some sort of operation performed so that "he would leave his wife alone" sexually. Whatever they operated upon, it did not affect his poetry. Morris was not obsessed with martyrdom, but in fact, he was so obsessed with his "mission" that it was the numerical equivalent of martyrdom. Rosenfeld had no desire to "re-deify Christ" or accept the olive branch held out by Paul to convert Jew and Pagan alike to the "new Jewish religion", using Christ as a focus. While many of Rosenfeld's themes were universal, they never included a universalism in which the Jew sublimates his beliefs, his traditions and his behavior into a newly synthesized being that was neither fish, fowl nor just plain meat. What came as a surprise to us, in delving into the YIVO archives, was the attention that Rosenfeld gave sympathetically to Jesus. He looked upon Christ as an embodiment of the Jewish soul. The fate of Christ has been the fate of the Jew. The poems he wrote about Christmas carry the same message: not a burden of hatred or anxiety, but a recognition of the Jewish role in the core of Christianity. Also, he "pulled no punches" in describing the role that Christianity, even Christmas Bells, played in the martyrdom of Europe's Jewish population through the centuries. Rosenfeld had no desire to investigate what might have been attractiveness in alien cultures or religions. He never lived to see the gradual disintegration of the Jewish culture in America, or elsewhere. Neither did his interest in the spirit of Zionism (the effort to create a legally established home in the Holy Land for any and all Jews who wish to reside there) last long enough to see that dream come true. Fortunately for him, he never lived long enough to witness any part of the European Holocaust which destroyed so many of the Jewish people that he loved. The only examples of snideness or angry criticism that Rosenfeld employed was at the expense of enemies who were patent in their cruelty to his people or himself:

the "bosses" and the "Junge" who plagued him. Basically, he was a troubador of love and nature, especially after his battles for labor seemed to be less imperative for him. And that's when his appeal waned as well. He was at his best as a curmudgeon for the laboring Americans.

Why didn't Rosenfeld write of the shtetl? Why did he not describe the beauties of a Polish lake or the beckoning prospects of a Polish road as it narrowed into a single line of mystery in the distance? Why did he not write much of the transports that brought him to America or the crowded, frenetic streets of the ghettos of Amsterdam and London? Why did he not condemn God for his tribulations or wrestle with the Devil as Job might have? He seemed to have left the all-powerful mystic forces of the netherworld to their own devices, only alluding to them occasionally in some of his most disturbing poems. He had apparently found his "niche", not in regurgitating the memories of the oppressed and sterile past in shtetl life, but in an exciting post as bard for the oppressed, struggling working class in America. His priorities were the immediacies of the workers' needs. His goals were the socialist goals of better pay, better working hours and better working conditions, a better home life, better opportunities for his children; better everything! And from these goals he devised poetry and wrote polemics for years, wherever he could get published. His was not exactly a one-track mind, but you had better agree with him or get out of the way!

In some of the poems to be shown in the next chapter it will be demonstrated that Rosenfeld was not all curmudgeon. He stopped to smell the roses. He paused to pay his respects to his Biblical antecedents. He doffed his hat to Whitman and Heine and other creative geniuses he admired. But like the sabra, the fruit of the Holy Land, he protected his soft sweet core with a tough, prickly exterior which he used to defend himself in his self-appointed mission for the underprivileged.

References

1. Reiss, E., "Elements of Liter. Analysis", Preface iii
2. ibid, p. 6, 7, 8
3. Leibowitz, NY Times, Book Review 9/5/89, p. C20
4. Adams, H., "Interests of Criticism", p. 55
5. Wisse, Ruth, "Sholem Aleichem", Introduction, xv
6. Wisse, Ruth, "I.L. Peretz", p. 29

SELECTED YIDDISH POEMS
BY MORRIS ROSENFELD

In Original Yiddish, Translations into English,
with Transliterations, Analyses and Critiques

8

Selected Yiddish Poems

The poems in this chapter were written in Yiddish by Morris Rosenfeld over the span of his life in America. Many of the poems here are printed in the original Yiddish with Hebrew characters. All the Yiddish will be placed in separate pages at the end of each section of his poetry. For all poems there is a transliteration using Roman (English) characters. Also, for most poems there will be a brief "critique" or "analysis." Over the course of the last century American Jews have generally become so assimilated that Yiddish is used less and less and so many of us cannot read Hebrew characters for either Yiddish or even for Hebrew prayers. For such people, and until recently, we have been among them, transliteration and translation are a "must" if one wishes to appreciate the scope and significance of important Yiddish writers.

Once these poems are read it will become a revelation that someone so long ago and from such a far-off background could be so vital to ours lives and so up-to-date in much of his thought. The immigrant experience still reverberates in our conceptions, in our preconceptions and in the way we are dealt with in this country. The problems of immigration, even now, are serious and even frightening. You will discover that Rosenfeld was a deeply emotional, religious, socially conscious individual. He seemed to cry, almost whine, ever so often. It occurs to us, after five years of reading his work that he took his subject matter too much to heart and often became overcome by it. This "attitude" of grief and woe not only reflected his own travail but was also used as an "approach" to reach the heavily burdened masses whose psyches were overtaxed with labor and frustration.

The reader will note here that in our "critiques and our analyses" we are occasionally rather light-hearted and almost "flip" in our approach. That is where Rosenfeld and his grandson differ—in their attitudes. No disrespect is ever meant, but the light-heartedness is part of Ed's personality and is, in a way, a result of Rosenfeld's success. In our overview of his life and his accomplishments we reveal that the economic security, social advances and broad education we have received have made us feel less intense and less victimized by the world we live in. We are more relaxed than our distinguished grandpa but we are aware that the very social benefits and psychological security we are heir to are a direct result of the fighting socialism and unrelenting pressure of men like Rosenfeld and his confreres. Just read his poetry in whatever language is comfortable for you. Try to put yourself into the context of *his* times, in the frame of reference that includes national and world problems and the historical problems of the Jews that seemed insoluble. Place yourself in the Jewish ghetto a century ago, with its crowds, its poverty, its noise and untidiness, its intensity and unbelievable strength. Then ask yourself how any man could rise above the tumult to view his people with such affection and offer them so much support and solace.

Many people have translated Rosenfeld's works into English. Some of those whose efforts we could identify include: Prof. Leo Weiner, Rose Pastor-Stokes, Helena Frank, Max Rosenfeld, Aaron Kramer, L. Trommer, Nathan Ausubel, Florence Kiper, Henry Greenfield, Belle Robbins, Itche Goldberg, Philip Raskin, Alice Stone Blackwell, Marc Syrkin, Leon Goldenthal and Edgar J. Goldenthal (known in this chapter as EJG). To all these artists and the many whose names have not been mentioned here we owe a deep debt of gratitude. Their works are in books in homes, libraries, schools, camps, theatres and institutions of many varieties the world over. And, best of all, so many of these poems are still in the memories of a multitude of Jews everywhere.

All poetry has been transliterated and translated by Edgar Goldenthal except where otherwise indicated.

HUMOR

If at any time we understated Rosenfeld's sense of humor we hereby apologize for it. His imagination was inexhaustable. The following is only a partial listing of some of the many hundreds of poems and prose works that contained a sometimes biting, sometimes zany sense of the oblique. His titles were not always indicative of the sharpness of his feelings on many subjects. He also used his poems and "fables" to exact "revenge" on some of his equally acerbic critics and detractors. One can not be sure, after all these years, whether his tales were just stories he created or formulae for sardonic thrusts at his "foes".

Morris had an interesting knack for inserting poems in the middle of the text of stories, speeches and essays. He simply found poetry more efficient for making pointed remarks. Whom else do we know who inserted poetry into his prose? Anyhow, just look at some of these titles of poems and prose we selected off-handedly from some of his books.

Legends from the Future	The Licker
The Lost God	Self-Help
Without Winter	Aw, Give it Back To Me
The Fox And The Goose	The Cat And The Bird
The Pessimist	The Noodnick (The Pest)
The Action	Collecting Rent
The First Day's Wages	Between Shleppers
False Thanks	The Hamentosh to The Reader of the Megilleh
Beryl The Fisherman becomes a Decadent	The Looker
The Tip	Do You Believe It?
The Lost One	The Mattress
The Dead Mattress	The Corset
The Second Wife	Fell In
Litvak and Daitch	

(The eternal internal competition between Germanic and East European Jews)

ONCE AGAIN
GUIDE TO YIDDISH PRONUNCIATION

This is a guide to reading and pronouncing Yiddish using the YIVO technique rather than the "sounds-like" or the Germanic methods:

Letters	Sound in English
kh	for the gutteral sound frequently spelled with a "ch", as in Germanic words like macht, nacht
oh	for the sound of "aw" as in draw, straw, or the short "o" as in done, won
ey	for the sound of "ay" as in play, stray
ay	for the sound of "aye" as in mine, shine, cry
uh	for the sound of the long "u" as in dune, rune
u	for the sound of the short "u" as in put
a	for the sound of "ah" as in calm, balm, mom
ih	for the sound of the long "e" as in peel, reel
i	for the sound of the short "i" as in hit, mitt. So many writters use the letter "i" as a long "i" that we occasionally do so too. This is no shandah, since it always is a variation of the sound "eee"; so "dih" or "di" sound like dee
e	for the sound of "eh" as in met, get and at the end of a word. As in German, there are no silent letters.
o	for the sound of "uh", as in mutt, gut
kn	sometimes an "e" is omitted after a consonant and before an "n", as in blikn, shikn, but the sound is identical with blicken, shicken
dt	sometimes a "dt" is placed at the end of Germanic words such as vandt, handt, but the sound is identical with hand, vand

GEMS FROM MORRIS ROSENFELD

(From a book compiled and rendered into English verse, copyrighted and with all rights reserved by Elbert Aidline-Trommer, in 1921)

There is no other poet in the Jewish or, perhaps the world's literature as versatile as Morris Rosenfeld. First known to fame as a singer of Labor and Rebellion, he shortly afterward began to pour out his songs of the Jewish Wanderer longing for his ancient land. Seven years ago his Yiddish version of the Song Of Songs was published and, together with it, a book of love poetry. At the same time he became a contributor to the Jewish Daily News and in its columns has given vent to the profound religious feeling that had been pent up in his spirit all these years. Thus now, in his sixtieth year, Rosenfeld has completed the gamut of a true poet's life-work.

In the selections that follow, the poet's soul is revealed through the medium of allegorical poems telling of his—of every artist's—spiritual experience. There is the majestic eagle soaring in inaccessible heights, yet compelled by dire necessity to descend to the earth; there is the canary, trilling free and unhampered in the woods, and his domesticated brother singing in captivity. A nameless stream flows through the mountains and what a wonderful, deeply reverent prayer Rosenfeld makes of it. The setting sun awakens a melancholy feeling in the poet and, finally at the thought of friends who have gone before him, whence no one returns, he craves to learn, "Where are they?"

(E.A.Trommer, interestingly enough, was the father of the young woman who wrote a delightful little monograph about Rosenfeld and one of his grandsons {guess which one.) That monograph is also included in this volume. If there are any Trommers left in the world we have just found a picture of Mr. Trommer with two of Rosenfeld's daughters in 1904! EJG)

LIST OF YIDDISH POEMS IN THIS CHAPTER
With Translations, Transliterations and Critiques

Page   *Poem In English Translation and Transliteration*

144   **Poetry of the Sweatshop** .... The World Of The Worker
146   The Pale Operator .... Der Bleykhe Opereytor
148   The Sweatshop .... Di Svett Shop
152   The Workmen .... Di Arbayter
153   The Teardrop Millionaire .... Der Trehren Millyunehr
155   The Lion .... Der Leyb
157   Red Terror .... Di Royte Beholle
160   What is the World .... Vuhs Iz Di Velt
163   Bread With Tea .... Broyt Mit Tey
164   Exile .... Golos
165   The Old Tailor .... Der Alter Shnayder
167   The Candle Seller .... Der Likht Farkoyfene
171   The Ghetto Tree .... Der Ghettoh Boym
173   The Bride Of The Hills .... Der Kale Fuhn Di Berg
176   A Teardrop On The Iron .... A Trehr Oyfn Ayzn
178   Shoot The Beast .... Shihst Di Bestih
179   Evening On The Hudson .... Abend
181   To The Workmen .... Tsum Arbayter
183   Selected Labor Poems In Original Yiddish

197   **Poems Of Family And Personal Life**
199   My Little Son .... Mayn Yingele
202   Lovesong In A Sweatshop .... Vehr Oyb Nit Du
203   My Resting Place .... Mayn Ruhe Plahtz
205   To My Beloved .... Tsu Der Gelihbte
207   A Dead Heart .... A Toyte Hartz
209   All Are Silent .... Alle Shvaygen
211   Earth .... Erd
212   Stealings .... Ganeyves
213   With My Child .... Mit Mayn Kindt
217   Selected Family and Personal Poems in Original Yiddish

223   **Poetry Of Thoughtfulness, Philosophy and Nature**
225   Autumn .... Herbst
226   The Purpose of Life .... Der Pasron Fon Leybn

229 Autumn Leaves...Herbst Bletlakh
231 The Eagle..Der Adler
232 Want And The Poet.................. Der Nuht Un Der Dikhter
234 A Dream .... A Dream
237 The Phantom Vessel ....Der Vandershiff
239 The Canary ....Der Kanarik
240 The Christmas Tree...........................Der Vaynakhtsboym
241 The Illegitimate Child ....Der Momzer
243 The Jew To Christ..........................Der Ihd Tsuhm Kristus
244 Christmas Bells..................................... Vaynakhts Gluhkn
246 Women's Suffrage .... Frauen Shtimrekht
247 In The Desert.................................... In Der Midbar
249 A Mirage—It's A Lie..S'iz A Lign
251 The Creation Of Man............................ Mayse Bereyshihs
255 Selected Thoughtful, Philosophical, Nature Poems in
    Original Yiddish

267 **Poetry About Jewish Subjects and Nationalism**
269 America...Amerika
270 Chanuka Lights ....Khanukah Likht
273 Israel ....Yisroheyl
274 Sfere.. Sfere
276 Yiddish.. Ihdish
279 Selected Poems of Jewish and Nationialistic Subjects In
    Original Yiddish

283 **Biographical Poetry**
285 Lincoln .... Linkohn
287 GeorgeWashington .... Dzshohrzdsh Vashingtohn
289 Heinrich Heine ....Haynrikh Hayne
291 Hertzl...Hehrtzl
292 Walt Whitman .... Valt Vitmann
295 Selected Biographical Poems in Original Yiddish

299 **Epigrams**.. Epigrammen
    Creating.. Shaffen
    Critics ....Kritik
    Translating.. Ihberzetzen
    The Fool.. Der Nahr
    She Lives Eternally .... Zi Leybt Eybig

The World .... Di Velt
Mankind .... Di Menshhayt
Ask Not .... Freg Nit
Hold Him .... Hahlt Ihm
Jews .... Ihdin

The etchings included in this section were done by Ephraim Lilien for Rosenfeld's book "Lieder Des Ghetto" in 1902.

POETRY OF
THE SWEATSHOP
THE WORLD OF THE WORKER

The poor workingman at his bench is here being "bled" by the "bloodsucker", the "boss" by the "bloodsucker", the "boss", who grows fat and bejeweled at the expense of his worker's blood and toil. And at the right you see that the poor tailor is caught in an ugly web of endless labor for poor wages. As intense as was Rosenfeld's poetry, Liliens drawings leave nothing to the imagination. They are simply brilliant.

DI BLEYKHE OPERATR
The Pale Operator

Ikh zey dohrt a bleykhn opereytr,
Farkokht ihn der arbayt, a shrek!
Un dayt ikh gedank ihm, altz neyt ehr
Un lihgt zayn kraften avek.

Es varren khdoshm farfloygen,
Vus loyfen dih yohren ahin,
Un nohkh zitzt dih bleykhr geboygen,
Un kampft mittn royen mashihn.

Ikh shtey uhn betrakht doh zayn tsuhre,
Zayn tsuhre farshmihrt un farshvitzt,
Un fihl ahz doh arbayt keyn gebora,
Der impot nohr pratzevet yetzt.

Dokh fallen dih troppen kasseydr,
Fon oyfgang biz untergang shpeyt,
Un zappen zikh ayn in dih kleydr,
Un trinkn zikh ayn in dih neyt.

Ikh bitt aykh, vih lang vet nokh yohgn
Der bleykher dem blutige rohd?
Oy, ver kan zayn ende mir zohgn?
Ver veys yenm's shreklikhen sohd?

A shver, zeyer shver, dohs tzu zohgn,
Dohkh eyns iz bevuhst un besheyt,
Ven ihm vet dih arbayt darshlohgn,
Zitzt taki a tzveyter un neyt.

Original Yiddish for this poem is on page 183

THE PALE OPERATOR

I see him there, a pale operator,
caught up in the work that he dreaded.
For long we have known he was stronger before,
and sharp as the needles he threaded.

Many indeed are the months that have flown,
the years go on longer and mean.
Yet there sits the pale one, sadly ingrown,
as he fights with his hateful machine.

I stand there and note his expression,
his face smeared and sweaty and grim.
I feel he is lost in depression,
No will, only habit guides him.

His eyes see the workplace with loathing,
from morn 'til the hours grow late.
His tears soak themselves in his clothing
as he mourns at his pitiful state.

I ask, how long can he take it,
so pale at that terrible wheel.
Who knows why he doesn't forsake it
or what the grim end will reveal.

It's hard, very hard to be truthful,
if one is alert and aware.
When he's stricken down someone more youthful
will sit and burn out in his chair.

THE PALE OPERATOR

This poem, the first we shall present in this book, sets the tone, in a way,
to demonstrate the painful, honest representation of immigrant life that
Rosenfeld used to arouse and inspire his people to a new and better life.
There are arch warnings of the end that can come to people who labor
under such dreadful conditions. Let no one think that this translation has
the power and personal "feel" of the original mother-tongue in which it
was written. This pale operator will be visited again and again in such
poems as, "Der Alter Schnayder.

THE SWEATSHOP

This is a most impressive poem, one of those enraged expressions of pain and humiliation at his gradual dehumanization while working as a "machine" at the machines. "I work and I work without rhyme, without reason; produce and produce and produce without end. For what and for whom? I don't know, I don't wonder. Since when can a whirling machine comprehend?" He finds that "tears that are seething soak into my thin little banquet of bread." Banquet indeed! He cannot resist being sardonic. Despite his pain he still shrieks for, "an end to enslavement, an end let there be!" He is not hopeless.

The clock that ticks his enslavement implies the possibility of a future of freedom. But here he cries, "I forget what I am, what I mean! Such tumult! Such battling! My ego goes under. I know not, I care not, I'm just a machine!" Read in Yiddish this poem is positively inflammatory. His inner writhing is almost explosively apparent. If the term elegance can be applied to restrained fury then this time Morris has done it. This was one of his earliest labor poems and it established his position in Yiddish belle-lettres.

DI SVET SHOP
The Sweatshop

Es roysht in shop azoy vild di mashihnin,
Az ohftma farges ikh in roysh dohs ikh bin;
Ikh vehr in dem shreklikhn tuhml farlohrn,
Mayn "ikh" vehrt dort botel, ikh vehr a mashihn !
Ikh arbayt un arbayt un arbayt ohn kheshbn,
Es shafft zikh un shafft zihh un shafft zikh ohn tzohl;
Fihr vohaws ? Un fihr veymn ? Ikh veys nit, ikh freg nit,—
Vi kuhmt a mashihn tzuh denken a mohl ?

Nishdoh keyn gefihl, keyn gedank, keyn farshtandt gohr,
Di bittere, bluhtige arbayt dershlohgt
Dohs aydlste, shennste un beste, dohs raykhste,
Dohs tihfste, dohs hekhste vohs leybn farmohgt.
Es shvindn sekuhndn, minuhtn un shtuhndn,
Gohl zeygl-shnell flih-en di nakht mit di tohg;
Ikh trayb di mashihnen glaykh ikh vill zi daryohgn,
Ikh yohg ohn a saychl, ikh yohg ohn a brohg.
Der zeygr in vohrkshop, ayr root nit afeele,

Ehr veyst altz un klapt altz un vekt nohkhanander,
Gezohgt hoht a mensh mihr amohl di bedaytung,
Zayn vayzn un vekn dohrt lihgt a farshtandt,
Nohr eppes gedenkt zikh mihr, punkt vi fon kholem,
Der zeygr ehr vekt in mir leybn un zinn,
Un nohr eppes,—ikh hohb fargessen—nit frahg es !
Ikh veys nit, ikh veys nit, ikh bin ah mashihn !

Un tzaytenveyz ven ikh darhehr shoyn dem zeyger,
Farshtey ikh gantz anders zayn veyzn, zayn shprakh,
Mir dakht az es nuhkt mikh dorten der uhnruh,
Kh'zohl arbaytn, arbaytn, meyrer a zakh !

Ikh hehr in zayn tohn nohr dem bohs's vildn beyzr,
Zayn finsteren kuhk in di veyzr di tzvey,
Di zeygr mir skruhkhet, mir dakht, az ehr traybt mikh,
Un ruhft mikh, "Mashihn !" un shraybt tzuh mir, "Gey !"
Nohr dan, ven's shtiller der vilder getuhml,
Avek iz der maystr, ihn mitohgtzayt shtuhndt,
Dan fangt ohn ihn kohp bay mir langsam tzu tohgen,
Ihn hehrtzen tzu tzih-en, ikh fihl dan mayn vuhndt;

Un bittere treheren, un zodike treheren
Tzu vaykn mayn magren mitohg, mayn broyt,
Es vargt mikh, ikh kan nit mehr essen, ikh kenn nit !
Oy shreklikhe pratze ! Oy bittere noyt !
S'ershaynt mir di shop in mittohgtzayt shtuhnde
A bluhtige shlakhtfeld, ven dohrt vert geruht,
Arum un arum zey ikh lihgn haruhgim,
Es liyarmt fon d'r erd dohs fargihsene bluht,

Eyn vayle un baldt vert gepoykt a trevohge,
Di toyte ervakhn, es leybt oyf di shlakht,
Es kampfen di truhpes fir fremde, fir fremde,
Un shtarytn un fallen, un zinken in nakht.
Ikh kuhk oyf dem kampf-platz mit bitteren tzohren,
Mit shrek mit nekome, mit hellisher payn,
Der zeyger, yetzt hehr ikh ihm rikhtig, ehr vekt es,
"A sof tzu di knekhtshaft, a sof zohl dohs zayn !"

Ehr mintert ihn mir farshtandt di gefihlen,
Un veyst vi es loyfen di shtuhndn ahin,
An eylendr blayb ikh, vi lang ikh voll shvaygn,
Farlohren, vi lang ikh farblayb vohs ikh bin . . .

Der mensh velkher shlaft in mir, heybt an ervakhn,
Der knekht velkher vakht in mir, shlohft dakht zikh ayn,
Atzindt iz di rikhtige shtuhndte gekuhmn !

A sof tzu dem eylendt, a sof zuhl es zayn ! . . .
Nohr pluhtzling,— der vistl, der bohss— ah trevohge !
Ikh vehr ohn dem seychl, farges vohss ikh bin,
Es tuhmlt, man kampft, oy, mayn "Ikh" iz farlohren,
Ikh veys nit, mikh art nit, ikh bin a mashihn !

Original Yiddish for this poem is on page 184

THE SWEATSHOP

So wild is the roar of machines in the sweatshop
I often forget I'm alive, in that din!
I'm drowned in the tide of the terrible tumult
my ego is slain; I become a machine.
I work and I work without rhyme, without reason,
produce and produce and produce without end.
For what? and for whom? I don't know, I don't wonder—
Since when can a whirling machine comprehend?

No feelings, no thoughts, not the least understanding;
this bitter, this murderous drudgery drains
the noblest, the finest, the best and the richest,
the deepest, the highest that living contains.
Away rush the seconds, the minutes, the hours;
each day and each night like a wind-driven sail;
I drive the machine as though eager to catch them,
I drive without reason—no hope, no avail.

The clock in the shop, even he toils forever
He points and he ticks and he wakes us from dreams.
A long time ago someone taught me the meaning:
His pointing, his waking are more than they seem.
I only remember a few things about it;
the clock wakes our senses and sets us aglow,
and wakes something else—I've forgotten, don't ask me—
I'm just a machine, I don't know, I don't know!

But once in a while, when I hear the clock ticking,
his pointing, his language, are not as before.

I feel that his pendulum lashes me, prods me
To work ever faster, to do more and more!
I hear the wild yell of the boss in his ticking,
I see a dark frown in the two pointing hands.
I shudder to think it: the clock is my master!
He calls me "Machine!", "Hurry up!", he commands.

But when there's a half-hour lull in the uproar,
at noon, when the boss turns his back on us, then,
oh then, the sun slowly rises within me,
my heart reaches out and my wounds burn again,
And tears that are bitter and tears that are seething
soak into my thin little banquet of bread.
I choke on the food—I can't swallow a morsel—
Oh bitter to be neither living nor dead!

At lunchtime the shop's like a grim field of battle,
the cannon are resting, I look all around—
Wherever I turn I see nothing but corpses;
the blood of the innocent shrieks from the ground!
One moment, and soon an alarm will be sounded,
the corpses awake, they return to the fight;
the dead rise to battle for strangers, for strangers,
they strive and are stricken and sink into night.

I look at the bloodbath with rage and with horror,
with grief, with a vow to avenge what I see.
At last I can hear the clock rightly, he wakes us—
"An end to enslavement! An end let there be!"
He ticks back to life my emotions, my senses,
and points to the hours that are hurrying past.
As long as my lips are sealed up I'll be wretched,
as long I am what I am I'll be lost.

The man who had slept in me slowly awakens,
the slave seems asleep that was wakeful in me.
The hour, at last the right hour is striking,
an end to misfortune! An end let there be!
But in comes the boss with his whistle, his bugle;
I'm lost—I forget what I am, what I mean.
Such tumult! Such battling! My ego goes under.
I know not, I care not—I'm just a machine. . . . !

Translated by Aaron Kramer

THE WORKMEN

He stands back looking over his years of outspoken struggle for the workingmen. "I have spoken out for him before God, I have opened up the Garden of Eden and spoken up on his great disasters. I have given my tongue to the nightingale to sing them freedom, to sing them pulsations of life—all without thanks." He enjoys his feelings of self-pity and is partly justified. He knew how few workers would be present at his funeral. Not really demanding, as some critics claimed, he sacrificed his all for a noble cause. Of course he wanted to be adored. He was widely appreciated for many years, but the public's memory is short. "What have you done for me lately?" Do you wonder about his talents? Just peek into the appendix of this book for a surprising summary of his achievements.

DI ARBAYTER
The Workmen

At shteyen zey far mir a bleykhr shreynge,
Dem eylend's shrekklikhe armey
Oh nit gehohlfene, genarte meynge !
Zi brekht mir duhkch dohs hartz mit vey.
Dohs zaynen mayne briheedr, blass un ohrem,
Di shvester mayne fon fabrik,
Ikh hohb a mohl geklapt in zey're kvorem,
Geruhfn zey tzum leybns glik.

Ikh bin in zey're veytag ayngedruhngn
In zeyr khuhrbn tihf arayn,
Ikh hohb far gohtt un layt tzuhkluhngn,
Dem groysen brohch fon zeyer "zayn".

Ikh hohb der nakhtigal mayn tzuhng gegeyben,
Tzu zingn zey a frayhayts lihd,
Tzu zingn zey di prakhtikayt fon leyben
Tzuh zingn az di tzayt farfliht.
Ikh hohb gemakht di kvorim reyden,
Di himlen oyfgerissen vaydt,
Ikh hohb gevekt di gruhb un deym ganeyden,
Alle eyduhs tzum gerekhten shtrayt.
Dohrch arehme shklaffen zaynen zi farblayben,
Un ikh bin eylendt, alt un krank,
Un vohs ikh hohb gezungen un geshrihbn,
Blaybt ihber ohn a dank.

THE WORKMEN

There they stand, a faded tableau,
misery's defeated force.
Heartbreaking they are, a painful source
of anxiety and woe.
Brothers mine—pale, poor, in gloom,
and sisters from the fact'ry,
I have at times knocked at their tomb
singing of life's vict'ry.

I've drawn into the pain of their existence,
their deepest desolation,
I have spoken well to God, with insistence,
of their tragedy, their vexation.
I have given the nightingale my tongue
to extoll the joys of life,
I have excited them with freedom's song,
carving time with my poet's knife.

I have brought voices from the earth
and opened heavens wide,
I've awakened Edenland and Death
to witness what's inside.
Still they exist, in unremitting slave'ry
in tired, sickly ranks.
I too am worn and what I wrote with brave'ry
remains without their thanks.

Original Yiddish for this poem is on page 186

THE TEARDROP MILLIONAIRE

This poem like most Rosenfeld poems, speaks for itself. That is to say that
it recites the struggles and the agony of one man who sees his life as a
paradigm of the immigrant workers' lives. Here he bemoans the money-
less recompense he receives for his writing. Nevertheless he exposes his
affection for his fellow-man and since their tears of appreciation add up to
the millions he is indeed a teardrop millionaire. In just a few lines, a gem
of a poem, Morris uses a minimum of verbiage to illuminate the plight of
a men living on the barest of rations. It takes true poetic imagination to
be sardonic and beautiful at the same time.

DER TREHREN MILYOHNER

The Teardrop Millionaire
A nit keyn gohldner kamertohn
Shtimt ohn mayn kol tzu zingn,
Es kan der vuhnk fon oyben ohn,
Mayn shtim nit makhen klingen;
Dem shklav's a krakhtz, ven ehr iz mihd,
Nohr vekt in mihr di lihdr,—
Uhn mit a flam leybt oyf mayn lihd,
Fihr mayne ohreme brihdr.

Derfar fargey ikh ohn a tzayt.
Defar vebt oyf mayn leben.
Vohs kennen mihr di ohreme layt
Fihr a beloynung geben ?
Zey tzohlen trehren fihr a trehr,—
Dohs alles vohs zey kohnen;—
Ikh bin a trehren-milyohnehr,
Un veyn oyf di milyohnen . . .

THE TEARDROP MILLIONAIRE

It's not a tuning-fork of gold
that sets my throat to sing,
or do my melodies unfold
to satisfy a king.
The groans of slaves when they are tired
awake my songs.
It's only then that I'm inspired.
I reckon up the wongs.

And this is why I pine away
and half-alive I linger.
What wages can the workers pay,
what pittance to their singer?
They pay for tears with every tear—
that's all they can afford.
I am a teardrop millionaire
and weep upon my hoard.

Translated by Aaron Kramer
Original Yiddish for this poem is on page 187

THE LION

In "The Lion", we see Rosenfeld as everyone remembers him; sharp, witty, unafraid and a touch irreverent. Here he is a lion. Of course he's a lion! Of course he's not a dog with trash-can teeth who licks the master's boots to show his gratitude! When he asks, "Why do you throw me bones and cram your belly full of beef?" there is your fighting socialist again. "Be careful, I'm a lion, Sir! Don't play your games with me, for all I have to do is stir and mince-meat's what you'll be!"

Can you place yourself in the ghetto ninety-five years ago, dear reader? Seat yourself with a glass of tea (ah glezzela tey) and a lump of sugar and the newspaper and then read this poem. He is telling you that YOU are the lion at rest. YOU are the creature who knows "each foot of forest ground, and since birth I've fled the hunter . . . . one day I'll break the cage and you'll all be lying dead!" He's telling you that you can take just so much of the boss' guff and then you'll, "break the cage" and trample your oppressors. His readers were not very sophisticated, but they certainly got the message.

DER LEYB
The Lion

Vus ruhkt yihr altz di fleysh in zikh
Un shmayst tsu mir di beyner ?
Vus meynt yihr, vus ? Ah hundt bin ikh,
Ah hundt mit kelsher tseyner ?

A hundt vus loyft arum in gass
Un nekhtigt oyf di bliklekh ?
Un ven ihm fallt a beyn tsum shpass
iIz ehr shoyn ibber gliklikh ?

A hundt vus khopt a viss un kikh
Erindering un shuffel,
Un lekt derfar dem virteh di shikh
Der nihrtahin di pantuffel ?

Oh tsittert ! Den ikh bin der leyb !
Nit shpihlt mit mir in shpitlakh !
Den oym derlang ikh mikh a heyb
Tsufleysh ikh oykh oyf pitzlakh !

Ikh ken di stepp, ikh ken dem vald,
Ikh bin in yekt geboren.
Ikh tu ah bruhm, es vert a gevald !
Un yihr derkent mayn tsorn !

Nit kuhkt zikh ayn vus ikh farshvayg,
Nit halt mikh far a shoyteh.
Es kumt der tug ikh brek di shtayg
Un yihr blaybt lign toyteh!

THE LION

Why do you throw me bones, and cram
your bellies full of beef?
What do you really think I am
a dog with trash-can teeth?

A dog that runs around all day
and sleeps in halls at night?
And when a bone is flung his way
gives thanks at every bite?

A straying dog that humbly chews
at filthy scraps of food,
and has to lick the Master's shoes
to show his gratitude?

Be careful! I'm a lion, Sir!
Don't play your games with me—
For all I have to do is stir
and mince-meat's what you'll be!

I know each foot of forest ground—
since birth I've fled the hunter—
My roar strikes terror miles around,
Well you'll know the growl I utter.

Don't think because I hush again
there's nothing in my head.
One day I'll break the cage, and then
you'll all be lying dead!

Translated by Aaron Kramer
Original Yiddish for this poem is on page 188

THE FIERY PANIC

When the Triangle Shirtwaist factory on the lower East side of New York City went up in flames, hundreds of women died in that fire. Some jumped out of windows, some landed on the pavement, others, in clusters, landed in fire-nets that could not handle so much weight. Some died in the inferno when their hair acted as so much kindling. It was, up to that time, the worst workplace tragedy in American history. Rosenfeld's poem, "The Red Hell" (here called the "Fiery Panic") was the major item, taking up the center of a whole page in the Daily Forward, the premier Yiddish-language newspaper. Any Jew who could read and saw that poem, wept. This was more than a quickly-written elegy. It was more than a frenzied scream at the world's intransigence. It was an indictment of the "Money-king" and the "Dollar-prince" and the whole system of abusive workplace conditions. "Cursed be the system! Cursed be the planlessness! Cursed be the world!", shrieked Morris, his ink mixed with vitriol and tears. What is remarkable, also, about this poem is its order and direction. He was excited and in emotional agony, yet his journalistic impulses forced him to direct his flow of words into acceptable norms for his emotions.

His words rise in an articulate crescendo that the ordinary excited writer might not be able to organize on such short notice.

Ultimately, from this fire came legislation on working conditions, and a wild jump-start for the socialist movement which was in need of such a stimulant. "Drape yourselves in black, O Golden Land! Too stark your crime, too terrible your shame!" That Morris could sure write.

DER ROYTE BEHOLLE
THE RED TERROR *(Only three sections shown here).*

1 Nit keyn shlekh, nit keyn ferteyfelte pogrohm
   Hut ungefihlt di grestes shtert mit kluggen,
   Di erd hut nit getsittert in ihr tohm,
   Es hoht key blitz, keyn dunner nit geshluggen,
   S'hubbn keyn shvatze vetter-velkhenms nit gekrakht
   Un keyne kannunen nit di lufe tsuakert,
   Oh neyn! Duhs hut ah moyredige hell ervakht,
   A shklaffen-nest mit shklaffen-vild geflakert,
   Dohs hut der gohld-gohtt mit a brand gelekhter
   Gefressen undzere zien un tekhter,
   Gelekt di lebens mit zayne royten tsungen—
   Zay zaynen in dem toyr geshprungen,

In zayn shoys gedringen,
Erh hut zey gekhapt, gelakht, gezungen,
Ehr hut zey farshlungen!

2 Zey zaynen gezessen in zeyer yokht fartihft,
Zeyer shveys hut getrift,
In dem fertoybenden geshum,
Fun mashinen arum
Ven tsehn shtok in der hoykh
Hut zey ferviklt der roykh,
Fershpunnen der flam,
Un ah glutigen yam,
Gefressen, genahsht,
Ferkoylt, ferasht!

3 Oyf dayn gevissen, raykher undzer troyer,
Oyf dayn gevissen undzer kluhg,
Es zohl durkh nakht un tuhg
Dikh shrekken der farbrennter moyer,
Un unzerer tekhter in di flammen
Zulln dayn leben farsammen,
Dikh zulln bay dayne frayden,
Bay dayne glikken,vargen shtikkn,
Unzere layde,bay di simkhes fun dayne kinder
Zullstu fihlen di klohle, fun der royte behohle,
Un tappen vi ah blinder divent mit shrekken
Biz vet dih, ven vet dikh fermekken!

Transliterated by EJG and Rifke Levine

THE FIERY PANIC
(The Red Hell)

Not a war, nor demoniacal pogrom
choked this greatest city with laments.
No cannons raked the air,
no tremors shook the earth,
no thunder rocked,
no bolt of lightning struck,
no clouds grew black.
No! A frightful redness glowed,
a slave-nest violently blazed.
The god of Gold, with mocking flames,
devoured pour sons and daughters,
licked their lives away with flaming tongues.

They leaped into the lap of death,
who caught them up and toyed with them
and swallowed them alive.
Into the deafening clatter of machines
where they waited, locked within their yokes,
the redness came!
The smoke enveloped them,
the grasping flames entrapped them
and a glowing sea of fire
nibbled, seared, cremated,
turned them into ash!
O my sisters! My young sisters!
O my young brothers!
Mourn for them, my songs!
Lament and mourn for them!
The worker's death lies in wait for him
in the dark corners,
lurks at his wretched door . . .
Woe to the world !
On a Sabbath eve the redness came,
a Sabbath for the working-man,
this his kiddush and havdalah.
Suddenly the fiery panic came,
sent by Money-king and Dollar-prince.
Flow, my tears! Weep, my soul!
O! Cursed be the system!
Cursed be the planlessness,
Cursed be the world!
For whom shall we grieve?
For whom shall we grieve first?
For those burned to death,
or those "beyond recognition?"
For those who now say kaddish,
or the "rescued" cripples?
Mourn for all of them, my sea of tears . . .
Drape yourself in black, Oh Golden Land!
Too stark your crime, too terrible your shame,
too deaf your conscience and too blind your law.
Too fiendish your business, too bloody the net
which traps your poor, your unsuspecting poor . . .
Your time will come! Your time will come!
Light the Yahrtseit candles in the Jewish streets!

This tragedy is ours,
this tragedy of the Jewish masses
of our people poor and wretched.
This funeral is ours, and the corpses.
The children,
snatched by fire from our arms
were ours, our blossoms . . . woe to us . . .
mourn our joys in rows of coffins!
Mourn our loved ones turned to memories of Hell!
You Men of Wealth!
Our grieving and our sorrow on your conscience!
On your conscience our lament!
By daylight and by dark of night
may the blistered walls affright you,
may the memory of our daughters in the flames
contaminate your lives.
May our anguish choke you
in your time of gladness!
May you taste the venom of that deadly glow
amidst your childrens' celebrations
May you grope about the walls
with blind and terror-stricken eyes
until the day of your obliteration!

Translated by Max Rosenfeld
Original Yiddish for this poem is on page 189

VUS IZ DI VELT
What Is The World

(The first three stanzas and last two stanzas)
Un iz undzer velt ah shluf-tsimmer, nohr—
Un iz ah kholem dos leyben?
Dan zohl mir, vil ikh mayn ikh mayn pohr yohr
In gute khaloymes farshvayben.

Dan vil ikh khaloymes fun frayhayt un glik,
Vi yene groysartike herren:
Dan vil; ikh in kholem ah lihblikher blik
Un vil nit mehr troymen fun trehren.

Un iz undzer velt ah simkheh, ah "bal",
Vi mir zaynen alle farbetten;
Dan vilt ikh mir oykh zitzen freylakh in tsahl
Um hubbn ah kheylik, ah fetten!

Un iz undzer velt ah milkhohmeh atsind
Vo shtarkereh un shvakherer shtrayten,
Dan art mikh keyn shturim, keyn vayb un keyn kind,
Ikh bloyt nit mit kalpkayt fun vayten.

Dan varf ikh in fayer zikh ven ikh ah held,
Un kempf vi ah leyb fun dem shvakhen;
Un treft mikh di koyl: ikh fall toyt oyfen feld
Dan ken ikh oykh shtarbendik lakhen!

Transliteration by Rifke Levine and EJG

WHAT IS THE WORLD

And if it's no more than a bedroom, our earth,
and life but a dream, but a slumber—
I also am ready for my few years' worth
of dreams that are good to remember.
Let me dream of luxury, dream of delight,
like those with the world in their keeping.
I want to see eyes that are loving and bright
and have no more nightmares of weeping.

And if it's a grand celebration, a ball,
where all are invited as brothers,
then I too shall sit in the banqueting-hall—
my portion as large as the others'.
I too am well able to eat what is good, a choice bit of meat
gives me pleasure.
The blood in my veins is as red as the blood
of those who are swollen with treasure.

And if it's a garden, surrounded by trees,
where all kinds of roses are growing,
I want to go freely wherever I please,
no sentries to keep me from going.
I'd like a fine garland of flowers to wear,
instead of those thorns that have crowned me.

I want to go strolling, my love always there,
with myrtle and laurel around me.

And if our world's nothing but bloodshed today,
Where bondsmen rise up in resistance,
no wife and no children will keep me away,
I won't watch the war from a distance.
I'll leap into battle, I'll make myself brave
and fight for the slaves like a lion;
and if I am hit and the field is my grave,
I'll know how to laugh—though I'm dying!

Translated by Aaron Kramer
Original Yiddish for this poem is on page 191

WHAT IS THE WORLD

How do we address "What is the World?". Is this poem philosophy? Is it
a puerile foray into understanding the complexities of life? Not at all. It is
a simple man with simple language telling what life offers him and what it
denies him. He is not the first poet to think of life as a dream. Wordsworth
wrote, "Our birth is but a sleep and a forgetting", and even the folksong,
"Row, row, row your boat gently down the stream. Merrily, merrily, merrily, merrily, life is but a dream . . ." preceded him. Morris is in good
company. He wants his share of the world, especially if the world is a
bedroom with good dreams and no nightmares. If life is a celebration, a
ball and a banquet-hall with choice bits of meat and garlands of flowers
with fine aroma he wants his share. "And if the world's nothing but bloodshed where bondsmen rise in resistance, I won't watch from a distance—
I'll know how to laugh when I'm dying!" He meant this. He lived this
way. This poem is his strong affirmation of his willingness to live life to
the hilt, even to die for it; which is what he did.

It amazes us that a man can use the language of the common man,
colloquialisms and simple terminology that one uses in the home, not in
the classroom or halls of the mighty, and yet he expresses the deepest and
noblest convictions with the assurance that he is playing the harp used by
the angels. We admire his Muse, too. She's the kind of woman we could
love. How many Jewish Muses do you know?

BREAD AND TEA

How in the world can Jewry ever forget this poet? "Bread and tea, bread and tea, what a menu, woe is me! I ask you God, is this a joke, to fix it so I'm always broke? Can't you spare a few sardines, a slice of lox, a can of beans?" He is on the verge of giving God a calling-down and then he uses a different tack. "Things are not so "extra" with you? And are you, yourself, in trouble too?" How delighted his readers had to be with this poet. Here he is trying to outwit God.

BROYT MIT TEY
Bread With Tea

(Only the first two stanzas transliterated)
Nohr broyt mit tey un broyt mit tey,
Dohs iz ah kest, zoh ikh un vey !
Den bistu, Gutt, oyf mihr in cass,
Vus du erloybst zikh dihzen shpass ?
Tsu zholleven sardines a box,
Ah shtikkel kez, a brekkel lox ?
Ah bissel milkh, a mohl an ey ?
Nohr brot mit tey un broyt mit tey,
Dohs is ah kest? Zoh ikh un vay !

Du shpielst es tkiffes, Gutt, mit mir ?
Ikh zoll zikh aynbetten bay dir?
Nohkh veynig hub ikh, tug un nakht,
In betten dikh alleyn farbrakht ?
Dohkh voyn ikh oyf dem finften shtuk
Mayn tfile, hehrstu vi in truk.
Mashmoes, Gutt, du bist alleyn,
Oykh mit alleman, Ikh meyn—
Di muz es oykh nit "extra" geyen. ?

Transliteration by EJG with Rifke Levine
Original Yiddish for this poem is on page 192

BREAD AND TEA

Bread and tea and bread and tea!
What a menu! Woe is me!
I ask You, God, is this a joke,
to fix it so I'm always broke?

Can't You spare a few sardines,
a slice of lox, a can of beans,
a little milk, a piece of cheese?
Just bread and tea and bread and tea?
What a menu, woe is me!

Is this a judgment You've decreed,
just to make me come and plead?
Haven't I sought You day and night,
praying that You ease my plight?
Yet here I am in a fifth-floor flat,
and You care less than does my cat!
Apparently, God, it must be true;
things are not so "extra" with You.
Are You, Yourself, in trouble too?

Translated by Max Rosenfeld

GOLOS
Exile

Ven tuhn man hin di mihde beyner ?
Ven glaykht man oyz dem ruhkn?
Di veyg zeyt oyz msuhkhn.
A yeydr trit iz fohl mit shteyner!
Vohin ? Vohin ? Du ar'mer veyner!
Helf dem nakud'n bruhdr!
Shtrekt ihm oyz a varme handt!
Shtell zikh bay zayn shiksals ruhdr

In zyn naye haymats-landt!
Ihr antloyft fon toyzend kluhlos
Fon dem toyfel's shvartzen raykh,
Helft ihm ptor'n dem golos
Ven ehr kuhmt aheyr tzu aykh !

EXILE

When can you straighten out your back
and rest your weary bones?
That road ahead looks dangerous,
each step is full of stones.
Whither? Whither, wanderer with
your tears and groans?

Help your homeless brother,
offer a warm hand.
Fate says, "Help each other
in this foreign land.

He flees a thousand curses,
the Devil's own domain,
Help him escape the exile.
He comes to you in pain.

EXILE

This poem is a simple expression of humanity towards his fellow immigrants. His meter and rhymes are flawless as he advises, "help your homeless brother, offer a warm hand, Fate says help each other in this foreign land." This is a lovely poem to interest the immigrant in someone else besides himself.

THE OLD TAILOR

This is one of thousands of labor poems that Rosenfeld wrote—but not "just another". The imagery here is sharp and direct. He speaks volumes in just a few lines. The "Old Tailor" here is the "Pale Operator" of another poem, grown older. The fight is gone. He has developed the cough of the tubercular. Those who work with him see "the blackened stamp which is the good man's punishment." What a conception! "His glasses cover up his tears, his pain hides in his breast." And for us, this exposes the heart and soul of the poet.

DER ALTER SHNAYDER
The Old Tailor

Ehr zitzt un neyt shoyn fihle yohren,
Un zayn bleykhr pohnm shvitzt,
Der bohrd iz ihm shoyn vays gevohren,
Vh der pohdim vohs ehr nitzt,
Nisht doh kimat in shtoht a maystr
Velkher ehr hoht nit gedint,
Un dohkh hoht ehr keyn sent in taystr,
Un keyn brot fir veyb un kindt.

Ehr kumt areyn in shop beginnen,
Un fardingt shoyn zeyn handt,
Ehr halt farayns in eyn fardihnen
Un farhultet keyn sent.
Un ehr shaft nohkh shpeyt bay nakht
Un immer, immer vu tsu borgren,
Zitst ehr troyrig un trakht.

Der maystr iz mit ihm tsufridn,
Dan ehr tohn't nit keyn zakh,
Ehr makht in shop nit keyn ycridn,
Un baleydikt nit zayn fakh.
Ehr kumt un geyt avec ihn shtillen,
Reyden, reydt fir ihm di khust,
Dem treyr fardekken ihm di brillen,
Un dem shmertz fardekt ihm di brust.

Di arbayts-laytr, alle kukn,
Oyf dem krankn mit ah vey,
Zey kukn oyf zayn mihdn rukn,
Velkher krimt zikh baym ganey,
Zey zayen shoyn dem shvartzen zihgl,
Fir zayn ehrlikhkayt di shtohf . . .
Zey zeyen punkt, vi ihn a shpigl,
In dem alteren zeyer suhf.

Original Yiddish for this poem is on page 193

THE OLD TAILOR

For many years he sits and sews,
His white face sweats in rivulets,
His craggy beard yet whiter grows
Like thread with which he knits.
Within this town no boss is there
For whom he has not served,
No coins has he to buy the fare
His hungry family deserved.

He's at the shop at break of dawn,
Already rents his hand,
He holds his pay lest it be gone,
For thrift is his command.

He works from gray of dawning,
He works 'til late at night,
From borrowing to pawning,
He juggles in his plight.

The Boss has satisfaction,
Complaints from him are rare,
No need for cruel reaction,
This worker's pride is there.
In silence always he appears,
Talking hurts his chest,
His glasses cover up his tears,
The pain hides in his breast.

All the workers now observe
The sick ones with their pain.
They see their weary backbones curve
With sewing's endless strain.
That blackened stamp their eyes detect,
The good man's punishment,
They see a mirror that reflects
Their latter years, broken, bruised and spent.

THE CANDLE SELLER

Here, in Rosenfeld's next poem (a terrific, emotional work) is a bitter, nearly hopeless tirade against "the existing false order of things," a desperately poor young woman, aged and worn beyond her years, sits on a cold night with her skeletonic infant bundled tight against her body, trying to sell candles. The pain of hopelessness written in her face, she gently begs for attention, to sell a few candles so she and her baby might survive. But her failure is in part a universal failure, where the world that is better off (the "rich", he calls them) hurry off to their homes, to the synagogue, to the shops—and no one even looks her way. "Where is the good?", is her plaintive cry.

The labor poet, the immigrant poet, knows that her only friend is the telegraph post, that cold, rigid, aloof carrier of messages to all but the poor woman. Somehow she considers it her only friend. It supports her back and also supports a lamp that illuminates her plight. The poet paints a hurried sketch of life on a ghetto street just before the Sabbath. He refers to "the princess, the Sabbath, from Heaven descended" . . . The socialist in Rosenfeld decries the injustice that, "millions are squandered in idle display; that men, all unheeded, must starve by the way." But the poet himself is not hopeless. "The great day of judgment will come at last!"

LIKHT FARKOYFENE . . . THE CANDLE SELLER

(Only first, fourth and fifth stanzas transliterated here)
In Hester street, neben ah telegraf sluhp,
Ahn oreme froy zitst dohrt glaykh tsu a trup.
A beynerer punim un bleykh vi der toyt,
Dohkh kentig di bakkengeven a mol royt,
Nohr voyltohg un frayndshaft un lihbe un prakht
Zey hubbn geviss duhs nit khorev gemakht,
Es zitst dohrt, di bleykhe, fun veyenen halb blind,
Ihr bruhst tsit a dar, a farmorites kind.

Duhs zoygt un duhs veynt un duhs shluhft un mit vey
Shpringt oyf duhs skeletal fun mama's geshrey.
"Koyf, vaybelakh! Likhtelakh! Tsvey far dray tsent!
Oyf mir iz ah mazel vi likhdig duhs brennt!"
Ikh bet aykh vi lang vet nokh handlen in gass
Di elend, geklibbene, kranklakh un blass,

Vi lang ken zi leyden nokh hunger un noyt,
Zikh ranglendik mit dem farbissenen toyt.
Vi lang, oh, vi lang vet dohs oreme vayb
Nokh shpayzen dem nefish vuhs ligt bay ihr layb?
A mol flegt dohs kind khutsh dershlingen a treher,
Dokh yetzt mama's oygen zey veynen nit mehr,
Nitoh mehr keyn treren, der moyekh iz leyer,
Dohs hertz iz tsybrokhen, der ohtem iz shver.
Di lippen nohr murmen nokh koym oykh mit vey,
"Koyf shabbes likht, vaybelakh, koyf khutsh ah tsvey!"

In Hester street shtil un farlozzen, alleyn,
A yusseml shteyt, dort a kurbele kleyn,
Derbay zitzt a kalter fun farglivverte trup,
Di oreme soykheste neben a slup,
Dervayle hut keyner bamerkt nohkh dem mehs,
Es zeynen di raykhe fertrun mit dem fress,
Hayndt ver redt di frume, di koshere layt,
Zey hubbn geviss erev shabbas keyn tsayt.
Azoy iz di drama avec unbetrakht,
Biz langsam un shtil iz gekummen di nakht,
Gekummen iz oykh fun dem heyligen zibul,
Di beys malke shabbes, yetzt geyt men in shul.

Transliterated by Rifke Levine with EJG

THE CANDLE SELLER

In Hester Street, by a hard telegraph post,
There sits a poor woman as wan as a ghost.
Her pale face is shrunk like the face of the dead,
And yet you can tell that her cheeks were once red.
But love, ease and friendship, and glory I ween,
May hardly the cause of their fading have been,
Poor soul, she has wept so, she scarcely can see.
A skeleton infant she holds on her knee.
It tugs at her breast and it whimpers and sleeps,
But soon at her cry it awakens and weeps.
"Two cents, my good woman, three candles will buy,
As bright as their flame, by my star in the sky!"
Tho' few are her wares, and her basket is small,
She earns her own living by these, when at all.

She's there, with her baby, in wind and in rain,
in frost and in snowfall, in weakness and pain.
She trades and she trades, through the good times and slack,
No home and no food and no cloak on her back.
She's kithless and kinless, one friend at the most,
and that one is silent, the telegraph post!
She asks for no alms, the poor Jewess, but still,
although she is wretched, forsaken and ill,
she cries, "Sabbath candles!" to those that come nigh,
and all that she pleads is that someone will buy.

To honor the sweet, holy Sabbath, each one
with joy to the market has gone.
To shops and to pushcarts they harriedly fare,
but who for the poor, wretched woman will care?
A few of her candles you think they will take?
They seek the meat patties, the fish and the cake.
She holds forth a hand with the pitiful cry,
"Two cents, my good woman, three candles will buy!
But no one has listened and no one has heard.
Her voice is so weak, it fails at each word.
Perchance the poor mite in her lap understood.
She hears mother's crying, but where is the good?

I pray you, how long will she sit there and cry,
Her candles feebly shown to all who pass by?
How long do you think it will be, e're her breath
Gives out in this horrible struggle with death?
How long will this frail one in mother-love strong
give suck to the babe at her breast? Oh, how long?
The child, mother's tears used to swallow before,
But mother's eyes, nowadays shed them no more.
Oh dry are the eyes now and empty the brain,
the heart well-nigh broken, the breath drawn with pain.

Yet ever, though faintly, she calls out anew,
"Oh buy but two candles, good women, but two!"
In Hester Street stands, on the pavement of stone,
a small orphaned basket, forsaken, alone.
Beside it is sitting a corpse cold and stark;
the seller of candles,—will nobody mark?
No, none of the passers have noticed her yet,
The rich ones on feasting are busily set.
And such as are pious, you may well believe,
have no time to spare on the gay Sabbath eve
No one has noticed and no one has seen,
and now comes the nightfall, quiet, serene.

The Princess, the Sabbath, from Heaven descends,
and all the gay throng to the synagogue wends.
Oh synagogue lights, be ye witnesses bold
that mother and child died of hunger and cold;
Where millions are squandered in idle display,
that men, all unheeded, must starve by the way!
So hold back your flame, blessed lights, hold it fast!
The great day of judgment will come here at last,
before the white throng, where imposture is vain,
ye lights for the soul, you'll be lighted again!
And upward your flames there shall mount as on wings
and damn the existing false order of things!

Translator is unknown to us, but the Victorian English gives us a hint that it might be Helena Frank or Rose Pastor Stokes.

THE GHETTO TREE

"In New York's teeming ghetto there stands a gnarled old tree," and it speaks to us! So Rosenfeld is now a tree. He's been a lion, a bird, a blotter, a machine—he uses any guise in his basic role as an observer of Man's fate, of the Almighty's broken promises, and of Man's struggle to survive. His lines on Nature are truly beautiful, "Where are you, saucy breezes? Oh come and stir my boughs! And you, so deep and tranquil, blue sky where are you now?" But, of course, this poem is not about a lonely, ignored old tree, but about a lonely ignored old man who has seen his comrades depart in the battle of life. Rosenfeld had a compulsive, unwavering obsession with freedom and social progress. He is unquestionably in the grasp of his Muse, who controls his passions and his dedication. In this man perhaps Plato was correct, that the poet is subsumed with an obsessive need to speak out with words that seem to be the inspiration of a Dybbuk-like alter-ego.

In this poem even a gnarled old tree is an instrument for social progress. Go argue with his Muse! Also, it is likely that this poem is an attack on those "intellectual pygmies" who denigrated the old "ghetto tree" who served his community so well for so long. And, not just accidentally, this translation by Aaron Kramer is superb.

DER GETTOH BOYM
The Ghetto Tree

(The first four and last two stanzas)
In hartz fun New York ghetto,
In engshaft un in kokh,
Dort shteyt ah boym, an alter,
Un zifst vey un oykh.
Ehr kukt zikh um far vunder,
Ihm redt alleyn tsu zikh,
Vi eylent un farlozzen,
Vi umgliklikh bin ikh!
Nohr mutneh gossen zey ikh
Un hehr ah mudnem gevald,
Vu zayt ihr, alte feygel?
Vu bistu, alter vald?
Vu zayt ihr vintlakh frishes?
Oh, kommt! Derlangen ah shtif.
Vu bistu rayner himmel, farklehrt un bloy un tihf?
Vos tu ikh, alter yossem,
Alleyn oyf dihzen flek.

Ikh hub di fraynt farloren,
Tuh, nemt mikh oykh avek!

Oh, shnayt mikh op vus gikhen,
Nit lozt mikh langer shteyn,
Ah troymende matseyre
Oyf frayhayt's grob alleyn.

Transliteration by Rifke Levine with EJG

THE GHETTO TREE

In New York's teeming ghetto there stands a gnarled old tree.
Unheard in all that tumult it sighs, "Ah, woe is me!"
It looks around in wonder and murmurs with a sigh,
"How wretched and neglected, how pitiful am I!

There's only gloom to look at, fantastic sounds to hear,
Where are you now, old forests, you birds that sang so clear?
Where are you, saucy breezes ? Oh come and stir my bough!
And you, so deep and tranquil—blue sky where are you now?

Where are you, mighty giants ? Why don't you gallop past
upon your speedy stallions and blow a trumpet-blast?
Time was, I still remember, before I learned to bend,
how freely rang the laughter of heroes through this land.

The larks, they trilled so sweetly! The sun, it shone so bright!
How wonderful the world was with so much joy and light.!
But now I watch the pygmies, they scurry here and there.
Debased are men and nature— Life's meaningless and bare.

What good am I, old orphan, still standing here alone?
I've lost my dearest comrades, so let me, too, be gone.
Oh cut me down, I beg you! This is no tree you save,
But one poor dreaming head-stone alone on Freedom's grave."

Translated by Aaron Kramer

THE BRIDE OF THE HILLS

A miner and his daughter's bridegroom are trapped in a mine and die in its cave-in. His lovely daughter now lives in a dream and even dances with her lover's ghost. This fantasy seems simple enough on the surface, but knowing grandpa as we now know him, we can detect a socialist impulse behind this poem. Morris creates this fantasy to point up the mine-owners' disregard for human life and safety as the miners experience frequent mine cave-ins. "Up she starts and flees the coal-mine with a shriek of "Murder!" No one can forget that outcry who but once has heard her!" Nice rhyme, "murder" and "heard her", thanks to Aaron Kramer.

Poe and Coleridge might have written this with references to Stygian nights or "Xanadu where Alph the sacred river ran through caverns measureless to man down to a sunless sea." but there are no such references here. His hero was killed in an underground passage and only his shadow dances with his lover in a meadow in the black of night. And if you believe Morris Rosenfeld maybe you can hear her shriek, "Murder!" in a spine-tingling voice when you walk up that mountain yourself, sometime in the dead of night.

DER KALE FUN DIH BERG
The Bride Of The Hills

(The first four and the last four stanzas only)
Oyf di Allegheny berger
Zet zikh ah ruine,
Dorten ligt an angefallene
Alten koylenmihn.
Un nit vayt fun dihzer khurbe
Aynzam un farluzzen,
Shteyt ah shtihbele, ah kleyne,
Tsvishen vilde grozzen.

Dorten fleg der alter bergman,
Ruh bay nakht gefinnen.
Dorten flegn ziftsen klingen,
Shtille trehren rinnen.
Doh di viste koylenmihne
Dort iz blut geflossen,
Unten ligt der guter alter
Un zayn tokhter's khossen.

Glaykh tret tsu der alter tate
Durkh gebrennt mit vunden,
Veynt un bensht di kinder zayner,
Ziftst un vert farshvunden.
Doh farstummen di klezmorim,
Un di glokken alle,
Alles shvindt un shvaygt, es blaybn
Nor di khossen-kale.
Un zey blaybn un zey tantzen,
Ruhig keyner shtert nit,
Biz es gibt ah vunk fun ergetz,
Un der chossen vert nit.

Doh shpring oyf dem toytens kale,
"Oh, di menshen's shekhter!",
Un farshvindet in de berger
Mit ah vild gelekhter!

Transliterated by Rifke Levine with EJG

THE BRIDE OF THE HILLS

There's a wreckage on a mountain
guarded by the raven,
once it was a busy coal-mine,
once, before the cave-in.
And, not far from this old ruin,
where no creature passes,
there's a small, deserted cabin
hidden by wild grasses.

Here each night a miner rested
from the pick and shovel,
tears have fallen here and sobs have
echoed through this hovel.
In the devastated coal-mine
blood once ran like water.
Trapped were both the miner and the
bridegroom of his daughter.

And his lovely pious maiden—
who can bear to hear it—
stumbles up the silent mountain,
sick in mind and spirit.
Rocks alone are her companions,
and to them she weeps now.
Late at night she finds the coal-mine;
only there she sleeps now.

But no sooner is she sleeping,
the musicians gather,
start a tune and from the grave-pit
rise both groom and father.

And with them the other miners
all surround her, singing,
and not far off, in the steeple,
bells are ringing.
Silent—as the grave is silent—
black and blood-becovered—
into his cold arms the bridegroom
takes his warm beloved.

Half burnt through by wounds, her father
greets the pair with tears then,
gives them both his benediction,
sighs and disappears then.
Suddenly the bells fall silent,
and the band stops splaying,
all grow still and vanish; no one
but the lovers staying.

Undisturbed, they dance together
down to the moonlit meadow,
'til the moment comes—he leaves her
dancing with a shadow.
Up she starts, and flees the coal-mine
with a shriek of "Murder!"
No one can forget that outcry
Who but once has heard her . . .

Translated by Aaron Kramer

A TEARDROP ON THE IRON

This is another of Rosenfeld's sad expositions on his life in the factory. He repeats the theme here (and in many such poems) that a heavy heart, endless travail, a cough and a groan and a numbed mind are part of the job. But here he has a charming twist in which he asks his tears, ". . . are there any more from whence you come? When will the lamentations end?" In this well-written little effort we are convinced that for Morris they will never end. We know for a fact that his Muse actually cried bitterly. when she read this.

A TREHER OYFN AYZEN
A Tear On The Iron

A, kalt un finster iz di shop!
Ikh halt dem ayzen, shtey un klop!
Mayn hehertz iz shvakh, ikh krakhtz un khuhst,
Es heybt zikh koym mayn kranker bruhst.
Ikh krakhtzt un chuhst un press un klehr,
Mayn oyg vert fikht, es fallt ah trehr,
Der ayzen gliht: dohs treherel mayn,
Dohs kokht un kokht un ziht nit ayn.

Ikh fihl keyn kraft, es iz farvuhnd't,
Der ayzen fahlt mihr fon der handt,
Un dohkh der treher, der haysser treher,
Der treher, der treher, kokht mehr un mehr.
Es roysht mayn kohp, es brekht mayn hehrtz,
Ikh frahg mit vey, ikh frahg mit shmehrtz,
Oy zohg, mayn frayndt, in noyt un payn,
Oy, treher, farvohs zihdst duh nit ayn?

Oy, shtuhmer treher, oy, shtuhmer sprakh!
Zohg, hob ikh dayne nokh a sakh?
Tzi duh bist shoyn di letzter haynt
Fon alle mayne heysse frayndt?
Bist efshe gohr a kuhryehr,
Zohg ohn mir, az iz kuhmen mehr?
Ikh vollt es vollen vissen, zohg,
Ven endigt zikh der groysser klohg?

Ikh vollt gefragt nokh mehr un mehr,
Bay'm uhnruh, bay dem vilden treher,
Doh hohben zikh darlangt a gohs,
Gohr teheren ohn a mohs,
Un ikh hohb shoyn farshteyen glaykh
Az tihf iz nohkh der trehren taykh.

A TEARDROP ON THE IRON

Oh, cold and gloomy is the shop
I press and press and never stop.
My heart is weak, I cough and groan,
my chest is heavy as a stone.
I cough and press and dream and doubt,
my eyes well up, a tear drops out.
The iron glows, my little tear
it seethes and does not disappear.

I have no strength, it's all used up.
My fingers let the iron drop.
And still the tear seethes on and on
as though it never will be gone
My heart is heavy and my brain
is wracked, I ask in grief, in pain—
"Oh friend in need and sorrow, say
oh tear, why don't you boil away?"

"Oh silent tear, oh silent tongue,
will others like you come along?
Are more of my hot friends to fall
or will you be the last of all?
"Are you the herald to proclaim
that there are more from where you came?
I want an answer: tell me, friend,
when will the lamentation end?"

Still other things would I have asked
the fiery tear of my unrest,
but all at once began to pour
tears without reason, more and more,
and it was very plain to see
how deep my well of tears must be.

Translated by Aaron Kramer

Original Yiddish for this poem is on page 194

SHOOT THE BEAST

"Don't spare the bullets! Load your gun and shoot the hungry miner dead!" This was written after miners were shot down during a famous Pennsylvania coal-strike. It demonstrates Rosenfeld's concern with all labor, not merely those in the garment area. He empathized with the abused miners, "Why should the miner fear the tomb? Has daylight ever glowed for him? A man who toils in total gloom and hears the great walls caving in!" Can you tell a great poem when you read it? The powerful cadence, the brave explicitness of his images go right to the heart of the matter here, and to the heart of the reader as well. His directness and simplicity of expression are essential elements of expository poetry. He does not need references to the spires of the orient, the marble palaces of Athens or to the fratricide of the Celts. To Morris the classics were the workers of the world, whose needs had to be addressed. Those who read this understood that it was meant for them.

SHIHST DI BESTIH
Shoot The Beast

Lohdt ohn di bihksen, shpohrt nit keyn blay,
Un shihst dem mayner in zayn noyt,
Ehr shtarbt dohkh zelten say vi say
Mit a natihrlikh, menshlikh toyt.
Vohs hoht a mayner far a vehrt?
Nit yetzt iz shpeyter, makht a sohf!
Ehr lihgt dohkh say vi say in d'r erd,
Ihr shihst a mas, aykh kuhmt keyn shtrohf.

Vohs art a mayner dan di nakht?
Vu treyst ihm likht? Vu kvikt ihm shayn?
A mensh vohs lihgt in shvartzen shakht
Un hehrt vi berg nohr fallen eyn.
A mensh shrekt der toyt nit, neyn!
Lohdt oh di bihksen, fayert ohp!
Zayn ohrtz iz uhntn, zohl ehr gayn
Un nit fardreyen dohrt a kohp.

Vohs darf a maynr vohs lihgt in gruhb?
Vohs vil a shklav, vohs hoht keyn tohg?
A sheyne kleyd, a fayne shtuhb,
A groyssen loyn? Tzuh velkhen klohg?
Oh, fayert ohp, shpohrt keyn blay!

A mayner's bluht meg rinnen fray,
Oh, fayert ohp, nit shpohrt keyn shroht—
Ihm hehrt keyn mensh, ihm helft keyn goht!

Original Yiddish for this poem is on page 195

SHOOT THE BEAST

Don't spare the bullets! Load your gun
and shoot the hungry miner dead!
A miner's life is seldom done
the same as other folks—in bed.
A miner's life—what is it worth?
This year or next, let it be finished!
He is a creature of the earth.
You kill a corpse you won't be punished.

Why should a miner fear the tomb?
Has daylight ever glowed for him,
A man who toils in total gloom
and hears the great walls caving in?
A miner flinch at dying? No!
Just load your gun and shoot away!
The ground's his country, let him go;
not bother us another day!

What does he need, down in the mine,
this slave whom sunlight never knows?
A home in which the sun can shine?
A higher wage? A suit of clothes?
Oh, shoot away, don't spare the lead
Its's safe to shoot a miner dead.
Oh, shoot again, in case you missed him!
No man will hear, no god assist him.
Translated by Aaron Kramer

EVENING ON THE HUDSON

This is a lovely poem in which he bids goodnight to the Palisade cliffs
which form the western shore of the Hudson river. Living in Yonkers,
New York, Rosenfeld had ample time to witness the beauties of the Hudson valley and other parts of Westchester in all seasons. It is not a great
poem, despite its imagery, but it has its moments of charm. It is of note
that he says, "Soon upon the cold horizon you will be a stain, red as blood.
A throb of pain hovers in the west." That's Grandpa, again, putting blood
and pain even in the sky.

AHBEND
Evening

Oyf di Palisaden ruhet di zunnen,
Varfenden yihr letzten zihssen blik,
Dem farlohzten Hohdson velkher ligt
In zayn kalte zilber-bet fartrakht.

Gute nakht dir, likht princessen, shtim
Vee ah yugend—hilum in di barg,
Zinkstu nemmendik mit zikh di freyd,
Leykhtendik fergessten in dayn prakht,
Lohzendik di velt alleyn—Gute nakht!

Bald bleybt ibber nohr ah royter plek
Oyfn hohryzant vi blut, ah shmertz
Vakhst zikh oys in merv un ah vey,
Vigt di felden shlefferik un vakht,
Un es sheptshet umetum: "Gut nakht!"

EVENING ON THE HUDSON

Upon the palisades the sun reclines
taking one last fond look
about the Hudson, lying lonely and bemused
upon its bed of icy-silver light
softly mumuring a sad good-night.

Goodnight! O princes of the light! Goodnight!
Silent, as a youthful dream, you sink
into the hill taking human joy along,
disappearing in your splendrous might,
leaving us alone again. . . . goodnight!

Soon upon the cold horizon, you
will be a stain, red as blood.
A throb of pain hovers in the west,
a twinge will rock the fields in sleepy rite,
and everywhere a whispering . . . goodnight, goodnight!

Translated by Max Rosenfeld

TO THE WORKINGMAN

"Be proud of your work. It gives you the right to enjoy the fruits of the earth!" This is Polonius speaking to his son Laertes. "Be proud, be brave, manly, but no man's slave . . . you should know the worth of your place . . ." A terrific little poem. He lets those immigrants know of their rights but does not neglect their obligations and responsibilities to be worthy ciizens. This was another time, another world, but people listened to this man and loved him. What more could a poet want? By the way, can someone really write poetry like this on a trolley-car?

TZUM ARBAYTER
To The Workingmen

Zay shtohltz oyf dayn arbayt; Zih giht dir ohs rekht
Dih fruhkht fon der velt tzuhgenihsen.
Zay muhtig, zay menshlikh un zay nit keyn knekht!
Dayn vert uhn dayn ohrt zohllstuh vissen!

Dayn vert tzu betzohlen farmohgt nit keyn trohn,
Dih kann dih natur nohr fargelten.
Dayn ohrt iz an ehren-ohrt gantz oyben-ohn,
Du goht fon dih ihrishe velten!

Mit vohs dikh belvinnen, ven alles iz dayn,
Duh flaysige handt mit dem hammer?
Tzu di ge-ihrt alles.dohs broyt un der vayn,
Dohs ayzen, dohs gohld un der marmer.

Derfohr magsuho shtohltz zayn un neymen mit rekht
Alsding, vohs dayn hartz kan ferlangen!
Zay muhtig, zay tapfer un zay nit keyn knekht,—
Un shmihd nit, un tohg nit keyn tzvangen

TO THE WORKINGMAN

Be proud of your work, it gives you the right
To enjoy the fruits of the earth,
Be gentle and brave but no man's slave,
You know your place, your worth.

To express your worth requires no "deed",
No man should you demean,
Your place is a pedestal on high,
You God of the earthly scene!

What should be your recompense
when everything is thine?
Your skillfull arm and industry
will bring you bread and wine.

Iron, gold and marble too
may be your rightful prize,
And ev'rything your heart desires
that in your power lies.

Be heroic and be brave
and be nobody's slave.
And neither make nor carry chains
to weigh you to the grave.

דער בלייכער אפרייטער

אָ יך זעה דערם אַ בלייכען אפרייטער
פערקאַכם אין דער אַרבּיים, אַ שרעק!
און זיים איך געדיינק איהם אלץ נייט ער
און לייגם זיינע קרעפטען אוועק.

עם ווערן חדשים פערפלויגען,
עם לויפען דיא יאָהרען אהין,
און נאָך זיטצם דער בלייכער געבויגען,
און קעמפּם מים'ן רויהען מאַשין.

איך שמעה און בעטראַכם דערם זיין צורה,
זיין צורה, פערשמירם און פעשוויצם,
און פיהל, אז דא ארבּיים קיין גבורה,
דער אימפעם נאָר פראַצעװועם איצם.

דאָך פאַלען דיא מראָפּענם כסדר,
פון אויפגאַנג בּיז אונטערגאַנג שפּעם,
און זאַפּען זיך אין אין דיא קליידער,
און מרינקען זיך אין אין דיא נעם.

איך בּעם אייך, ווּא לאַנג וועם נאָך יאָגען
דער בלייכער דעם בלוטיגען ראַד?
אַ. ווער קען זיין ענדע מיר זאָגען?
ווער וויים יענעם שרעקליכען סוד?

אַ. שווער, זעהר שווער דאָם צו זאָגען
דאָך איינם איז בעוואוסם און בעשיידם:
ווען איהם וועם דיא ארבּיים דערשלאַנגען,
זיטצם תּכף אַ צוווייטער און נייט.

דיא סוועם שאם

עס רוישען אין שאם אזוי ווילד דיא מאשינען,
אז אפטמאהל פערגעס איך אין רויש דאס איך בין;—
איך ווער אין דעם שרעקליכען טומעל פערלארען,
מיין איך ווערם דערם במל, איך ווער א מאשין:
איך ארבייט און ארבייט, און ארביים אהן חשבון,
עם שאפפט זיך, און שאפפט זיך, און שאפפט זיך אהן צאחל:
פיר וואס? און פיר ועמען? איך ווייס ניט, איך פרעג ניט,—
ווא קומם א מאשינע צו דיינקען א מאהל?

ניטמא קיין געפיהל, קיין געדאנק, קיין פערשטאאנד גאר;—
דיא ביטערע, בלוטיגע ארבייט ערשלאגט
דאס עדעלסטע, שעהנסטע און בעסטע, דאס רייכסטע,
דאס טיעפסטע, דאס טהכסטע וואס לעבען פערמאגם.
עס שווינדען סעקונדען, מינוטען און שטונדען,
גאר זענגעל־שנעל פליהען דיא נעכטם מים דיא טעג;—
איך טרייב דיא מאשין גלייך ווי ווי זיי דערשנעג,—
איך יאג אהן א שכל, איך יאג אהן א בּרעג.

דער זייגער אין ווערקשאם, ער רוהט נים אפילו,
ער ווייזם אלץ און קלאפּם אלץ און וועקם נאכטענאנד;—
געזאגט האם א מענש מיר אטמאהל דיא בעדיימונג:
זיין ווייזען און וועקען, דערם לינעם א פערשטאַנד;
נאר עטוואם געדיינקט זיך מיר, פונקם ווי א פון חלום,—
דער זייגער, ער וועקם אין מיר לעבען און זינן,
און נאך עפעם,—איך האב פערגעסמען,—נים פרעגמם עם!
איך ווייס נים, איך ווייס נים, איך בין א מאשין!......

און צייטענוווייז ווען איך דערהער שוין דעם זייגער,
פערשטעהע איך גאנץ אנדערש זיין ווייזען, זיין שפּראַך,—
מיר דאכם, אז עם נוקעם מיך דערמען דער אונרוה,
כ'זאל ארבייטמען, ארבייטמען, מעהרער, א סך !
איך הער אין זיין מען נאר דעם באטס'ם ווילדען בייזער,—
זיין פינסמערען קוק אין דיא ווייזער דיא צווייי;—
דער זייגער, מיר זקרוכעם, מיר דאכם, אז ער טרייבם מיך
און רופם מיך "מאשינע!" און שריים צו מיר: "נייי!"

נאר דאן, ווען ס'איז שטילער דער ווילדער געטומעל,
אוועק איז דער מיסטער, אין מיטאָג־צייט שטונד,
דאן פאנגם אן אין קאם ביי מיר לאנגזאם צו מאגען,
אין הארצען צו ציהען,—איך פיהל דאן מיין וואונד;—
און ביטערע טרעהרען, און זודינע טרעהרען

צו וויקען מיין מאגערען מיטטאג, מיין ברויט, —
עם ווערגט מיך, איך קען ניט מעהר עסען, איך קען ניט !
אַ, שרעקליכע פראצע ! אַ, ביטערע נויט !

ס'ערשיינט מיר דיא שאפ אין דער מיטטאג-צייט שפונדע
אַ בלוטיגע שלאכטפעלד, וען דארט ווערט גערוהם :
ארום און ארום זעה איך ליעגען הרונים,
עם ליארמט פון דר'ערד דאם פערגאסענע בלום.....
אייו וויילע, און באלד ווערם נעפויקט אַ טריוואַנע,
דיא טויטע ערוואכען, עם לעבם אויף דיא שלאכט,
עם קעמפפען דיא מרופפען פיר פרעמדע, פיר פרעמדע,
און שטרייטען און פאלען, און זינקען אין נאכם.

איך קוק אויף דעם קאמפפ-פלאץ מים ביטערען צארען,
— ; מים שרעק, מים נקמה, מים העלישער פיין
דער זייגער, יעטצם הער איך איהם ריכטיג, ער ועקט עם :
"אַ סוף צו דיא קנעכטשאפט, אַ סוף זאל דאם זיין !"
ער מינטערם אין מיר מיין פערשמאאנד, דיא געפיהלען,
און וויים וויא עם לויפען דיא שטונדען אהין :
אן עלענדער בלייב איך, וויא לאנג איך וועל שוויינען,
פערלאצרען, וויא לאנג איך פערבלייב וואם איך בין.....

דער מענש, וועלכער שלאפם אין מיר חייבם אַן ערוואכען,
דער קנעכט, וועלכער וואכם אין מיר שלאפט דאכם זיך
— ; אייו
אצינד איז דיא ריכמיגע שמונדע געקומען !
אַ סוף צו דעם עלענד, אַ סוף זאל עם זיין !...
נאָר פלוצלינג — דער וויספעל, דער באם — אַ טרעוואַנע !
— , איך ווער אַן דעם שכל. פערגעם, וואו איך בין
עם מומעלם, מען קעמפפפם, אַ, מיין איך איז פערלאצרען. —
איך וויים נים, מיך ארם נים, איך בין אַ מאשין...

די אַרבײַטער

אָם שמעהען זיי פֿאַר מיר אַ בלייכע שרײַנגע,
דעם עלענד'ס שרעקליכע אַרמיי.
אַ, ניט געהאַלפֿענע, גענאָרטע מענגע !
זי כרעכט מיר דורך דאָס האַרץ מיט וועה.

דאָס זיינען מיינע ברידער, בלאָם און אָרעם,
די שוועסטער מיינע פֿון פֿאַבריק ;
איך האָב אַ מאָל געקלאַפט אין זיי'רע קברים,
געראָפֿען זיי צום לעבענס גליק.

איך בין אין זייער וויימאַנ איינגעדרונגען,
אין זייער חורבן טיעף אַריין,
איך האָב פֿאַר גאָם און ליים צוקלונגען
דעם גרויסען בראָך פֿון זייער „זיין".

איך האָב דער נאָכטינגאַל מיין צונג געגעבען,
צו זינגען זיי אַ פֿרייהיימס-ליעד,
צו ווייזען זיי די פֿרעכמינגקיים פֿון לעבען,
צו צייגען, אַז די ציים פֿערפֿליהם.

איך האָב געמאַכם די קברים ריידען,
די הימלען אויפֿגעריסען ווייט.
איך האָב געוועקם די גרוב און דעם גן-עדן
אַלם עדות צום נערעכטען שמרייט.

דאָך אַר'מע שקלאַוועו זיינען זיי פֿערבליבען,
און איך בין עלענד, שלאַם און קראַנק,
און וואָם איך האָב געהונגען און געשריעבען
בלייבם איבער וואָנעלען אָהן אַ דאַנק.

דער טרעהרען-מיליאנער

אַ נים קיין גאָלדענער קאַמערטאָן
שטימט אָן מיין קעהל צום זינגען,
עס קען דער וואָנק פון אויבען אָן
מיין שטים נים מאַכען קלינגען ;
דעם שקלאַוו'ם אַ קרעכץ, ווען ער איז מיעד
נאָר וועקט אין מיר דיא ליעדער, —
און מים אַ פלאם לעבם אויף מיין ליעד,
פיר מיינע אָר'מע ברידער.

* * *

דערפאַר פערגעה איך אָהן אַ ציים.
דערפאַר וועבם אוים מיין לעבען :
וואָס קענען מיר דיא אָר'מע ליים
פיר אַ בעלוינונג געבען ?
זיי צאָהלען טרעהרען פיר אַ טרעהר, —
דאָם אללעם, וואָס זיי קאָנען :—
איך בין אַ טרעהרען-מיליאנער
און ווין אויף דיא מיליאנען ....

פרויען-שטימרעכם

גים איהר שטימרעכם, גים עם גערן !
לאָזם די פרוי נים זיין געקנעכטעם !
דען איהר שטים איז וואָם מיר הערן
ווען מיר פאלען אויף דער וועלם.

אַ. איהר שטים איז וואָם בעגריסם אונז
דורך דעם לעבען'ם ווייטמען גאַנג,
און דערקוויקם אונז און פערזיסם אונז
יעדען וועה ווי אַ געזאַנג.

לאָזם די מומער און די שוועסמער
העלפען פיהרען אונז דאָם לאַנד,
דען דאָם איז דער וואונש דער גרעסמער
און דער מענשהיימם העכסמער שמאַנד !

דער לייב

וו אם רוקם איתר אלץ דיא פלייש אין זיך
און שמיסם צו מיר דיא ביינער ?
וואס מיינם איהר, וואס ? א הונד בין איך,
א הונד מים קהל׳שע צייהנגער?

א הונד וואס לויפם ארום אין גאס
און נעכמינם אויף דיא בריקלאך,
און ווען איהם פאלם א ביין צום שפאם
איז ער שוין איבער גליקליך ?

א הונד וואס כאפם א ביס אין קין,
ערנידעריגם און שפל,
און לעקם דערפאר דעם ווירמה דיא שיך,
דער ווירמהין דיא פאנםשפעל ?

א, צימערם ! דען איך בין דער לייב, —
נים שפיעלם מים מיר אין שפיצלאך,
דען קום דערלאנג איך מיך א הייב,
צופלייש איך אייך אויף פיצלאך !

איך קען דיא ספעם, איך קען דעם וואלד,
איך בין אין יאכם געבאטרען,
איך מהו א ברום, עם ווערם א גוואלד, —
און איהר דערקענם מיין צארן.

נים קוקם זיך אייין וואס איך פערשווייג,
נים האלם מיך פאר א שומה. —
עם קומם דער מאג, איך כרעך דיא שמייג
און איהר בלייבם לינגען מומע....

די רויטע בהלה

(אויף פערברענטע פאבריק-מיידלעך אין ניו יארק)

———

נים קיין שלאכם, נים קיין פערטייפעלמער פאָגראָם
האָט אָנגעפילם די גרעסטע שטאָדם מים קלאַנגען;
די ערד האָם נים געצימערם אין איהר תהום,
עס האָם קיין בליץ, קיין דונער נים געשלאַנגען;
מ'האָבבען קיין שווארצע וועטער־וואָלקענס נים געקראָכם,
און קיין קאָנאָנען נים די לופט צוצאָקערם —
אָ, ניין! דאָם האָם א מורא'דינע העלל ערוואַכם,
א שקלאָפֿאַק־נעפעסם מים שקלאַפֿען וויילד געפֿלאַקערם;
דאָם האָם דער גאָלד־גאָם מים א בראַנד־געלעכמער
געפֿאָרפֿטען אונו'רע זיהן און מעכמער,
געלעקמם די לעבענס מים זיינע רויטע צונגען —
זיי זיינען אין דעם פֿויס געשמאָרבענגען,
אין זיין שויס געדרונגען,
ער האָם זיי געכאַפֿם, געלאַכם, געזונגען...
ער האָם זיי פֿערשלונגען.

זיי זיינען געזעסען אין זייער יאָך פֿערמיעם,
זייער שוויים האָם געמריפֿם —
אין דעם פֿערמויבענדען געמשום
פֿון מאָשינען אָרום, —
ווען צעהן שמאַק אין דער הויך,
האָם זיי פֿערוויקעלם דער רויך,
פֿערשפֿונגען דער פֿלאַם,
און א גלומינער ים
געפֿרעסען, גענאַשעם,
פֿערקוייהלם, פֿעראַשעם!

שוועסמער מיינע! יונגע שוועסמער!
מיינע יונגע ברידער!...
מרויערם מיינע לידער!
יאָמערם און מרויערם!...
זעהם ווי עם לויערם
פֿון מונקעלע נעפסמער
דעם ארבייטער'ס מוים;
ווי ער האַלם זיין ברוים...
ווי ער גלאַצם ביי זיין מהיר,
ביי זיין אָרעם געצעלם —
וועה, וועה אין מיר!
וועה, וועה דיר, וועלם!
א שבת איז דאָם געווען,
אן ארבייםמער'ס א שבת
זיין „קידוש" !... זיין „הבדלה" !...
די רויטע בהלה

אין פֿלוצלונג געשעהן,
געשיקם פֿון דעם רייכען,
דעם פֿרינץ פֿון געלד.
אַ, ווען אַך אַ גליכען!
פֿליסם פֿערעדמייכען,
אַ פֿלוך דער אָרדענונג!
אַ פֿלוך דער אונאָרדענונג!
אַ פֿלוך דער וועלם!

אויף וועמען זאָל מען פֿריהער קלאָגען?
אויף די פֿערברענמע?
אויף די נימ-דערקעננמע?
אויף די, וואָס קדים זאָגען?
אויף די פֿערקריפעלמע,
פֿון „זיין" געפֿראָגען?
מיין פֿערערדמיר
אויף אייך אַלעמען גליך!

פֿערהיל זיך אין שווארצען, דו גאָלדען לאַנד!
צו מיעף דיין פֿערברעכען, צו שרעקליך דיין שאַנד,
צו מויב דיין געווייסען, צו בלינד דיין געמעק,
צו מיפֿעלש דיין „האָוון", צו בלומינ דיין נעק,
דיין נעק, וועלכער פֿאַנגם דיינע אַרעמע ליים —
ס'וועם קומען די ציים! ... ס'וועם קומען דיין ציים! ...

צינדם יאָהרציימ-ליכם אָן אין די אידישע גאָסען!
דער בראַך איז דער בראַך פֿון די אידישע מאָסען,
פֿון אונזערע מאָסען פֿער'חושך'ם און אַרעם.
ס'איז אונזער לויה, יאָ, — אונזערע קברים.
ס'האָם אונזערע קינדער, ווה, אונזערע בלומען,
דער פֿיער פֿון אונזערע אַרעמם גענומען.
ווה! אונזערע ליעבע פֿער'שרפֿה'מע קיהלען,
ווה! אונזערע פֿריידען אַ העללע מים גרהילען,
ווה! אונזערע גליקען אַ בצרג מים ארונות,
ווה! אונזערע זיסע — גיחנום זכרונות! ...

ס'איז אונזער לויה, יאָ, — אונזערע קברים.
ס'האָם אונזערע קינדער, ווה, אונזערע בלומען,
דער פֿיער פֿון אונזערע אַרעמם גענומען.
ווה! אונזערע ליעבע פֿער'שרפֿה'מע קיהלען,
ווה! אונזערע פֿריידען אַ העללע מים גרהילען,
ווה! אונזערע גליקען אַ בצרג מים ארונות,
ווה! אונזערע זיסע — גיחנום זכרונות! ...

אויף דיין געווייסען, רייכער, אונזער מרויער,
אויף דיין געווייסען אונזער קלאָג.
עס זאָל דוךֿ נאכם און מאָן
דיך שרעקען דער פֿערברענמער מויער,
און אונזערע מעכמער אין די פֿלאַמען
זאָלען דיין לעבען פֿער'סם'ען!
דיך זאָלען ביי דיינע פֿריידען,
ביי דיינע גליקען,
ווערגען, שמיקען
אונזערע ליידען!
ביי די שמחות פֿון דיינע קינדער
זאָלסמו פֿיהלען די קללה
פֿון דער רוימער בהלה,
און מאַמען ווי אַ בלינדער
די ווענם מים שרעקען,
ביז די ציים
וועם ברענגען די ציים
וואָס וועם דיך פֿערמעקען!

וואָס איז דיא וועלט

וון איז אונזער וועלטמיל אַ שלעפּצימער נאַר,
אַון איז נאַר אַ חלום דאָס לעבען ;
דאַן זאָלען מיר, וויל איך, אויך מיינע פּאַר יאָהר
אין גוטע חלומות פערשוועבען.

דאַן וויל איך חלומות פון פרייהיים און גליק,
וויא יענע גרויסאַרטיגע הערררען :
דאַן וויל איך אין חלום אַ ליעבליכען בליק
און וויל נים מעהר פרוימען פון פרעהרען.

און איז אונזער וועלטמיל אַ שמחה, אַ באַלל,
וואו מיר זיינען אַלע פערבעמען ;
דאַן וועלם זיך מיר אויך זימצען ברייטלאַך אין זאַל
און האָבען אַ חלק אַ פּעמטען.

אויך איך קען פערדרייהען אַ זאַך, וואָס איז גומ,
אַ ביסמ'ן אַ פּעמם'ן פערמראַגנען ;
איך האָב אין מיין גוף אויך דיא זעלביגע בלומ,
וויא דיא, וועלכע אורצרות פערמאָגען.

און איז נאַר אַ נערמען אַצינד אונזער וועלם,
וואו ס'וואַקסען אויך אַלערהאַנד ראָזען,
דאַן וויל איך שפּאַציערען דערם, וואו מיר געמ'עהלם,
און נים, וואו דיא רייכע מיר לאָזען.

דאַן וועלם זיך מיר מראַגען פון בלומען אַ קראַנץ,
איך וויל זיך מים דערנער נים ציערען ; —
דאַן וועלם זיך מיר אויך מים מיין ליעבסמע אין גלאַנץ
פון מירמען און לערבען שפּאַציערען.

און איז אונזער וועלם אַ מלחמה אַצינד,
וואו שמאַרקע און שוואַכערע שמריימען ;
דאַן מרם מיך מיך קיין קיין שמורעם, קיין ווייב און קיין קינד,
איך בלייב נים מים קאַלמקיים פון וויימען.

דאַן וואַרף איך אין פייער זיך, ווער איך אַ העלד,
און קעמפּף וויא אַ לייב פיר דעם שוואַכען ;
און מרעפם מיך דיא קויל — איך פאַל מוים אויפ'ן פּעלד,
דאַן קען איך אויך שמאַרבענדיג לאַכען.

ברויט מיט מהעע

אָר ברויט מיט מהעע, און ברויט מיט מהעע
דאָס איז אַ קעסם זאַ אַך און וועה.
דען ביטטאָ, נאַטאָ, אויף מיר אין כעם,
וואָס דוא ערלויבסטאָ זיך דיעזען שפּאַס ?
צו זשעלעוועז סערדינם אַ בּאַקם,
אַ שפּיקעל קעה, אַ בּרעקעל לאַקם,
אַבּיסעל מילך, אַטאָל אן איי !
נאָר ברויט מיט מהעע, און ברויט מיט מהעע,
דאָס איז אַ קעסם זאַ אַך און וועה !

דוא שפּילסט עם תקיפות, נאַטאָ, מיט מיר ?
איך זאָלל זיך אייַנבעטטעַן בּייַא דיר ?
נאָר ווייַניג האָב איך מאַג און טשכם
און בעטטעַן דיך אַליין פערגראַטעכם ?
דאָך וואָרין איך אויף דעם פינפטטעַן שטאָק,
מיין תפילה הערטטטאָ וויא אין טראָק, —
משמעות, נאַטאָ, דוא ביסט אַליין
אויך ניט מיט א ל ל ע מ ע ז, איך מיין,
דיר מוז עם אויך ניט ע ק ס ט ר א געהן. . . . .

נאָר ברויט מיט מהעע, און ברויט מיט מהעע,
וואָס מויט דיא קאַטצעַן, איך פערשטעהע :
דוא וואָלסט נעגנעבען, גומער נאַטאָ,
דיא צייַם איז שלעכם, דוא ביסט באַנקראַטם.
דוא בּיסם און מוזם דאָך זיין גערעכם
וואָס חעלפּם עם, יאָ, דיא צייַם איז שלעכם !
כ'האָב וועקסמעלאָך זאָגאַר פערטאָל,
איך האָב אַ „מאַרגיידרוש" אויף דיין שמוהל,
נאָר געה און קריך מיר אַוש אין זבול !

נאָר מהעע מיט ברויט, און ברויט מיט מהעע,
דאָך ווילל איך וויסען דיעזעז דרעה :
דוא גיבּסט דאָך עטעם מאַנכעַן יאָ.
פיר מ י ר נאָר איז בּי דיר נישטאָ !
אויף דעם בּין איך שוין נאָר ניט קלוג,
אַ שווינדעל, האַ ? בּיי נאַטאָ בּעמרוג ?
נין, יעטצם פערשטעהע איך, נאַטאָ, איך גלויב,
אַז ערד'ם עשירות קומט דורך רויב, —
איך קריך ניט מעהר פאַר דיר אין שטויב.

דער אלטער שניידער

ע ר זיצט און נייט שוין פיעלע יאהרען,
און זיין בלייכער פנים שוויצט. —
דער בארד איז איהם שוין ווייס געווארן,
וויא דער פאדים, וואס ער נימצט.
נישטא קמעט אין שטאדט א מייסטער,
וועלכען ער האט נים געדיענט
און דאך האט ער קיין סענם איין מייסטער
און קיין ברוים פיר ווייב און קינד.

ער קומט אריין אין שאפ בענינען
און פערדיענגט שוין זיינע הענד; —
ער האלם פאראיינם אין איין פערדיענען
און פערהולמעוועם קיין סענם.
ער שטעפם שוין ווען עם גראט'ם דער מארגען
און ער שאמם נאך שפעט ביי נאכם,
און אימער, אימער, וואו צו בארגען
זיצט ער פרוויערינ און טראכם.

דער מייסטער איז מים איהם צופריעדען,
דען ער מענה'ם נים קיין סך.
ער מאכם אין שאפ נים קיין יריד'ן
און בעליידינם נים זיין פאך.
ער קומם און נעהם אוועק אין שמילען, —
ריידען, רעדם פיר איהם דער הוסמ !
דעם טראהר פערדעקקען איהם דיא ברילען
און דעם שמערץ פערדעקם דיא ברוסם.

דיא ארבייטם־לייטע, אלע קוקען
אויף דעם קראנקען מים א וועה,
זיי קוקען אויף זיין מיעדען רוקען,
וועלכער קריסם זיך ביי'ם געגעה.
זיי זעהען שוין דעם שווארצען זיעגעל,
פיר זיין עהרליכקיים דיא שמערצ.... .
זיי זעהען, פונקם וויא אין א שפיעגעל,
אין דעם אלמען זייער סוף.

א טרעהר אויפ׳ן אייזען

קאלט און פינסטער איז דיא שאפ!
אַיך האלט דעם אייזען, שמעה און קלאפ!—
מיין הערץ איז שוואך׳ איך קרעכץ און הוסט;
עס הויבט זיך קוים מיין קראנקע ברוסט.

איך קרעכץ און הוסט און פרעס און קלעהר,
מיין אויג ווערט פייכט, עס פאלם אַ טרעהר,
דער אייזען גליהם: — דאם טרעהריל מיין —
דאם קאכם און קאכם און זידט נים אייַן.

איך פיהל קיין קראפט, עס איז פערווענד׳ט׳ם;
דער אייזען פאלם מיר פון דיא הענד,
און דאך דער טרעהר, דער הייסער טרעהר,
דער טרעהר, דער טרעהר, קאכם מעהר און מעהר.

עס רוישט מיין קאפ, עס ברעכם מיין הערץ;
איך פרעג מים וועה, איך פרעג מים שמערץ:
„אַ, זאָג, מיין פריינד אין גוים און פיין,
אַ, טרעהר, פאראוואם זידסטו נים אייַן?

אַ, שטומער טרעהר, אַ, שטומע שפראַך!
זאָג, האָב איך דיינע נאָך אַ סך?
צי דו ביסט שוין דער לעצטער היינם,
פון אַלע מיינע הייסע פריינד?

ביסט אפשר גאָר אַ קוריער,
זאָגסט אָן מיר, אז עס קומען מעהר?
איך וואָלם עס וועלען וויסען, זאָג:
ווען ענדיגם זיך דער גרויסער קלאַג?

איך וואָלם געפרעגט נאָך מעהר און מעהר
ביי׳ם אונ־רוה, ביי דעם ווילדען טרעהר,
דאָ האָבען זיך דערלאנגט אַ גאָם
גאָר טרעהרען, טרעהרען שאָן אַ מאָם
און איך האָב שוין פערשטאַנען גליַיך,
אז טיעף איז נאָך דער טרעהרען מייַך.

שיסט דיא בעסטיע

———

אַדם אָן דיא ביקסען, שפּאַרט קיין בלײַ
און שיסט דעם מיינער אין זײַן נויט,
ער שמאַרבט דאָך זעלטמען סײַ ווי סײַ
מים אַ נאַטירליך, מענשליך טויט.
וואָס האָט אַ מיינער פֿאַר אַ וועראַמה ?
נים איצם איז שפּעטער, מאַכם אַ סוף !
ער ליגט דאָך סײַ ווי סײַ אין דר׳ערד,
אַהער שיסט אַ מת, אײַך קומם קיין שטראָף.

וואָס אַרם אַ מיינער דען דיא נאַכם ?
וואו מרייסט איהם ליכם ? וואו קוויקם איהם שײַן ?
אַ מענש וואָס ליגם אין שוואַרצען שאַכם
און הערם ווי אַ בערג נאָר פֿאַלען אײַן.
אַ מיינער שרעקט דער טויט נים — נײַן !
לאַדם אָן דיא ביקסען, פֿײַערם אָפּ !
זײַן אַרם איז אונטען, זאָל ער געהן
און נים פֿערדרעהען דאָ אַ קאָפּ.

וואָס דאַרף אַ מענש, וואָס ליעגם אין גרוב ?
וואָס וויל אַ שקלאַוו, וואָס האָם קיין מאַג,
אַ שעהנע קלייד, אַ פֿיינע שטוב,
אַ גרויסען לוין ? צו וועלכען קלאָג ?
אָ, פֿײַערם אָפּ, נים שפּאַרם קיין בלײַ !
א מיינער'ם בלום מעג רינען פֿרײַ,
אָ, פֿײַערם אָפּ, נים שפּאַרם קיין שראָם —
איהם הערם קיין מענש, איהם העלפֿם קיין גאָטם.

PERSONAL
AND FAMILY
POETRY

This is an idealized version of Rosenfeld's son Joseph. Etching by Lilien.

MAYN YINGELE

Ikh hob ah kleynem yingele,
Ah zunele gor fayn,
Ven ikh derzey ihm dakht zikh mir
Dih gantze velt iz mayn!

Nor zelten, zelten zey ikh ihm,
Mayn sheynem ven ehr vakht,
Ikh tref im tomid shlufndik
Ikh zey ihm nor bay nakht.

Dih arbet traybt mikh frih aroys,
Un lozt mikh speyt tsurik,
O, fremd iz mir mayn eygn leyb,
O, fremd mayn kinds ah blik!

Ikh kum tsuklemterhayt aheym,
In finsternish gehilt,
Mayn bleykhe froy dertseylt mir bald
Vih fayn dohs kind zikh shpilt.

Ikh hehr es tsu un ayl—es muz—
Yoh, Yoh es muz geshehen!
Dih faterlihbe flakert oyf,
Es muz mayn kind mikh zeyn !

Ikh shtey bay zayn gelegerel
Uhn zay, uhn hehr, uhn shah!
Ah troym bevegt dih lippelakh,
"O vu, O vu iz pa?

Vih zis es ret, vih klug es fregt,
"O mame, gute ma,
Ven kumt uhn brengt ah penny mir,
Mayn guter, guter pa?"

Ikh kuhsh dih bloye eygelakh
Zey efenen zikh, "O kindt!"
Zey zehen mikh, zey zehen mikh!
Uhn shlissen zikh geshvint.

"Doh shteyt dayn papa, tayerer,
Ah pennele dir, na!"
Ah troym bevekt dih lippelakh,
"O vu iz, vu iz pa?"

Ikh blayb tseveytikt uhn tseklemt,
Farbitert uhn ikh kler,
Ven du vakst oyf amol, may kind,
Gefinst du mikh nit mer!

Transliterator unknown to us.

MY LITTLE SON

I have a son, a little son,
a youngster mighty fine,
And when I look at him I feel
that all the world is mine.

But seldom do I see him when
he's wide awake and bright.
I always find him sound asleep,
I see him late at night.

The time-clock drags me off at dawn,
At night it lets me go.
I scarcely know my flesh and blood,
His eyes I hardly know.

I climb the staircase wearily,
a figure wrapped in shade,
Each night my haggard wife describes
how well the youngster played.

How sweetly he's begun to talk,
how cleverly he said,
"When will my daddy come and leave
a penny near my bed?"

I listen and I rush inside,
It must—yes, it must be!—
My father-love begins to burn,
my child must look at me!

I stand beside the little bed
and watch my sleeping son,
when, Hush! a dream bestirs his mouth,
"Where has my daddy gone?"

I touch his eyelids with my lips,
The blue eyes open then,
They look at me! They Look at me!
And quickly shut again.

"Your daddy's right beside you, dear.
Here, here's a penny, son!"
A dream bestirs his little mouth,
"Where has my daddy gone?"

I watch him, wounded and depressed
by thoughts I cannot bear;
"One morning, when you wake, my child,
you'll find that I'm not there."

Translated by Aaron Kramer
Original Yiddish for this poem is on page 216

MY LITTLE SON

This is one of Rosenfeld's most popular poems. It recounts how a father leaves for work early in the morning, before his youngster is awake and returns from work so late in the evening that the child is already asleep. Every worker could identify with the parent who must dedicate his time to a job that keeps him from his family and homelife. This poem is intense and effective in its simplicity and economy of verbiage. It has been translated into many languages and several melodies have been set to it. The "Yingele" (Youngster) whose he refers to was our mother's only brother, five years older than she. A couple of ancient pictures of him are included in this volume. He was a talented writer and aroused the jealousy of some Polish-American boys who waylaid him and threw him down a flight of stone steps. He developed a sarcoma of the shoulder from this incident and died at age fifteen. His death nearly destroyed his father. This poem is not simply Rosenfeld's problem: it is a cry at the injustice of life which afflicted most of the immigrants.

VEHR, OYB NIT DUH?
Who, If Not You ? *(Lovesong In A Sweatshop)*

Duh iz keyn nakhtigal, nit duh,
Keyn foygel zihs un lihb.
Nuhr mashihnen shver un groh,
Zey kuhkn kalt un trihb.

Oyf himmel un erd un velt
Zey zaynen aygen shtohl,
Der niggun fun leben fallt,
Nitduh keyn nishumeh, kuhl.

Es huzshet, es fayft un es shrayt,
Es kloppt un roysht fun yogt,
Men hehrt nohr redn tsu tsayt
Der imfet traybt un shohgt.

Un vollst du oykh nit zayn
Vi vohllt ikh hoykh geshtrebt ?
Ver vohllt mir geshikt di shayn
Vohs shtarkt mikh un beleyt.

Der geroysh vohs gib ikh um ihm ?
Vohs art mihr kokh un fayf ?
Ikh hehr dayn gebenshteh shtim
Un mayn gezang vert rayf.

Original Yiddish for this poem is on page 218

LOVESONG IN A SWEATSHOP
(Who, If Not You?)

No nightingale here preens
himself and sweetly sings.
Only iron-gray machines,
looking cold and frightening
at sky and earth and all;
and, like an unsheathed knife,
cast a discordant pall
upon the melody of life.

The repetitious rain
of sounds, their urgent whine,
makes every note the same,
except the murmuring of time.

I too, were you not here,
would one day cease to strive,
to see, to feel, to hear,
to keep my hope alive.

No matter now the noise,
the rush, the clatter. When
I hear your blessed voice
my song resounds again!

Translated by Max Rosenfeld

LOVESONG IN A SWEATSHOP
(Who, If Not You)

What saves many a poem by Rosenfeld is his imagery. This might have been a pedestrian poem, with nothing special to recommend it, since there is nothing really going on here. Ah, but there is his brilliant imagery in this tender lovesong. Don't overlook his lines that say that those machines in his shop are "iron-gray, looking cold and frightening . . . and like an unsheathed knife cast a discordant pall upon the melody of life". And how about this line, "The repetitious rain of sounds, their urgent whine makes every note the same, except the murmuring of time."?

How dare this tailor take his mind off those clothes he was pressing, to think of more "pressing" subjects, such as the murmuring of time! How could a poetic soul even survive under such conditions? Frankly, we in the family of Morris Rosenfeld never for a moment realized the greatness of that man who could conceive of the murmuring of time while struggling so to make a living. In addition, we hope you have been noting the brilliant, poetic translations of Max Rosenfeld.

MY RESTING PLACE

Apparently this poem was a favorite of our Dad, Dr. Leon Goldenthal. He took several lines from it and "adapted" them for the inscription on grandmother Bessie Rosenfeld's tombstone. He used different lines from this poem for our mother's monument so there was no way they could escape Rosenfeld's poetry. Here Rosenfeld combined his love for nature with the dreadful life of immigrant workers, who are constantly reminded here of the gloomy, slave-like atmosphere of their places of work. He uses terms like, "lives are fading", "chains are clanging ", "Tears are flowing and teeth are gnashing", all evidence of the humiliating, frustrating, emasculating daily struggle for existence. This was not hyperbole. This is the way it was. The word, "ruhe" means calm, peacefulness, as contrasted with the frenetic, disturbing atmosphere of the work-place.

MAYN RUHE PLATZ
My Resting Place

Nit zuch mich vu di mirten grinen!
Gefinst mich dorten nit, myn shotz!
Vu lebens velkn bay machinen,
Dorten iz myn ruhe plotz.
Nit zuch mich vu di faygl zingen!
Gefinst mich dorten nit, myn shotz!
Ah shklof bin ich, vu kyten klingen,
Dorten iz myn ruhe plotz

Nit zuch mich vu fontanen shpritzen,
Gefinst mich dorten nit, mayn shotz!
Vu treren rinnen, tsayner kritzen,
Dorten iz myn ruhe plotz.
Un leebst du mich mit vorer leebe,
Zoh kum tsu mir myne gter shotz!
In hyter oyf myn hartz dee treebe,
Un mach mir zees myn ruhe plotz.

Transliterator unknown
Original Yiddish for this poem is on page 219

MY RESTING PLACE

Seek me not 'mid blooming meadows,
Not there my spirit can you trace,
Where workers toil like spectral shadows,
'Tis there you'll find my resting place.
Seek me not where birds are singing,
Not there my spirit can you trace,
A slave am I, where chains are ringing,
'Tis there you'll find my resting place.

Seek me not 'mid fountains dashing,
Not there my spirit can you trace,
Where tears are falling, teeth are gnashing,
'Tis there you'll find my resting place.
And love'st thou me with love's true passion
Thy steps unto my spirit trace.
Bring joy with thee; in love's true fashion
Make sweet to me my resting place.

Translated by Belle Robbins

TSU DER GELIHBTE
To My Beloved

Oh zay gebensht, Oh zay gegrist,
Mayn glik, mayn treyst, mayn goldner sheym!
Du kumst atsind kumst umzist
In dumpfen shop bay mihr tsu zayen.
Doh roysht es, kohkht es, zihdt es brennt !
Duh iz ken ohrt fihr di tsu shteyn.
Ferdingen zaynen mayne hendt.
Ikh tohr dikh nit umarmen-neyn!

Ohbvohl Ikh bin ohn dir vi toydt,
Dohkh muz ikh es ferlangen: Neh!!
Doh hersht der herter kampf fihr broyt,
Doh muz men tsafflen baym geneh.
Kum shpeyter elsht, oh kum bay nacht
Tsu mir aheym, dohrt bin ikh fray,
Mayn hertz lebt ohp. mayn gayst ervakht,
Mayn lihbe flahkhert fun dohs nay.

Dahn gib ikh mir tsu dir ah yohg,
Un fahl begeystert oyf dayn bruhst,
Un mayne leyden fun dem tohg
Zay veren alle der bevust
Un mayne kushen hustu dan,
Un mayne treyeren ohn ah shi-ur,
Dem beste vus es iz faran,
In mayn neshume shenk ikh dihr.
Mayn shenstes lihb tret bahld aroys

Un grist dir hays baym ershten blik,
Un yedes vohrt vus du redst oys
Vert mir fervandtlt in musik.
Dohkh itzt, gelihbte, mustu geyen,
Doh hut di lihbe nit keyn makht,
Ikh tor dikh nit uhmarmen—neyn!
Mayn leben kuhmpt ersht mit der nakht.

TO MY BELOVED

How good to look at you again
my love, my joy, one bright dream!
You come now and you come in vain
to be with me at my machine.

There's steam and smoke and madness here—
there's no place for a guest to stand.
I can't so much as touch you, dear,
for I have rented out my hand.

Come to me later! Come at night,
for then my darling, I am free.
My spirit wakes, my heart is light,
the flame of love revived in me.

I'll sing as I have never sung
the moment that your face appears,
and every word upon your tongue
shall turn to music in my ears.

I'll greet you then in such a way
as I would now, if I could dare.
Then all my troubles of the day,
my inmost wounds, will be laid bare.

And you will have my kisses all,
and tears enough, you'll have those too.
Whatever good is in my soul
I'll offer as a gift to you.

But now, beloved, you must go,
love has no business in a shop.
I can't so much as touch you—no!
My life starts when the treadles stop.

Translated (beautifully) by Aaron Kramer

TO MY BELOVED

Once more a lovely poem to his beloved is prisoner to the pervasive depression of life in the shop. "I can't as much as touch you, dear, for I've hired out my hand!" But he does love, he does look forward to those hours away from work. "I'll sing as I have never sung, the moment that your face appears, and ev'ry word upon your tongue shall be as music to my ears." Rosenfeld's language here is not Victorian, stilted obeisance to Webster's dictionary. He speaks colloquial Yiddish, the way he would speak to Bessie if she had suddenly come into his shop and said, "Nu, Morris, what time do you finish up here?" He'd have to anwser, "I'm rented out for the day, but my life starts when the treadle stops." There is no elegance here, just a passionate young man in his twenties forced into a life of denial and despair

A DEAD HEART

This is a painful acceptance of a loss of inner fire to express inner grief. He says, "I seek my former "me", the younger one, from which the older "me" has run." It has not run away. It was worn away. How long can one have the koyach (strength) to fight? His tears "come from the head, not from the heart. This heart of mine is dead." Maybe so, but his ability to tell about it is in first-rate style. However, in a way, this concern is a foreboding for him.

AH TOYTE HERTZ
A Dead Heart

Mayn harfe hoht amohl geshpihlt,
Un hoht dih velt farkluhngn,
Mayn gantze zeyle hoht gefihlt,
Mayn gantze hartz gezuhngn.

Mayn oyg hoht alle un altz gezeyn,
Mayn oyer altz farnuhmn,
Mayn lihd iz mit a vildn bren
Bay mir oysgekuhmn.

Ikh zing, di harfe mayne shpihlt,
Nohr nit dem zelben nigen,
Nitoh, es feylt der ershter bren,
Ikh zuhch, ikh aker un ikh kan

Ihm mehr nit tuhorik kihegn.
Vu bisuho ergets yuhnges lihd?
Gezuhngn mit a fayer,
Vohs hoht geshtrebt, vohs hoht gegliht
Di velt tzuh makhen frayer?

Vu iz di brokhe, vu der fluhkh,
Vohs hoht mayn vunsh geshponnen?
Ikh zuhkh mayn ershter "Ikh" un zuhkh,
Un oyz ehr iz faruhnen.
Farlohshn iz der shtarker flam,
Bezihgt fohn vilden leybens-yam,
Ehr iz dem shiksals korbm.
Yetzt kuhmt mayn treher kalt arohp,
Fon hehrtzen nit,—ehr kommt fon kohp,
Dohs hehrtz iz mir geshtohrbn.

A DEAD HEART

My heart once played what the world required,
My whole heart sang what my soul inspired,
My eyes explored with great desire,
all sounds my ears took in.
My songs burst forth with wild fire
that leapt up from within.
My harp plays and again I sing
but the melody has a diff'rent ring,

Gone are the early flames that burn,
I search, I labor and I yearn
to recover that old flame of truth.
Where are you, song of youth

that had brightly burned and glowed
to light for the world a free-er road?
Where is the blessing, where the curse
'pon which my early will would nurse?
I seek my former "me", the younger one
from which the older "me" has run.

Departed is that stronger flame that burned
'til conquered by the sea of life.
Fate's victim for his youth has yearned
while embers cool through years of strife.
So now when tear-flows coldly start
they don't come from my heart,
They originate within my head,
That heart of mine is dead.

ALL ARE SILENT

This poem has to be the saddest, most poignant poem we have ever read. The poet's only son, the "Yingele" (Youngster) of one of his most famous poems, has died at fifteen. Joseph Rosenfeld was a high school student in Yonkers when some Polish-American roughnecks, threw him down a flight of stone steps. His death from complications almost destroyed his father. Rosenfeld, beside himself with grief, could not hold it within himself at all. Possibly the only therapy was to tell the world about it, to get it off his chest. This exquisite little poem asks the world, "Have you not met, wandering somewhere, a young prince calling, "Daddy!"? My son, my first son, has disappeared. Maybe you know where he is?" We could not sustain a dry eye while writing this. He wonders where his son is now, even though he knows the youngster is buried. He asks the stars, "Haven't you even once found a blonde cherub stumbling along searching for his home and his sick Daddy?" Oy vay!

ALLE SHVAYGEN
All Are Silent

Vinden fohn di vayte steppes,
Khivales fohn der groysen yam,
Zohgt! Oyf ayer shtuhrm-vahndern,
Hoht ihr nit begegnet vu
Blohndshandik a yungr melekh,
"Tate!" shrayendik? Mayn kindt!
Mayn ben-yikhid iz farshvuhndn!
Efsher veysst ihr vu ehr iz?

Zohgt! Oyf ayere shtralen veygen,
Himmel's likhtig pihlgrihr,
Troymer fohn di hekhster sfihren,
Shteren! Treft ihr nit a mohl
Klihpendikh cheruhb, a blohndn,

Zuhkhendik tsuhrik zayn heym,
Un a krankn tatens lihbe,
Treft ihr nit a mohl mayn zuhn?

Shneller um di vinden,
Hastig roysht die yam, uhn blaykh,
Mitleydig di shterren kuhkn
Oyf der shtuhmer erd arohb,
Vendt ikh zikh tsuh dem beyss olem,
Dohrt shteyt a kalter shteyn,
Ernst glohtst mihr in pohnm,
Glohtst un shvaygt.

Original Yiddish for this poem is on page 220

ALL ARE SILENT

Winds from the far steppes,
Waves from the great sea,
Speak up! On your storm-wanderings
have you not met somewhere
a young wandering prince
calling, "Daddy!"? My son,
My first-born, has disappeared,
Maybe you know where he is?

Speak up! Perhaps on your sunny paths,
You Heaven's shining travelers,
dreamers of highest spheres,
Stars! Have you not once found
a blond lad stumbling about,
searching for his home
and a sick father's love?
Have you never, even once, seen my son?

The winds race around quicker,
The seas roar angrily and the stars
seem pitifully pale
to the quiet earth below.
I drag wearily to the graveyard
and there stands a cold stone,
steadily staring in my face.
It stares, and it is silent.

EARTH

The death of his son left Rosenfeld permanently obsessed with the feeling of loss. Here, in one of many poems on this subject (we only include a few here) Morris is not acceptant of his tragedy. He hates the earth, he despises that all-inclusive desolator of life and hope, beauty and joy, yet he is afraid to out-and-out curse the dust in his grief. ". . . my only joy, who now is also earth, and no more." Well expressed, but if we are drained by his repetitive sorrow how must he have felt?

ERD
Earth

Fardammte frasserdikke, oh, beyse erd,
Vohs dayn tsuhritste hals shlingt altz arayn,
Un lohzt nohr ihbr lebedig di payn;
Vohs in dayn groyssen boykh vert altz tsushtert,
Un nohr matzseyvos zohgn, vohs duh hohst fartsert,
Farshohltn vohlt ikh dikh, oh duh marshas,
Farfluhkht dayn shtoyb mit veytig un mit khas,
Dohkh vi zohl ikh farshihltn dikh atzindt,
Az in dayn shvartzn boykh ruht mayn kind ?
Farshluhngn hastuh, vey, dem zihssen blik,
In veymes likht es hoht getrohnt mayn glik,
Vohs iz yetzt oykh nit mehr vi erd a shtik.

Original Yiddish for this poem is on page 219

EARTH

Oh, damned, all-consuming evil Earth,
Who snatches all away and casts it into your angry maw!
Who leaves naught behind but pain and awe,
In whose great gut dissolves everything of worth
and only tombstones signify what you have taken. How we are sore!
I would curse you! How you desolate!
I would curse your dust, with your grief and hate!

Yet how can I utter such an attack
when my child rests in your breast so black?
You have taken away, oh, woe! that sweet boy
in whose light has been enthroned my only joy,
who now is also earth, and no more.

GANEYVES
Stealings

Ikh ganveh a shmaykhl fun dayn punim,
Un behalt ihm tihf in hertzen.
Kh'ganveh dem shohten fun dayneh lukken
Un behalt ihm in mayn zeyle.

Kh'ganveh a shtrahl fun dayne oygen,
Ikh behalt ihm in di nehrven,
Ikh ganveh ah tsitter fun dayn buzim,
Un behalt ihm in di gefihlen.

Un fun di dohzigeh ganeyvis verren
Dee flammen fun mayn lihbe.
Ikh trohg dikh in zikh, mayn gelihbte,
Un du bist dokh nit mayne !

Ganevis zihse ! Heylige ganeyvis !
Makht raykh mihr di neshuhme,
Ikh vill aykh tsurik mehr nit ohpgeven,
Ikh nem aykh mit in keyvr!

Original Yiddish for this poem is on page 220

STEALINGS

I steal a smile from thy fair face
    and hide it deep within my heart.
I steal a shadow of thy grace
    and hide it deep within my soul.

I steal a ray from thy bright eyes
    and hide it deep within my mind.
I steal the echo of thy sighs
    and weave it softly in my dreams.

A word from thy sweet lips I steal
  and hide it deep within my thoughts.
I steal the rapture of thy thrill
  and drown it deep within my blood.

And from all these sacred "stealings"
  are born the bright flames of my love.
And the fount of all sweet feelings
  and the stream of my life's joy.

Translated by Henry Greenfield

STEALINGS

Another of Rosenfeld's brief poems, this is an interesting approach for a lovesong. It might have been entitled, "A Kleptomaniac's Romance". The poet steals a smile, a shadow, a ray, an echo, a word and rapture, and together they feed the fires of his ardor. It's a nice effort, and a cute idea, but from this calibre of a poem one does not get famous.

WITH MY CHILD

It is depressing to read so much almost unrelieved sadness. If it is tough to read it for a few hours think how difficult it must have been to live that way. It is almost too much for us to absorb all this gloom and doom. Here Morris takes his boy out for a walk and their poverty is so extreme that even such a nice event becomes a trauma. We have begun to wonder, after working so long on his works, whether Morris didn't lighten up once in a while and actually enjoy his life a bit. His daughters never gave us the impression that he was gloomy. According to relatives whom we contacted he was actually quite charming. A cousin, Lillian Rebold, now well over eighty, recently told us that when she was about eight years old she visited Rosenfeld. He took her on his knee and charmed her with his stories about his home in Poland. That was in about 1920.

MIT MAYN KINDT With My Child
Dohs vetter iz lihblikh, ikh gey mir in gahss,

Mit mir geyt mayn ingele, kranklikh un blass.
Baym veyg oyf a kornr, darzeyt ehr a standt,
Un fangt ohb tzu veynen, un shtellt oyz di handt.
Ehr tziht zikh ahihn, vu es lihgn di frukht,
An apfel, nebekh, vi vohllt ehr farzuhkht !
Es kharesht dohs hehrtzl, es brikht nebekh shihr,
Ehr kuhkt oyf di frukhten mit vey un oyf mir.
Oh, kindt maynes, ikh veys vohs du vilst, vohs dir felt
Dohkh neyn, nit fir unz iz di frukht fon di velt.

Mir gehen zikh vayter, mayn ingele shvakh
Zayt vihdr a fenster mit tzatzkes a zakh.
Ehr kuhkt oyf di glikn mit kindersheyn kheyn
Un kuhkt mir in pohnm tzu veys ikh zayn meyn.
Ehr ploydert, ehr plapelt, ehr veynt un ehr lakht.
Un tziht mihr dehrvayle tzuhm fenster bezakht.
Advihdr shpiltzayg apart lohkt ihm ohn,
Ikh kuhk mit yessorim. oh vohs zoll ikh tohn ?
A tzatzkele, nebbakh, dohs kindt iz gekvelt,
Dohkh neyn, nit fir unz hoht zi tzatzkes di velt.

Nuhn, hohb ikh mit ehrgernis zikh un mit khass,
Farshvehrn mayn kindt nit tzu neymen in gass.
Ehr bayt zikh un shrayt, "Mit dem tatenin geyn!",
Es rirt mikh, dohs antfer, ikh troyrig, Neyn !".
Ikh antfer ihm, "Neyn !" un ikh fihl ikh fargey,
An afele, nebbakh. Gargihrt, vi vey !
Vi bitter un vey iz mir un vi vindt
Tzu zeyen un tzu fihlen dohs tzuhr fon mayn kindt !
Un dohkh mit a kol halb dehrshtikt fon a veyn,
Ihm antforen, "Shah !" Un ihm antforen, "Neyn !"

Original Yiddish for this poem is on page 221

WITH MY CHILD

I go for a walk, it's a beautiful day,
My son walks beside me, he's sickly and gray.
When one of the corner-stands catches his eye
he stretches his hand out and tries not to cry.
He goes where the fruit have all neatly been placed.
An apple, alas! How he longs for a taste.!

His little heart's ready to break, I can see,
With sorrow he looks at the fruit and at me.
Oh, Darling, I know why your hands are stretched forth,
but no, not for us are the fruits of the earth.

We go a bit further, my sick little boy
discovers a window with toy after toy.
He looks at the gifts with the glee of a child
and then his eyes ask if I know why he smiled.
He chirps and he chatters, he laughs and he cries
and pulls me along to admire each prize.
Each charm in the window excites him anew.
With pity I watch him; Oh, what shall I do?
My child sees a toy and his eyes fill with mirth,
but no, not for us are the toys of the earth.

Well, gloomy and bitter I vainly swore to keep him inside and go walking
   no more.
He tugs at me, begs me, "Please, Daddy, let's go!"
It moves me, yet sadly I always say "No!"
I keep saying,"No, son! We're staying inside!"
For each of his tears I've my own tears to hide.
How painful it is for a father, how sad
to see the distress of my own little lad,
And yet, with a voice almost smothered by woe,
to answer, "Be still!" and to keep saying, "No!"

Translated by Aaron Kramer

מיין אינגעלע

———

אַיך האָב אַ קלייגעם אינגעלע,
אַ זוהנעלע גאָר פיין!
ווען איך דערזעה איהם דאַכם זיך מיר,
דיא גאַנצע וועלם איז מיין.

נאָר זעלטען, זעלטען זעה איך איהם,
מיין שעהנעם, ווען ער וואַכם.
איך טרעף איהם אימער שלאָפענדיג,
איך זעה איהם נאָר ביי נאַכם.

דיא אַרבייט טרייבם מיך פריה אַרויס
און לאָזם מיך שפעם צוריק;
אָ, פרעמד איז מיר מיין אייגען לייב!
אָ, פרעמד מיין קינד'ס אַ בליק!

איך קום צוקלעממערהייד אַהיים,
אין פינסטערניש געהילם, —
מיין בלייכע פרוי דערצעהלם מיר באַלד,
וויא פיין דאָם קינד זיך שפיעלם,

וויא זיס עם רעדם, וויא קלוג עם פרעגם:
„אָ, מאַמאַ, גומע מאַ,
ווען קומם און ברענגם אַ פעני מיר
מיין גומער, גומער פאַ ?"

איך הער עם צו און אייל — עם מוז, —
יאָ, יאָ, עם מוז געשעהן!
דיא פאַטערליעבע פלאַקערם אויף:
עם מוז מיין קינד מיך זעהן !.....

איך שטעה ביי זיין נילעגעריל
און זעה, און הער, און שא !
א מרוים בעוועגם דיא ליפעלאך :
„א, וואו איז, וואו איז פא ?"

איך קוש דיא בלויע אייגעלאך,
זיי עפּנ'ן זיך — „א, קינד !"
זיי זעהען מיך, זיי זעהען מיך,
און שליסען זיך געשווינד.

„דא שטעהם דיין פאפא. מהיירערע,
א קענגילע דיר, נא !"
א מרוים בעוועגם דיא ליפעלאך :
„א, וואו איז, וואו איז פא ?"

איך בלייב צרזועהמשגם און צוקלעהמם,
פערבימערם און איך קלעהר :
„ווען דו ערוואכסם א מאהל, מיין קינד,
געפינסטו מיך נים מעהר"......

וועד, אויב ניט דו?

דאָ איז קיין נאַכטיגאַל ניטאָ,
קיין פֿויגעל זיס און ליעב,
נור מאַשינען שווער און גראָב,
זיי קוקען קאַלט און טריב

אויף הימעל און ערד, און וועלט.
זיי זיגנען אייזען, שטאָהל,
דער נגון פֿון לעבען פֿעהלט,
ניטאָ קיין נשמה־קול.

עס הוזשעט, עס פֿיפֿט און עס שרייט,
עס קלאַפּט און רוישט און יאָגט,
מען הערט נור ריידען די צייט....
דער אימפעט טרייבט און שלאָגט.

און וואָלסט דו דאָ אויך ניט זיין,
ווי וואָלט איך הויך געשטערעבט?
ווער וואָלט מיר געשיקט די שיין
וואָס שמאַרקט מיך און בעלעבט.

דער ג'רוזט, וואָס גיעב איך אום איהם?
וואָס צאַרט מיך קאָך און פֿייף?
איך הער דיין געבענשטע שמים
און מיין געזאַנג ווערט רייף.

מיין רוהע פלאמץ

נ
יים זוך מיך, וואו דיא מירטמן גרינען !
געפינסט מיך דארטמן נים, מיין שאמץ ;
וואו לעבענס וועלקען ביי מאשינען,
דארטמן איז מיין רוהע פלאמץ.

זוך מיך, וואו דיא פויגעל זינגען !
געפינסט מיך דארטמן נים, מיין שאמץ ;
א שקלאוו בין איך וואו קייטמן קלינגען,
דארטמן איז מיין רוהע פלאמץ.

זוך מיך, וואו פאנטאנגען שפריטצען !
געפינסט מיך דארטמן נים, מיין שאמץ ;
וואו פרעהרען רינען, צייהנער קריטצען,
דארטמן איז מיין רוהע פלאמץ.

און ליעבסטו מיך מיט וואהרע ליעבע,
מא קום צו מיר, מיין גוטער שאמץ !
און היימער אויף מיין הערץ דיא טריעבע,
און מאך מיר זים מיין רוהע פלאמץ.

ערד

פ
ערדאטטע פרעטטערקע, א. בעזע ערד,
וואס דיין צורייטצטע האלז שלינגט אלץ אריין,
און לאזט נאר איבער לעבעדיג די ביין ;
וואס אין דיין גרויסען בויך וועדם אלץ צושטערם
און נאר מצבות זאגען, וואס דו האסט פערצעהרם ;
פערשאלמען וואלם איך דיך, א. דו מרשעת,
פערפלוכם דיין שמויב מיט וועהמאג און מים כעס,
דאך ווי זאל איך פערשילטמען דיך צצינע,
אז אין דיין שוואַרצען בוזים רוהט מיין קינד ?
פערשלונגען האסטו, ווה, דעם זיסען בליק,
אין וועטטע ליכם עס האם נעמהרטאנע מיין גליק,
וואם איז יעצם אויך נים מעהר ווי ערד א שמיק.

גנבֿת

איך גנבֿ'ע אַ שמייכעל פֿון דיין פּנים
און כ'האַלט איהם טיעף אין האַרצען.
כ'גנבֿ'ע דעם שאַטען פֿון דיינע לאָקען
און כ'האַלט איהם אין מיין זעעלע.

כ'גנבֿ'ע אַ שטראַהל פֿון דיינע אויגען
און כ'האַלט איהם אין די נערוון.
איך גנבֿ'ע אַ ציטער פֿון דיין בוזים
און כ'האַלט איהם אין די געפֿיהלען.

און פֿון די דאָזינע גנבֿת ווערען
די פֿלאַמען פֿון מיין ליעבע.
איך טראָג דיך אין זיך, מיין געליעבטעסטע,
און דו ביזט דאָך נים מיינע.

גנבֿת זיסע! הייליגע גנבֿת!
מאַכט רייך מיר די נשמה!
איך וועל אייך צוריק מעהר נים אָבגעבען,
איך נעהם אייך מים אין קבר.

מים ליעבע

דער גריל קלאַפּט אין פֿעלזען־שטיין.
עס הודשעט דער זשוק אין דער לופֿם.
דאָך איך געה אום איינער אַליין
און זינג פֿון געווויירצינגען דופֿט.

עס האָבען קיין זשוק און קיין גריל נים
קיין ניגון פֿאַר בוים און פֿאַר בלום;
זיי האָבען קיין נייסם, קיין געפֿיהל נים,
און טומלען משוגע אַרום.

איך וואַלם ווי דער גריל דאָ געווען,
אָם ווי דער משוגענער זשוק.
ווען איך וואַלם דאָ דיך נים דערזעהן
און זיך נים געקוויקם מים דיין קוק.

יאָ, דו האַסם מיך גייסטיג נעמאַכם:
מיין האַרץ ווי די זונען־בלומע בליהם,
איך פֿיהל פֿון די פֿעלדער די פֿראַכם,
און זינג זיי מים ליעבע אַ ליעד.

אלע שווייגען

וווּ יעדען פון די ווייסע סטעפעס,
קוואלים פון דעם גרויסען ים,
זאגם! אויף אייער שטורעמזושאנדער,
האָט איהר נים בעגעגענם וואו
בלאָנדזשענדיג א יונגען מלאך,
„מאמע"! שרייענדיג ? מיין קינד!
מיין בן יחיד איז פערשוואונדען!
אפשר ווייסט איהר וואו ער איז ?

זאגם! אויף אייי'רע שטראחלענדוועגען,
הימעל'ם ליכם'גע פילנער איהר,
מרוימער פון די העכסטע ספערען,
שטערען! מרעפם איהר נים א מאל
קליפענדיג א כרוב א בלאנדען,
זוכענדיג צוריק זיין חיים
און א קראנקען מאמענס ליעבע; —
מרעפם איהר נים א מאל מיין זוהן ?

שנעלער ליופען אום די ווינדען,
האסטיג רוישם דער ים און בלייך,
מימליידיג די שטערען קוקען
אויף דער שטומער ערד ארּאָב—
וואנד איך זיך צו דעם בית עולם,
ערטען שטומם א קאלטער שטיין,
ערטּם בלאזם ער מיר אין פנים,
גלאצם און שווייגם...

THE POETRY OF
THOUGHTFULNESS, PHILOSOPHY
AND NATURE

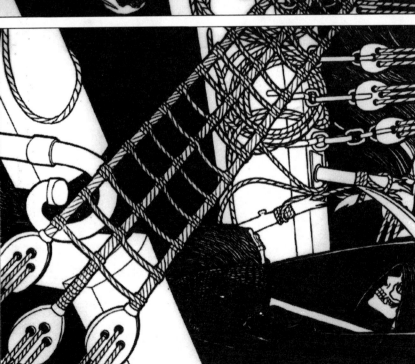

In *Der Sturm* two men wait for death in a dreadful storm while Death itself waits unobserved with its toothy grin and inexorable hold on their lives. This is more than an incipient shipwreck that Rosenfeld describes. It is the ship of life itself coming to another of its heartless conclusions, a universal expression of the absurdity of life. These etchings by Lilien are from Rosenfeld's *Lieder des Ghetto*.

HERBST
(Autumn)

Mit kalte blikken kommt der herbst getzoygen,
Ehr kommt un luhst, un freylikhkayt fargeyen.
Es kommt der toyt fun zayne chemurne oygen
Di lihbe shtarbt mit yeyne zihsse veyen.
Durkh vald un feld tsuklingt es shmertzlikh fraykhen,
Es lesht di zunen. Es brekht dem zuhkh dem shtayfen.
Di lohnke kohrtshel zikh, es glivveren di taykhen,
Der vindt dershrayt zikh, far zayn eygene fayfen.

Der barg shpringt oyf ah naketter, tsushrukken,
Fun shluff geshtert durkh groyligeh illis.
Es nellkt dee letzteh royz in zummer's lohken,
Di luft-kapelyeh geyt avek in golos.
A ven di shtahde hut zikh fray gefittert,
Der pastikh hut gesvishtshet glik in greyden.
Loyft um der herbst mit metushetsh un gevittert,
Un shrayt, un redt, un ver farshteyt zayn redn ?

AUTUMN

This is much more than a competent poem. Rosenfeld's images are nothing less than brilliant. In this brief little poem he says what a prose writer
might express in pages. Morris writes poems about everything; holidays,
seasons, and the artifacts of man and nature. But here he describes in min-
iscule phrases the changes from summer to winter during the Autumn
months when the earth is cooled and a sense of wintry forboding arrives,
when, "the last red rose in summer's tresses fades the winged chorus into
exile goes." Yes, the birds go to a warmer exile as, "the meadow shrivels
and the lake congeals and the wind is frightened by its own delirium . . .
"This, by any standard, is a first-rate poem. This is Morris in elegant
guise. One can sense winter lurking right around the next page in the
calendar. We must also tell you that Max Rosenfeld's translation here is
exceptional.

AUTUMN

Autumn comes in cold and piercing guise,
Autumn comes and life and joy are slain,
Unwelcome death peers from its clouded eyes,
Love perishes, and love's sweet pain.

Its tortured gasping rips through wood and fields,
It splits the oak, extinguishes the sun,
The meadow shrivels and the lake congeals,
The wind is frightened by its own delirium.

The hill leaps up, naked and afraid,
The fearful wails have shattered its repose,
The last red rose in summer's tresses fades,
The winged chorus into Exile goes.

And where the shepherd piped his happy tune
And grazed his flock in peaceful pasture-land,
Autumn, in a frenzied storm of doom
screams, and speaks . . . but who can understand?

Trans. by Max Rosenfeld
Original Yiddish for this poem is on page 265

DER PASRON FUN LEBEN
The Meaning Of Life

Der tuhg iz farshvunden, fun dunkele grunden,
Hub shtil oysgebunden, ihr shvaygen di nakht,
Un shtum un fertrakht, fartihft in ruhnus.
Fun lebens gevaldige, shvere khezshboynes,
In aynzame shtunden vi khshuf gebunden,
Als ikh bin gegesses un hub halb gevakht,
Hut pluhtzling mayn likht zikh alleyn ohngetsunden.

Un ikh hub ah hand in der luften derzehen . . .
Zi hut ah papihr mit fihr zihglen fermakht.
Derlangt mir un mehr iz ihr shpur nit geveyn.
A shtimme nor hub ikh fernummen gantz zakht.
"Ikh hub dir dem pasron gebrakht.
Dem pasron fun leben, di var alte frage,

Di eybige retenish, eybige flage
Vohs mattert di mensh-hayt azah lange tsayt.
Atsind, zollstu vissen vus leben bedayt,
Nitmehr zollstdu griblen un finsternis flihglen,
Doh hohstu dem emes, nu, effen di zieglen!"

Dem pasron fun leben, vus toyzende shtreben,
Zayn entfer tsu geben, dohs hub ikh atsind—
Ikh, erden-kindhohb dohs skhie tsu vissen,
Dem sohd vos hoht velten mit moykhes tsurissen,
Dem tsihl fun dem kumer, dem tsihl fun fershveggen,

Dem tsvik fun dem zayn doh, fun layd un fun payn doh,
Nokh velkhen mir forshen un blayben als blind!
Ah sohf tsu di nahrishe sirutsim vohs veben,
In kup nohr ah tummel fun roykh un fun vindt,
Oh gelikhes shtimme! Vi hohb ikh fardinnt?

Oh, ganohd! Vohs vet endlikh mayn tsukunft fergessen.
Un oht brekht ah zihgl! Ah tsveyter! Ah dritter!
Dohkh vus zoll bedeyten mayn innigster tsitter ?
Gelest mir ihr verren, der retzel geshvindt.
Den eybige tsveyel iz veytig un zind!
Un ikh hub tsubrokhen di zihglen—un—vohs?!
Ah blanke papihr, keyn eyn eyntsiger mohs!!

Transliterated by Rifke Levine with EJG

LIFE'S PURPOSE

In a sinister moment the Muse hands Morris an envelope as in the Academy Awards and says, in a tremulous voice, "You'll find in this paper the purpose of life!" The poet builds up the tension and the expectation that this little tailor from the East Side Ghetto, this emotional refugee from a shtetl in Poland, will tell us the purpose of life. After opening the three seals.. "a blank piece of paper and not a word to me!" If neither the Muse nor the poet know the answer why should we? As a matter of fact, if Morris had been a philosopher or a cleric he would have been slipped the same piece of blank paper. Perhaps life does mean nothing, but there is a blank piece of paper at the end of this book where one may write in the answer one's self, if one likes. Sorry.

LIFE'S PURPOSE

The day is gone.
From dark corners, stealthily,
the night unbinds in silence,
as if shrouded in demure quiet
with thoughts incomprehensible,
bewitched and perplexed,
to solve some problems,
to shed some burdens

E'er the dawn comes anew.
In such a sinister moment
a sealed envelope sways before me
and a tremulous voice says,
"You'll find in this paper
the PURPOSE OF LIFE!
Just open the seals. . . ."
The hand disappears.

Oh! Mysterious voice, why choose me
to get such treasure, sought by so many?
I, poor mortal, to know the answer
which has perplexed the geniuses of the world?

The purpose of our coming, our goal to find,
our spirit immortal, of which we are blind?
Oh! Angelic voice, you find me worthy
to discover the reason for my suffering and pain,
the salvation that will brighten my domain!

In agony I break the one seal, a second and a third—
But what is the meaning of my trembling so fiercely?
The envelope is now open and oh! What do I see?
A blank piece of paper and not a word to me.

Translator unknown to us. It was "improved" somewhat by EJG because some of the words we tried to read on an old, yellowed page were almost illegible.

AUTUMN LEAVES

Rosenfeld wrote several poems about autumn leaves and about the season, autumn. Many philosohers have used autumn as an allegory for the next to the final stage of life. Morris was an unquivical lover of nature since his years as a boy in the countryside of Russian-Poland. There was no affectation here. He used natural phenomena as allegories in many poems: he was a ghetto tree, his birds sing of freedom, he himself is a leaf about to fall, his setting sun bears the running blood of a dying day and so on. That is what poets are supposed to do. His nature poems are frequently deceptively simple, and sometimes utterly simple. Here the allegory is his own life superimposed on the world of nature. Did you notice how rarely he uses classical references in his nature poems? Possibly his readings in the classics, untutored by any "professors", did not work their way into his subconscious except for those which had a direct bearing on Jewish history.

You must have enjoyed the language of this poem. "My spirit calls unanswered calls . . ." This sets the scenario for fear and insecurity. Autumn is the season that intimates the chill and the storms of winter. It takes a first-rate imagination to set the stage for a cold winter in the minds of people in any season, even three-quarters of a century later.

HERBST BLETLAKH
Autumn Leaves

(Only sec's I, II,VI here)

I

Eynzam zitz ikh vi gefangen,
Fun ah veltzammen gefihl,
Eppes hub ikh eyn farlangen,
Dokh ikh veys nit vuhs ikh vill,
Zaynen freyden, zaynen leyden,
Ergetz vu fihr mihr bashtellt ?
Krank iz eyner fun uns beyden,
Zugt: Bin ikh es, tsu di velt?

Shtunden kumen un ferinnen,
Nayhe—naye kumen tsu,
Dokh keyn eyner brengt mayn zinnen,
Un am,ayn kranken buhzm ruh.
Veynen muz ikh, kennen redden,
Kennit vissen vohs mir fehlt,
Krank iz eyner fun uns beyder,
Zugt: bin ikh es, tsu di velt ?

II

Ikh lihb dem vindt, ikh lihb dem yam,
Den vi dem ershten bin ikh eylend,
Un vi der tsveyten roysht mayn hertz.
Ikh lihb di volken, lihb di nakht,
Den vi di ershten ken ikh veynen,
Un vi di tsveyten iz mayn velt.

VI

Der veg iz vayt, der tuhg iz kurtz,
Di zun zinkt bald arunter,
Dos vasser roysht, tsum breg iz vayt,
Mayn shif, mayn shif geht unter.
Doh helft es mehr keyn ranglen zikh,
Der vindt iz ah gezunter,
Der yam iz groyss, der yam iz vild,
Mayn shif, mayn shif geyt unter.

Oh zay gezunt, du sheyne zuhn,
Du sheynst nokh vihder munter.
Mokh ikh bikhvalyas royshen shrek,
Mayn shif, mayn shif geht unter.

Transliterated by Rifke Levine
Original Yiddish for this poem in on page 255

AUTUMN LEAVES

Alone, I sit as summer falls,
with feelings strange, unknown.
My spirit calls un-answered calls—
a fear within has grown.
My share of troubles and of luck
must have somehow gone awry.
One of us has gotten sick—
Is it the world? Or I?

Time's persistent flow I find
Destroys the hours without surcease.
Yet none affords my aching mind
and heart a moment's peace.
Weep I must, I cannot speak.
What I lack I can't deny.
I know that one of us is sick—
Is it the world? Or I?

DER ADLER
The Eagle

Ven di rizenvelken yohren
Oyben un dem hekhster ohrt
Shvebt der kayzer fun di foygel
Fliht der groysser adler dohrt.
Mit di shtarke fliggl fohkht ehr
In der luften un ehr fliht,
Elender, ah huhtz di himmlen
Hehrt ehr keyn khaverim nit.

Vert ehr mihd fun shvereh reyzen
Ruhet ehr eynzam un alleyn
Bay dem zoym fun tihfeh vassern,
oyf ah hoykhen barg fun shteyn.
Mit ferakhtung kuhkt ehr unter,
Shohkendig zayn shmoltzen kohp.
Ohft nohr, ven ihm tsvingt der huhnger
Lohzt ehr zikh mit vey ahrub.

THE EAGLE

The gigantic clouds are roaming,
   Where the thunder wildly roars,
There the king of all the feathered,
   The majestic eagle soars.
With his mighty wings aflutter,
   All alone, he flies above
Has no comrades, knows no friendship,
   God's free sky his only love.

And when tired of ever flying,
   He reposes all alone
On the banks of deep swift waters,
   Or a lofty cliff of stone.
He surveys the vale below him,
   Shakes his head with cold disdain,
Only oft—by hunger prompted—
   He descends with gnawing pain.

Translated by L. Trommer
Original Yiddish for this poem is on page 257

THE EAGLE

We tend to let first impressions affect us. But this is not simply an eagle that Rosenfeld talks about. Even though at first glance it is a pleasant but pedestrian poem, we know it is far from that. Of course most eagles would have chortled at the little Yiddle in his workshop trying to describe the power, the majesty, the cold existential life of this great bird. Rosenfeld does a commendable job of appreciating that this creature is lonely, cold and sometimes hungry. But is that cold, lonely, hungry existential creature not the poet himself swooping down when pangs of hunger grip him? Does the poet not soar with beauty and power, grasping with his claws onto a high promontory to view the world below him; to study and concentrate, with objective eyes, on the mountains and plains of our existence and then, with passion and keenness plunge down to make his direct hit on the subject that interests him most at that time?

You know, in this book Rosenfeld has been a lion, an eagle, a ghetto tree, a canary, a bird in the desert and many more alter-egos who view the world, describe it for us, offer commentaries that either solve problems or simply cause us the pain of recognition of the sometimes intractable aspects of human life. Morris was not a simple man. Actually, we need observers and philosophers of his character now, more than ever, because our problems have become indurated. A brave, perceptive troubador would help us understand our world better.

WANT AND THE POET

Translator unknown, but it is Victorian in age and the translator could be Helena Frank and Rose Pastor Stokes. It is just as professional and full of understanding as it can be. There is something akin here to Poe's "Raven", but it is "want" who comes to his door, not a mysterious black bird. "I love thy black and curling hair" is the paragon of evil speaking directly to Morris. This is a fine poem in terms of tone, purpose, intensity, rhyme and meter. This is not a simple poem, for it shows the personal relationship of the poet to the evil angel whom he has known so well for so long. He knows how "I love to swallow thy tears and all thy songs to follow!"

DER NUHT UN DER DIKHTER
Want And The Poet

(*The First Stanza*)
Hay! Hay! Vehr vel es dohrt probihren
Mit gevalt tsu uffnen mayne tihren?
Vehr kumt es dohrt mayn ruh tsu shterren?
Du nuht? Ikh hehr, ikh ken es shverren.
Ah, duhs iz zi, Oh du megeyfeh!
Avek! Du alteh makhsheyfeh!
Vohs zuhkhst du doh in guttes tsoris?
Avek tsu ahll di shvartzeh yohren!
(*Next to last stanza*)
Avek du cringeren fun trehren!
Kh'hub fraynd berimteh, millyunehren
Zey vellen shtendig mayne zohrgen,
Ikh zull nit leyden, zull nit bohrgen,
Ikh zull nit shvartzen mehr mayn punim,
Tsu kvikn mayne dume sohnim,
Vuhs velten mikh in keyvr bringen.
(*Last stanza*)
"Dertzeyl mir nit fun millyunehren,
Zey vellen dikh gevis fergessen.
Zey hubbn anderer interesten.
Dervayl bistu zeyer shpilkhul:
Dukh bald dreyt ibber ziklh dos milkhel,
Tsuribben vert dayn gantze freyde
Un mir farblaybn endlikh beyde!"

Original Yiddish for this poem is on page 258

WANT AND THE POET

Who's there! Who's there! Who was it tried
to force the entrance I've denied?
And 'twere a friend, I'd gladly borne it.
But no—'twas want! I could have sworn it!
I heard thy voice, old witch! I know thee!
Avaunt, thou evil hag! Beshrew thee!
God's curse! Why seekest thou to find me?
Away, to all black years behind me!

To torture me was thine endeavor,
My body from my soul to sever,
Of pride and courage to deprive me
And into beggary to drive me.
Begone! where thousand devils burn!
Begone! nor evermore return!
Begone! most wretched one of creatures
and hide for aye thine hateful features!

"Beloved, ope' the door in pity!
No friend have I in all the city
Save thee. Then open to my call!
The night is bleak, the snowflakes fall,
Ah, what delight, willt thou receive me?
I found, when I from thee had parted,
No friend but he was fickle-hearted!"

Away, old hag! Thou liest so,
Thou harbinger of pain and woe!
Away— am I thine only friend?
Thy lovers pale, they have no end!
Thou vile one, may the devil take thee!
Begone, and no more visits make me!
"'Tis true! Yet those must wait my leisure.
To be with thee is now my pleasure.
I love thy black and curling hair,
I love thy wounded heart's despair,
I love thy sighs, I love to swallow
Thy tears and all thy songs to follow.
Oh great indeed, might I but show it,
My love for thee, my pale-faced poet!

Translator unknown—it sounds Victorian

A DREAM

For some reason, though this is one of Rosenfeld's best poems, it was not
included in any anthology we have seen. Perhaps the publishers were short
of space, but we find this a first-rate poem. It has rhyme and meter, allegories galore, and a ringing defense of Freedom, as though Freedom were a
living entity itself. The point of view is that of a friendly observer who
then becomes a champion of the victim. "Come, let in the light! Arise,
you have the might! Set Freedom free!"

AH TROYM
(A Dream)

Ven alts iz shtil arum
Vi oysgeshtorben shtum,
Keyn shokh, keyn pips, keyn riuhr,
In tihfkayt fun der nakht,
Vi durkh ah tsoybermakht
Bayvayst tzi zikh far mir.

A blondeh, sheyneh vayb,
Vi shney iz veys yihr layb,
Nohr blass di bekken, blass—
Di shulter fest un klohr
Fartsihrt mit goldne hohr,
Nohr nass di oygen, nass.

Zi kukt mikh ohn un shvaygt,
Heybt oyf di hendt un tsaygt,
Es hengt ah keyt arup,
Ikh fihl, ikh veys yihr meyn
Un endlikh mit geveyn.
Farlangt zi, "Shliss mikh op!":

Mayn hertz vert heyss, tsugliht,
Ikh loyf mit shnelle trit
Un khap zikh tsu der keyt
Oh vi ikh fall tsurik!
Oh shlang—ih lang, ih dik
Iz dort arum gedreyt!

(last three stanzas)
Ikh shray, ikh vek, ikh shtrohf,
Ikh hehr ah kropheray,
"oh hebt zikh, hebt zikh shnell!
Un zoll es vehren hel,
Kumt makht di frayhayt fray!"
Es shvaygt! Nor Ikh alleyn

Tsuplatz—nor vek ah shteyn!
Es rihrt zikh nit fun flek,
Oh, ruf zey, "Yoh tsu nit?"
Es heybt zikh nit ah trit,
Es nemt keyn zohf, keyn ek.
Dohkh ver ken zeyn dohs bild

Un zol nit verren vild?
Ah sohf zoll zayn, ah sohf!
Ikh varf zikh in gefahr,
Doh shrayt es, "Vilder nahr!"
Ikh khop zikh oyf fun shlohf!

Transliteration by Rifke Levine and EJG

A DREAM

When night and silence deep
hold all the world in sleep
as though Death claimed the hour,
by some strange witchery
her form appears to me,
as though Magic were her dower.

Her beauty, heaven's light,
her bosom, snowy white,
but pale her cheek appears.
Her shoulders firm and fair
a mass of gold, her hair;
her eyes, the home of tears.

She looks at me, nor speaks,
Her arms are raised; she seeks
her fettered hands to show.
On both white arms a chain,
she cries and pleads in pain:
Unbind me! Let me go!

I burn with bitter ire,
I leap in wild desire
the cruel bonds to break.
But, God! Around the chain
is coiled, and coiled again
a long and loathsome snake!

I shout, I cry, I chide!
My voice goes far and wide,
a ringing call to Man:
"Oh come, let in the light!
Arise! You have the might!
Set Freedom free again!"

Alas! None came to her release;
and hope for her is none!
Now up! For Freedom's sake!"
I spring to take her part:
"Fool!" cries a voice. I start,
and in anguish I awake.

Translator unknown to us

THE PHANTOM VESSEL

The sensitive soul recognizes his youth as it flies from him on a phantom vessel—Time. The ship of life is indeed a lonely vessel. Its destination and its schedule will always remain a mystery. It takes a poet of Rosenfeld's calibre to describe the evening sky and note "the footprints of a dying day." The colorful array of sunlit clouds are "bloodstained banners, torn and battered . . ." He might have described the evening sky as a display of nature's talent with a luminescent brush of the sun's rays, but he thinks of bloodstains, tatters and tears, "with parched and burning edges." There is just a single reference to God and none to classical illustrations.

Morris finds in his own life and his own observations a universal theme—aging, dying, vanishing to an unknown clime amidst a beautiful display of Nature in a universe that will forever be renewed, whether he is around to observe it or not. This bitter-sweet point of view is akin to Heine, only it is more intense and more personal.

DER VANDERSHIF
The Phantom Vessel

(First three stanzas)
Shoyn di letzten zunnenshtrahlen
Shtaygen oyf di shpitzen boymen,
Un di grohe abendshattens
Veben zikh arum der erd.

Oyf der shpitz fun yene berger
Iz nohkh fun der vaytens meglikh,
Tsu derkenen royte shpuhren
Fun der zunen di letzte trit.

Lange blutig-royte pahsen
Hengn dohrt in merb-vinkel
Tunken ohp di haysse bregen
In dem kalten ohkean.

(Last four stanzas)
Busset di shif, men zeyt keyn manshahft,
Nohr ah kind ehr shteyt gebrokhen,
Neben mahst boym un ehr yohmert
Mit ah bitteren gefihl.

Langeh gohld gekroytzeh lohken
Kayklen zikh oyf zayne shulter,
Ziftzendik fun hinten kuhkt ehr
Un di shtille shif zi fliht !

Mit ah zilber-vayseh tikhel
Velkhe flahtehrt in der luften,
Glist der sheyner mihr fun vayten,
Ehr gezenent zikh mit mihr.

Un mayn hertz fangt ohn tsu klohpen,
Eppes veynt zikh—zohgt, vus iz dohs ?
Yenes sheyneh kind—ikh ken ihm—
Gohtt ! Mayn yugend fliht es dohrt !

Original Yiddish for this poem is on page 260

THE PHANTOM VESSEL

Now the last long rays of sunset
to the tree-tops are ascending,
and the ash-gray evening shadows
weave themselves around the earth.

On the crest of yonder mountain
now are seen, from out the distance,
slowly fading crimson traces;
footprints of the dying day

Blood-stained banners, torn and tattered,
hanging on the western corner,
dip their parched and burning edges
in the cooling ocean wave.

Smoothly roll the crystal wavelets
through the dusky veils of twilight
that are trembling down from heaven
o'er the bosom of the sea.

As by magic moves the rudder.
Borne upon her shiny pinions
flies a ship, as though a spirit
drove her onward at its will.

Empty is she and deserted.
Only close behind the mainmast
stands a lonely child, heartbroken,
sobbing loudly and bitterly.

Long and golden curls are falling
down his neck and o'er his shoulders.
Now he glances backward, sighing,
and the silent ship flies on!

With a little, shining kerchief
fluttering upon the breeze,
unto me he sends a greeting,
from afar he waves farewell.

And my heart is throbbing wildly.
I am weeping, tell me wherefore?
God ! That lovely child, I know him
'Tis my youth that flies from me!

Translated by Rose Pastor Stokes

THE CANARY

Rosenfeld had a canary, we remember that. He might have stared at that bird long and hard to be able to detect changes in his mood. After all, that bird was in captivity, which might have affected his song. To paraphrase Rosenfeld's poem, "IF", "If birds were not imprisoned what would their carols be? Would joys of freedom savored inspire their melody?" But simple as this poem is let us look at it from another point of view. Is he really singing about a canary? Is this an allegory for mankind or the eternal Jew in some form of bondage? Does the poem then produce a different appreciation? Just recently (May, 1993), we found, among Leon Goldenthal's papers, a note about this poem. It said that Rosenfeld used to recite or sing this poem wherever he went. Ah then, it is not really a canary, is it?

DER KANARIK
The Canary

Es trillert der kanarik
in frayen valdt alleyn;
Ver kan zayn simkha fihlen ?
Ver kan zayn freyd farshteyn ?
Es trillert der kanarik
In raykhtsten palast sheyn;
Ver kan zayn veytig fihlen ?
Ver kan zayn shmertz farshteyn ?

Original Yiddish for this poem is on page 257

THE CANARY

Alone, a fair canary
is trilling in a tree—
Oh, who can feel his gladness
or understand his glee?
A fair canary, trilling,
Is heard 'midst riches rare—
Oh, who can feel his sadness
Or know his deep despair?

Translated by Max Rosenfeld

THE CHRISTMAS TREE

Rosenfeld pulls no punches when he swings. He looks at the Christmas tree, so beautiful that it sparkles with the inner green of life. It blooms when all about are winter-dead. But he shudders. He thinks the tree is red. "Yes, red and wet with blood . . . I see hatred, envy, scorn. The love of Christ is what I see!" Oh yes, the greatest irony of all is that the religion based on the man of love and gentleness has but reflected all the basest instincts of mankind to survive as an institution, while Christ's love is but a tool. Does Rosenfeld speak the truth, or does history lie?

DER VYNACHTSBOYM
The Christmas Tree

Es lihgt a sheyne troym
In grihnm Vynakhtsboym:
Ehr grihnt ven altz iz toyt.
Ikh shtey un kuhk ihm ohn,
un muhz a tzitr tohn.
Mir dakh az ehr iz royt !

Yoh, royt un nahs fon bluht.
Ikh zey in ihm di ruht,
Vohs hakt mayn leyb uhmzihst.
Ikh zey in ihm dem khass—
Di lihbe fon dem Krist.

Original Yiddish for this poem is on page 261

THE CHRISTMAS TREE

There is a lovely fantasy
about the greening Christmas tree:
he blooms when all about are dead!
When I gaze at him I quake,
My mind implies it's a mistake;
It seems to me he's red!

Yes, red and wet with blood is he,
I see the rod of misery
which drives me to futility,
I see hatred in each arm,
The envy, scorn and urge to harm
The love of Christ is what I see.

THE ILLEGITIMATE CHILD

The next is an unusual poem devoted to the pain and suffering of a "mom-ser", an illegitimate child, who is baffled and hurt by his outcast state. He is unprotected except by his mother, "a weak woman who loves me. . . . Why don't I say kaddish (the prayer for the dead) for my Daddy?" A prayer for the dead for someone not dead? This is a strange topic to write about but appropriate.

DER MOMSER
The Illegitimate Child

Di khaydr kindter villen zikh mit mir nit shpihln,
Der rebbi shtakt mikh duhrkh mit zayn blikn,
Nit doh fir mir keyn hartz mit menshlikhe gefihln,
Di beste vohlten geren mikh darshtikn.

Fon kiduhsh-bekher vu di kinder alle zuhpn,
Yohgt mikh mit vilde chas avec der shammos,
Kh'hays, "Momser". Tohr rum arum kodesh zikh nit shtupn,
Farshalten zaynen mayne d'amos.

Der khazen trohgt tzum "Layenen" di seyfr toyrah,
Un yeydr eynr kuhst ihr mit a kduhshah,
Ikh shtel di lippen oyz, man kuhkt oyf mir, a moyrah!
Ikh kehr zikh ohp mit veytik un mit uhshah.

Ikh trakht un trakht, un kan mayn khet zikh nit erklehren;
Vohs heysst: A momser? Zohgt: Fihr vohs mir plohgn?
Un frag ikh es mayn muhtr, veynt zi bittre trehren,
Zi kuhsht mikh heyss un vil es mir nit zohgen.

Fihr and're kinder hoht a tate vohs tsuh zohgn,
Un fihr a yussem shtelt zikh yeydr eynr,
Nohr bin ikh hafkr, vi a blat fohn vindt getrohgn,
A khuhtz eyn shvakhe froy, oy, lihbt mikh keyner!

Un vu iz dohch mayn tate ehrgetz hingekumn?
Nishtoh keyn siruhtz fihr dem na vneyd'n?
Iz ehr avek, hoht ihm der himmel tzuhgenumn?
Farvohs zohg ikh keyn kaddish nohkh mayn tate?

Nohr frag ikh dem vindt. Dih velt iz shuhom tzuh mayne shmertzen,
Ikh hehr keyn antfer, hehr keyn eynem reyden,
Dem emes nohr farneym ikh tihf bay mir ihn hehrtzen;
Bin uhnshuhldig un leyd uhmzihste leyden.

THE ILLEGITIMATE CHILD

The school-kids will not play with me,
The teacher stabs me with his glance,
There are no human feelings towards me,
They'd kill me if they had the chance.

The deacon drives me from the holy cup
which all the children taste.
A "bastard" can't approach the Ark,
A curse has me embraced.

The cantor shows the Torah,
with veneration kissed.
My lips are out . . . they shame me!
I'm scandalous! I'm hissed!

I concentrate and wonder why all this hostility,
What do they mean, "a bastard"? Why do they harass me?
And when I ask my mother she pours out bitter tears,
She kisses me so warmly but doesn't ease my fears

Other children have a Dad, can open up their hearts,
When something happens orphans are protected by us all,
Only I am like a stray, a dog from other parts,
Except by one weak woman, I get no love at all.

So where in all this universe has my Daddy gone?
For an outcast there's no answer. I'm lonely and forlorn.
Is he dead? Has Heaven taken him and carried him away?
Why shouldn't I say kaddish for my Daddy ev'ry day?

I ask the world for answers. It's silent to my pain.
There are no decent answers. I'm questioning in vain.
I only guess the truth somehow, but still don't comprehend.
I'm guiltless and suffer torment that simply will not end.

Original Yiddish for this poem is on page 262

DER IHD TZUM KRISTUS
The Jew To Christ

Tzuhm Krist geneyglt mit a bleykhm pohnim,
Mit vildn shmertz in di gekvalte glihder,
Betrakhtsu dayn unehrbarmigen shonim,
Vohs ruhfn zikh mit uhnrekht dayn brihder.
Di ruhfst duhrkh tihfn ohmr, payn un kvahlen:
"Mayn Goht, Mayn Goht, vohs hastu mikh farlohzn?"
Dohkh dan gebeyt vert mit dem vindt farblohzen
Un dayne trupns bluht tsuhm bodn fahlen;
Tsum kaltn bodn, fon dayn guhf dem reynm!

Es lohben zikh di payniger un freyen
Mit dayne ihbermenshlikh bitt're veyen,
Un shpoht farneymstu nohr, keyn treyst fon keynm,
Kh'kuhk troy'rig dikh ohn un kuhk oyf zikh,
Man zohgt dohs bistu, dohkh dohs bin ikh!

THE JEW TO CHRIST

Oh, Christ, white-faced and with wild pain nailed
up by your twisted limbs beneath the sky,
Can you contemplate those enemies you wrongly hailed
as brothers, who mercilessly let you die?
You call through lament, torture and agony,
"Oh God! Oh God! Why has thou forsaken me?
Your prayer is blowing in the wind, which dulls the sound,
and your noble blood drips in silence to the ground,
from your shining body to the cold and hungry earth.
Your executioners revel in your pain, their mirth
knows no bounds. No pity do you get, only scorn,
and you shall hang there, bled to death until morn.
I look upon you sadly and wonder what I see.
They say that it is you, but still I know it's me!

Original Yiddish for this poem is on page 263

THE JEW TO CHRIST

Here Rosenfeld superimposes the dying, tortured Christ with the tortured
dying Jews of history, where the executioners rejoice in his pain and he
gets scorn, not pity from everyone. Talk about telling it straight! In four-
teen lines, the length of a Shakespearean sonnet, a man summarizes the
historical sickness of anti-Jewishness and says, for his people, "Oh, my
God! Why have you forsaken me?!' You want him to smile and rub his
hands obsequiouly, like Donald Meek, when he looks at a cross with
Christ upon it? Not Morris!

CHRISTMAS BELLS

"Ring out you Christmas bells. Tell heaven and earth how many times you
have frightened the world and awakened the sword . . . Oh, woe! how the
world has sinned when it has heard your clanging!" One cannot be a Jew
from the oppressive Europe and feel any other way but this. Such fear and
disquietude never leaves your psyche. This is America but Morris remembers how churchbells would signal the start of a pogrom. When, indeed,
will civilization begin? (In this analysis we have quoted from a translation
by Aaron Kramer)

VAYNAKHTS-GLOHKN
Christmas Bells

Kling oyz, kling oyz ihr Vynakhts- glohkn!
Zohg ohn di himmel un di erd,
Fihle mohl ihr hoht di velt geshrohkn,
Fihle mohl ihr hoht bevekt dem shverd!

Kling oyz, un zohlen alle shteren
Behalten zeyer zihsen prakht!
Zohlt di lavohne duhnkl verren
Un nit belikhten ohp di nakht!

Den finsternis hoht ihr farkindigt
Zayt yohren un zayt doros lang.
Oh vey, vi hoht di velt gezindigt,
Dohs zi muhz hehren ayer klahng!

CHRISTMAS BELLS

Ring out, ring out, you Christmas bells,
Your guilt to Heav'n and Earth it tells!
How many times you've the world scared,
How many times the sword you've bared!

Ring out that all the stars should hide
their splendor, and the moon beside
should darkened be and not light
up the night until eternity!

The black impulses you inflamed
for all those generations still unnamed
have roused the world to scorn and sin
when your harsh klangings there begin!

Original Yiddish for this poem is on page 263

WOMEN'S SUFFRAGE

How many other poets living a hundred years ago do you know about who were vocal about women's rights? He felt that women had an innate right to speak up and to vote. This man was 'way ahead of his time! Incidentally, if this translation sounds a little clumsy it is because some of his idiomatic expressions are not translateable accurately. For instance, the last line of stanza one, if exactly translated, would read, "When we fall off the world!" This poem has more impact in Yiddish but it is still not a great poem. It says all the right things but misses on the artistic side.

FROYEN SHTIMREKHT
Women's Suffrage

Git yihr shtimrekht, git es gern !
Lohst di froye nit zayn gekvohlt
Den yihr shtim iz vus mihr herren
Ven mihr fallen oyf di velt.

Oh, yihr shtim iz vohs begust uhns
Durkh dem lebens vayben gang,
Un derkvikt uhns un fergihst uhns
Yeder vey vi ah gezang.

Lohst di mutter un di shvester
Helfen fihren uhns dus land,
Den dus iz der vuhnsh der greste
Un der mensh-hayt's hekhster shtand !

WOMEN'S SUFFRAGE

Grant her the right to speak!
Grant it with good cheer
Should not the woman revel also,
knowing her voice is what we hear
from birth 'til from this earth we go?

Ah, her voice brings pride to us,
as through life's journey so long
she delights and sweetens thus
and softens each pain like a song.

Allow this sister and this mother
to help lead us in this land,
toward that wish, greater than any other,
that is Mankind's highest stand.

Original Yiddish for this poem is on page 187

IN DER MIDBAR
In The Desert

Es shteyt in vayten midbar
Ah foygele alleyn
Un kuhkt zikh um faruhmert
Un zingt a lihhdl sheyn.

Zayn himmel-zisse shtimme,
Vi reynste gingeldt flihst,
Un vekt di shtille toytkayt,
Di steppe leyr un vihst.

Ehr vekt di toyte himmeln
Di shtuhme steppe's aruhm,
Dohkh blayben toyt di toyte,
Di shtuhme blayben shtuhm.

Fihr veymen, zisse zinger,
Zohg, klingt dayn heller tohn ?
Vehr hehrt dikh un vehr fihlt dikh,
Un veymn gaystuh ohn ?

Duh magst dayn gantze zeyle
Arayntohn in dayn lihd,
In dem farlohrn'm midbar
Keyn hehrtz darvekstuh nit.
Nisht lang vestuh doh zingen,
Ikh fell es, ikh farshtey;
Dayn hehrtz vet gihkh tzuhshpringen
Far eylendt un far vey.
Uhmzihst iz vohs duh flayst zikh,
Dohs vet nit helfen, neyn !
Alleyn bistu gekumn,
Un vestu alleyn fargeyn.

IN THE DESERT

Alone in the far-off desert
  there stands a little bird
Who to himself sings sadly
  the fairest music heard.
His heavenly sweet singing
  flows like purest gold
to wake the quiet deadness,
  the prairies bare and cold.

He tries to wake dark heavens
  and silent steppes all 'round,
The dead stay dead, the silent
  stay dead, without a sound.
Say, for whom sweet singer
  your sprightly warbles ring?
Who listens there and feels you,
  for whom is it you sing?

You fill your song with all your soul
  to 'rouse this lifeless waste,
There is no heart to wake or stir,
  your efforts are misplaced.
You will not keep on singing long,
  I sense. I understand.
You're wasted on the desert air,
  You're singing to the sand.

Your heart will break, you sing in vain
  and naught can help you, no.
All alone it is you've come
  and all alone you'll go.

Original Yiddish for this poem is on page 264

IN THE DESERT

Naturally he's not talking about a bird singing all alone in the desert. This is another allegory. It is himself, the poet, the singer of social songs that are not always what people want to hear at that moment in time. In this dry and uncaring world he sympathizes with himself by saying, "You're wasted on the desert air, you're singing to the sand . . ." Poor Morris Jacob Rosenfeld! But he used many ploys to get attention. One of them was to castigate an inattentive audience. "Your efforts are misplaced." might have been a way of irritating his editor to a more responsive attitude. He knew what he was doing.

IN DER MIDBAR S'IS A LIGN
(It's A Lie!)

(A folklorized version of a poem, Fata Morgana, by Rosenfeld)
In Sahara, vu men vandert
in der haysen midbar-zamd,
treft ah mol du verst farvundert
zeendik's s'bavynte land—

Shepsen pashen oyf der lanke,
Undem pastech zestu koym
un dir ducht zich, as iz emes
az du zest es nit in troym .

Azoy oych treft in lebn,
refst ah mol ah milden blik,
heybst on boyen goldene shlese,
verst farkisheft funem glik

(Refrain) S'iz ah lign ! S'iz ah lign !
S'iz ah puster troym !
Der midbar hut kayn feld,
kayn zangen un kayn boym!
Transliterator unknown to us

Original Yiddish for this poem is on page 265

MIRAGE

Now here is a lovesong with a reverse twist. Like a mirage in the desert his love's promise is a delusion—a figment of his imagination. This is a delightful poem to read after all those heavy works we have been reading here. He admits that the course of true love may not always be easy. . . .or even what it seems to be. But is this another of his allegories, of a mirage that always entices the dispersed Jews in the desert of the world? In every generation a bright hope arises; of honorable, fair treatment, and as the heart swells and the eyes brighten and the pulse pounds, as in love's delusion, so we learn that it is all a lie! There is no oasis, there is only the cruel sand. It is just a mirage. Hopefully the Arabs and the rest of the world will allow the present oasis to materialize. But we know better. "S'iz ah lign!"

MIRAGE
(It's A lie)

A straggler in the barrens
of the hot Sahara sand
will suddenly be startled
by the sight of verdant land.

The trees are always fruitful
and the gardens always green,
the towers all of marble
and the water blue-marine.

The lambs frisk in the meadow
and the shepherd plays his fife,
and everything is in its place
just as in real life.

Just so, I am bewitched
by the promise in your glance
and my eager eyes see visions
of enravishing romance.

But your promise is delusion
and my wretched heart is torn
as you leave me in my wilderness,
wandering and forlorn.

(Refrain)
But Oh! It lies! It Lies!
There's nothing there to see!
It's one of Nature's tricks,
A dazzling fantasy!

Translation by Max Rosenfeld

THE CREATION OF MAN

We have to give Rosenfeld credit: he never ran out of ideas. In this poem
the Lord is going to put a poet in his Heavenly Senate! That's a pretty
good thought. Anyone in mind? What surprises us is the modernity of
his wild concepts. That idea of the Chairman of the Board wanting *you*,
particularly, to be on his Board because of your special qualities could be
on TV at any time. With a man like Woody Allen or Robin Williams it
could be quite a comedy. The two ladies who translated this poem kept
the whole whimsical poem intact, with rhyme and meter and tongue-in-
cheek reverence too.

MAYSE BEREYSHIS
The Creation Of Man

Ven der hut beshaffen
Unzer vundersheyner velt
Hut ehr nit gefregt bay keynem
Nor getun vi ihm gefehlt.
Alles nokh zayn eygene villen,
Nokh zayn eygenem plan betrakht,
Ehr hut lang genug ge-arbet,
Un ehr hut es gut gemakht.

Ven ehr iz tsu mensh gekumen,
Iz ehr nit gegangen glat,
Un ehr hut tsunoyfgeruffen,
Zayn geflihglten senat.
"Hert mikh oys, ihr mayne gedoylim,
Aykh hub ikh aher gebrakht
Ihr zoll mir an eytse geyben,
Vi der mensh zoll zayn gemakht.

Helft mir, kinder, im beshaffen,
Ubber kuhkt zikh gut arum,
Ehr zol zayn in uns gerohten
Un khasrunus un ah muhm.
Den ikh kroyn im als ah hersher,
Un ikh shenk im fun mayn flam,
Ehr zoll fray behershen kennen,
Luft un erd un oykh dem yam.

Der pohet zol zayn geflihglt (Last two stanzas),
Ehr bekommt mayn hekhsten rang,
Effnen vil ikh mayne himmlen
Far dem mayster fun gezang.
Un ikh vel fun aykh ah molokh,
Ehr zoll greyt zayn tug un nakht,
Ihm di fliggl untsushefften
Ven zayn heylig lihd ervakht.

Transliteration by Rifke Levine

THE CREATION OF MAN

When the world was first created
by th'all wise Eternal One,
asked he none for help or counsel—
simply spake, and it was done!

Made it for his own good pleasure,
shaped it on his own design,
spent a long day's work upon it,
formed it fair and very fine.

Soon he thought of Man's creation—
then perplexities arose.
So the Lord his winged Senate
called, the question to propose!

Hear, my great ones, why I called ye,
Hear and help me ye who can,
hear and tell me how I further
shall proceed in making Man.

Of my holy fire I'd give him,
crowned monarch shall he be,
ruling with a sway unquestioned
over earth and air and sea

"How? This toy of froth and vapor,"
thought the Senate filled with fear.
"If so wide his kingdom stretches,
shortly he will break in here!"

To the Lord they answered, saying,
Mind and strength thy creature give,
Form him in our image
Lord, but wingless let him live!

"Lest he shame the soaring eagle
let no wings to man be given.
Let him o'er the earth be ruler,
Lord, but keep him out Heaven!"

"Wisely said", the Lord made answer,
"Lo, your counsel fair I take.
Yet, my Senate, one exception—
one alone I will to make.

"One exception, for the poet,
for the singer shall have wings.
He the gates of Heav'n shall enter,
highest of created things.

"One I single from among ye,
one to watch the ages long,
Promptly to admit the poet
when he hears his holy song."

Translated by Rose Pastor Stokes and Helena Frank

הערבסם בלעטלאך

.I

אָ ייננזאָם זימץ איך, ווי׳א געפֿאנגען

פֿון אַ זעלמזאָמען געפֿיהל :

עפּעם האָב איך אייז פֿערלאָנגען.

דאָך איך ווייס נים, וואָם איך וויל.

זייׂנׂעׂן פֿריידען, זיׂינׂעׂן ליידען

ערׂגׂעׂץׂ וואָו פֿיר מיר בעשׂמעלם ?

קראַנק איז איז איינער פֿון אונז ביידען ! —

זאָגׂמׂ : בין איך עם, צו דיא וועלמ ?

שׂמוׂנׂדׂעׂן קומען און פֿעררינען, —

נייׂע, נייׂע קומען צו ;

דאָך קיין איינע ברענגם מיין זינען

און מיין קראַנקען בחום רוה. —

ווינׂעׂן מׂח איך, קעׂן נים רייׂדׂעׂן,

קעׂן נים ווימׂעׂן, וואָם מיר פֿעהלם.

קראַנק איז איז איינער פֿון אונז ביידעׂן ! —

זאָגׂמׂ : בין איך עם, צו דיא וועלׂם ?

.II

איך ליעב דעם ווינד, איך ליעב דעם ים,

דעׂן ווׂיא דעׂר ערשׂמׂעׂר בׂין איך עלעׂגׂד

און ווׂיא דעׂר צוׂוׂיׂיׂמׂעׂר רוׂיׂשׂם מיין הׂערׂץׂ.

איך ליעב דיא וואָלקען, ליעב דיא נשׂכׂם,

דעׂן ווׂיא דׂיא ערׂשׂמׂעׂ קעׂן איך ווׂיׂינׂעׂן

און ווׂיא דׂיא צוׂוׂיׂימׂעׂ איז מיין וועלׂם.

.III

דׂיא וועלׂם איז זׂאָ אַלם און אׂומעׂגׂלׂיׂך ;

דאָם לעׂבׂעׂן זׂאָ קאׂלם און זׂאָ קלעׂגׂלׂיׂך ;

דׂיא ערׂד אזוׂי שׂמוׂצׂיׂג און קׂלׂיׂין ;

דׂיא צׂייׂם אזוׂי קׂרׂום, אזוׂי שׂוׂייׂבׂיׂג ;

דעׂר מעׂנׂש אזוׂי דׂום און נׂיׂשׂם אׂיׂיׂבׂיׂג —

וואָם מׂהׂו איך דאָ אׂיׂינׂעׂר אׂלׂיׂין ?

IV

האָב פֿׂיׂעׂל געׂלׂאַׂכׂמׂ, דאָך זׂעׂהׂר פֿׂיׂעׂל געׂוׂוׂייׂנׂמׂ

אַ, שׂמעׂנׂדׂיׂג איז בׂיׂי מׂיׂר געׂוׂוׂעׂן פֿעׂראׂיׂינׂמׂ

מׂיׂן לׂאַׂך מׂיׂמ מׂיׂינׂעׂ מׂרׂעׂהׂרׂעׂן....

נׂׂישׂמׂמׂ, וואָם צו הׂעׂרׂעׂן !

האב פיעל גערעהם, דאך פיעל געשווינ׳עגען שטיל,
מיין שוויינגען אַבער האט געמענה׳ם פיעל,
איך קען איין שוהערען.
נישטא, וואם צו הערען!

האב פיעל געהאכם, דאך פיעל אַ, פיעל געליעבם!
קאנצפראסמען חאבכן מיר דאם חערץ צוקניפם.
איך האב פערביירם זיך ווהערען...
נישטא, וואם צו הערען!

V

וואו איך פאַהר און וואו איך געה נאר,
וואו איך זיצק און וואו איך שטעה נאר,
שוועבם פאר מיר אַ בלייך געשטאלם.
אימער בלייכער, בלייכער, ווערם עם,
פון דיא מיעדע אויגען מרעהרם עם,
מים דיא דערע באַקקן צוקם עם,
מים דיא שמארע בליקען קוקם עם
און עם ווינקם אין מיר אַ כוואלם.
שרייב איך, אויף מיין שרייבען לעבם עם;
לעז איך, זעה איך אויפ׳ן בוך עם;
נאר בחנום, וואם איך זוך עם
אויסצומיידען; אימער שוועבם עם
פאר דיא אויגען מיר, — אַ וועה!
וואו איך געה און וואו איך שטעה!
ווען איך ליעג אין קבר קאלם.
דאן פערשווינדעם דאם געשטאלם.

VI

דער ווענ אין וויים דער מאַנג איז קורץ;
דיא זונן זינקם באַלד ארונטער;
דאם וואסער רוישם, צום גרענ אין וויים —
מיין שיף, מיין שיף געהם אונטער!

דא העלפם עם מעהר קיין ראנגלען זיך, —
דער ווינד איז אַ געזונדמער;
דער ים איז גרוים, דער ים איז ווילד —
מיין שיף, מיין שיף געהם אונטער!

אַ, זיי געזונד, דוא שעהנע זונן!
דוא שיינסם נאך וויעדער מענמער;
נאר איך, — דיא כוואלעם רוישען שרעק —
מיין שיף, מיין שיף געהם אונטער!

דער אדלער

וואו די ריעזענוואלקען יאגען
אויבען, אין דעם העכסטען ארם,
שוועבט דער קייזער פון די פייגעל,
פליהם דער גרויסער אדלער דארם.

מים די שטארקע פליגעל פאכט ער
אין דער לופטען און ער פליהם.
עלענדער, צ הון די הימלען
האם ער קיין חברים נים.

ווערם ער מיעד פון שווערע רייזען
רוהם ער איינזאם און אליין
ביי דעם זוים פון מיעפע וואסערם,
אויף צ הויכען בארג פון שמיין.

מים פעראכטמונג קוקט ער אונטען,
שטאלצענדיג זיין שטאלצען קאפ,
שטם נאר, ווען איהם צווינגט דער הונגער,
לאזט ער זיך מים וואה אראב.

דער קאנאריק

עס טרילערט דער קאנאריק
אין פרייען ווּאלד אליין;
ווער קען זיין שמחה פיהלען ?
ווער קען זיין פרייד פערשטעהן ?
עס טרילערט דער קאנאריק
אין רייכסטען פאלאסט שעהן;
ווער קען זיין וועהמאטק פיהלען ?
ווער קען זיין שמערץ פערשטעהן ?

דיא נוים און דער דיכטער

היי, חיי ! ווער וויל עם דערם פראַבּירען
מיט נוואָלם צו עפּ׳נען מיינע מיהרען ?
ווער קומם עם דאָרם, מיין רוה צו שמערען ? —
דיא נוימח ? איך הער, איך קען עם שווערען !
אַ דאָם איז זיא, אַ דיא מנפת !
אַוועק, דו צלמע מכשפה !
וואָס זוכּםמו דאָ אין נאַממעם צאַרען ?
אַוועק צו צלל דיא שווארצע יאהרען !

דו האָםם מיך לאַנג נענת געמאַמערם,
מיין לייבּ און לעבּען שיער נע׳פמר׳ם,
מיין מומה נערויבּם, מיין שמאַלץ צוםרעמען,
נעצוואונגען מיך אויף בּרוים צו בּעמען ! —
יעצם נעה, וואו מויזענד שדים ברעננען !
אַוועק, איך וויל דיך מעהר נים קענען !
פערשווינד, דו שמוצינע ארורה,
נעהם צו פון מיר דיין שווארצע צורה !

„אַ, עפּען אויף, נעליעבּמער, עפּען !
איך קען חוץ דיך קיין חבר מרעפּען ;
דיא נצכם איז קצלם און איך וועל ערפרירען :
אַ, מאַך מיר ווידער אויף דיא מהירען !
איך בּין דיין צלמע נוים דיא מרייע,
בּיי דיר צו זיין איז אַ מחית ! —
אַ, זיים איך בּין פון דיר נעשיעדען,
האָבּ איך נים מעהר קיין פריינד בּיי אידען".......

אַוועק פון מיר מים דיינע שקרים,
פערנרייממערין פון מוים און קברים !
אַוועק ! איך בּין בּיי דיר נים איינער,
דיך קענען מויזענד בּלייכע וויינער,
פערנעה, פערשווינד, אַ ווער פערשנימען,
און מאַך דער וועלם מעהר קיין ווייממען !
דיך קענען פיעל, דו בּיםם קיין חידוש,
ווער רעדם פון דיא, וואָם שרייבּען אידיש....

„מיך קענען פיעל, דאָם איז קיין ליענען,
דאַך איז בּיי דיר מין פערנעענינען ;
איך ליעבּ דיין קרויזעלקצפ דעם שווארצען,
איך ליעבּ דיא וואונדען פון דיין הארצען ;
איך ליעבּ צו שלינגען דיינע מרעהרען,
איך ליעבּ דיין זיפץ, איך ליעבּ צו העהרען
דיין ליעד פון מרוירינע נעזיכּםער, —
איך האָבּ דיך ליעבּ, דו בּלייכּער דיכּםער !"

אַ ערגםע פֿון דעם מײַסעל'ם ווײַבער,
צוזק! בין מעהר קײן פֿערזענשרײַבער,
א_יך שאַף קײן ברטטען מעהר, אַ מערק עם!
איך האָבדעל מעַבטק און צוקערקעם.
עס איז מיר זים, עס איז מיר בימער:
איך בין קײן פֿוהר קײן געניטער,
דאַך פֿינקפֿליך און צו גוטער צחלער,
לעב רעכם און שלעכם און שמאַר צו דאַלער.

„און שרײַבטטטו נים, דאַן וועטטטו שרײַבען;
וועטטם, פֿרײַנד, קײן קרעמער נים פֿערבלײַבען;
איך קען זײ גום, צ דיא געשיכטען:
דהא וועטטם נאַך לײַדען און וועטטם נאַך דיכטען
דו וועטטם זיך נאַך אַ מאַל פֿערמהיידיגען
פֿיר דײַן מיך יעצט בעלײַדיגען.
אַ, זײ קײן שוטה, בעטסער עפֿען!
וועטטטו מיך א מאַל'ל נאַך מחנן מרעפֿען!"

צוזק, דו ברינגערין פֿון מרעהרען!
כ'האָב פֿרײַנד בעריהממע מיליאָנערען:
זײ וועלען שפענדיג מײַנער זאַרגען,
איך זאַל נים לײַדען, זאָל נים בטרגען
איך זאַל נים שווטרצען מעהר מײַן פֿנים
צו קווישקען מײַנע דומע שונאים.
וואָם וועלטמען מיך אין קבר ברינגען
אויִם קנאה צו מײַן שעהנעם זינגען.

„דערצעהל מיר נים פֿון מיליאָנערען!
וואָרם אויִף! זײ וועלען קעלטער ווערען,
זײ וועלען דיך געוויים פֿערגעסטען, —
זײ האָבטן אנד'רע אינטערעסטען.
ערהווילע בּיטטו זײַער שפּיעלכעל;
דאָך בַּעלד דריום איבּער זיך דאָם מיחלכעל, —
צוריקבַּען וועטטם דײַן גאַנצע פֿריידע
און מיר פֿערבלײַבען ענדליך בּיידע!"

דיא וואונדער שיף

שוין דיא לעצטע זונענשטראהלען
שפיגלען אויף דיא שפיצען בוימער,
און דיא גרוים אבענדשטמענם
וועבען זיך ארום דער ערד.

אויף דעם שפיץ פון יענע בערגער
איז נאך פון דערווייטעגם מעגליך
צו דערקענען רוימע שפורען
פון דער זון, דיא לעצטע פרים.

לאנגע בלומיג-רויטע פאטען
הענגען דארם אין מערב-ווינקעל,
פונקען אם דיא הייסע ברעגען
אין דעם קאלמען שקעטן.

ס'קייקעלם זיך דאם גלאטע וואסער
דורך דיא דונק'לע אבענדשלייערם,
וועלכע צימערען פון אויבען
אויפ'ן בוזים פון דעם ים.

רוהיג בלאזם אַ לינדער ווינטעל
דורך דיא הרובנע שטילע וועלען
וועלכע שעפטשען, מורמלען עפעם, —
ווער פערשטעהם דיא וואסער-שפראך ?

אויסגעשפרייט דיא ברייטע זעגעל
געגען שמילען אבענדהימעל,
איילט אַ שיף נאר אהן מאטראזען
דארטען ווייט, — ווער ווייס ווהר, ווהו ?

נאר דער רודער ווא מים כשוף
ער בעוועגם זיך ; — ווא מים פליגעל
פליהם דיא לאטקע, ווא דיא רוחות
וואלמען איהר נעיאגם אהין.

וואם דיא שיף, מען זעהם קיין מאטשטפם ;
נאר אַ קינד אַ שמעהם ער געבראקען
געבען פאמם בוים און ער יטמערם
מים אַ בימערן געפיהל.

לאנגע, געלד געקרויזטע לאקען
קייקלען זיך אויף זיינע שולטער ;
זיסצענדיג פֿון הינטען קוקט ער...
און דיא שפּילע שיף זיא פֿליהם !

מיט צ זילבערווייסע מיכעל,
וועלכע פֿלאטערט אין דער לופֿטען,
גריסט דער שעהנער מיר פֿון וויימען,
ער נעעעגנעט זיך מיט מיר...

און מיין הערץ פֿאנגט אן צו קלאפּען, —
עפעס וויינט זיך — זאגט, וואס איז דעם ?
יענעם שעהנע קינד — איך קען איהם —
נשמם ! מיט יוגענד פֿליהם עם דארם !...

דער וויינאכטס-בוים
——————

עם ליעגט צ שעהנער פֿרוים
אין גרינעם וויינאכטס-בוים :
ער גריגם וון וון אלץ איז מויט.
איך שטעה און קוק איהם אן
און מח צ צימער מחשן :
מיר דעכם, אז ער איז הדים

יא, הדים און נשם פֿון בלום,
איך זעה און איהם די רוס,
וואם השקט מין לייב אומוים,
איך זעה און איהם דעם חשם,
די קנוה און דעם כעם—
די ליעבע פֿון דעם קריסם.

דער ממזר

אידי חדר קינדער ווילען זיך מיט מיר ניט שפּיעלען,
דער רבּי שטעכט מיך דורך מיט זיינע בּליקען ;
ניט פֿיר מיר קיין הארץ מיט מענשליכע געפֿיהלען, —
דיא בּעסטע וואלטען גערען מיך דערשטיקען...

פֿון קידוש־בּעכער וואו דיא קינדער אלע זופּען,
יאגט מיך מיט ווילדען כעם אַוועק דער שמש, —
כ׳חיים: „ממזר". מאר צום ארון קודש זיך ניט שטופּען,
פֿערשאלטען זיינען מיינע ד׳ אמות.

דער חזן טראגט צום „לייענען" דיא ספֿר תורה,
און יעדער איינער קושט איהר מיט א קדושה ;
איך שטעל דיא ליפּען אויס, מען קוקט אויף מיר, א מורא !
איך קעהר זיך אַפּ מיט וועהמאג און מיט בּושה.

איך טראכט און פֿראַכט, און קען מיין חטא זיך ניט ערקלערן;
וואָס הייסט: א ממזר ? זאָגט : פֿיר וואָס מיך פֿלאָגען ?
און פֿרעג איך עם מיין מומער, ווינעם זיא בּיטערע מרעהרן,
זיא קושט מיך חייס און וויל עם מיר ניט זאָגען.

פֿיר אַנד׳רע קינדער האָט א מאטע וואָס צו זאָגען.
און פֿיר א יתום שטעלט זיך יעדער איינער. —
נאָר איך בּין הפֿקר, ווא א בּלאָם פֿון ווינד געטראָגען.
א חוץ איין שוואכע פֿרוי, א, ליעבּט מיך קיינער !

און וואו איז דאָך מיין טאטע ערגעץ הינגעקומען ?
נישטא קיין תירוץ פֿיר דעם נע ונד׳ן.
איז ער אַוועק, האָם איהם דער הימעל צוגענומען ?
פֿארוואָס זאָג איך קיין קדיש נאָך מיין טאטען ?

נאָר פֿרעג דעם ווינד. דיא וועלט איז שטום צו מיינע שמערצען
איך האָר קיין ענטפֿער, הער קיין איינעם ריידען,
דעם אמת נאָר פֿערנעהם איך טיעף בּיי מיר אין הערצען:
בּין אונשולדיג און לייד אומזיסטע ליידען.

דער איד צו קריסטוס

צום קרייץ גענאגעלט מיט א בלייכען פנים,
מיט ווילדען שמערץ אין די געקװעלטע גלידער,
בעטראכטסטו דיינע אונערבארמדיגע שונאים,
וואס רופען זיך מיט אונרעכט דיינע ברידער.
די רופסט דורך טיעפען יאמער, פיין און קװאלען:
„מיין גאָט, מיין גאָט, וואס האסטו מיך פערלאָזען"?
דאך דיין געבעט װערט מיט דעם װינד פערבלאזען
און דיינע מאראבענע בלום צום בָאדען פאַלען;
צום קאַלמען בָאדען, פון דיין גוף דעם ריינעם!
עם לאבען זיך די פײנינגער און פרייען
מיט דיינע איבערמענשליך בימ׳רע וועהען,
און שפאם פערנעהמסטו נאר, קיין טרייסט פון קיינעם.
כ'קוק טרוי'רינג דיך, און איך קוק אויף זיך,
מען זאגם מיר דאם ביזט ו, דאך דאס בין איך...

ווינאכטס-גלאָקען

קלינגט אויס, קלינגט אויס, איהר װיינאַכטס-גלאָקען!
זאגט אן דעם הימעל און די ערד,
פיעל מאָל איהר האָם די וועלט געשראקען,
פיעל מאָל איהר האָם געוועקט דעם שװערד!

קלינגט אויס, און זאָלען אלע שטערען
בעהאלטען זייער זיסען פראכט!
זאָל די לבנה דונקעל װערען
און נים בעלייכטען אם די נאכט!

דען פינסטערניס האָם איהר פערקינדיגט
זייט יאָהרען און זייט דורות לאַנג.
א, װעה, װי האָם די וועלט געזינדיגט,
דאָם זי מוז הערען אייער קלאַנג!

אין דער מדבר

עס שטעהט אין וויסטען מדבר
א פעלזעלע אליין
און קוקט זיך אום פעראומערט,
און זעבט צו יעדער שעהן.

זיין הימעל־זיפּע שטימע
וויא רייכספער גינגאלד פליסט,
און וועקט דיא שטילע טויטקייט
דיא סטעפּע לעער און וויסט.

ער וועקט דיא טויטע הימלען
דיא שטומע ספּה'ם ארום,
דאך בלייבען טויט דיא טויטע,
דיא שטומע בלייבען שטום :

מיר וועמען, זיסער זינגער,
זאג, קלינגט דיין חעלער מאן ?
ווער הערט דיך און ווער פיהלם דיך ?
און וועמען געהסטו אן ?

דו מעגסט דיין גאנצע זעעלע
אריינטהאן אין דיין ליעד, —
אין דעם פערלאָרנ'ם מדבר
קיין הערץ דערוועקסטו ניט.

ניטש לאַנג וועסטו דא זינגען,
איך פיהל עס, איך פערשטעה :
דיין הערץ וועט זיך צושפרינגען
פאר עלענד און פּאר וועה.

אומזיסט איז וואס דו פלייסט זיך,
דאס וועט ניט העלפען, ניין !
אליין ביסטו געקומען
און וועסט אליין פערגעהן.

ס׳איז צו לינן!

אין מעהרערע, וואו מען וואנדערט
אין דעם הייסן מידבר־זאמד,
מראפט א מאל, דו ווערסט פארוואנדערט,
וועגנדיק ס׳כשווינמע לאנד.

רעפרײן:
ס׳איז צו לינן, ס׳איז צו לינן,
ס׳איז א פוספער מרוים —
דער מידבר האמ קיין פעלד,
קיין זאנגען, קיין בוים!

שעפסט מעשען אויף דער לאנקע,
און דעם פאספער זעפסו קיים!
און דיר דוכם זיך, אז ס׳איז אמת,
אז דו זעפסם עס נים אין מרוים —

עם אזוי אויך מרעפם אין לעבן,
מרעפם א מאל א מילן בליק,
חייבסם אן בויען געלדענע שלעסער,
ווערסם פארישוועלם פונעם גליק.

הערבסט

מים קאלמע בליקען קומם דער הערבסט געצווינגען,
ער קומם אן לוסם, און פריילעכקיים פערגעהען,
עם קוקם דער מוים פון זײנע כמורנע אויגען,
די ליעבע שפעארבם מים איהרע זיסע ווענהען.
דורך וואלד און פעלד צוקלינגם א שמערצליך פראיכען,
עם לעשם די זונ, עם ברענכם דעם דוב דעם שמײסען,
די לאנקע קארמשעפם זיך, עם גליווערען די מייכען,
דער ווינד דערשרעקם זיך פאר זיין אייג׳צעם פייסען.

דער באצם שפרינגם אויף א נאקעמער, צושראקען,
פון שלאף געשטארם דורך גרוילינג ילעם,
עם וועלקם די לעצטע רויז אין זומערם לאקען,
די לוסם־קאמעליע נעהם צורעק אין גלות...
אראו די סמאדע האם זיך פריי גענמערם,
דער פאספוך האם געסווישעששעם גליק און פריידען,
לויפם אום דער הערבסם ממשמש און נעוויסערם,
און שרים, און רעדם, און ווער פערשמעהם זיין ריידען?

POETRY OF
JEWISH SUBJECTS
AND NATIONALISM

❖

In many poems and in his prose Rosenfeld wrote of the eternal plight of the wandering Jew, the man who is a "man without country," in constant hope of returning to his true home, Israel. Here Lilien shows that the "Wanderer" is beset with brambles and frustration while the Paradise of Israel seems so enticing but unattainable.

AMERIKA
America

Amerika, du land fun tsuker,
Amerika, du land fun gohld,
Vi bitter iz in dir dohs leben!
Vi shlekht vert doh der mensh batsolt!
Oh land vus dayne shiffen, bahnen,
Durch kreytzen shnell ih land ih fluhss
Vi hintershtellig iz dayn fohlk nohkh!
Vi geyt der ulam doh tsu fuhss!

Oh land fun predines un reduer,
Fun glahte frohzen hitren tsihl,
Vi leydt doh shveygenden di mahsse!
Vi shtorbt dem fohlk far huhnger shtil!
Oh vunderland ! Oh vundermenshen!
Unshtoht dem lebens tsuker-roh,
Vi lang vestu, oh, kalter Yenke,
Doh kayen shiksals tabak nohr?

AMERICA

America, Oh sugarland!
America, Oh goldenland!
How bitter it is for me to say
how Man must struggle for his pay!
Oh land where speedy ships and trains
traverse the rivers and the plains!
And yet how backward folks can be,
how poor your people, basic'lly.

Oh land where preaching speakers' goals
as smooth, cold guardians of our souls,
allow the suff'ring silent masses
to starve to death . . . .and time just passes.
Oh wonderland! Oh wondrous men we thank!
How long will you, too, be a frigid Yank?
Instead of life, to offer "sugar-cane",
Chewing Fate's tabac' to slowly die in pain.

AMERICA

Now here is a disappointed, angry immigrant who found that the Goldene Medina was not the Golden Land that he expected. He digs at the phony preachers of morality and freedom while men starve. He implies that neither the speedy trains or sugar-coating can suage the starving workers' pains. This poem was a guarantee for Rosenfeld's popularity among his proletarian friends in his own time Some poets live in the clouds and write in an esoteric manner. Not Morris. He lived among men, suffered among men and wrote the unvarnished truth about what he saw.

CHANUKAH LIGHTS

In Chanuka Lights you will see that Rosenfeld is at his most endearing, and not only to the Jews of his time. This is one of his most popular and enduring poems. Music has been written to it by composers in many countries. It is so simple, evoking memories of a "heroic" Jewish past and holding up those little lights of hope for a brighter future. Morris appeals to children as well as to a childlike chauvinism in the displaced adults of the ghetto. To this day it is sung wherever there are Jews who understand Yiddish. "Ah yihr klayne likhtalakh! Yihr dertzeylt geshikchtalakh!" Go translate "likhtalakh" and "geshikhtalakh"! The best I could do was, "Oh you candles, small and bright, telling tales with such delight!" Even accurately translating such a couple of phrases is impossible. There is an affectionate, personal relationship to those diminutive candles that cannot cross language barriers.

DI KHANUKA LIKHT
The Chanuka Lights

A ihr kleyne likhtalakh !
Ihr dartzeylt geshikhtalakh,
Myse'lakh ohn tzohl,
Ihr dertzeylt fon bluhtikkayt,
Berye'shaft un muhtikayt,
Vuhnder fon amohl !

Ven ikh zey aykh shmihklingdik,
Kuhmt a kholem fihnklingdik,
Reydet eyn alter troym;
"Ihd, du hohst gekrihgt amohl,
Ihd du hohst gesihgt amohl,."
Gohtt ! Dohss gloybn zikh koym !

S'iz bay dir a tohlk geveyn,
Bist amohl a fohlk geveyn,
Hohst amohl regihrt,
Hohst amohl a landt gehat,
Hoht amohl a handt gehat!
Akh, vi tihf dohs rihrt!

A, ihr kleyne likhtalakh!
Ay-ere geshikhtalakh
Vekken oyf mir payn,
Tihf in hehrtz beveykt es zikh,
Uhn mit treheren frehgt es zikh
Vohs vet itzer zayn?

Nit eyvik zaynen mir, vi haynt,
Geveyn a fohlk vohss kan nohr klohgn,
Mir hohbn oykh amohl dohs fayndt
Gevihzn, dohs mir kannen shlohgn.

Mir hohbn oych mit tapferkayt,
Mit tihgrmuht, fir unzer gloybn
Gevohrfn zikh in gresten shrayt
Un hoykh di fohn fon zihg erhoybn.

Nohr doros zaynen zeyer fihl
Avek, fargangen zayne yohren,
Mir zaynen shvakh gevohren, shtill,
Dem alten riheeznmuht farlohren.

Farlohrn hohbn mir dem muht,
In golos tzvishn di rshihm,
Dohch iz fareyrbrt in unser bluht,
Der fayer fon di Hasmonihm.

Un khohtkh es habn shtarker handt
Mit dreshrs unzer layb gedrohshn,
Dohkh yeynr alter fayer brennt,
Ihm hoht der bluht-yam nit farlohshn.

Yoh, emess, tihf iz unzer fahl,
Mir zaynen kerperlikh nohr flihgn,
Zohkh leybt in uns eyn ihdahl
Dohs kant ihr, fohlkr, nit bezihgn!

CHANUKAH LIGHTS

Oh you candles, small and bright,
Telling tales with such delight,
Tales we cannot count,
Tales of massacre and pain,
Of skill and brave'ry proved again,
Wonders to recount.

When I see you glimmering,
A spectre rises, shimmering,
Like a dream of old,
Saying, "Jew, you've fought before,
Conquered worlds in peace and war!"
God! What stories we are told!

You were once a nation strong,
A people with a hist'ry long,
Once YOU held the reins!
Once you held, with iron hand,
Held your own, your native land.
Oh, how deep that pains!

Oh you tiny little lights,
Burning brightly days and nights,
How your stories ache!
In my heart old mem'ries stir,
Tears and fears and pains occur,
What road will the future take?

We've not always been so weak,
Absorbing endless blows,
We were the strong and not the meek,
And our armies struck the foes!

We have lived with bravery,
With tiger-spirit for our faith,
Thrown ourselves in battles great
and hoisted flags of victory.

Generations have gone by,
Many years in darkness lie,
We've become the weak and still
And lost our voice, once strong and shrill.

Our spirit, once so keen
Has lost its edge in bondage mean,
Yet somewhere in our deepest souls
Are Hasmonean burning coals!

And though today a stronger hand
Flails and beats us down,
Those fiery coals of yesterday still stand
And in that sea of blood won't drown.

Though our fall is deep and real
We can't stand idly by.
We must not simply bow and cry,
But rise for our ideal!

Original Yiddish for this poem is on page 279

YISROYEYL
Israel

Ah zohg, mit vohs iz balzamihrt
Mayn fohlk, mayn eyvik fohlk gevohrn?
Azoy lang toyt un ekzistihrt,
Zayn fats un marekh nohkh nit farlorn . . .

Es lihgt in truhne fon der tzayt,
Ah muhmih vih alt Mitzrayim,
In fremde velt-muhzeyuhms vayt,
Un khohlm't fon Yerushalayim.

ISRAEL

Ah, tell me how my people are preserved,
My eternal people, have they this deserved?
So long dead and yet existing,
Flesh and bones are still persisting.

Live, we lie in the casket of Time,
Mummy-like in Egypt's parch-ed clime,
Far away, in strange world-museums,
and still dreaming of Jerusaleum.

Original Yiddish for this poem is on page 280

ISRAEL

This is a brilliant poem. Every line is a treasure. Just read the English as though it were prose and it is still a poem. "Oh tell what has preserved my people, my eternal people? Have they this deserved? So long dead and yet existing, flesh and bones still persisting . . . we live in the casket of time, mummy-like as in Egypt's parch-ed clime . . . far away, in strange world-museums and still dreaming of Jerusaleum." This is elegant and exquisite. There is no mourning, no excess of language: a crystalline essence of a pinched soul is cast forth.

SFERA

We have a lot of disasters to commemorate. What has happened recently in Hamas, Somalia, India, Rwanda and South Africa "ain't nothin'" compared to what has befallen our ancestors and recent relatives. We specialize in being humiliated and decimated. Yet there is something bothersome about this well-written poem. It is the poet's attitude. He is not openly sad for this occasion. He attempts to be sardonic, but does it fall flat? He asks his Muse if she objects to his laughing at such a sad time. She doesn't reply, but we do. At first blush we want to say, "If you're going to laugh, Morris, let us in on the joke. If your Muse didn't reply, don't write this poem."

But then the depth of his thinking came through: He has found another answer to lamentation: laughter. That is the one release from the destructiveness of despair. Laughter is a recogniton of absurdity. The truth is, as Rosenfeld here states, "Laughing and groaning are with him the same." As our mother would have said, "In a meshugina velt kennen mir nor lakhn." (In a crazy world we can only laugh.")

SFERE

(first three stanzas)

Ikh vollt dakht zikh velln yetzt betten mayn lihreh
Zi zol etvas lakhen es geyt ubber nit.
Yoh, brihderlakh, erstens iz bay undz Sfere.
Un shtamm eppes, zugt mir, vi lakht es ah Yid?

Yoh, tatteh, du lakhst? S'iz ah klug tsum gelekhter.
In Yiddishe freyd iz den duh eppes rekht?
Der Yiddisher lakh iz den eppes ah rekhter?
Ah mish-mosh dokh nohr fun ah zifts mit ah krekhts.

Ah shpass hut ah tam gohr dus Yiddishe leben.
Ah shpass hut der Yiddisher mazel, ah kheyn.
In ihm, vel di zilberne volkendlakh shveben
In feld iz ah khihs, dir zitz nohr un veyn.
(last two stanzas)
Un vus ehr zol zingen un vi shnell lakhten,
Un vi ehr shpielen gohr freylakhdik ziss.
Der hertmen in lid zaynen plutzlung ervakhten,
Ah "tefilleh leni": dohs hertz git a riss.

Ikh vollt, dakht zikh, vellen yetzt betten mayne lihreh
Zi zoll etvas lakhen, es geyt ubber nit,
Yoh, brihderlakh, ersten iz yetzt bay undz Sfere.
Haynt shtamm eppes, zugt mir vi lakht ah Yid?

Transliteration by Rifke Levine with EJG

SFERE

I asked my Muse had she any objection
to laughing with me—not a word for reply!
You see, it is Sfere, our time for dejection
and can a Jew laugh when it is the rule to cry?
You laughed then, you say? 'Tis a sound to affright one.
In Jewish delight what is worthy the name,
The laugh of a Jew is never a right one,
for laughing and groaning with him are the same.

You thought there was zest in the Jewish existence?
You deemed that the star of a Jew could be kind?
The Spring calls and beckons with gracious insistence,
Jew—sit down in sackcloth and weep yourself blind!
The garden is green and the woodland rejoices,
how cool are the breezes, with fragrance how blent,
But Spring calls not you with her thousand sweet voices
with you it is Sfere—sit still and lament.

The beautiful summer, this life's consolation,
in moaning and sighing glides quickly away,
What hope can it offer to one of my nation?
What joy can he find in the splendors of May?

*Translated by Helena Frank Sfera is a period of mourning commemorating the
disasters in Israel during the Crusades.*

YIDDISH

We devoted a whole chapter to Yiddish, many pages that took weeks to research and write and that is so formal and inquisitive. This poet writes a few lines and tells it all better. That is the wonder of poetry. Sometimes we devote more lines to explain what a poet has said than there are in the poem itself. Poetry is crystalline compared with prose. There is mo doubt that Rosenfeld, a pioneer in the use of Yiddish as a modern poetic medium, understood fully the techniques of his craft and the resources of his language. Just today, a friend of ours was demcaning Yiddish as a language in comparison with German. Although Jewish, his German back-ground would not let him appreciate Yiddish. We read him this poem but obviously could not get through to him. Yiddish is just not his language nor can he identify with Yiddishkeit (Jewishness)

IHDISH
Yiddish

Es klohgen mankhe grammenflekhter,
Dohs unzer loshn iz a shlekhter,
Dohs "Ihdish" iz tzuh prohst, tzuh trohkn,
Es hoht keyn bluhmn uhn keyn farbn,
Un kratzt dee zeyle vih a sharbn,
Un iz farzoyrt uhn mzuhkn.

Es feylt uhns, zohgn zey, dohss sheyne,
Dohs eydle vohrt, dohs zanfte, reyne,
Un dohs beshreynkt zey di gezangen . . .
Es hoht nohr rapnikis tzu raysen,
Nohr rihtr, zohgen zey, tzu shmaysen,
Un nit keyn hehrtzedike klangn.

Oy vey ! Di velt nohkh tzu farbluhndn !
Di muhtr-shprakhe frakh tzu shendn.
Un zikh fartaydigen duhrkh lihgn !
Oy ihdish ! Du mayn bester khelek !
Vi bistu raykh, vi bistu heylek !
Vohs kan ikh mit dir nit bezingn ?

Dohs leybn kan keyn zakh mihr bringn
Ikh zohll nit kannen dohs bezingn.
Mayn shprakh iz brayt vi alle yam'n
Un sheyn vi May in follen blih'en,
Ikh zing un mayne lihdr glih'en
In toyzend-farbedike flammen!

YIDDISH

There are rhymesters who complain, all
say our tongue is banal,
it has no flowers, shades or class,
and scrapes the soul like broken glasss.
They say it's common, plain or dry.
They cannot sing and wonder why.

They say our language lacks allure,
the noble word, the rich and pure,
It circumscribes their singing.
They hear but harsh words ringing.
They say it's just a stick, a sabre,
to chill the heart or hurt a neighbor.

Oh, dear! To so delude the world is wrong,
It's rude to so abuse your mother-tongue
and so demean yourself with lies.
Oh Yiddish! To your portals my heart flies!
How rich you are, how holy too,
What songs can't I create with you?

Your range of colors makes others pale,
The prettiest flowers on hill or dale
I sharply paint. My palette's full.
The poet's heart and love can pull
the colored threads of sound, and conceive
from language heaven-large a tapestry to weave.

Life could give me nothing if I could never sing.
My language,wide as all the seas,
put images and memories
like May in bloom and children heard in gleaming cantos of the soul,
Its thousand-colored flames enhance the poet's role.

Original Yiddish for this poem is on page 281

דיא חנוכה ליכם

א

איהר קליינע ליכמעלעך !
איהר דערצעהלם נעשיכמעלעך,
מעשה'לאך אהן צאהל,
איהר דערצעהלם פון בלומינקיים
ברית'שאפם און מוחהינקיים,
וואונדער פון אמאל.

ווען איך זעה אייך שמינקלענדיג,
קומם א חלום פינקלענדיג;
רעדם איין אלמער פרוים:
„איד, דוא האסם נעקריענם אמאל,
איד, דוא האסם נעזיענם אמאל"
נעמ, דאם נלויבם זיך קוים !....

ס'איז ביי דיר א מאלק נעוועןּ,
ביסם אמאל א פאלק נעוועןּ,
האסם אמאל רעניערם :
האסם אמאל א לאנד נעהאם,
האסם אמאל א הׂאנד נעהאם,"
אך, ווִיא מיעף דאם ריהרם !

ב

אּ. איהר קליינע ליכמעלעך י
אייערע נעשיכמעלעך
וועקען אויף מיין פייןּ ;
מיעף אין הערץ בעוועגם עם זיך,
און מים מרעהרען פרענם עם זיך :
וואם וועט אימצמער זיין ?....

נים אײביג זײנען מיר, װיא הײנם,
געװען א פֿאָלק, װאָם קען נאָר קלאָגען ;
מיר האָבּען אױך אַמאָל דעם פֿינד
געװיזען, דאָם מיר קענען שלאָגען.

מיר האָבּען אױך מים מאַשפֿערקריים,
מים מינערמומה, פֿיר אונזער גלױבּען
געװאָרפֿען זיך אין גרעסמען שמרײים
און הױך דיא פֿאָהן פֿון זיעג ערהױבּען.

נאָר דורות זײנען זעהר פֿיעל
צוריק, פֿערגאַנגען זײנען יאָהרען, —
מיר זײנען שװאַך געװאָרען, שמיל,
דעם אלמען ריעזענמומה פֿערלאָרען.

פֿערלאָרען האָבּען מיר דעם מומה
אין גלות צװישען דיא רשעים
דאָך איז פֿערערבּם אין אונזער בּלוס
דער פֿיער פֿון דיא חשמונאים.

און חאָמש עם האָבּען שמאַרקע הענד
מים דרעשערם אונזער לײבּ געדראָשען ;
דאָך יענער אלמער פֿיער בּרענם, —
איהם האָם דער בּלום־ים נים פֿערלאָשען.

יאָ. אמת, מיעף איז אונזער פֿאַל,
מיר זײנען קערפֿערליך נאָר פֿליעגען ;
דאָך לעבּם אין אונז אײן אידעאַל,
דעם קענם איהר, פֿעלקער, נים בּעזיעגען !

א זאָגם, מים װאָם איז בּאַלזאַמירם
מיין פֿאָלק, מיין אײביג פֿאָלק געװאָרען ?
אזױ לאַנג מוים און עקזיסמירם,
זײן פֿעמם און מאַרך נאָך נים פֿערלאָרען...

עם לעבּם אין מרונע פֿון דער צײם,
א מומיע װי פֿון אלם מצרים,
אין פֿרעמדע װעלם־מוזעאָומם װײם
און חלום'ם פֿון ירושלים...

אידיש

עס קלאַנגען מאַנכע גראַמען־פֿלעכטער,
דאַס אונזער לשון איז אַ שלעכטער;
דאַס „אידיש" איז צו פּראָסט, צו טרוקען,
עס האָט קיין בלומען און קיין פֿאַרבען,
און קראַצט אַם די זעעלע ווי אַ שטערבען,
און איז פֿאַרהוּיערט און מסוכן.

עם פֿעהלט אום אונז, זאָגען זיי, דאָס שעֶנע,
דאַס עֶדלע וואַרם, דאָס זאַנפֿטע, ריינע,
און דאָס בעשריינקט זיי די געזאַנגען...
עס האָט נאָר ראָפּניקעס צו רייסען,
נאָר ריסער, זאָגען זיי, צו שמייסען,
און ניט קיין האַרצעדינע קלאַנגען.

אָ, ווען! די וועלט נאָך צו פֿערבלענדען!
די פֿומערשפּראַכע פֿרעך צו שענדען
און זיך פֿערסיידינגען דורך ליטען!
אָ, אידיש, דו מיין בעסטער חלק!
ווי ביסטו רייך, ווי ביסטו היילינ!
וואַם קען איך ניט מים דיר בעזינגען?

די שעֶנסטע בלום פֿון אַלע מוּהאַלען,
מיר פֿעהלם קיין פֿאַרבען זי צו מאַלען,
אָ, מערקם דאַס אייך, איהר ניסטערמער פּלאַכע!
און קום זאָל זיך מיין הארץ פֿערליעבען,
מיין ליעבע וואָלם ניט שטום געבליעבען,
דען הימעל־גרויס איז מיר מיין שפּראַכע!

דאַם לעכען קען קיין זאַך מיר ברינגען,
איך זאָל ניט קענען דאָס בעזינגען;
מיין שפּראַטך איז ברייט ווי אַלע ימ׳ן
און שען ווי מאָי אין פֿולען בליהען,
איך זינג, און מיינע ליעדער גליהען
אין פֿוייענד־פֿאַרבּעדינע פֿלאַמען.

ציון

פריי נאָך ר' יהודה הלוי.

װעז װילסטו, ציון, גאָר בײ מיר ניט פֿרעגען
אױף דײנע עלענדע, װאָס זיפֿצען שװער?
איך טראָג דאָך זײַ׳רע גרוסען דיר אַנטקעגען —
דײן רעשטעל, װעה, דו האָסט דאָך שױן ניט מעהר!

פֿון מזרח, מערב, דרום און פֿון צפֿון,
איך ברענג דיר ברכות, ברכות אָהן אַ שיעור, —
דיא קינדער דײנע בײנקען שטאַרק און האָפֿען,
אַ יעדעס הערץ נאָר ציהט אַהין צו דיר.

אױך איך, געבונדענער אין גלות־קײטען,
בעקלאָגענדיג דײן שרעקליכען בעשטאַנד.
װיל דײנע לאָנג פֿערלאָש׳נע בערג בעשפֿרייטען
מיט מרעהרען, װעלכע פֿליסען נאָכאַנאַנד.

(Only first three stanzas included)

BIOGRAPHICAL POEMS

A man of the book.

LINKOHN
Lincoln

Ziftzend hoht der areme neyger,
Zayn farlohrenkayt gemeynt,
Un hoht oyf zayn vihst geleyger,
Duhrkh di shtille nakht geveynt
Mit der vaysser tseyner bayssen
Fleygt ehr ohft zayn shvartzen layb,
Fleyg oyf zikh di hoyt tsuhrissen,
Un dem suhd fartroyt zayn vayb.

Nohr dem yohkh hoht ehr getrohgn,
Shtil un ruhig vi a lam,
Fleygt zayn shiksal nit beklohgen,
Hoht geshtikt in zikh di flam.
Afrika hoht ihm getzoygen,
Nohkh zayn heym hoht ehr gegart,
Duhrkh di mihde zeynzuhkht's oygen
Hoht der vey zikh duhrkhgeshpart.

Dohkh der hillel hoht farnuhmn,
Dem farlohrenm's gebeyt,
Un a melakh iz gekuhmn,
Un hoht "fray" dohs vert gereydt.
Oyf Kentucky's grihne vihzn.
In a shtihble oyf'n feld,
Iz der rihz fon frayhayt rihzn,
Angekuhmn oyf der velt.

"Lohz ihm loz!" hoht ehr gelyarmt,
Vert duhrkh zayn fargeyen nit raykh!
Goht hoht Zikh oyf ihm darbarmt,
Shvartz tzih vys, mir zaynen glaykh!"
Un ehr hoht di kayt tzuhrissen,
Un gelohzen geyn dem knekht,,
Un befrayt a fohlks gevissen,
Uhn gekroynt dohs menshenrekht!

LINCOLN

The poor negro, sighing
has thoughts about his plight,
and lying in his shabby bed
has wept throughout the night.
And biting with his white teeth
the skin that marred his life,
he tore the hated black away,
and trusted just his wife.

Peaceful as a lamb he lived
and quietly drew the yoke,
By not not complaining of his fate
the flames of freedom choke.
Africa has suckled him,
He yearns for his home ground,
Through the desolation in his eyes
pours the pain, without a sound.

Still, the Heavens noticed
and saw his bended knee,
A leader bold has risen
and spoken the word, "Free!"
To Kentucky's fields, so lush and green,
To peon's huts, so bare and mean,
Came the giant of Freedom,s giants
like the world has never seen.

"Set him free!", he bellowed,
"By his loss shall no man gain!
God has taken pity on him,
Black or white we are the same!"
And thus the chain is broken,
Humanity delights,
He freed the nation's conscience
and crowned our human rights!

Original Yiddish for this poem is on page 295

LINCOLN

As a descendant of a people often wracked with the same pain and humiliation as the negroes Rosenfeld shows understanding and hope for the future, now that Lincoln, "the giant of freedom's giants" has cried out "Set him free!". This is a thoughtful, respectful song to liberty for the poor and embittered. "Through the desolation in his eyes pours the pain, without a sound." This is just as timely today. Now a confused, chaotic revolution is arising. A snarl of deserved hatred curls about the lips of a black nation still in partial subjugation a century and a half after Lincoln. A cataclysmic revolt is at our doorstep. America has mishandled the Lincolnian spirit of fair play. If Lincoln were alive today he would be assassinated, like JFK, RFK, Martin Luther King and . . . Lincoln.

GEORGE WASHINGTON

In the next poem Rosenfeld expresses his admiration for George Washington, who was not only the father of our nation but a role model for generations to come. The poet notes that although born to a form of nobility, Washington has become far nobler than mere family and wealth could create . . . and "his grave is larger than his cradle." What a charming way to state that by his own achievements the man increased his noble stature beyond his birthright. The patriotic immigrant cautions us that "no evil power should close the door" that Washington opened, that we should not."demean his soul which rests in peace." Rosenfeld was a genuine patriot, not for the dramatics that created our nation but for the principles that underlie its foundation. This was no cheap hack writing. The immigrant who longed for freedom celebrates it, not by mere flag-waving but by flaunting the Constitution and The Bill of Rights, in song.

DZSHOHRZDSH VASHINGTON
George Washington

A nohbleman fon hekh'ren gayst gebohren,
Aristokrat geveyn ihn ohnfang fon zayn leyben,
Dohkh hoht der yikhuhs zikh in ihm farlohren;
Ehr hoht dem fohlk zayn eydle hartz avekgegayben,
Ehr hoht zayn grihren "Ikh" tzu hilf genuhmen:
Dem mensh, di frayhayt hoht ehr loyz gemakht di flihgl,
Ehr iz avek fil nohber vi gekuhmen,
Zayn keyvr iz a folle gresser vi zayn vihgl.

Gekampft, regihrt, dohkh nit gehersht oyfn keynm,
A khavr tzuh yuhkhbd's zuhn; vi fon mitzrayim,
Befreyt a fohlk, geleybt mit ihm in-eynm,
Un oyfgemakht der velt a nay Yeruhshalayim.
Oh, groyser gayst, vohs hoht a velt geshaffen!
Oh, reyn, uhnbeflekte zeyle ohn a glaykhn!
Du zingt a lihd a yeydr frayer haffen,
Der Hohdsohn roysht dayn loyb, es royshn alle taykhn!

Dir flattert oyz a loyb der sheynster banner,
Es reydn alle berg fon dihr, di tihfer fluhtn.
Oh, du unshterblikher Amerikaner,
Fon velkhen alle fohlker denken ven zey bluhtn!
Oh, zohl dayn gayst bay dihzn toyer vakhn,
Baym toyer, vohs du hohst ge-afnet far dem mihdn,
Un zohl keyn beyze kraft ihm nit farmakhen,
Nit lesteren dayn zeyle velkher ruht in frihdn!

GEORGE WASHINGTON

A nobleman, of a higher spirit born,
Aristocrat from earliest of days,
Yet lineage at times received his scorn.
His noble heart to his folk was given,
To will himself to share has he striven.
To man was he devoted and freedom loosed his wings,
More noble grew he, honest, selfless, brave,
Much larger than his cradle was his grave.

He fought and ruled with full democracy.
A friend to sons of Jewry, as though 'twer really he
was freed from Egypt, he kept that memory
and constructed for the world Jerusalem anew.
Oh pure, untarnished soul we sing a song to you,
To you who had no equal our song of hope we raise,
The Hudson roars your honor, all rivers join in praise,
A beauteous silken banner is flown for you in praise!

The mountains all speak well of you, and, too, the oceans deep,
Of that eterne American who God's own trust did keep,
Of whom all people dream when trouble roils their sleep.
May your spirit guard that door, that door you opened wide,
When the needy crossed the seas and landed with the tide,
And let no evil power attempt that portal close
or demean your soul which rests in peace, in surcease and repose.

Original Yiddish for this poem is on page 296

HAYNRIKH HAYNE
Heinrich Heine

A mohnuhment fir Haynrikh Hayne,
Vi lekherlikh, vi duhmb di taneh!
A mohnuhment fon kalter marmer,
Fir ihm, vohs zayn gezang iz varmer,
Iz heysser vi di hitzt fon zuhmer,
Fon ihm vohs hoht dem tihfsten kuhmer,
Gegohssen in a gotlikh fayer;
Vohs hoht getzohllt ih fihle, ih tayer
Fir lihbes haylige shlihkhos;
Di sheynster kroyn fon frayhayts zinger,
Fehr ihm vilt ihr mit menshenfinger
In kalten shteyn vohss tzayt tzuhfressed es,
A daynkmal makhen, shat, farges es!

Farges es dan a Haynrikh Hayne
Makht zelbst di mohnuhment zayne.
Ehr hoht geshmihd't ihn gohldn'e hiruhzim,
Mit flammen fon zayn eygen'es buhzim,
A mohnuhment fihr zikh oyf immer.
In "Nohrdzey" tihf, in himmel's shimmer,
In yeydr hartz vohs lihbt un laydet,
In yeydr zeyle velkhe maydet
Dem veyg fon khnuhfah un gemaynhayt.
Ehr darf keyn shteyn, Ehr darf keyn tzaykhn,
Ihm kan fargessenhayt nit graykhen.
Ehr leybt un ehr vet eyvik leyben
Vi Der vohs hoht ihm unz gegeyben!

HEINRICH HEINE

A monument for Heinrich Heine!
How laughable! Such a dumb thought!
A monument of cold marble
for him whose song is warmer,
is hotter, than the heat of summer,
for him who has the deepest grief
quenched in a godly fire,

Who has spoken much and dearly
for Love's holy mission?
For him, with men's fingers,
would you make a memorial
in cold stone which time eats away?
Forget it! Forget it for Heinrich Heine!
He makes his own monument.
He has hammered, in golden verses,
with flames of his own heart,
a monument for himself in eternity,
In Northsea deep, in Heaven's shimmer,
In every heart which loves and suffers,
In every soul which shuns
the road of flattery and baseness,
In every spirit in love with beauty.
He needs no stone! He needs no sign!
Forgetfulness cannot reach him,
He lives, and will always live
as He, who has given him to us!

Original Yiddish for this poem is on page 297

HEINRICH HEINE

This is a paean to that great German-Jewish poet whose work was revered in Europe and the world over. This poem is not the free verse of Rosenfeld's tribute to Whitman but it is, never-the-less, a change in his style of writing. It is still Victorian in language but modern in tone and form. It shows that Rosenfeld, had he been so inclined, might have extended his influence further afield by adapting himself more often to different types of poetry than you will see throughout this book. Incidentally, this translator did not rhyme these lines the way Morris did. He got carried away with the spirit of the thing and may have made it even more modern sounding.

We are not sure how much influence Heine had on Rosenfeld. Heine and Goethe were the first German poets he read. He also wrote a monograph on Heine, whom he admired. Heine wrote in the early 19th century, in a more formal use of the rhyming quatrains than Rosenfeld uses. He had a light, charming touch although his subject matter was often very sad. Heine's "punchlines" were often like a kick in the solar plexus. Rosenfeld's were more like having someone pulling your fingernails out. It was Heine who wrote, "Ich vays nicht vas zoll es bedeuten das ich zo traurig bin . . .", which somehow sounds familiar in Rosenfeld's personality.

HERTZL
Herzl

Avek der troymer un zayn troym,
Der tzoyber is shoyn tsurohnen,
Der kampf, vohs hoht a fohlk gevonnen—
A kholem, velkher gloybt zikh koym !
Der heldt un der shrayt
Dohs feldt un di tsayt,
Der muht un der zvek,
Allsding iz avek !
Der gayst, vohs hoht tsuhm likht geshtreybt,
Hoht oyzgeduhmft, iz oyzgeveybt !

HERTZL

Gone is the dreamer and his dreams,
The magic dissolved in foam,
Mirage is never what it seems,
So died our Jewish home.

Gone is the hero in his fight for life,
The siege of the ages—the eons of strife—
continues, continues. We've suffered a blow,
The light of our candle is flickering low.

Original Yiddish for this poem is on page 298

HERTZL

This is a perfunctory, simple credit to a founder and prime mover of modern Zionism. It is honest but without any passion, especially when you consider that Hertzl personally told Rosenfeld that if he had to be any Jew in the world Rosenfeld is the man he would have wished to be. Of course Morris returned the compliment. Our own feeling is that he wrote this in a hurry immediately after the event and rather than erupt in a maudlin exposition he wrote this simple, basic little note. It doesn't satisfy us at all as a tribute. This poem was written after the tragic sudden death of the young Zionist leader in 1904. Hertzl was only 44 years old. Rosenfeld was only 42 himself.

VALT VITMAN
Walt Whitman

Oh dus, in vemes shtarke zinger-brust
Es hobn zikh tsvey upgunden fareynt
Di tihfkayt fun farkehrten himmel
Di shtill farvigte tihfkayt fun der erd.
In vemes hertz es hoht gesheynt di zunen—
Der mundt un vemes hohben hel geglantzt,
Di shterren, gantze velten ohin ah tsohl,

In vemes hertz es hut gegrinnt der May
Un vu dem duners bruhm hoht zikh tsumisht
Mit dem getshvitzer fun dem nakhtigal,
Un vemes vunder-shtarkes lihd men fihlt
Di almakht un di kraft fun der Natur.
Prohfet unshtarblikhen, ikh gib dir loyb !
Ikh fall in shtoyb itzt fun dayn shtoyb, un zing !

Transliterated by EJG with Rifke Levine

WALT WHITMAN

Oh thou, within whose mighty poet-heart
two fathomless abysses intertwined:
the deepness of the pure blue heavens and
the softly cradled deepness of the earth;
within whose heart arose the sun, the moon,
and where, in all their bright magnificance,
stars without number blazed, whole worlds of stars;
within whose heart the buds of May awoke,
and where the harsh voice of thunder sang
beside the twitter of the nightingale;
within whose overwhelming chant one feels
the pulse of nature, its omnipotence;
immortal bard, I honor thee: I kneel
upon the dust, before thy dust, and sing.

Translated by Aaron Kramer
Original Yiddish for this poemis on page 298

WALT WHITMAN

This is a friendly new form of writing for Rosenfeld, who here honors the great American poet, Walt Whitman. It takes a truly great bard to inspire Rosenfeld to say to him, "I honor thee! I kneel upon the dust, before thy dust, and sing!" The more we read of Morris Rosenfeld the more aware we become of his originality, especially in his use of language to emphasize a point. His mind must have worked very quickly because it does not seem to us that he planned his poetry in advance the way Wordsworth and Tennyson did. To say, "I kneel in the dust, before thy dust" must have been an inspiration of the moment. Also, in order for his talent to grow and mature he must have done considerable reading of other poets' works. We have a number of books that were his, thanks to our parents, and we know he read widely.

אייברעהעם לינקאָלן

צו זיין הונדערטם יאָהריגען געבורטסטאָג.

יעמצענד האָט דער אר׳מער נעגער
זיין פערלאָרענקייט געמיינט,
און האָט אויף זיין וויסטען נ׳לעגער
דורך די שטילע נעכט נעוויינט.

מיט די וויסע צייהנער בייסען
פלעגט ער אָפט זיין שוואָרצען לייב,
פלעגט אויף זיך די הויט צורייסען
און דעם סוד פערטרויט זיין ווייב...

נאָר דעם יאָגד האָט ער געטראָגען
שטיל און רוהיג, ווי א לאם.
פלעגט קיין הויכען וואָרט ניט זאָגען,
שטיל געשטיקט אין זיך די פלאם.

אפריקא האָט איהם געצוינען,
נאָך זיין היים האָט ער געגאָרט,
דורך די מירע זעהנזוכטס אוינען
האָט דער וועה זיך דורכגעשפאָרט.

דאָך דער הימעל האָט פערנומען
דעם פערלאָרענעם׳ס געבעט.
און א סלאָף איז געקומען
און האָט פריי דאָס וואָרט געערדט.

אויף קענטאָקי׳ס גרינע וויזען,
אין א שטיבעל אוים׳ן פעלד,
איז דער ריזן פון פרייהיימס ריעזען
אנגעקומען אויף דער וועלם.

„לאָזט איהם לויז!" האָט ער גערלאיארמט,
„ווערט דורך זיין פערצעהן ניט רייך!
„נאָט האָט זיך אויף איהם דערבארמט,
„שוואָרץ צי ווייס, מיר זיינען גלייך!"

און ער האָט די קייט צוריסען,
און געלאָזען געהן דעם קנעכט,
און בעפרייט א פאָלקס-געוויסען,
און געקרוינט דאָס מענשען-רעכט.

דזשארדזש וואשינגטאן

אַ נאָבעלמאַן פון העכ׳רטען גרעסם געבאָרען,
טריסטאָקראַטם געוואָרען אין אָנפאַנג פון זיין לעבען,
דאָך האָט דער יהום זיך אין איהם פערלאָרען ;
ער האָט דעם פאָלק זיין עדעל האַרץ צוועקגעגעבען.
ער האָט זיין גרעסם׳רען ״איך״ צו הילף גענומען :
דעם מענש, די פרייהיים האָט ער לויז געמאַכם די פליגעל,
ער איז צוריק פיעל נאָבלער ווי געקומען,
זיין קבר איז אַ פולע גרעסער ווי זיין וויעגעל.

געקעמפט, רעגיערם, דאָך נים געהערשם אויף קיינעם,
אַ חבר צו יוכבד׳ם זוהן : ווי פון מצרים
בעפריים אַ פאָלק, בעלעבם מים איהם אידעאַיינעם,
און אויפגעמאַכם דער וועלם אַ ניי ירושלים.
אַ גרויסער גיים, וואָס האָט אַ וועלם געשאַפען !
אַ ריינע, אונבעפלעקמע זעעלע אָהן אַ בלייכען !
דיר זינגם אַ ליעד אַ יעדער פרייער האַפען,
דער האַרמאָן רישם דיין לויב, עם רוישען אַלע מייכען !

דיר פלאַמערם אוים אַ לויכ דער שענסמער באַנער,
עם רעדען אַלע מערג פון דיר, די מיעפע פלומען.
אָ, ה אונשטערבליכער אַמעריקאַנער,
פון העלכען אַלע פעלקער דענקען, ווען זיי בלומען !

אָ, זאָל דיין גרעסם ביי דיעזען מהויער וואַכען,
ביים מהויער, וואָס דו האָסם געעפענם פאַר דעם מיעדען,
און זאָל קיין בייזע ברעכם איהם נים פערמאַכען,
נים לעטמערען דיין זעעלע, וועלכע רוהם אין פריעדען !

הײנריך הײנע

א מאָנומענט פיר הײנריך הײנע,
װיא לעכערליך, װיא דום דיא מענה !
א מאָנומענט פון קאַלטען מאַרמאָר,
פיר איהם, װאָס זײן געזאַנג איז װאַר׳מער,
איז הײמער װיא דיא היטץ פון זומער,
פיר איהם, װאָס האָט דעם מיעססמען קומער.
געגאָסען אין א געממליך פייער ;
װאָס האָט געצשאהלם אי פיעל, אי מהײער
פיר ליעבעס הײליגע שליחות ;
װאָס האָט פעדיינעם דיא העכסטע סמיכות,
דיא שעהנסטע קרױן פון פרײהײטס זינגער —
פיר איהם הילם איהר מיט מענשעסאפינגער
אין קאַלמען שטיין, װאָס צײט צאַרעסם עס,
א דײנקמאַל מאַכען, שאם, פערנעסם עם !

פערנעסם עס, דען א הײנריך הײנע,
מאַכם זעלבסם דיא מאָנומענטען זײנע.
ער האָט געשמיד׳ם אין גאָלד׳נע חרוזים
מים פלאַמען פון זײן אײנ׳נעם בוזים
א מאָנומענט פיר זיך אױף שיטער.
אין „נאָרדזעע״ טיעף, אין הימעלם שיטער.
אין יעדער האַרץ, װאָס ליעבם און לײדעם,
אין יעדע זעעלע, װעלכע מײדעם
דעם װעג פון חנופה און געמײנהײים,
אין יעדען נײסט בעלעבם פון שעהנהײים.
ער דאַרף קײן שטײן, ער דאַרף קײן צײכען,
איהם קען פערגעסםענהײם נים גרײכען.
ער לעבם און ער װעם אײביג לעבען
װיא דער, װאָס האָם איהם אונז געגעבען.

וואלט וויטמאן

(אמעריקא'ס גרויסער דיכטער).

א
הו, אין וועמעם שטארקע זינגער־ברוסט
עם האבען זיך צוויי אבגרונדען פעראיינט :
דיא טיעפקייט פון פערקלערטען הימעל און
דיא שטיל פערווירטענדע טיעפקייט פון דער ערד ;
אין וועמעם הערץ עם האט געשיינט דיא זונן,
דער מאנד און וואו עם האבען העל געגלאנצט
דיא שטערען, גאנצע וועלטמען אהן א צאחל,
אין וועמעם הערץ עם האט געגרינט דער מאי
און וואו דעם דונערס ברום האט זיך צומישט
מיט דעם געמשוויטשער פון דער נאכטיגאל ;
אין וועמעם וואונדער שטארקעם ליעד מען פיהלט
דיא פלמבען און דיא קראפט פון דער נאטור,
פראפהעט, אונשטערבליכער, איך גיב דיר לויב,
איך פאל אין שטויב יעצט פאר דיין שטויב און זינג.

ה ע ר צ ל

א
ווען דער טרוימער און זיין טרוים,
דער צויבער איז אין שוים צורונען,
דער קאמפף, וואם האט א פאלק געוואונען —
א חלום, וועלכער גלויבט זיך קוים !
דער העלד און דער שפרייט,
דאם פעלד און די ציים,
דער מזם און דער צוועק,
אלסדינג איז אוועק !
דער גייסם, וואם האם צום ליכם געשטרעבט,
האם אויסגעדומפפם, איז אויסגעזוועבם.

EPIGRAMS
IN VERSE

————◆————

EPIGRAMS

According to Webster an epigram is a "concise poem dealing pointedly and often satirically with a single thought or event, often ending with an ingenious turn of thought" Well, these epigrams of Rosenfeld do precisely that. However we had a problem with them. Translation was much more difficult than with a lengthy poem where one has more room to "work around" an idea. Here, because the point of each epigram often ends with some wild colloquialism, we have had to use far more imagination and research than we used for his other poetry. They are all fun and quite sardonic.

Apparently Rosenfeld used this medium to get back at some of his pet nudnicks who bothered him. He had a sharp sense of humor but was no Woody Allen. But neither is Woody Allen a struggling immigrant with the weight of the world on his shoulders. I think Morris and Woody would have respected each other, with Woody poking fun at Rosenfeld's constant "crying" and Morris wondering aloud whether, at times, Woody has either of his feet touching solid ground. All translations of these epigrams were done by Ed Goldenthal with the help, particularly with the idiomatic expressions, of Sandy Greenberg.

CREATING

If gold alone inspires your art
    then pureness from your work will part.
If you create for fame alone
    you fool yourself—you'll be unknown.
Creation for itself is just,
    if you create because you must!

CRITIQUE

If your poems just "won't do"
    and blessings aren't said for you,
then curse and scream and write "critiques"
    for those endowed with lucky streaks.

TRANSLATING

If you translate just "the word"
    it's dead—the meaning isn't heard.
An artist true can sense the role
    not of the word but of the soul.

THE FOOL

The head of a fool fills with smoke
when success strikes him and wiser folk.
No sooner does understanding come
than luck arrives, just for the dumb!

SHE LIVES ETERNALLY

Stupidity will long endure,
    her changing guise gives new allure,
off'ring masses her newer forms.
    In every century she changes,
evoking wonder at her talent's ranges,
    and so to ev'ry age conforms.

Original Yiddish for these epigrams on pages 302 and 303

THE WORLD

The world is mute when they praise you
   and hears when you are opposed,
The world is blind when they raise you
   and sees when your casket is closed.

MANKIND

The world doesn't know you're wise
   until it begins to apprise
that you are man enough
   to show how craftily you bluff.

ASK NOT

The world's advice you need not ask,
   your own counsel you should consult.
On your shoulders must weigh each task
   and you must vouch for the result.

HOLD HIM

When you have fortune in your grip
   hold him fast, don't let him slip!
If you forget yourself a while
   he'll run away ten thousand miles!

JEWS

Reb Yek says, "The world's a wonder!"
   Reb Tudros says, "She's a fright!"
I stand listening and ponder
   and think that both of them are right!

עפּיגראַמען

שאַפּען

אוז שאַפֿפֿסטו פֿאַר געצאַהלם אַלייז,
דאַן איז דײַן שאַפֿעז זעלמעז רייז.
אוז שאַפֿפֿסטו, ווײַל דו זוכּסט אַ שם,
דאַן נאַרסטו זיך זאַגאַר מים דעם,
דעז שאַפֿעז האָם נאָר דאַן אַ האָפֿם
ווען איינער שאַפֿם נאָר, ווײַל ער שאַפֿם.

קריטיק

אויב דײַן קענסם איז גים קיין „אי אי",
מעז מאַכם אויף איהר קיין ברכח...
מאַ שרײַב „קריטיק" אוז שילם, אוז שרײַ
אויף דעם, וואָס האָם האַצלחה!

איבערזעצען

ווען דו איבערזעצסם דעם טוימע וואָרם,
דאַן פֿערנעמסטו נאָר אומזיסם אַז אָרם;
וואָרום קינסמלער בּיסטו ווען דו ווייזם,
נים יענעמס וואָרם, נאָר יענעמס גײַסם.

די וועלם

די וועלם איז מויב ווען מעז לויבם דיך,
אוז האַרם ווען מעז איז דיר צרוויידער;
די וועלם איז בּלינד ווען מעז הויבם דיך,
אוז זעהם ווען מעז לעגם דיך אַנידער...

סאַרזאַכטיג

זײַם ערנסטם מים דער אונשולד סיי ווי סיי,
דעז אָפֿטמאַל מאַכם זיך לומפּערײַ,
אום אַבצומאַכאַז אַ זאַך אַ „בּלאָטע"—
גע'פֿגר'ם, שטיל אוז תם'עוואַטע.

פרעג ניט

ניט פרעג די וועלט קיין עצה,
נאָר פאָלג דיין אייגענעם ראָט,
ווייל נאָר דיין אייגענע פֿליַיצע
מוז טראָגען דעם רעזולטאַט.

דער נאַר

ביַי'ם נאַר ווערט אַ פולע קאָפּ מיט רויך,
ווען איהם איז גוט און דעם חכם אויך,
דען ליַים ווי ער קען די זאַך פֿערשטעהן,
קומט דאָס גליַיק נאָר דער דומהיַים אליין.

זי לעבט איַיביג

די דומהיַיט, זי וועט לאַנג נאָך האַלטען,
און אַלץ אין אַנדערע געשטאַלטען
ערשיַינען פאַר די מאַסען.
אין יעדען אַנדערען יאָהרהונדערט
וועם זי אַלץ אַנדערס זיַין בעוואונדערט
און וועם זיך שמעענדיג פֿאַסען.

אידעען

ר' יעקעל זאָגט: די וועלט איז פֿיין,
ר' טודרום שריַיט, אַז זי איז שלעכט,
איך שטעה פֿאַרטראַכט און חער זיך איַין —
מיר דאַכט זיי האָבען ביַידע רעכט.

האַלט איהם

און האָסטו געכאַפּט דאָס גליַיק פֿאָר'ן קאָפּ,
מאַ האַלט איהם פעסט און לאָז איהם ניט אָב,
דען קום פֿערמראָכמסטו זיך אויף אַ וויַיל',
אנטלויפט ער פֿון דיר צעהן טויזענד מיַיל.

9

Poetry Written in English

The following poems are but a few of the many hundreds Rosenfeld wrote in English. In the beginning he struggled and even wrote some poems declaring his admiration for the language of Shakespeare and admitting he would like to be a bard in that language. The shallowness of his vocabulary and his problems with grammar and spelling were gradually overcome with the years. His rhymes at times teetered on the brink of doggerel, even though his ideas and images were frequently excellent. Some of his syntax showed that either he had not yet mastered the English syntax or that he had, on occasion, actually translated Yiddish poems into English. In those instances, which we cannot prove, the position of the verb, the nouns and adjectives, seem to give it away. There is an undeniable German syntax in a few of his English poems, which may represent his inability, at certain earlier times, adequately to grasp English as we know it.

We include some of these poems as an example of his persistence and his talent. He was actually quite good-spirited about his efforts. Morris completed several collections of poems in English. The first was called, "PILGRIM", which was never published. Some of those poems are included here. Then there were many hundreds more, also never published, which we discovered at the YIVO and in some papers left by Dr. Leon Goldenthal, an earlier biographer of Rosenfeld. To think that for over half a century these treasures were in our home and we never knew about them! Many poems written after "PILGRIM" are superior in terms of syntax, vocabulary and general feel of the language. His poetry became less Victorian in manner, more modern in style. We also noted more "free verse" and a radical change in his approach to love-poetry. Earlier love-poetry (not only Rosenfeld's) was stilted, overly sentimental, written in the love-formula of the time. He changed with the times and his love-poetry was more daring and more exciting.

Rosenfeld was so appreciative of America's largesse to the Jewish immigrants that he became openly patriotic. He wrote glowingly and in good English about Lincoln, Whitman, the Alleghenies and America's physical beauty. He wrote to support our efforts in World War I, to support the miners in the coal pits, the blacks in their ongoing troubles and, amazingly, he wrote a remarkable poem on women's rights! Yes, women's rights! He called it, "THE MAN", and you must read it.

Rosenfeld was Jewish to the core but most of his English poems were not about Jewry's problems, nor were they even about Labor's problems! He expanded his themes to include Nature and philosophical topics. In fact he wrote, and never had a chance to publish, a whole work of philosophical concepts that came to him in his latter years. How we wish we had gotten to know the real Morris better! How we wish the world had gotten to know him better! That is a major reason for writing this book in the manner we have chosen. We wanted to let the world "in" on the human being, the vibrant persona of the man behind all those poems and other writings. We've never met his Muse, but I feel that her granddaughter is a close friend of mine.

Most of the English poems included here will not have written individual commentaries; only those whose subjects seem to require it . Each appended note will put the poem in context with his life and his times. Introducing "PILGRIM" is a written report from a professional "reader" from a publishing house, expanding on what we have been trying to state. The "reader" concludes with, "perhaps the poet can perfect some of the poems in which he has struggled in vain." This strikes a chord in my mind. The temptation to "correct" or "improve" some stanzas of Morris' poetry has been immense. But that would not be honest or respectful to Grandpa. Certainly, after years and years of college it would be a cinch to rewrite a few lines here and there. No way, dear reader, will we sink that level. Rosenfeld was a great poet, deserving to be read, good or not so good, as he was at times.

EJG (the author of this book) did have enough chutzpah to attempt a translation of his grandfather's poetry. However even in the translation he tried to hew as closely as possible to the vocabulary, meter and sense of Rosenfeld's Yiddish poetry. We make no apologies for Rosenfeld's shortcomings but are frank about our own. The decision was made not to demonstrate Ed's ability as a poet but to try to replicate the unsophisticated, impassioned, simple style of Rosenfeld. Remember, *he* was the great bard. But something important must be stated at this juncture. In translating Rosenfeld from the Yiddish we became acutely aware of a factor that distinguishes his poetry from many other poets: he never tried to be "poetic"! It became evident to us, when reading other translators' efforts, that they often added fancier words than he would use. They went off into typical "descriptive modes" to add an elegance or floweriness that he never put into his work. The man spoke a simple colloquial Yiddish and he wrote in exactly those words for his poetry.

He definitely had a dictionary. We have in our possession the very copy of Harkavy that he used, but it seems to us that he hardly ever used it. This is why he repeats certain pet words ad nauseum. Perhaps he should have owned a thesaurus. When we translated Rosenfeld from the Yiddish we used (as exactly as possible) the meaning and the word he employed. Our talents as a poet may be limited but we never (well, hardly ever!) put our own poetic license to work. It would not be fair or honest to add a 1997 imagination or expression to a Victorian-age poet's creations. In a couple of instances the type-written words on the moldering paper it was written on obscured the sense of the poem, so a word or two was placed in the appropriate spot. Also, in one poem it seemed to this author that the poet was very upset when he wrote. Some thoughts did not sound organized. Since the thought behind the poem was adequate justification to print it, three or four words here and there put sense into it. The poems involved have been adequately described for the reader when he gets to it.

In this section we are simply writing a heartfelt appreciation of Rosenfeld. His English poetry shares much of the passion, simplicity and lack of sophistication of his Yiddish works but one can sense here the struggles of a pioneer in a new culture, a PILGRIM, if you wish, who even in his later years, is clearing the land, cultivating the soil and describing the beauties of his new home-land as he creates a new life for himself. As we read his poetry we cannot help but sense the personality behind all those words; the ego to succeed, the love he wants to express, the disappointment and frustration that eats at him while he struggles to reassert his leadership in the medium of his choice.

To those who may have never had to emigrate to an alien land, we suggest that you attempt to write even a business-letter in some foreign language, using proper vocabulary, syntax, imagery and up-to-date feel. And then, *imagine yourself actually thinking in that alien language* so that you can express emotional or descriptive ideas that are original and worth reading. *Rosenfeld had to think in English*, he simply could not translate his thoughts into English or the whole effort would have been transparent and a failure. We only included those poems of Rosenfeld that seemed to rank as acceptable English poetry and publish them without excuses.

COPY OF A "READER'S" REPORT ON
"SONGS OF A PILGRIM"*

The effort represented by this verse is, as Mr. Tobenkin suggests, rather pathetic and to me it is rather appealing as well. That the Yiddish poems of the writer are very well known and loved is easy to believe, because one sees, behind the imperfect expression of these attempts at English verse the soul of a true poet who has something to say which common humanity can feel and understand. These poems have a simplicity, a beauty and a universality suggestive of folk poetry.

I have been over them carefully twice and find work of two widely different qualities. About half of the hundred poems achieve a degree of perfection in artistic expression. The others are often so crude as to be pathetically absurd. They suggest a blundering, verbatim translation of a masterpiece in which the beauty of the original is hopelessly lost. It is possible that the best poems were those which the poet composed in English and the others the result of the poet translating his own work.

The moving spirit of this poet and his verse is his intense love for America. This work represents a gift of the immigrant to America and one would like to accept it gratefully without hesitating for commercial reasons. And I am not at all sure that it does not have commercial value. *The poems represent something new in American poetry;* (italics inserted, ed.) they are wonderfully genuine and simple and they mean something which may touch and win the public. I believe that enough poems could be selected to make a significant little volume, with perhaps an introduction by Mr. Tobenkin. Perhaps the poet can perfect some of the poems in which he has struggled in vain to "sing in Shakespeare's tongue".

*This is a letter from a "reader" for the F.A. Stokes publishing house in about 1920.

SONGS OF A PILGRIM
A Selection

THE PILGRIM

I am a Pilgrim. To the holy shrine
Of English literature's my way.
My Heart, my soul and all the feelings mine
Are yearning there to come and sing and pray.

I wish my trembling knees there to bend down
Where Milton knelt during his life-long night.
I wish to put one more gem in the crown
That glitters in eternal light.

A NEGRO CHILD

Without guile or patronization Rosenfeld writes this charming little poem
to a Negro child. His sensitivity was touched despite an initial inclination
to overlook the child. He didn't HAVE to write this poem. There was no
large Negro constituency out there to impress with his liberalism. Nobody
even knows he wrote this poem. He simply wrote what came naturally,
even though his rhymes were forced. This a very early, experimental poem
in English.

A NEGRO CHILD

I once observed a Negro child,
He looked to me most strange and wild.
I turned in disgust away
But when I saw the same child play
And heard him laugh and saw his joy
With which he kissed his pretty toy
I cared not for his skin or blood,
I saw a soul, a part of God.

A LEAF OF GRASS

The pen is trembling in my fingers,
I fear to write an English line,
I dare not walk the paths divine
The starry paths of English singers.

But still ,"sing on, you are not liable,
Sing on, sing on!" I hear a voice,
"Select sweet English as your choice,
Make Shakespeare your poetic Bible."

My courage grew, my heart is stronger,
I sing in English without fear,
The Muse is good to me and dear,
My soul is new, my feelings stronger.

I care not if the critic lingers
To fix my place. I wish to pass
Not more than a humble leaf of grass
In the garden of the English singers.

TWO TREES

Said the willow tree with great pride
to an apple tree close by its side,
"Disfigured creature! Gaze at me!
Behold my graceful symmetry.
You are twisted, bent and small,
but I am strong and straight and tall!"
Said the apple tree, "I will not dispute,
but let me remind you that I bear fruit!

This is not a great poem but it is pleasant and not at at all foreign in its
syntax. The rhythm of the last two lines suffers from his desire to rhyme
fruit and dispute.

I KNOW NOT WHERE

I studied the map there to find
the land where life to all man is kind,
where strange the sigh is, strange the tear,
and people have not whom to fear,
where days give zest and nights give rest,
and things are of the very best.
I looked for that most blessed spot
and looked in vain: I found it not.

I crossed the seas to find the land
where Fate rules with a milder hand,
a kinder God looks down with love
on ev'ry mortal from above,
where silvery bells softly ring
and sweeter songs the warblers sing.
I did not find her here nor there.
O Happy Land! Where are you, where ?

There is something of German or Yiddish syntax in "I Know Not Where", but it does seem that he is thinking in English, mostly, since he does not frequently place his verbs at the end of the sentence.

TO MAN

The following poem is a work we mentioned earlier. Read it aloud and with vigor, the way "Morris the Declaimer" used to do. See how up-to-date it is, how incisive. The women's movement today could use a poem such as this in its fight for equality. This poem came as a total surprise and a delight to us, about ninety years after it was written. It has never been published before. This is proof that Rosenfeld *could think in English*. His frequent rhymes in this and other poems of joy with toy and the use of the word "woe" are distressing, especially today, when a thesaurus would provide a multitude of better rhymes. Did they have thesauruses in his day?

TO MAN

You never did consider her your equal, no,
You looked upon her as a toy,
To play with and to have your sport, your joy.
You never took to heart her deep and human woe,
You didn't care, you made her cheap, and sore,
She was to you a woman, nothing more.

You raise your hat to her you, pay her great respect,
But never think to give her equal rights,
She is a plaything through your days and nights,
And her correct demands you wilfully reject.
You did deny her rightful place in life,
She was to you no more than just a wife.

She is the mother of generations, all,
She nursed the ages with her milk, she gave
Her love, her care, her all, but was your slave,
She is the source of life, her joys enthrall
Us, the mother of the human race is she
But never recognized, yea, never free.

Yes, Man, but now she comes to say that you are wrong,
Now history stands up for her and pleads
And gives the facts of all her mighty deeds,
And claims her proper place that was denied her long,
For she keeps up the world and makes it new,
It's time that she be deemed as good as you.

The future will condemn your grave mistake
And look unkind upon your bitter wrongs.
Oh help her, Man, to come where she belongs.
Turn on the light! The hour has struck. Awake!
Don't leave upon your name a shameful stain,
Don't mar our time of spirit, heart and brain!

The centuries look down indignantly and ask
"Will her humiliation never cease?
Will she remain as helpless as she is?
Will her oppressors not be called to task?"
And Justice cries, "Is this the woman's Fate?"
Yea, must her freedom come so very late?

THE POET'S LEXICON
Music

Music, heaven's sunny daughter,
Holy language of higher souls,
Sweet laughter of young cherubs,
Murmur of unbodied spirits
Mixed with the voice of thunder,
With weeping of babies,
And fire of lovers,
And roars of the ocean !

Music, herald of peace and war,
You have a melody
For the slaves and the free
For the free and the slave,
The cradle and the grave.

MUSIC

In many ways this is a departure for Rosenfeld: no worries about meter, no fighting to find a rhyme in an alien language, no searching for a more appropriate word. This is a modern poem with a universal concept of poetry and music. We see here interesting images and this form of expression could have been the future for Morris, if only he had lived long enough.

POETRY WRITTEN IN ENGLISH
(Not from "SONGS OF A PILGRIM")

THE RAVEN

'Tis night, the woods are dense and still,
The birds are all at rest,
But from some hidden nest
From time to time comes a shrill,
Comes a most terrible scream.
The Raven talks in his dream!

The trees are quiet, undisturbed,
The birds are fast asleep,
The lonely clouds do weep.
The night is in itself absorbed
But the darkness knows the screams
And what the black raven dreams.

THE RAVEN

This poem might be an allegory. Perhaps those who are considered dark and unpleasant by the world have their own deep-throated screams of terror in the tense stygian blackness of an endless night. While not a great work of poetic art this poem does lead one to the well of thought.

IF
(Reprinted from "The Survey")

If hope would fly and sorrow stay,
If stars were dark and days were gray,
If love would vanish like a breath,
What would life be, and what would death?

If songs would die out in the nest,
And pleasure in the human breast,
If flowers were to lose their hue,
What would I be, and what would you?

IF

Morris is good at asking tough questions. Here again he slips us the piece of blank paper without any explicit answers. This poem exhibits the mature seriousness with which he considers life. There is a positive for every negative; for sorrow there is hope, for gray days there are bright stars at night, for a vanished breath there is undying love. In this way he really answers his own questions but it is important for us to ask ourselves the same old questions so that, periodically, we may become re-acquainted with the valuable positive answers we can actually give ourselves. This is a fine poem in mature English.

JEALOUSY

I'll take the sun's rays and will weave
Rich silk for you my darling and will give
To the tailor the azure blue,
That he may make a dress for you;

THE POET OF THE GHETTO / 316

Veins from the planets I shall pull
And spin them 'round a golden spool,
To sew it and to make it strong—
And iron it smoothly with a song;

All the bright stars will partake
In its sweet artistic make;
I'll buy you sandals of pure light
And see that they should fit you right;

From Eden's gardens I shall take
Flowers, a wreath for you to make;
I'll harness the cherubs up on high
In the heavens, with you to fly.
I want to pride myself above
And make them jealous of my love.

JEALOUSY

Morris has written here a delightful love poem; not quite like Solomon's
Song because Solomon wasn't a tailor. And he would not have wanted to
make the Heavenly Delegates jealous of his love because he knew what
happened to Annabel Lee when "they envied her and me, so that her high-
born kinsmen came and carried her off to a sepulcher, there by the sounding sea." It takes a broad imagination to drape your love with filaments
from the stars and the gold of the sun woven as only a Muse-driven poet
can weave, and then iron the fabric with a song!

THE PRESENT ONLY

Said Moses: "Lord of Love and Grace,
I pray show me Thy holy face.
My wish is, God, to look at thee
And at all things that are to be.
The curtain of the future, raise,
And far ahead O let me gaze."

Said God: "No living man can see
My face, or what there is to be.
What you may see is but my back.
Yea, of the past you may keep track.
I've granted to the mortal eye
To see but things that have passed by."

THE PRESENT ONLY

This poem is deeper than it appears at first glance. We must not be put off by the brevity and simplicity of so many of Rosenfeld's poems. He did not have the characteristics of those great English poets who have been quoted for their "deathless" lines. Rosenfeld's ideas are secure and mature. His observations are accurate, his expressions are without guile or pretense, without sophistication This poem has a ring to it like a bell wrought of noble metal. The little tailor has graduated from labor poems to the profound thoughts that lie behind philosophy and religion.

I CHASE

In sad moments when I find no grace
In heaven, with a full heart I chase,
I chase the billows of the ocean,
The wind in the prairies I chase,
My soul chases on with emotion
The sun in yon western space.
I want to keep pace with them all
On this troublesome, accursed ball.
Perhaps I'll be able to reach the door
That leads to where sorrow is no more.
I chase and chase, I chase and I chase,
And only a shadow do I embrace.

I CHASE

There is something about this poem that would best be examined by a psychiatrist. You know how dreams are, sometimes, when you are on an endless, unfulfilled chase. You know it is the epitome of frustration. You are not sure this will be gone when you awaken. You are not sure you are asleep. Something is always keeping the object of your search just a little beyond your reach. This is more than a poem. It is a bad dream. It is Rosenfeld's life and it is Jewish history in rhyme and meter. It is also a fine poem.

LIKE THE MOON

You are so pale, my love,
But like the moon above
Walking pale on high
Lends splendor to the sky.

So are you on this earth,
You give it greater worth,
You are sweetness and grace
With a heavenly face.

LIKE THE MOON

Did you ever feel this way about your love? When you get lots older this seems adolescent. But when you are adolescent this is how you feel. Your love is "sweetness and grace with a heavenly face." There is a Yiddish song, "Sheyn vi di lavuhneh"; pretty like the moon. But our Muse tells us that you don't have to be an adolescent to be in love.

I KNOW NOT WHY

This poem was set to music and as a song was published by the NEW YORK HERALD in its issue of June 11, 1899. This is the first of Rosenfeld's poems written in English that received national recognition. It was published in Stedman's "AN AMERICAN ANTHOLOGY" in 1900. It is simple, to the point, no affectation. If a true philosopher offered Rosenfeld's answers to eternal questions on the imponderables of human existence he would lose his tenure and his pension too. "I Know Not Why" is an honest answer from a simple poet to a complex question. By the way, the answer you and I might offer today would probably be the same, "I know not why."

I KNOW NOT WHY

I lift mine eyes against the sky,
The clouds are weeping—so am I;
I lift mine eyes again on high,
The sun is smiling—so am I.

Why do I smile ? Why do I weep ?
I do not know, it lies too deep.
I hear the winds of autumn sigh,
They break my heart, they make me cry.

I hear the birds of lovely Spring,
My hope revives, I help them sing.
Why do I sing? Why do I cry?
It lies so deep, I know not why.

THE ANT

Poor anty, I could not help killing you.
You were in my way when I trod.
It was a murderous act, it is true,
But 'twas the holy will of God.

Little things are not considered at all.
They mustn't creep where people walk.
As a rule, we step on those that are small,
And have no voice, and cannot talk.

THE ANT

Do you really think this poem is about an ant? Or is it about our poorly
civilized civilization? Rosenfeld can say serious things with whimsy, the
way every grandfather can do. Here the poet has truly thought in English
when writing this poem. He must have felt encouraged that his efforts to
write in our language were becoming more successful.

THE WORKING GIRL

Every busy weekday morning
When the masses went to work,
Did I espy a sweet young girl
Hurry too along with them.

Weeks and months and years were passing
But not much the girl did grow
Small her stature, pale and sickly
Was her face. I thought it cried,

"Cruel world! Why did you squander,
Say, the roses of my youth?
Why did you, with hate, extinguish
Say, the fire in mine eyes?"

I remember this same sidewalk
Where she trod when young and sweet:
Cold and mute the stones as ever.
She is silent just as they.

Will you make her restitution,
Bloody murderess, O world!
Will you give her fire and courage,
Youth, beauty and color back?

THE WORKING GIRL

We are not sure about this one. First impulse is to say, "This would make a great poem, someday." It has all of Rosenfeld's images and intensity. It doesn't need rhyme, but needs meter. Would it have sounded better in Yiddish? It has a Yiddish syntax and so falls a trifle short in English. But read it again and take it seriously. Suppose we translate it into Yiddish: Read the third stanza in transliterated Yiddish:

Rotskhisher veldt! Far vus hustu tsutrenzlt,
Zug, di royzen fon mayn yugend ?
Far vus hustu, mit khasse, oysfarleshen,
Zug, der fayer fon mayne oygen?

Our Yiddish is not too good, but that sounds more like Rosenfeld, doesn't it?

A QUESTION

This is a flying leap forward in Rosenfeld's English style. He ceases his struggles for rhymes, satisfies his ambition with firm, important questions, cool imagery and a near irreverence towards the Power that creates all good and evil. Why does he bring in Satan? Does he grant that the universe is schizophrenic, with both sides battling for control? Is he even implying that God is a split personality with both halves of Him at odds with each other? We think we know which side has won so far, but this is really your decision to make as well. Rosenfeld mentions Tophet, that Hell, that place of endless perdition. We know what was on his subconscious agenda. Anyone who is familiar with Jewish history recognizes that place. This is a first-rate poem for Morris.

A QUESTION

Eternal, who dost speak in trembling silence
Soul of light, great Spirit of the universe
to born and unto unborn generations,
that carries the worlds within thy ethereal self,
God, creator of all the orbs from chaos
and life from Thine own perpetual fire—
A crumb of nothingness, a shameful mortal
dares to left his humble voice to thee—O list.

They claim Thou castest Satan from the heavens
into the depth of Tophet, with his presence
not to mar the sunrays of Thy corridors;
Not to lead Thy children on his paths;
Oh Lord, how does he manage blood and horror
on the earth to sow? Yes, how did he return
to wield his serpent rod in gory battle fields
and poison human hearts with hate and terror?

Or is it Man who wars on thy creation,
destruction who does seek, who does want himself
to tear the strings of life's invisible lyre
who hates to die by inches, old and feeble,
who does prefer to perish with sword outstretched,
not a forgotten frog in stagnant waters,
who hates the sickbed, which is waiting, yearning
for every mortal who does live and struggle.

However, man or devil, both are haters
of thy mysterious rulings. One does envy
Thy power and Thy celestial kingdom.
'Tis Satan, but Man, yea, the miserable Man,
who can but weep, who walks twixt graves and sorrow,
who swallows tears and groans and disappointments,
Man, chases his own shadow with a question;
He knows not why he was at all created.

ORIENTAL SONGS

This must have been written in the early twentieth century, having so many Victorian overtones and cloying expressions and approaches to the subject of love. But it also has excellent control of English so it is difficult to place it in time. There is much here to remind us of Solomon's songs: the frankness about passion and its attributes, the neglect of any worldly concerns except for love itself. As a bard for his time Rosenfeld wrote this for the people of his time. As such it is excellent. We sense the free style of Whitman, the escape from meter and rhyme. It sounds very modern.

ORIENTAL SONGS

I

Thy cheeks are like blossoms of Eden—
with heavenly perfume they spray,
Thou art like a flower delightful
adorning the garlands of May.
I see thee and breathe thy aroma
with sacred desire I am blest—
I wish that a butterfly were I
to dwell on thy white, heaving breast.

The world I'd forget in thy beauty,
creator's most exquisite art,
Inhaling thy fragrance I'd listen
to music of love in thy heart.
I'd wring all the truth of thy being
from secret and glowing repose,
O glorious flower of flowers
how splendid thy passion there blows!

I

I drank of the exquisite nectar
that flowed from thy red lips so sweet,
I kissed thine eyes burning, bewitching,
I kissed thy white hands and thy feet.
I made me a wreath of thy tresses,
thy ringlets my neck did embrace,
The wounds of my heart were forgotten,
I soared in the infinite space.
I lay on thy bosom enchanting,
I revelled in heavenly bliss,
The universe owning entirely
I lived in thy fiery kiss.

Thy breast was refreshingly glowing
and heaving and soothing and white,
It quelled all my ardorous yearning,
It thrilled me with wildest delight.

These moments I'll ever remember,
unearthly and sweet was their flood,
Their memory fills me with longing
igniting my passion with blood.

THE PICTURE

This is an interesting poem The poet simply does not seem very poetic.
He does not make any effort to polish up his verse with the finesse we
know he possessed. He was undoubtedly very depressed over the loss of
his son Joseph. However the whole concept of the poem is original even
though the poet does not seem to have the "koyakh" (strength) to deal
with it adequately. We must confess to correcting three or four words here
because the lines lost their coherency. This will not reduce the Bard's
reputation nor enhance ours.

THE PICTURE

I looked at the picture of my dead child
that hung upon my chamber wall.
I looked at the picture of my dead boy
that hung in a frame on the wall.
I knew that it would, tomorrow,
break me as it does now,
make heavy my heart with sorrow
and my life's flame burn very low.
My spirits are all very low
and fill my soul with woe.
So I turned my eyes away from the wall
that speaks of a grave that keeps my all.

I even thought of taking the picture down
to try to forget the past.
For what is the use of having it there?
It must not forever last.
It will rend my heart in twain
and do my soul good.

It will but increase my pain
and further darken my mood.
I'll take it off the wall—I must have rest,
Hide it from view and ease my wounded breast.

I stretched my hand to remove it, but lo!
It moved in the frame and said,
"Do not, Papa dear! Let me be here,
Oh let me be here!" He said
"No use in hiding me, father,
or taking me from your view.
Yes, leave me here, leave me, rather,
so I'll still remain with you
with a love that is more than true!"
So that dear picture hangs still on my wall,
and I dream of a grave that holds my all.

MY AMERICA

Be thou, New World, by heaven blest!
Thy threshold doth on freedom rest.
America! Thou hast my love
And if my valor thou wouldst prove
And ask my life as sacrifice
It shall be yielded in a trice.
No "wherefore" and no "Why" Ask,
I shall obey, whate'er the task.
     refrain
Thy wish is holy, thy command
I deem as writ by God's own hand
With thee in peace, with thee in strife,
Blest nourisher of freedom's life!
I am with thee, with thee, with thee,
Yea thou art precious unto me.

Thou sanctuary of the earth!
Thy voice to men has sacred worth
Like that which did from Sinai sound.
Thy every span is sacred ground.
What scepter and what throne shall dare
With thy bright banner to compare?

No other friend but thine I know.
Thy foe—I hate him—is my foe!
    refrain
Thy wish is holy, thy command
I deem as writ by God's own hand.
With thee in peace, with thee in strife,
Blest nourisher of freedom's life!
I am with thee, with thee, with thee,
Yes thou art precious unto me.

MY AMERICA

This poem was published in the Jewish Morning Journal in March 1917, (The week this author was born!). It was submitted with a speech by the Hon. Isaac Siegel to the House of Representatives in Washington as a possible new American Anthem. He wrote, in part: "Mr. Speaker, about thirty years ago there came to the U.S. an immigrant whose name is Morris Rosenfeld. He found employment as a sewing machine operator but when the long hours of work were over he took to writing poetry to depict the life of the workers in that trade. Men risen high in public life learned of his work and encouraged him. Among these was Col. Theodore Roosevelt and the late Gen. Frederick Dent Grant. He wrote this hymn which has met the approval of President Wilson."

Prose Writings by Morris Rosenfeld

——————————————

10

Prefatory Remarks to Rosenfeld's Prose Writings

Before we invite you to read Rosenfeld's prose we have to inform you that these charming little pieces are as new to us as they probably are to you. We, as children, always knew that Grandpa was a well-respected poet. But why didn't Mom ever read any of these pleasant stories to us years ago? It's a puzzlement. They tell us so much about the New York City of the immigrant experience. And they tell us so much about the Grandpa that we barely knew. We were very young and thought of him an old man. Is 61 really so old? We never knew he had a "cute" sense of humor, or that he was a frank critic and satirist. We never were told that he was so very observant of his own Jewish world and the great world beyond.

They never told us that he was so steeped in the history and religion of the Jews. We knew (by observation) that he was not religious in terms of frequent trips to the synagogue. Neither were we very observant of religious matters ourselves. However when you read these few brief stories you will note his references to every aspect of Jewishness, of his religion, of our history as Jews. These references simply rolled off his tongue. As a second-generation American Jew I have been relatively uninformed by early training and have had to study and "look-up" aspects of Yiddishkeit that were as much a part of Rosenfeld's life as was the air he breathed. As you can see from his writings, he could rattle off dates and names and historical and Biblical facts and events as though they had been something he had actually lived through himself. None of these events was an artifact to him. For me there is an almost subconscious historicity to all of our past. These facts, although they had to be learned in later life by the author, found such a receptive soil that it seems as though I always knew them. I am a Jew by accretion; by the accumulation of historical sedimenta. But Rosenfeld was a Jew by construction. The way every aspect of a spider's web is connected to even the most distant junctures at its periphery, so Rosenfeld's Yiddishkeit was connected by actual experience and positioning in the center of that web to every aspect of Jewish life and history. He could never escape it. Morris could move to America, to Yonkers, to Europe: his Yiddishkeit went with him. In the stories you are about to read he is not a comedian who takes a trip to the lower East Side just to find material for a comedic monologue. He visits the ghetto to absorb the human warmth that brings the taste of a delectable fruit to his lips, and that taste is warm and sweet—and funny!

Rosenfeld's Jewishness was evident in every aspect of his persona because he actually lived an unmistakably Jewish existence all his life and these little vignettes demonstrate what I actually envy in his Yiddishkeit. You must also be informed that all is not what it seems in these stories. When he writes about a nudnik or an individualist these are not "bubbe-mayses" (grandmother's tales). He was probably referring to some actual immigrants who rubbed him the wrong way. He was often critical of "Die Junge" and wrote thinly-veiled satires with them in mind, especially when they seemed to have come to an already existent Jewish community ready to criticize it, take it over, offer scant respect or appreciation to those whose suffering made it all possible. For those interested in the immigrant experience this collection is more a serious cluster of allegories than mere humorous documents. Even, "Chanukah, Jewish self-defense" is really a prescription for Israel to defend itself wherever it is located.

So now please read his stories, of which we have included only a very few. But first be aware that many of these prose writings were translated by Max Rosenfeld with exquisite fidelity to the language and the sensibilities of the times during which they were written.

THREE GENERATIONS

A long, long time ago Jewish immigrants "ran" to America, (gel-oyfn). Some time later they "walked" to America,(gegangen). Now they "ride" to America (men fort). There is a big difference! Those who years ago "ran" to America are almost all gone. Their children and grandchildren now play a role as rich American "Yahudim", "highly-placed citizens". Most of them are well-off financially and look down on the East Side with a microscope.

Those poor unfortunates who "walked" to America—because Fate and persecution drove them from their homes without money enough for the journey—are almost all still here. They are the ones who paved the way in America for Jewish learning, Jewish journalism, Jewish art. Not all of them are happy. Many, very many, fell on the battlefield of livelihood and progress, and many remained suspended in mid-air without a firm foundation under their feet.

Those who "ran" to America managed to amass wealth in various ways, just as they had been accustomed to doing at home. But those who had to "walk" to America had to fight bitterly merely to exist.

It is quite different now for those who "ride" to America. These people come to a place where everything is "ready" for them. They don't know and don't want to know what happened here before they came. As soon as they arrive they begin to interfere and give advice. They refuse to recognize, with gratitude, what was done here for their benefit and immediately begin to "kick" and complain as though they helped to build something, to create something.

It is certain that the coming generations of the three categories of immigrants will become so interfused that they will not be able to tell "who is who". But in the meantime, those who "ran", those who "walked" and those who "rode" are three distinct classes.

The first class worked its way up to the "high places" of the West Side and the elegant places of the East Side. The second class is slowly moving away from Hester Street. And the third class, more and more, remains the sole ruler of the East Side, the so-called ghetto. These Jews find ready newspapers, ready unions, ready theaters, ready organizations, lodges, societies, hospitals, institutions. They do not know how much blood and sweat, how much labor and thought it cost to create all this in a strange country under the most adverse conditions. These new arrivals do not concern themselves one bit with the history of the East Side, with the many sacrifices which were brought upon the altar of Jewish progress in the New World. They snatch it all up as though it were their own and most of the time do not even have a kind word for their predecessors.

Up until recently nothing was heard about the East Side. No sooner does it become famous, however, and the Jewish name begins to achieve some prominence, than the early arrivals, those who "ran", come to demand a portion of recognition. All of this happened, they say, because of them. It was their light, shining down on us from above, that inspired us. And many of the new greenhorns, the "unknowns", even have the chutzpah to come and "teach" us and "enlighten" us and insult us in the most shameful language. We sacrificed ourselves for many years for our people. We created an extensive, first-rate journalism, we wrote books while living in poverty and want, fighting hunger and inundation, and those who harvest the fruits of our bloody toil now pay no attention to us whatsoever.

Well, the "important people" from uptown, the "big-shots" of the Golden Ghetto, have by this time discovered that we do not want them as partners in the Genesis of our culture. We have given them to understand that we want to be our own bosses. Now it remains for us to remind the new immigrants not to forget the brave pioneers. We are at present getting some puffed-up "maskilim," and just plain Jews with pretensions, who are stirring up a storm against the old fighters for progress in the Jewish quarter. These "maskilim" should take off their hats to those who paved the way for them.

Every Jewish newspaper on the East Side has its story of suffering and every writer who is today making a modest living by his pen went through long years of famine. Every union has a record of bloody pages and a tear-filled history. Every Yiddish actor who now wears a diamond stick-pin and a gold watch contended long with Destiny and struggled fiercely for a living. All the true Yiddish poetry in our "exile-tongue", which was created in the damp tenements of the Jewish quarter bears the stamp of sacrifice. And every textbook written here to teach the greenhorns the language of the country is a monument to a piece of lost life.

The producers of all these good things on the East Side are

slowly but surely withdrawing. They have grown weary. A little longer and their work will be taken over by other, younger hands. Soon the first quarter-century of labor and travail, of ceaseless struggle, will die. You, the new Americans, do not forget your courageous foregoers! Do not forget what we did for you! Don't be so high and mighty! Have respect for the good things you find here. The achievements we leave to you, even though they may not be complete, are still tangible, visible. What you do with them is not foreseeable. Have reverence for the martyrs of the East Side! Bow your heads to an immortal quarter century!

A BOUQUET OF ROSES

August 31, 1908, toward midnight, I left the stage of the Cracow Folks-Theater with my head full of bravos and my hands full of roses. The bouquet was presented to me by the Academic-Zionist Society with the Polish-Hebrew name, Przedoswit-HaShachar (Dawn) which had arranged the Literary evening. No doubt the society meant well with its fragrant gift, but the flowers had too many thorns. After I had perspired all evening for an audience of over a thousand people, I now had to carry with me a whole mountain of Cracow recognition. Had they at least have allowed me to go "home" to my hotel room, which I appreciated most at night, it wouldn't have been so bad. But the Dawn people decided to drag me to a coffee-house somewhere at the edge of town. The Cracow working-people escorted me, singing workers' songs and I became so excited with the singing, with this honor shown me by the poor people of Cracow, that I was moved to present them with my flowers. But this gesture, I realized, would have been misunderstood and would have aroused criticism, so I refrained. Until long past midnight, sleepy and falling off my feet, I carried the bouquet like a lulav on Succos wherever I went. Finally I got to bed, but could not fall asleep. I was too apprehensive. What would I do with the flowers in the morning?

Sleepless all night, I rose at dawn, gathered up my few paltry belongings and went out into the street to hail a droshky and transport my two suitcases to the railroad station. (I had to leave my room early in the morning because my "tenancy" expired then. They did not even bring me water to wash myself!).

With the Polish droshky standing in front of the house, I went back into my room to pick up my bundles. But I stopped at the bouquet, perplexed. What was I to do? Where was I to bury my academic honor? Take the flowers with me? Leave them behind? Outside, the droshky was waiting. I picked up both suitcases, managed to get the bouquet, my cane and umbrella under my arms and instructed the droshky-driver to take me to the station.

It was still very early. There were only a few people in the station and as soon as I alighted from the droshky the porters attacked me from all sides. This one wanted to carry my cane, that one my umbrella, another one, even me! This was no everyday occurrence—such a Squire who comes to the railroad station with a two-story bouquet of roses!

And having no other choice, I let myself be served and waited-upon and paid each attendant as much as he asked.

But my flower troubles had just begun. My bundles safely in the hands of the porter, I remained again helplessly staring at my bouquet. In one hand a cane and an umbrella, in the other hand a strange bundle of flowers, I began to stroll slowly and sleepily toward town. Wherever I went I met the same quizzical stares: What kind of creature was this? Where was he going? For whom were the flowers intended?

Whenever the thought crossed my mind to toss them away I felt ashamed of myself. If anyone were to see me do it they would take me for mad. What sane man would throw a bouquet of living roses into the gutter? No one with a soul!

I wanted to go into a coffee-house for breakfast, but how could one enter a restaurant carrying a huge bouquet of flowers? What would I do with it after I got in?

Deep in puzzlement I suddenly noticed, near the post office, two barefoot girls, looking for all the world like two unwanted flowers, fresh, pretty, fragrant flowers, which Fate held in its hands and did not know where to put down.

One of the girls, the younger of the two, suddenly stretched out her hand to me and with a sweet, "Please, Sir", asked for a flower. This was the most pleasant, the most charming, the most welcome "Please, Sir" that I heard in Cracow. With indescribable joy, with a deep inner happiness, I handed her the bouquet.

"Here, child," I said. "Take all of them. You and your companion are as lonely as these flowers."

And standing near the two friendless young girls I felt as though the three of us together were a superfluous bouquet. . . .

UNITY

"Proletarians of all lands, unite!"

Wait! Don't think this is an invention of the Later Prophets. Make no mistake. The idea of unity is older than Karl Marx or Bakunin.

Be so good as to ask that old perennial student there, in the corner by the stove, to open up the Midrash T'hillim. He'll be only too happy to do it for you.

What a story that Midrash has to tell! And the waters "grew strong" and rose to the Celestial Throne.. and God hovered over them and said, "Let the waters assemble!"

When the Earth heard this she hurled forth mountains and valleys. Great canyons formed and the waters came and filled them. Then the waters again grew proud of their strength and boasted, "We are the mightiest of all creation ! Come, brother waves, let us cover the entire face of the Earth. We are too confined. We need the whole Earth. . . . all of it!"

"Quiet, young whippersnappers!", thundered the Creator at the upstarts. And a wind rose over the surface of the Earth. "I will send the sand to make a barricade! You will be powerless against it!", the Creator stormed at the quarrelsome depths.

And when the brazen waves saw the grains of sand, each one tiny and insignificant, they grew even more insolent. "What can this small-fry do against us? This will be a picnic! The smallest of our fellows will move against them and make an end of them with no trouble at all!" When the largest grain of sand looked around at his brothers and saw how frightened they were he called out to them, "True, brothers, it's true. We're very small and each of us alone is worth nothing. But let us stay together, let us never separate. Then the waves, those braggarts, will feel our strength. We can throw their sneers back into their teeth!"

When the grains of sand heard this they came running from all ends of the earth. They assembled in great, limitless armies and besieged the mighty upstarts on all sides. The waves hurled themselves at the sandy banks and recoiled with an angry growl.

Then a voice was heard over the waters, "Consider well the wise plan of the grains of sand. Even the smallest forces become a mighty power when they are united!"

"Amen! . . . . Amen !" sang the grains of sand, as the crest of a mighty wave struck the beach and broke into a thousand pieces . . .

THE NUDNICK

He is the most pleasant person in the world—from the back; and the wisest man in the world—when he sleeps. His company makes you sick and his complaints bore you to death. He is a nudnick. He always has something to tell you, but you never have anything to hear. You don't hear him, really, because before he comes to the point you're unconscious. And the point itself is one tremendous chunk of boredom.

If he tells you, for instance, about his arrival in America, he begins with his parents' betrothal contract. He beats your ear until it comes out the back of your head and he doesn't give up until you start snoring. He is a nudnick.

To look at him you wouldn't think he could add 2 and 2, but when he opens his mouth he shoots straight up to the millions. He doesn't mind one bit that your jaw is breaking from yawning. Most people are not always in a mood to argue. The nudnick, however, is forever on a search for ears to listen to his arguments, and the longer the ears the better he likes it.

The nudnick is not limited to one type of nudick activity. The Creator has blessed him with all the psychic qualities needed for his chief virtue, his main purpose in life, his raison d'etre—to bore the rest of humanity. He is a writer, a critic, a lecturer, a "doer" and a reformer. He is a nudnick on all fronts and will bore you—and you—and anyone else who lets him. You sit and listen to him and you must suck a lemon to keep from fainting. You lose your patience and would gladly beat him up for having the gall to charge a fee for wearying the public. The rickety chair on which you sit breaks under the weight of your burden and you feel like doing violence to the newspaper which printed the announcement that brought you up to this God-forsaken third-floor meeting-room to hear a sermon on "The Decadence of the Stringbean". You want to leap up onto the platform, grab the nudnick by the legs and hurl him back to Lithuania where he came from.

Yet as soon as you look at him closely your heart softens and you are moved to give him a pinch of snuff to clear his head and liven him up a little, because, all things considered, this little man is pale and fragile as a sardine. You can see at once that he has not had a good meal in days and you wonder where you can get him a quick cup of coffee and a bagel. You immediately forgive him. You become practically a disciple of the Indian law-giver Buddha. The latter let himself be devoured by a hungry beast out of sympathy for God's creatures and you would let yourself be bored to death out of pity for one of God's nudnicks who came to America with the intention of plaguing the Jewish streets of New York. It is true that we Jews are not the only people in the world afflicted with nudnicks. But the genuine nudnick is to be found only among us; he is almost exclusively a Jewish character. He is a Diaspora product of Jewish sadness, of the monotonousness of Jewish life which stretches like tar and bores you to distraction. Among us, boring the public has become a profession.

In the old days, a Jew down on his luck, without a source of livelihood, used to become a melamed. Now he becomes a nudnick; that is, first he bores himself! Later he learns to bore others. He begins his career in his own home—on his family, his friends, his lodge-members, his union brothers. Gradually he bores his way into a newspaper office, then onto a platform and finally, little by little, he becomes a Community Nudnick and bores all Israel.

And with us, once a man becomes a well-known nudnick, it is impossible to get rid of him. He is ever and eternally on the ready. He manages to find his followers; people who are sick of life and looking for an easy, painless end. He is perfectly willing to be their Angel of Death.

In the celestial realms, where people live and enjoy it, where every moment is used for pleasure, there is no time for nudnicks. In our poor Jewish quarter, however, where the interest in life limps along and the days and years drag interminably without a moment's real happiness, or a single taste of pleasure—here the nudnick is for the soul what skim-milk is for the body; it's insipid, but filling. And the nudnick has an unlimited field for his activity.

THE MAN WITH PRINCIPLES

He is a man with principles. He is full of them, from his collar to his galoshes. His principles hang from his nose, and in order that the world may see he has principles he never wipes his nose. He is one of those extreme radicals whose principles extend to the year 9900. He belongs to the holy, world-renowned principled martyrs who once became incensed at the baker on the principle that he had too much bread and they had none.

Principled bakers, he used to think, should unite and every day bake several trays of buns for greenhorn intellectuals who never got used to work here in America. They cannot become shoemakers, tailors, or furriers or peddlers. They are men with a principle and for people like them the coffee-house was invented, perhaps also the lecture platform, but never the factory. If I were a baker, he once resolved, I would bake a cake with a principle. I would supply the intelligentsia with free butter-cookies, buns, candies, apple-pie, pretzels, tarts and spongecake. Moreover, I would bake only principled bagels: with tiny holes, or no holes at all. I would fill up the holes with bagel.

Eventually he would become a manufacturer and proceed to drive his workers according to the principle of "the worse the better". When the workers would make demands of him he would personally descend all the stairs himself to deliver his rejection. Poor, weak workers! He would save them the trouble of climbing up the stairs. A man must have principles.

Like every poor immigrant he did all sorts of things to make a living, but he remained consistently principled throughout. He sold stocks to the poor Jewish workers in a "sure thing", but on two principles. First principle: Why not let the poor people "work themselves up in the world" too? Let them live a little; there's enough to go around for everybody. Later, when the "sure thing" turned out to be a fiasco, he enunciated the second principle: "Let them see, those jackasses, the falseness of contemporary society. Let them realize how they are deceived, taken for suckers, swindled out of their hard-earned pennies. Let them learn to be more cautious. My principle is to educate the masses."

When he took to selling pianos to poor people on the installment plan he did it, naturally, with a principle: "Don't think, God forbid, that I am doing this to make money, that my only concern is the commission! Perish the thought! To me money is worthless. Feh! I can make a living in a thousand other ways. The main thing, as far as I'm concerned is the principle.

"The life of the Jewish worker is a long stretch of unhappiness. I want to cheer him up a bit. Is there any reason why an operator's missus shouldn't learn to play the piano? It won't hurt. An operator's wife is just as entitled as Mrs. Vanderbilt, Mrs. Gould or Mrs. Rockefeller. My principle is equality and happiness. Yes, equality for all husbands and wives. The husband churns his guts out all day at the sewing machine, then let his missus or his daughter, right after supper, play him Hatikva or the Marseillaise or "Somebody Was There Before." Sometime later this principled man sold principled real estate lots in a swamp swarming with mosquitos. As was his habit, he sold them with a principle: "I sell these lots to poor people to prevent them from becoming landlords. I hate a landlord worse than a cockroach. Whenever I pay rent my heart bleeds. Therefore I'm selling these swamps so as not to increase the number of landlords, and the principle is a correct one. First, they never will be able to build on this kind of lot; they will never get a building loan. Seconds, if they do manage to build there, they will never rent. And if they do manage to get a tenant, they'll never collect the rent. And if they do collect the rent they'll only turn it over to the doctor to cure their nerves and their chronic ulcers. It is my principle that we have enough capitalists—too many—we don't need any more and I'm working day and night to prevent their growth. A man must live according to an idea, a principle.

For a short time, before he found the proper business; he sold snuff, and of course with a principle. His main idea, as he himself explained it, was to keep people alert, prevent them from falling asleep. These are his own graphic words, "My principle is to get people accustomed to using their noses, because only in that way can they detect the rotten smell of the present economic system. There is often more principle in a pinch of snuff than in a dozen tiresome lectures or artificial agitational speeches. Let the workers and Jews in general get used to good tobacco and they will be more wide-awake, more hopeful for the future, more optimistic. The nose was not built into the face just for charm's sake; certainly not the Jewish nose. It should be used. . . ."

Once he decided to go into the trouser business, but since he could not find the correct principle immediately he had to put off the venture. Finally he did find the proper principle and went into the pants business "I sell pants to the organized Jewish workers," he explained, "because I know that without this garment they will be unable to march. As a principled person it is my wish to see Jews march through the East Side without having people laugh at them. Imagine a march to Rutgers Square in those awful American short jackets and three-year-old worn-out pants. It would create a humiliating scandal! Anti-semites and capitalists would be laughing up their sleeves. Selling pants is a matter of principle."

TRAVELS IN THE JEWISH QUARTER: SUCCOS

Stanley may have described his travels in "darkest Africa", Alexander von Humboldt his scientific expeditions, Swift his adventures among the Lilliputians and Mendele Mocher Sforim his Travels of Benjamin the Third—but I will will tell you about my trip "back home" in our own Jewish Quarter.

Other artists, writers, and travelers go to Italy and Switzerland, or they make a tour around the world to gather new impressions, to take a fresh look at the old places, creatures, events. A Jewish writer, however, can find everything his imagination desires in the Jewish Quarter. Who needs Africa, Asia, the North Pole or even the mysterious mountains at the edge of the world? In this tremendous, strange cauldron known as the East Side he can find more Asians, Africans, Eskimos, Indians, giants and Lilliputians than you could ever imagine.

Nor does it cost very much. The traveling expenses are minimal. For a nickel you can make a trip from the Bronx to Rivington Street, for instance, and get your fill of "new impressions" and "expressions". There you will find an eternal jostling and crowding which squeezes out the little bit of soul, life and strength brought over from Galicia, Bukovina, Roumania or Lithuania—although the Litvaks here crowd and squeeze themselves in another neighborhood under the same conditions but in another dialect.

Our Jewish Quarter is even more interesting than usual on Sabbath or holiday eves, when young and old, men and women, come out to "shop" and incidentally to see what's going on "in the streets" or to see how the "market" is faring around the fish and chicken pushcarts, since Yiddishkeit nowadays is mostly a "kitchen-religion". Succos, however, is a holiday which is not completely devoted to the stomach. The Jewish market, in addition to the fragrant fish, also has fragrant esrogim, lulavs, myrtle-branches, green grass and. . . . green Jews who bid the prices of these articles sky-high. They are the "bulls" of the Jewish stock-market.

So it was on a Succos eve that I chose to make my tour around the Quarter to observe anew all the old, familiar things. I wanted to visit Rivington and Peat Streets, which on a market day afford a rare panorama of Jews and Jewish articles, a sort of human ant-heap, a confusion, a Tower of Babel, where all the "600,000" dialects of our Mother Tongue conjoin. Rivington Street is the border of the various Jewish ghettos which make up the great, single ghetto of New York.

Here you can find Galician, Roumanian, Lithuanian, Hungarian, Bessarabian, Bukovinian, Russian, Caucasian, German, Turkish Jews, and Jews from "the whole world". Here a philologist, on on Erev Shabbos, could put together a complete dictionary of our Yiddish language, which could serve everywhere—In Jassy, in Minsk, in Czestochova, in Calveria and in Brownsville. There, for instance, you can hear all the various pronunciations of the words VOS, EICH AND LEKACH. You will hear VUS, VOOS AND VOO'ES; EICH, ACH; LEKACK, LEYLACH. LAIKACH AND LIKICH.

In Hester street, if you do not give a merchant the respect due him, you will get a dressing-down in a Kapulier Lithuanian. In Rivington street, however, you will be greeted by a language which never existed even in your wildest dreams . . . You will hardly know whether you are being blessed or cursed.

I therefore chose Rivington street for my Erev-Succos expedition, because in my opinion, Hester street is better for Erev Yom Kippur. You cannot, however, simply descend upon Rivington street like a barbarian for his booty. You have to approach it tactfully from one of our other honored streets. Thus, as I turned a corner I suddenly came upon two small, twin-like synagogues. These were old, two-story, crumbling houses which had been leaning on each other this way for years, like two old Hebrew-teachers in a prayer-house; bent over, tubercular, dirty and tattered. The synagogues were on the second floor of the houses and on one of the holy places hung the following sign, in a Yiddish of sorts: HERE IN THIS SHUL SERVICES ARE SAID EVENINGS

AND MORNINGS BETWEEN 5 and 6 O'CLOCK
STRAIGHT. OTHER BUSINESS, INQUIRE BELOW.

The "other business" consisted of the following: a mattress
"factory", an old-furniture store, a Ladies Tailor, an engraver, and,
of course, many male and female boarders in the rooms. I looked at
God's dwelling-place on the East Side and my heart ached for the
poor spirit. . . . unfortunate Shechina! What a place Destiny had
brought it to!

As I stood and observed this "sight" of the East Side I noticed
on the collapsed balcony near the synagogues several tattered posters advertising a Yiddish play. On one of the posters, yellow and
dirty as many of the plays themselves, I could still see the words,
"King Of The Shnorrers", (a play which was the most popular in
the theatre) and a role which the Jew himself played in the world.
Yes, I thought to myself, as I hastily left the scene, "King of the
Shnorrers".

I headed in the direction of Rivington street. On both sides of
the street was an over-abundance of tiny food-stores and basement
restaurants, most of them milchege (dairy). In the window of one
of these restaurants was a chunk of cheese, and on the cheese so
many flies that the question arose in my mind, "Was the cheese
actually milchig or fleishig?" Across the street was a dairy store. In
the window stood a plaster cow, on which hung the following sign:

FRISSE PITER FOON UNDZ ALEYN GEMACHT.
UNZERE.
MELCHEKES FOON BOR OF HEL UNTERGEZUCHT
(Fresh butter Made By our Own Hands. Our Milchigs
Inspected by "Bor of Hel")

What do you say to that for Yiddish? But I was still able, by
some divination, to under-stand that BOR OF HEL meant Board
of Health, and that the SS in FRISSE and the I in PITER were a
compromise between Minsk and Jassy. At the corner of Rivington
and Suffolk I saw the first sign of Succos. The roar of the market-
place came toward me like a sea. I was almost deafened by the pre-
holiday tumult, the screams and shouts of buyers and sellers. I could
barely understand a word. On one of the corners stood a Chassid
selling esrogim and lulavs. Apparently he could not afford to rent
the entire corner for himself, so he shared it with an Italian boot-

black with two chairs. On one chair the bootblack shined shoes; from the other the Chassid sold his wares to a crowd of Jews who swarmed around him, picking and bargaining for the purest and best esrog for the holiday. The Italian had probably not foreseen what kind of partnership he was getting into. The crowd completely hid his "establishment" and no one could get near his chair. He grew angrier by the minute and his eyes flashed stilletos at the Chassid. It was a blessing from the Eternal Himself that the bootblack was able to control his wrath and confine his attack to Italian epithets.

From this corner I made my way across the street to a Jewish drugstore, the most remarkable apothecary I have ever seen in my life. It had only one window and that window contained only one item: Cockroach Poison. In the center of the window stood a sign with this most interesting advertisement in Yiddish:

THE BEST ANGEL OF DEATH FOR COCKROACHES!
STRONGER THAN CARBOLIC ACID AND ALL OTHER
POISONS! 10 CENTS A BOTTLE BUY SOME AND
CONVINCE YOURSELF!

Reading this amazing information I grew exceedingly thoughtful. This was actually the first time I had ever seriously thought about our cockroaches. What a world we had lived to see—a world where death did not come naturally to cockroaches; where a special Angel of Death had to be created for them, with a special Apothecary on Rivington street.

Somewhat removed from the tumult and confusion, a little off to one side of the crowd, stood a pushcart containing remnants of various kinds of cloth—wool, percale, silk, gingham, etc. It was attended by a young woman whose face was pale as death: the embodiment of Want.

She did not permit the women shoppers to handle the merchandise too freely. She seemed to be anxiously keeping them away from the pushcart, although it was obvious that she was sorely in need of customers. Not that there were many customers to keep away. It was erev Succos—who needed remnants now? The little girls' holiday dresses or the curtains for the window were already finished.

Suddenly a rather stout old lady leaned over the pushcart with a loud request. "Missus, do you have a nice piece of goods for a chalah-cover?" The pale young woman grew even paler and stared angrily at the old woman, apparently for having shaken the pushcart too violently; then she quickly tried to disguise her anger with a weak little smile. "May I have as many good years as I have fine pieces of cloth! Here is a wonderful little piece, suitable even for a jacket." She reached into the cart to select the cloth, but the old woman wanted to do her own selecting. Suddenly, fishing through the remnants, she stepped back frightened and uttered a little scream. Her hand had touched the face of a sleeping baby, who woke with a cry.

"My God ! Is this the place to keep a baby?"

With a trembling voice, her eyes swimming in tears, the young woman replied, "Where else should I keep it? . . .

ELECTION EVE

Berdichev and America woiuld be hard pressed to equal our East Side either in "Yiddishkeit" or in "Yankeehood". On Sabbath and holiday eves the East Side is more like Berdichev than Berdichev itself. On election eve it is more New Yorkish than New York.

If Moses and George Washington were suddenly to descend from heaven into Rutgers Square they would both be overjoyed; the former by the piety of the Rutgers Square fountain, which dries up every Sabbath and holiday (and also on Mondays and Thursdays) and waits only for someone to dress it up in tallis and yarmulke; the latter, by our Jewish newspapers, who have gotten so deeply in-volved in American politics that they sell the same newspaper to three political parties and still have enough space (and gall) left to preach "integrity".

The Jewish Quarter is the election-factory of New York. Here are manufactured speakers, speeches, campaign literature. . . . and citizens. Although the real benefits of the elections, city or national, accrue to the millionaires on the elegant avenues, still the actual labor is done, just as with shirts, pants or caps, on the East Side. Here you will find the "real craftsmen" who can manufacture the products "good and cheap"!

A Christian clergyman or literary personality, a Christian newspaper publisher, must be given "real money"; Esau still loves to receive gifts. A Jewish Rabbi, however, can be bought for a dollar and a quarter and a Jewish writer for a five-spot. A Jewish newspaper can be bought in various sections—for the same price you can get either the front page or even the "insides". The Jewish Quarter has become the "Reclining Couch of the American political Seder, and under Max the presser's mattress lies the key to political salvation. Proof of this is the fact that a "big" Christian politician (who is, incidentally, a big liar) lives in the same house with an old synagogue shammes (rector) and attends all the circumcision parties looking for votes . . . and getting them.

It should not therefore be surprising that I decided to take a trip through the Quarter at election time to see "what was doing". It was on a Friday afternoon, when the Jewish neighborhood is always interesting, even outside of election time. My main purpose was to observe the big political rally which was to take place that evening at Rutgers Square, the focal point of Yiddishkeit in the New World. But since the meeting was still some hours away I decided to take a walk to the Jewish market.

Strolling through a Jewish street I was abruptly blocked in front of a bookstore by three trash barrels standing in a row in the middle of the pavement. Most interesting was the center barrel, which was so full it wore a crown. And indeed it seemed to have something special about it; it was a Jewish barrel, full of Yiddishkeit of all kinds. Although it was already two weeks after the holidays the barrel still contained l'shona tova (happy New Year) cards, pages of Slichos leaflets, holiday parodies, pieces of lulav, myrtle leaves and bundles of hoshanas. Inside the barrel I could see pieces of discarded talleisim (prayer shawls), printed songs from Yiddish concert-halls, Simchas Torah flags, damaged mezzuzas and the front cover of a sensational novel which was being printed in endless installments. All this was inside the barrel. On the outside, however (in Yiddish) was a political poster which read thusly:

COME TONIGHT AFTER KIDDUSH TO THE CORNER OF RUTGERS SQUARE. A GREAT FRIEND OF THE JEWS WILL SPEAK. HE HIMSELF IS AN IRISHMAN, BUT THE JEWISH CANDIDATES CAN'T HOLD A CANDLE TO HIM. COME AFTER KIDDUSH. THE REVEREND FAKEROVITZ WILL SPEAK ABOUT SHABBOS AND THE ELECTION.

I read the poster, with all its mistakes in spelling, backwards and forwards until I could remember it by heart. This was the most interesting trash-barrel I had ever seen. It contained, in capsule form, all of American Yiddishkeit, literature and politics.

Leaving the scene of the trash barrels I cut over to Canal Street. It was about three o'clock in the afternoon. All was hustle and bustle. Jews carried on various businesses in the middle of the street; baking potatoes, frying pancakes, pickling cucumbers, making marmalade, playing barrel-organs, drawing lots, exhibiting trained white mice and talking parrots, removing warts, selling Yiddish theatre-songs, infants bibs, ladies underwear and "holiday leaflets".

In the midst of the "tumel" stood a peddler, an elderly Jew, busy with a pushcart of "nothing". He had sold out his little bit of merchandise. In the corner of the pushcart still lay several overripe pears, but these he was apparently saving for himself for the Sabbath. Whenever anyone approached his pushcart he shouted, "Gornit! Gornit! (Nothing!) Go away!" But the "businessman" had not yet had his midday meal. His wife came and brought him, covered with a napkin, a plate of hot fish, from the very fish she had just prepared for the Sabbath. The peddler removed the covering and the steam rose from the hot fish in puffs, as though the pushcart were smoking a pipe. He was about to attack his meal when, seemingly out of the earth, arose an old lady, a "greenhorn", munching on a baked potato.

"Mister, how much is your gefillte fish?"

The hungry peddler, confused, angry and surprised, did not know which to devour first, the fish or the woman. I burst out laughing and went on my way, praying God that I would never have to be a "green" old woman "shopping" for my lunch.

A PASSOVER JOURNEY

In a carriage through the Jewish Quarter. This was my firm resolution. And I carried it through. I did not use a carriage, god forbid, for the sake of elegance. When I was able to walk through the East Side on my own two legs, calmly, securely, I did so. I don't like to ride when I can go on foot. Now, however, I find it rather difficult. . . .

Anyway, it was a Jewish holiday, and I decided to ride through the Jewish "pale" to see how my poor brothers live, how they celebrate their "Day of Freedom." I could have gone on an ordinary weekday, but their weekday appearance was all too familiar to me; it has cost me much pain. When the Jewish Quarter comes to my mind my mood is far from festive. I see its bitter, oppressive crowdedness, its want, its unending toil to keep body and soul together. So I went during a holiday.

My journey was apparently destined to be completely Jewish, from beginning to end. Even the carriage was Jewish. I will not say that the horse was orthodox, or that its shoes had a kosher stamp; nor will I say that the carriage was protected by a mezzuza. I cannot even say that I rented the carriage on a Jewish street. No. I made the arrangements at that most Gentile Grand Central Depot. I approached a coachman in a livery with a high hat and yellow buttons.

"Do you know where Peat Street is?

"Sure. Ridge Street too!"

"Essex Street?"

"Ludlow too!"

"Monroe Street?"

"Cherry Street too!"

"And the Yiddish newspaper offices?"

"You must think you're talking to a goy!" the coachman replied in a hurt tone. "I want you to know that I am a Yahudi!"

"A Yahudi!", I gasped, and couldn't take my eyes off him. I'm afraid of a Yahudi. That is a German Jew who doesn't know German and isn't a Jew. I know that Yahudim hate the Jewish Quarter and one of their sort might take me on a wild goose chase to God knows where. Especially the New York Yahudim, who are always trying to upset everything the other Jews have set up. The coachman saw my embarrassment and explained knowingly that his father came from Sapetnik and his mother from Minsk; that he was born and bred among nothing but Litvaks!

A weight dropped from my heart. I began to bargain with my Minsker Yahudi—in English, naturally. He spoke only English, since he was born on Forsythe "Strasse." In brief, we reached an agreement and I crawled into the carriage. As I did so I took a quick look at the "equipage" and at the horse. Everything seemed to be in order, and in the horse's bowed head I recognized him to be Jewish.

The carriage was an open hansom cab, so that I could observe everything without obstruction. The coachman sat on a high seat in the back.

"Where to first?", he asked.

"To the Galitzianer neighborhood," I replied, and he cracked his whip.

Soon we were on Houston street. He rode several blocks and stopped. Houston street was impassible. A mountain of living beings swarmed in the middle of the street and the sidewalks were packed solid. In the midst of the mass stood a policeman wielding his stick repeatedly on an old tattered coat in which lay a bundle of bones called a "Thief." What this pale, frightened boy had stolen I still do not know. I could see that they had caught him and were beating him unmercifully. A thief, yes—but my heart was clamped in a painful vise and I might have fainted from revulsion had my eyes not been distracted by a most incongruous sight.

In the center of this human ant heap, close by my carriage, stood an old-maidish girl. She was sporting a massive Spring hat, a veritable meadow of flowers, grass and green leaves. And my horse, of course, was munching peacefully upon this rare feast.

A city-bred horse, I thought. It doesn't even know the difference between real grass and imitation. Then I began to fear for him. My horse might be lynched for eating "chumetz" during Pesach, and in the middle of the street! My coachman finally extricated the carriage from Houston street but my mind would not let go of those two "images'—the brutally-beaten thief and the innocently-devoured Spring hat.

Riding along in the carriage I looked for signs of the usual holiday atmosphere of the Jewish street, at least the artificial happiness of the Jewish poor. But even that was absent. It was the second day of Passover. The weather was fine. It was a perfect day for young men and women promenading, but instead of the joy of life, mournfulness filled the air. There was certainty that this was the traditional season of the "Song Of Songs". Life seemed to have shrunk. The streets gasped harshly, spasmodically, asthmatically. Here and there Jews stood or walked in groups, Galitzianer Jews, with shaven necks and impressive beards, with high hats on their heads and long pipes in their Hassidic mouths. They conversed heatedly, gesticulating, emphasizing their words with the thumb, shrugged their shoulders, smiled. But in general they did not seem to be in a "God's-in-his-heaven-all's-right-with- the-world" mood. Children swarmed underfoot. I thought of Egypt, where the Jews "were fruitful and multiplied" just to spite Pharaoh. Very few of the children wore new suits or new shoes. Most of them were not especially dressed up for the holiday. Their wan faces were not shining with the holiday spirit.

Nevertheless, they were children, running, leaping, climbing, screaming, pushing, playing ball. It seemed to me, however, that the ball did not fly as swiftly as it should, that they did not have the strength to throw it as it should be thrown. And I thought to myself: a ball thrown with the strength of Passover charity does not travel very far.

Riding through the Galitzianer neighborhood my eyes were filled with the hundreds of restaurants, their "Kosher l'Pesach" signs,and their thousands of curious inscriptions on their windows. As I read these announcements I thought: if the cooking inside is as bad as the spelling, outside then immediately after the holiday there will be a boom in the epsom-salts industry. Mostly I was amazed by the hundreds of Quick-Lunch restaurants, the eat-on-one-foot kitchens. In the old days Jews did not know of such things. This is an American innovation. Hurry-up restaurants are a product of Americanization.

In the old days in a Jewish restaurant you could eat for at least a half-hour and drink the meal down holding the folded pages of the Arbeiter Freint. Today, however, you're expected to be finished within three minutes. In short, we're progressing.

Most intriguing was a Dairy restaurant which had in its window the following remarkable sign:

KOSHER DIAREA FOR PESACH AND KWIK LUNCH COUNTER MILCHIGS A SPECIALITY. BIGGEST KALB-BRATTEN IN THE CITY. COME QUICK AND PROVE YOURSELF!

I began to ask myself the Four Questions: First, does the word Diarea mean Dairy or does it mean a belly-ache? Second, what are fleishige dishes doing in a dairy restaurant? Third, what is Kalb-bratten, the biggest in the city, doing in a quick-lunch counter? And fourth, why do we need a Quick-lunch Room during an economic crisis ? Everybody has plenty of time. . . .

THOUGHTS ABOUT EVERYBODY AND EVERYTHING

It is not good to be chained, even when the chain is made of gold.

Not everyone who deals in sugar has a sweet life.

As long as the whip remains the same it makes no difference to the horse who the driver is.

If all you think about is how bad the world is, you'll have no time to see what's good about it.

The main thing is : fly ! The goose and the eagle both have wings.

The wise man seeks the cause of his mistake. The fool doesn't even know he made one.

Don't tell us what you are. Show us!

Humor is the sober philosophy of life. Satire is drunk with bitterness.

Hardness alone does not make a diamond. Without its fire it would be merely another stone.

Poetry is the art of telling the truth so beautifully that the world will think it is a lie, and pay attention.

Dogs always bark at something or someone; human beings often at nothing.

To drown right off shore is not only a misfortune, it is a humiliation.

As long as an empty nut has not been cracked open it is just as important as the full one.

Don't let yourself sink too low; you will find it too difficult to get up.

Many people think it is so difficult to be honest that they don't even try.

An ignoramus is not a man who has received no education but one who has betrayed it.

The poor support the rich, who don't work. This would be a commendable act of charity if it weren't such a terrible crime.

Steal a wall, they pay you double.

Steal a brick and you're in trouble.

Not everyone who has studied geography knows where he is in the world.

To translate merely the cold printed word is a waste of time and paper. To translate the spirit is an art.

When you're being praised the world is deaf. When you're being criticised it regains its hearing. When you're being lifted up the world is blind. When you're being laid away it regains its sight.

Reb Yonkl said: "The world is good!"

Reb Todris said, "The world's a fright!"

From which debate I understood

The simple truth: they both were right!

(At this juncture we wish to disclose that all the preceding prose by Morris Rosenfeld has been translated brilliantly by Max Rosenfeld, no relative. As

Morris would have wished, Max has shown that "to translate the spirit is an art." Max is a fine poet himself. He is an added inspiration for the writing of this volume. Max has succeeded in bringing the authenticity that was in the original Yiddish ninety years later to English-speaking Americans. There was a naivete and open-eyed wonder to Morris Rosenfeld that belied his satirical tone. Nothing we can say about Morris will be as revealing as his own prose stories. EJG)

PRETENSIONS

From the epilogue of Leon Goldenthal's "Toil and Triumph", the novelized biography of Morris Rosenfeld, we wish to quote some remarks about Rosenfeld's forays into prose writing, and then we shall include a few of those charming little articles he called "Pretensions."

"While Rosenfeld believed that poetry was the only true medium for his cherished thoughts, and that poetry was his starlight and sunlight, he also attempted to express himself felicitously in prose. One day he took his courage in hand and offered an article on a philosophic theme to a friendly newspaper editor. It was received enthusiastically and he was asked to contribute a series of such articles. The writing was in a style all his own.

"He referred to the inanimate world, to tools and objects we come in contact with in our everyday life. He endeavored to make them articulate and to speak their feelings as though they were alive. He wrote about them in a feature column for the newspaper and, when the series was completed, he collected them in a book called "The Silent World", which he planned to publish; but death cut short his plans. Here, in translation, are three of these essays."

PRETENSIONS OF A MACHINE

I am but a man-made machine, a true expression of your civilization. I make no claim to godliness nor to strange spirits but I dare observe that if the whole world was created in six days it could not have been done with machines; and if done by hand, it surely could not have been done on time.

And I also observe that the Bible says that God took some dust from the earth, mixed it with water and patched out the form of man from the mixture; and patched he became, as you can see from the many imperfections. I sympathize with him. I am a machine!

You also cannot pride yourself that you invented me with ease. You suffered many hardships and disappointments and you attained me step by step, every part separately and then jointly, and I am still far from perfection. Your so-called "humanity" has invented so many machines, for almost every purpose, that in its anxiety it has become mechanized itself. You eat, you sleep. you work, you live—all by machine!

But the best machine of all, how to introduce a true and honest society of mankind, you have not invented yet. I know that sometimes you get embittered at your dependence on me and that some of your idiots get so exasperated with us that they want to break us up and our whole families. In despair they cry out that we are their troublemakers. They do not realize that we are made only to help them and free them of oppressive labor; we help build for them so many convenience.

We are innocent in it all—we are only machines. We only regret when you use children, young and tender girls, the future mothers of your infants, to work us, and we are exasperated when you use us to destroy so many innocent people and so quickly. We burst with shame, but we are only machines, the brainwork of man ! We are bitter that you not only enslave yourselves to the machines but kill yourselves trying to imitate us. You become living robots and forget the higher purposes of life. You become inhuman.

We also cannot bear to have you imitate us and convey such inhuman traits as: mechanized tears, mechanized laughter, mechanized love, morality, religion, honor, politics, charity, education, poetry and literature: even mechanized applause! You can do much with us and much to imitate us but not to change human feelings nor gain spiritual comfort nor true love or fraternalism.

I know it, because I am only a machine. When we see the troubles you get from your latest invention, the automobile, we take revenge on you for the trouble you gave the poor horse during the horse and buggy days. You cannot whip this machine into submission, nor can you overwork or abuse it. You must suffer all its caprices, serve it and pay for all its shortcomings. If a horse had given you half the trouble you would have whipped it to death. We laugh at you the way your Biblical hero laughed at the Philistines in his blindness.

PRETENSIONS OF A BLOTTER

I am a piece of soft, absorbent, unsized blotting paper, used to absorb the excess ink which escapes from a writer's pen. Although I often appear blotched and saturated with ink I am of no less importance than a clean sheet of paper. I am an equal sufferer.

Like a clean sheet of paper I have to absorb the writings of the good and the bad, even the most sinful thoughts and criminal deliberations like the incrimination of an innocent person, a contract of extortion of an usurer, an insincere declaration of love or the blemishing of a literary reputation, and so on.

I cannot lie on fresh, wet ink without absorbing such poison. Especially do I, poor blotter, suffer from political campaign literature or in the editorial room of some of your newspapers. Woe is me! What lies! What insincere flattery; what conniving mischief! I shudder at the thought! And when I have absorbed their ink they have no use for me and throw me away. But I am not the only one the world uses up, smears and throws away. The fate of many people is but to be a blotter of hard luck and to succumb in need or die prematurely. Corrupt people use the finest and noblest of men to blot out their iniquities,

Many an employer uses his working people like absorbent paper. These people are helpless for they depend on him for their livelihood. He forces them to absorb all his caprices, stubbornness, ineptitude and insults, and when they are weakened with sorrow or when they grow older he throws them away like a used-up blotter.

The property of absorption is also given to a sponge, but sponge can eliminate as well as absorb, and it is made by nature and fed most of the time with clear water, while I can only absorb manmade, manufactured stuff. In your world, too, there are men like the sponges who not only absorb but under the proper inspiration can project the product of their knowledge and genius, like many a literary man or poet. But you don't always appreciate these exceptional people except when they are philanthropists. You bow before these men, even when their riches are derived from the sweat and blood of their workers.

There are also amongst you people who absorb very much more than they give up. They like to take but hate to give! Anyhow, there are more of the blotter type among you than the sponge type. I, as a blotter, take courage when I think that your entire earth is nothing more than a large, a very large blotter. It absorbs your sweat, your tears, the blood you spill in your often senseless wars, and remains dry as if nothing happened. And what are your graves but blotters which take into their bosom the master and the servant, the rich and the poor, the strong and the feeble, the wise and the simple, leveling all distinctions.

But the greatest of all blotters is limitless eternity. She draws in the greatest and the best and little remains discernible. Oh, you eternal blotter! You endless, unexplainable, uncompromising, unattainable, undiscovered blotter.

PRETENSIONS OF A MIRROR

I am something that gives a faithful reflection or true picture of somebody or something. If you'd rather not look at me it is not of my concern, and if you do, I can only reflect whom or what you show me. Images of my own I do not possess. When you look at me you look at yourself. I am only a mirror, usually only a piece of glass with a metallic backing.

I know that some people dislike me because I reflect their ugly or dirty face, or other unpleasant features, but that is no fault of mine. I flatter no one. I have the same reflection whether a prince or a pauper looks at me. Furthermore, I induce no one to mirror himself. I stay mutely in my place and I come into use only when you care to observe your body or your features. That is what I am made for. I am only a looking-glass.

And it is a good thing that I am only a piece of glass, without feeling or sensation, otherwise you might perhaps destroy me. People do not always care to be shown-up, or to show their faces, because sometimes I must show you such unpleasant images, like a wrinkled face, prematurely gray hair, swollen eyes after a beating or from shedding tears.

It is a good thing I am not alive or I would burst with laughter when some of your old women work on their make-up with my reflection. They want to fill in the lines in their faces caused by inheritance or by age. With paint and rouge, with false eyelashes and false eyebrows, they attempt to fool the world. They try to make believe they are what they are not! They cannot fool me. I am only a piece of glass.

I have to laugh when some of you show your crooked faces, unkempt hair, dirty shirts and clothes and get exasperated at me. I cannot help it. I am only a mirror. Keep your face and body straight, keep clean and spotless and you will like me better.

I, the mirror, am a thing that dares to reflect the image even of the sky! Nothing is too high or too exceptional for me. Place me against the sky and I will even show you spots in the sun!

I will show you displeasing clouds that hide the sun or the stars. With the help of some lenses I will show you parts of the whole astronomical world. I will also show the ugly, unwanted balls of lead and fire that trouble the heavens above.

This is the scope of a mirror: the clearer and truer it portrays, the greater its value. Naturally, like everything else, there are cheaper mirrors too, mirrors which reflect distortion, but no sensible person will mirror himself by such means.

The trouble is, however, that people neglect to look into the mirror. They do not take the opportunity to see the truth and correct their blemishes. They say that the face portrays a person's soul. But what kind of a soul can a person have who shows no face? A person's best mirrors are his good deeds. Let him keep a good record of them and we will know how he looks.

"Oh, how long will the earth reflect itself in the sky and still remain dirty and smudgy?", I often complain to my Maker, my Inventor, because the world does not understand me . . .

She does not understand the usefulness of a mirror.

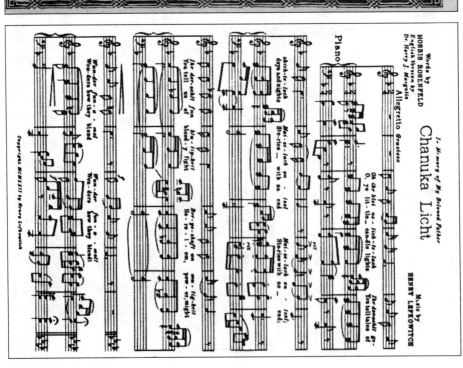

This is the front page of the Forward, a Yiddish Daily, the day after the horrendous Triangle Shirtwaist factory fire. Hundreds lost their lives. Rage and consternation filled the Jewish community. Rosenfeld wrote his explosive poem, The Red Panic, expressing his people's pain and sadness. This poem took up the full length of the third page.

News of the Yivo No. 81

MORRIS ROSENFELD EXHIBITION OPENS

In the first half of February 1962, the opening of the Exhibition "Morris Rosenfeld (1862–1923) and His Time" will take place in the Atran Exhibition Room, Yivo. The Exhibition will commemorate the centenary of the birth of the renowned Yiddish poet, who spent the last 37 years of his life in America.

As the name indicates, the Exhibition provides not only a cross section of the life and work of Rosenfeld, but also a bird's-eye view of that era and of the social and literary milieu of the poet, particularly of the first period of his creative activity The Eastern European Jewish immigrant masses in the 1880's and 1890's, the Jewish literary and journalistic scene of those years, the ideological and literary currents prevailing on the East Side—are generously represented.

Morris Rosenfeld in his first years in America.—*From the Yivo Archives.*

The Exhibition comprises 1,227 objects, arranged in 29 divisions, exhibited in more than 30 showcases and some 50 frames on the walls. It tells of Rosenfeld's family and of his life prior to his coming to America, of the year 1886, when he settled in America, of his first poems, of the life of the immigrants, the squalor of the tenements houses and the sweatshops, of the East Side, its charm and despair. Central in the Exhibition is the literary work of Rosenfeld in its manifold aspects: the poet of the sweatshop, the East Side, the class struggle and revolution on the one hand, and of national and religious sentiments on the other; and in a category quite apart Rosenfeld's nature and love poetry. In addition we see Rosenfeld's manifold activity as editor, journalist, satirist, writer of poems on the happenings of the day.

Several divisions are devoted to Rosenfeld in translation into European languages, beginning with the English translation by Professor Leo Wiener, of Harvard University. The divisions on his incipient blindness (in 1907) and on his tour of Europe (in 1908) provide a measure of his popularity with the Jewish public the world over, even in the circles of the assimilated in Western Europe and America. Lastly come the divisions telling of the loneliness and misery of his last years.

The Exhibition consists of several hundred photographs, paintings and pictures of Rosenfeld and his social and cultural ambience, manuscripts, periodicals, newspaper clippings with Rosenfeld's notations, the various editions of his works in Yiddish—including the rare first editions—and in other languages and sundry other documents. Noteworthy is the division on music to Rosenfeld's poems.

Most of the objects exhibited are from the Yivo collections. However, every possible effort was made to supplement deficiencies by borrowing rare objects from leading libraries, art galleries and private collectors. To them all go the thanks of Yivo.

To Prof. E. R. A. Seligman
My Dear Sir,—
No vain praise
or flattery is my tribute to you in
my preface of this book. It is the
expression of sincere gratitude for
many favors and genuine friendship
— Morris Rosenfeld.

New York
January 14th 1899

Prof. Seligman
My Dear and Honored Sir
Your letter and the Nation at hand.
I was already informed about the article in the Nation
by my friend Dr. Studynsky of Wiesbaden (Germany)
and I was very eager to see it. I am therefore very grateful to you for sending it to me. And I thank you
in advance for the articles you have promised to send
me.... As to what I am doing now:—well, I do some
thing — that is nothing. I work at the Columbia
University Library. I am cataloguing Hebrew books
there. God knows how I hate this dry and tiresome
work! When will the publishers read in some account?
May let me hear from you. Yours sincerely
Morris Rosenfeld

These two letters are from Rosenfeld to two of the best friends he ever had. Prof. Weiner was his "discoverer" and mentor. Prof. Seligman was not only an encouraging force but also asked his brother, the "banker, Seligman" to help provide Rosenfeld with an annual stipend to save the poet and his family from absolute poverty.

The letters on this page, from Rabbi Stephen S. Wise and Miss Jane Addams, are but two of the hundreds of letters to and from Morris Rosenfeld. The voluminous correspondence between Rosenfeld and many notables reposes in the files of the YIVO in New York. Two more such letters, from Edwin Markham and Upton Sinclair, are on following pages.

The paper trail of Rosenfeld's life begins with this map, based on the Encyclopedia Britanica's own map. It shows the town of Suwalki in Poland, where he was reared. He was born in the hamlet of Buksha about twenty mile away. See how close Suwalki is to Lithuania and to Russia itself.

92 Waters Avenue
West New Brighton, N.Y.
May 7, 1919.

My dear Morris Rosenfeld:

For long months I have been driven as a leaf in a whirl-wind---part of the time I have been lecturing thru New England with a wide swing cut into the Middle West.   Yet all this time you have been darting again and again into my memory like a ghost into a wood, and at each apparition of you I have been restless and un-happy.   I knew too well that I should have written to you long ago to thank you with happy words for the translation you made of my poem, The Man with the Hoe.   You translated it into Yid-dish and thus loosened it for a flight into new winds.

Let me assure you, dear and honored poet, that I was touoht and gladdened by this comrade kindness.   I was fully sensible of the distinction that you had conferred upon the poem.   I know of no one in America so well qualified as you were for this task of translation.   You not only felt the pas-sion of my poem, but you are also a poet with the power to choose the potent word.   Pray accept my heart's deep thanks for your distinguished service.   I shall keep the copy of the translation that you sent me, for I expect to use it---to-gether with other translations of the Hoe-poem---in the collec-ted edition of my poems.

I am greatly interested in what you told me of your purpose to bring out a volume of your poems in English.   I am hoping some day to see you at my home here some Sunday af-ternoon when my friends---some of them---shall be making a pil-grimage to this woodland haunt.   I will send you notice of our next reception.

Your comrade-in-arms,
Edwin Markham

Croton on Hudson NY
Jan 15 [915]
(1)

Dear Comrade:

I want to quote one of your poems in my collection. I suppose you will let me. Also I want to use that relief drawing which is in Mrs Stokes translation. Can you lend me all of the work that you have? And I will be grateful if you will refer me to the work of any other — to me here or abroad. Please reply at once, as I am beginning to print soon.

Fraternally

Upton Sinclair

To
Morris Rosenfeld

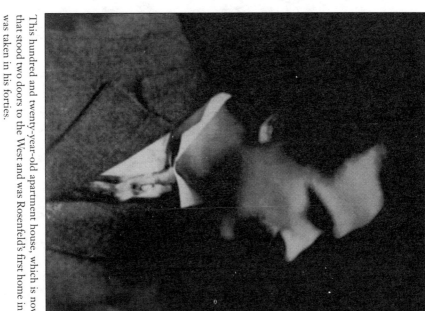

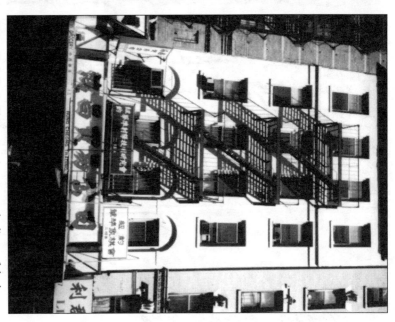

This hundred and twenty-year-old apartment house, which is now a part of New York City's Chinatown, is an exact duplicate of the house that stood two doors to the West and was Rosenfeld's first home in America. It is number 128 Catherine Street. The photograph of Rosenfeld was taken in his forties.

BROOKLYN ACADEMY OF MUSIC

Sunday, November 12, 1961 • 2:00 P.M.

The Jewish Cultural Clubs and Societies Present Their

Grand Concert

Dedicated to the Centennial of the Civil War and of Morris Rosenfeld

PROGRAM

• OPENING REMARKS by Chairman, Sonia Schechter

• GROUP OF CIVIL WAR SONGS
    WILLIAM WOLF, bass-baritone

• SHER - - - - - Folk
    EDITH SEGAL DANCE GROUP
    (Dancers participating listed on page three)

• DENMARK VESEY
    Based on poem "Denmark Vesey," by Aaron Kramer
    MORRIS CARNOVSKY AND PHOEBE BRAND

• ADDRESS - - - - Gedalia Sandler

• AUCTION BLOCK - - - Negro Spiritual
                                  Negro Work Song
    Choreographed by Edith Segal
    Eugene Young, baritone, and Roberta Frank, pianist
    Set by Samuel Kamen and Bobby Gainer
    EDITH SEGAL DANCE GROUP
    Charles Greene, Robert Heisler, Sally McGuire
    Nina Richardson, Michele Palmer, Sheri Saltzberg

Intermission

• THE TAILOR AND THE POET - - Itche Goldberg
    Musical Direction — MAURICE RAUCH
    JEWISH PEOPLES PHILHARMONIC CHORUS
    MAURICE RAUCH, Conductor   WILLIAM WOLF, soloist
    The Tailor — MENASHE OPPENHEIM
    The Poet — HENRY KELLERMAN
    At the piano — EUGENE KUSMIAK

Arranged by Committee for Jewish Education and Culture

THE ZUKUNFT

(The Future)   25 East 78th Street, New York 21, N. Y.
Tel.: LEhigh 5-4642

February, 1962

Dear Friends,

You are cordially invited to the

ROUND TABLE SYMPOSIUM

Sunday, March 11th, 1962, at 7:00 P.M.

HOTEL ASTOR

Broadway and 44th Sts. (at Times Sq.), New York

Topic:

*YIDDISH LITERATURE FROM MORRIS ROSENFELD
TO THE PRESENT DAY*

(The 100th Anniversary of the Poet Morris Rosenfeld)

SPEAKERS:

JACOB GLATSTEIN, *Poet and Essayist*
    Introductory Remarks.

MICHAEL CHERNICHOV-ASTOUR
    Professor Brandeis University, Waltham, Mass.
    Morris Rosenfeld — Social and National Poet of his Generation.

RABBI EMANUEL S. GOLDSMITH
    Member Editorial Board, Reconstructionist magazine
    Morris Rosenfeld and his influence upon the Development of Yiddish Poetry.

* * *

We hope that you will accept the invitation to our Yearly Symposium.
Kindly return the enclosed reservation blank as early as possible.

    Cordially yours
    THE ZUKUNFT

L. Segal, Co-Chairman   N. Chanin, Chairman
Ch. Pupko, Exec.-Sec'y

Sandwiches, Coffee and
Cake will be served   Subscription $2.50   (Tips included)

The Zukunft (The Future), Yiddish monthly, established in 1892

Our oldest couple
Ninety-two she. Hundred and four he!
Rachel and Ephraim Rosenfeldt, the parents of Morris Rosenfeld and Joseph Rosenfeld

Rose Rosenfeld Goldenthal, Rosenfeld's youngest daughter.

Rosenfeld's "middle" daughter, Freda Iona Hurwitz, at age 96, holding earlier photo of herself.

This nine-year-old boy was Rosenfeld's son Joseph, who was known world-wide was the "Yingele" of his father's poetry.

Morris Rosenfeld in his thirties.

Bessie Rosenfeld with her ten-year-old daughter Rose (Reyzele).

11

Epilogue

And so we come to the conclusion of this lengthy labor of love. We can emphasize both "labor" and "love." We have not asked ourselves "What have we accomplished?" or "Who is really interested in this kind of a work?" We have been so immersed in this subject for such a long period of time that we can no longer imagine that there is not a large potential audience "out there" to enjoy with us this vital subject of the immigrant experience of the Jewish people and the place in it of the talented, emotional poet, Morris Rosenfeld. But there is much more, which we never realized until this book had been nearly completed. We have discovered more about Morris Rosenfeld than anyone had an opportunity to know except his wife and children. Yet even they were too close to him, too close to the times they lived in, to see any of that in perspective.

Who knows his own place in history? Who knows how he will be thought of, if indeed anyone will care enough to think about him—when three-quarters of a century will have elapsed after his death? We hope that we have provided an accurate, sympathetic description of Rosenfeld, his life and times and his niche in history. We have the almost eerie sensation of having read the diary of a long-gone individual who had no realization that his writings and public expressions were indeed an almanac that could be read and interpreted by descendants many years later. Neither my wife and help-mate, Janice, nor I would ever have the temerity to read one of our sons' love-letters. Nor would Ed ever read Janice's journal.

But here, in reading Rosenfeld's schrifter (writings), we feel as though we had intruded upon his privacy.

Every idea that came to him he would put into a poem, or an article, whether it was love, pain, fear, suffering, excitement, love of nature, respect for some person or hatred of others, love for his Jewish brethren or America, respect and anxiety for the working-men, wonder about life, death, God or the blackness of the tomb. Nothing escaped his observation and his pen, from his flight from Europe's ghetto to his interests in the New York ghetto; all this and so much more was poured into Rosenfeld's writings. Mortimer Cohen, in his book of transliteration of some of Rosenfeld's poems, suggested that Rosenfeld might have been the first man to write poetry in the Yiddish language using accepted forms of meter and rhyme. Cohen's theory, we believe, needs more research than we have time to devote to that subject. To be a precursor in any field is a great responsibility for a young man in his teens. This we never realized. Rosenfeld was just Grandpa to us, a well-known poet and a man with a pretty-good temper. But as we read his poetry we cried with him—genuine, bitter tears—as he worried about his little boy who was dying of bone cancer. We wept when he wrote later that he had expected, like all parents, to predecease his offspring, but that here his youngster went to "the blackness of the tomb" before him. And we got excited with him when he exhorted his fellow workingmen to rise to the occasion and "make something more of their lives." We suffered with him when we read the nasty, personal, uncalled-for insults that "Die Junge", the left-wing exis-tentialist poets, heaped upon him in the press and in lectures. And we shrank in embarrassment when we read his own diatribes and uncouth writing in retaliation.

We marvelled at how highly developed his poetry became, coming as he did from a land where Yiddish was indeed a jargon. He took a coarse but expressive language and created beauty, ex-citement and inspiration with it. Yet it was only when we visited the YIVO that we discovered the thousands of items of literature, music and art that Rosenfeld created and inspired. One of his severest critics, Leivick, a fine writer and a member of "the Junge" in his early years, feeling a degree of remorse and a newfound respect for Rosenfeld, actually wrote a play about Morris, calling it "The Blind Poet." Also, at the centenary of Rosenfeld's birth the great Yiddish poet Glatshtein, who was also a founder of the original "Inzich" group, delivered a beautiful oration about the "great poet" Rosenfeld. It must be noted here that although "Die Junge" and the "Inzichist" groups were publicly excessively critical of Morris, when these young men reached a degree of maturity even the most bitter of them finally expressed their debt to and admiration for the older poet, whose life had been virtually extinguished by that time.

This volume is about more than Rosenfeld. There is occasion here to be proud of the millions of immigrants who had the courage to uproot themselves and emigrate to the West. This was a true phenomenon. Many peoples have been forcefully torn from their homes and forced to migrate elsewhere. But here was a people with age-old hope and faith in the future, in their God and His beneficence—who did not wait to be driven out. They pulled stakes and moved on their own. There is indeed occasion here to be proud of our recent ancestors who made that move.

And there is occasion here, as we tried to demonstrate in this book, to be proud of those same people who, once they had arrived in this alien land, did not become a burden to America but were industrious, creative, law-abiding and good citizens. They brought dedication, a firm belief in one God and a social consciousness that helped shape the future of this great American society. They helped bring our awareness of Man's responsibility for his brother's well-being, of the Golden Rule and of the philosophy of a loving family life and all it implies to become a part of the American ethos.

We are proud of the creativeness that so suddenly sprang from these humble working people, as though they were common soil that had been magically fertilized and invigorated with the inspiration for creativity of art, music and literature. We have earlier listed just a few of the thousands of such creative individuals who, but for the immigration to America, might still be "nobodies" living in "nowhereland" in Eastern Europe. Think of the intellectual and social loss that the world suffered when Hitler caused the destruction of six million of those he considered "nobodies." Those lost brethren were our kin, our blood and part of our history. Obviously, after glimpsing the racks of books and artifacts at the YIVO concerning Morris Rosenfeld we realized that even such a work as this is insufficient to pay him due homage. Someone, perhaps, will have an epiphany, such as we did, and devote a few years' time to do a complete translation of Rosenfeld's works with an update of his lingering effects on his people. Certainly translations and critiques of his plays, his philosophical writings and a study of his original music would add new dimensions to Rosenfeld's body of works.

When we read Rosenfeld's ideas and manner of expression, when we studied his reactions to praise and criticism, it all seemed so familiar to us. We recognize a "familial" personality there. He is no stranger to us. There is in several of his descendants much of his talent and personality. Many of his descendants have excelled in one or more forms of the arts. Every day, as our grandchildren mature, we notice some of the creative talents that distinguished Morris Rosenfeld, although none has reached his level of distinction yet. Several of our cousins have excelled in music and literature, some others have excelled in the graphic arts, one has become a Rabbi and many have found a niche in the field of medicine and allied disciplines.

Joan Harris Torres writes for Hollywood, and wrote a bestselling book called "Men Who Hate Women and the Women Who Love Them." Mario Torres dances on the Broadway stage. Dr. Andrew Harris, Professor of English at a Texas university has written a play, "Albee's Women" which is scheduled by the Schubert's for Broadway. Both Andrew and Joan recently had a play produced in Chicago under the auspices of the Schuberts. It is called "Better Half Dead" and was a great success. Their father Dr. Earle Harris, the eldest grandson of Morris Rosenfeld, was a founder of the HIP (Health Insurance Plan) in New York. He was also a talented watercolorist. Rebecca Goldenthal's pilot was a success for a new series on television to be shown soon and her designer earrings are exceedingly popular at Bloomingdale's in New York. Evelyn Hurwitz DeBoeck performed as a pianist for many years, in lounges and theaters in New York and elsewhere. She was selected by Eleanor Roosevelt to entertain at the White House. Allan Benarria Goldenthal was a pharmacist, a cryptographer for the American Military Intelligence during WW II, wrote a definitive work on how to read, write and speak in Chinese, was a poet and musician, ran an all-girl orchestra, created an advertising agency and, believe it or not, was an agent in the CIA after WW II. Talk about talent! His daughter Lisa is a writer for a New Jersey newspaper and his son Adam is a staff reporter. Dr. Mark Goldenthal is a musician, a poet and a psychologist. Dr. Jonathan Goldenthal is a composer who has had some music accepted for a movie. Joel Goldenthal is a talented pianist, composer and bandleader who also has his own advertising agency. Dr. Michael Goldenthal, a molecular biologist, writes with a whimsy that verges on the surreal. These are just a few of Rosenfeld's grandchildren and great-grandchildren who have have exhibited creativity. With a little more poverty and aggravation in their lives who knows what new genius will arise?

There were some aspects of Morris Rosenfeld that must be delineated before we close this work. We must admit that starting in about 1915–1918 his capacity to write first-rate poetry began to deteriorate. This followed some severe illnesses that sapped his strength. Most of the great Yiddish-American poets had already died prematurely. In his fifties he was already "the old man." He never expected to live into his sixties. Morris had noticed that he was no longer needed as a labor poet. Much of what he had fought for had been achieved. Labor was an increasingly viable force. He began to concentrate on Nature, Love and Philosophical topics, none of which drew much attention from his readership. He lost the "fire in his belly" and even admitted this in some of his poems. He was successful with his prose, but only to a modest degree. He also began to write increasingly in English, but never reached the success he had achieved in Yiddish. Almost everyone, except some of the avant-guard "modernists," was now writing in English and the "fire" was not replaceable by intellectual forays into philosophy or socially commendable concepts. If he had only retained that sardonic sense of humor he had when he (years before) edited a "Humor Magazine" with Sharkansky he might have well survived the change in his fortunes. But he did not. Morris' ego, which became over-weaning after his phenomenally successful European tour in the first decade of this Century, could not tolerate the neglect he began to receive, justifiably so in many cases, when his output was no longer as competent or as frequent as formerly. The embers were dying before the poet himself died. This realization ate at his soul and led to a premature death at 61. It seems premature to us, but he may have welcomed death. No one had to tell him he was "over the hill". No one had to tell him he was passe, although plenty of nasty men did so in the mistaken belief that their careers would rise on his ashes. They passed on to a secure oblivion while Rosenfeld's star still twinkles to us from afar.

As we think of Rosenfeld and his times and his creativity; as we think of Glatshteyn and his times and his creativity, we must ask,

"For whom do we qvell? (quiver with appreciation)? And for whom do we cry?" The answer is we qvell and we cry for the Jewish people, for Yiddishkeit, for that sad and wonderful, tragic and marvelous Jewish ethnic group that defies accurate definition. Even when they are great we have to cry tears of joy mingled with the inexpressible sadness that lies behind our joy. Glatshteyn expressed, in a very beautiful and highly developed Yiddish, the utter helplessness of "dos pintele Yid" (that tiny dot of a Jew) in the kaleidoscopic existence of our people. He saw us as without much real hope, without justification, without the determination of a true existentialist that some basic meaning does underlie all this and that it will somehow work its way to a useful and desirable conclusion.

Rosenfeld wrote in a far less pessimistic vein of the very same people in the very same world. However, he did not live to see the Holocaust, which threw all reasoning individuals into a new cauldron of intellectual ferment and should lead to some re-evaluation of Man as a justifiable creature. Neither Rosenfeld nor Glatshteyn depended upon a God for ultimate salvation. They looked to Man, without using the word "existential", for his own salvation. Glatshteyn, even before the Holocaust, was not very confident that this salvation would occur. Rosenfeld, a simpler poet, dealing with simpler but basic urges and desires, looked for Man to cure his own ills, even, "cholili vechas" (by chance) with a gentle upward nudge of the Almighty's elbow.

Knowing Rosenfeld as we have come to know him we feel that had he lived through the Holocaust and the developing freedom of the Jews in the Western world he would only have intensified his efforts to fight for Jewish survival and the creation of the Jewish State. He would have fought to increase Jewish identity both in Israel and in the diaspora. He would unquestionably have attuned his poetry to the times as he did for the immigrants a century ago. He was indeed a bard for his time and we could use one like him today.

In all honesty, very few modern, twentieth-century Yidlach (Jews) filled with the restless yearning for newness and creativity, despite years of education and training in both the understanding and appreciation of poetry and prose, would find that Rosenfeld's poetry would strike their fancy. Those not comfortable with Victorian age poetry might feel that the style of his earlier poetry is "dated." However, his subject matter and his approach to the lives and problems of his contemporaries are strikingly brave and vibrant. As an interesting sidelight on Rosenfeld's writing, his prose was remarkably "twentieth century" modern. We have the bizarre notion that had he devoted himself entirely to prose—stories, essays, polemic articles—his career might have lasted for many more years of popular acceptance.

We enjoyed reading Rosenfeld for what he said as much as how he said it. We read most of it in English translation. He was less the intellectual than Peretz, Bialik, Leyvik and Leyeles. His overheated mind led his overheated hand. None of his contemporaries except perhaps Yehoash, Winchevsky and Bovshover flailed as relentlessly as he did against an uncaring world. His sincerity could not be doubted since each "excitement", each terrible experience cost him "a piece of life." How long could such an ember burn on? Rosenfeld's poetry was an instrument, a tortured voice hoarsely berating the mailed fist of destiny. He did not "all alone beweep his outcast state." He shrieked to heaven! He ranted to the stars! He screamed his epithets to the powers that be, to awaken his fellow men to the tragic insufficiency of their lives. Although he did not write in an expressionist mode he shared in the "geschrai" (the scream) of German expressionists in the face of inhumanity.

Where some of his Yiddish poems in translation trembled on the brink of doggerel we must be certain that it is really the way he wrote them. Was the Yiddish more musical than the translation? Were the idiomatic expressions and rhymes translated with fidelity? Most of his early English poems were indeed not in the same league with his Yiddish works. He took an awfully long time to master English for creative purposes. It was Rilke who stated that he knew of the "old curse of poets" who use language for the description of their hurts instead of "transforming themselves into hard words as the stone-mason of a cathedral obstinately translates himself into the equanimity of the stone."[1] No way could Rosenfeld translate himself into the hardness of the stone. He, at the behest of his Muse, translated himself into the flame of rebellion and the steel edge of the sword that he used to slash a path for his downtrodden fellowmen.

We come away from this experience as souls affected by the sad life and the brilliance of a common man who was touched by the Muse and who, despite every adversity, drove himself to love, to observe, to fight and to create poetry, music, plays, prose and . . .

excitement! And not merely for himself was he a creative force; he lived for his people and society at large as well. What a legacy this is for Grandpa to leave us!

Referencespage

1. Preminger, Alex, Poetry and Poetics"

Appendix

Catalogue from YIVO on Rosenfeld Anniversary   382

Outstanding Dates in Rosenfeld's Life   384

Recollections of An Admirer   407

CATALOGUE BY THE YIVO INSTITUTE FOR JEWISH RESEARCH ON THE OCCASION OF THE CENTENARY OF MORRIS ROSENFELD'S BIRTH

This catalogue of the exhibition at the YIVO headquarters in New York City was prepared by Z. Szajkowski and staff and it not only describes all the items in the massive exhibit, it summarizes Rosenfeld's life, his achievements, his image before the world. There are forty-nine pages in the catalogue, which we will only partially use, with the permission, graciously given, of the YIVO. The research that was performed was tremendous, using data from all over the civilized world. We include this abbreviated summary of "Morris Rosenfeld And His Time . . . 1862–1923" for several reasons. Firstly, it provides the location of a wealth of material that others may wish to use for the creation of new documents on Jewish writers and the history of our people . Secondly, only by reading such a summary can one begin to grasp the immense connection between this one little man and the whole of Jewish culture and development during the immigrant experience. Lastly, we are proud to be able to demonstrate that our our newly-discovered appreciation for a grandfather who died in 1923 is indeed justified. Please believe us when we aver that we feel as though we had previously been leading a life nearly devoid of consciousness of the ramifications of that immigrant experience with our own selves and our families. Merely to read Howe's "World Of Our Fathers" was informative. But to read and study all the material involved in writing this volume has been nothing less than inspiring and provocative. We are literally provoked into extending ourselves into all directions of Jewish life. What is more, we are involving our children and grandchildren in a greater awareness of their history; into a realization of the debt they owe to their forebears. The following material, in its entirety, is taken from the YIVO catalogue, dated 1962.

FROM THE CATALOGUE
(Prepared by Z. Szajkowski for the YIVO)
(These are all quotes, with occasional comments by Dr. Ed Goldenthal)

On the centenary of the birth of Morris Rosenfeld the YIVO Institute for Jewish Research has arranged this exhibition..Morris Rosenfeld was not merely a distinguished poet, but also a pioneer of Yiddish Poetry in America. He was not merely a worker-poet, but also a national poet. His poems were not only a solace to all categories of the Jewish preople, but also a call to battle for a better future. They were declaimed and sung in the sweatshops, at home, at meetings and demonstrations of workmen and nationalist Jewish groups. Rosenfeld, the tailoring workman, put his pen at the service of his class, helping in the organization of unions and the like, as well as at the service of his people, the Jewish people. The translation of his poems into English and other languages not only spread the fame of the poet but helped to introduce the Yiddish language and its literature to the non-Jewish world and to arouse its interest in the tragic plight of the Jewish workman, in particular, and the Jewish people in general. Although Morris Rosenfeld was fortunate in surviving long after the premature death (of the "proletarian disease, tuberculosis) of his fellow pioneer singers of Yiddish social poetry in America, the long years of toil in the sweatshop exacted its toll. His artistic growth was arrested and he could not become the leader of a new generation of writers-immigrants.

Notwithstanding the fact that Rosenfeld continued writing to his end, his last years were pathetic and sad. These were years of poverty, misery and obscurity in an environment that was not able to overlook the petty foibles of a pioneer of Yiddish poetry. And thus Rosenfeld died poor, embittered and forsaken. In arranging this exhibition I have sought to give a picture of all aspects of Reosenfeld's life within the context of his time; the impact of great events on him and his participation in them; the poet as a public figure and in his workaday moments—a flesh and blood man and not a lifeless apology. To this end several divisions are devoted to general events in Rosenfeld's time. However his poetry and prose are illustrated by documents, pictures, drawings and contemporary objects of which Rosenfeld sang.

The major difficulty in arranging the exhibition is due to a lack of an authoritative biographic and bibliographical work on Rosenfeld. Only a part of his many poetical and prose works have been included in his collected works. Several collections of his poems, manuscripts of his plays, and several publications that he edited are no longer extant. Even some of the Yiddish publications of the 1890's, in which Rosenfeld appeared are no longer available. Nor are some of his "pen names" known any longer. Hence the lacunae in the exhibition. Fortunately there remained the notes of the historian and bibliographer, Kalman Marmor, who had devotedly gathered materials for an edition of Rosenfeld's poems and for a biography and bibliography of the poet. A part of Rosenfeld's personal archive was preserved in Marmor's library and archive, which he donated to the YIVO.

I wish to express my sincerest thanks (as we express ours, ed.) to Dr. Max Weinreich, E. Lifschutz, Jacob Gladstone and Abraham Kin, whom I have consulted freely about the character of the exhibition, as well as Dina Abramowitz, Judith Fink, Berl Kagan, Hillel Kempinsky, Moyshe Kligsberg, Dr. Shlomo Noble, Pinkhos Schwartz and Jonas Turkov, who in various ways offered their assistance. Z. Szajkowski, February, 1962. (Because Zosa Szajkowski specifically mentioned the need for an authentic biography and bibliography, we include here the many sources we have referred to and a number of other excellent tomes for specific reference. We suggest that any interested persons may contact the YIVO for items that we cannot, for reasons of space, present here. ed.) All objects (in this exhibition) are from the archives and Library of the YIVO, primarily the Kalman Marmor Collection, which contains the Morris Rosenfeld sub-collection; the Morris Rosenfeld Collection donated by his son-in-law, Dr. Leon Goldenthal; the episolary collection of Professor Leo Wiener and others, except the following items borrowed from these institutions and individuals:

A.C.A. Gallery, N.Y.: Archives of the Jewish Labor Bund: Bloch Publishing Co., N.Y.: Educational Alliance: The Harvard Univ. Library, Cambridge The Hebrew Union College Library, Cincinnati: ILGWU, New York: The Jacob Michael Collection of Jewish Music, N.Y.C.: The Jewish Labor Committee, N.Y.: The Jewish Museum, N.Y.: The Jewish Theological Seminary, N.Y.: The Jewish Division of the New York Public Library: The Music Library, The Picture Division: The Tamiment Institute Archives and Library: Mr. Arie Abrahamson, N.Y.: Dr. Leon Goldenthal, N.Y.: Mr. Aaron Kramer, N.Y.: Prof. B. Mark, Warsaw: Mr. M. Rauch, N.Y.: Mr. Joseph Rosenfeld, Newark: Mr. David Rosenstein, N.Y.: Mrs. Ruth Rubin, N.Y.: Mr. Leo Stein, N.Y.: Mr. Z. Szajowski, N.Y.: Mr. Artor Wolf, N.Y.

Also exhibited were objects from the American Jewish Archives, Cincinnati; Harvard Univ. Library.: The Yidishe Folks Bibliothek, Montreal: The Museum of the City of New York: The New York Historical Society: The New York Public Library: The Zionist Archives, Jerusalem: Dr. Hyman B. Grinstein, N.Y.: Jacob Epstein's Illustrations to the "Spirit Of The Ghetto, by Hutchins Hapgood, N.Y.-London: "Pioneers of Yiddish Poetry In America" by N.B. Minkoff, N.Y.1956 (3 vols.): ILGWU New History, Atlantic City.

OUTSTANDING DATES IN ROSENFELD'S LIFE AND WORK

1862 Born on Dec 28 or 30 1862, village of Buksha, district of Suwalki, Poland
1876 Wrote his first poem. Di Zelneray, which remained unpublished
1880 Married, divorced his first wife 6 months later (we have "family" information that he was married the year before and the marriage was "annulled". ed.)
1882 Married Rebecca Basye Beyle Yavorosky (Called Bessie, ed.)
1882 Spent 3 mo. in Amsterdam, went to America, returned home
1883 Spent 6 mo. in London, returned to Suwalki, returned to London
1886 Rosenfeld's three children, Sarah, Abe and Lilly, died in London,1886. Settled in America, published two poems, active in labor movement

1887 Published a third poem
1888 Press published several poems, first collection of poems, "Die Glocke" appeared.
1890 Published "Die Blumenkette", his second collection of verse
1892 Edited the magazine, "Di Zun" (the Sun)
1893 Published third volume of poetry, "Poezyen Un Lieder"
1894 Edited,with Sharkansky, humorous publication, "Der Ashmeday"
1896 Presents Operetta,"The Last High Priest/ Religion and Love"
1897 Publishes fourth collection of poetry, "Dos Liderbuch"
1898 "Songs From The Ghetto", English translation by Dr. Leo Wiener appeared. Brought Rosenfeld's name to non-Yiddish-speaking world.
1898 Rosenfeld writes an English poem, "I Know Not Why"
1900 Delegate to fourth Zionist Congress
1900 Publishes, together with Sharkansky, "Der Pinkes"
1902 "Lieder des Ghetto", major work, edited by Berthold Feivel illustrated by Ephraim Lillien, Berlin
1904 "Gezamelte Lider" (collected works), New York
1904 "Cintece din Ghetto", Iasi, Rumania
1905 His son Joseph, (Mayn Yingele) age 15, dies
1905 "Geklibene Lider" published, Warsaw
1905 Edited the "Nuyorker Morgenblat"
1905 "Zpevy z Ghetta", Prague
1906 "Piesni Pracy", Warsaw
1906 "Pjesme iz Geta", Zagreb
1907 "Heinrich Heine", N.Y. (Biography
1907 "Yehuda Halevi", (Biography), New York
1907 Onset of blindness
1908 Triumphal tour of Europe
1908 "Piesni z Ghetta", Warsaw
1908 "Shriften" (writings),, 3 vols., New York
1908 "Koltemenyei", Budapest
1909 "Gedichte", Prague
1910 "Shriften" (writings), 6 volumes, New York
1912 "Geveylte Shriften" (selected writings), 3 vols., New York
1913 Celebration of Rosenfeld's fiftieth anniversary
1914 "Dos Buch fon Libe: (The Book Of Love), New York
1914 "Songs of Labor", Boston
1914 Resigns from "Forwards" staff
1919 "Grine Tsores un Andere Shriften"(tales of immigrant life), New York
1921 Dismissed from "Tageblat" staff, March 4
1923 Celebration of his 60th birthday, N.Y., May 26 1923 Rosenfeld's death, June 22

(The accumulated data in Szajkowski's YIVO catalogue is divided into many divisions, listing works by Rosenfeld and about him, events of his times and other pertinent data. This could bore the casual reader but we feel it is imperative to include this, brief though it may be, to round out our picture of the life and times of Rosenfeld.EJG)

I. ROSENFELD PRIOR TO HIS SETTLEMENT IN AMERICA

Professor B. Mark writes to YIVO in 1961 that, "Older peasants in Boksha (where R. was born) recall that prior to the war several Jewish families lived there. Now no Jews live there." In 1882 R. visited New York, landed at "Castle Gardens", Brooklyn. At R's centennial photos of fishing villages in Poland, ships that plied between Europe and America, crowded ghetto scenes in Poland. In London, where R. lived and in New York. R. was busy, even in 1884, "writing letters to the editor" under assumed names. Some of those were exhibited, where the name "M. Ros. Leeds" was seen. (Leeds was a British town where he had lived). In this division are exhibited documents and pictures of Jewish life on the East Side: also a photo (which we have in this volume, ed.) of R and wife and eldest daughter, Dora, from 1886.

II. THE YEAR 1886 ON THE EAST SIDE

In 1886 R. settled in New York, where he became active in the labor movement. Same year he published two poems. That year was noted for its fierce social struggles, in which Jewish workers became involved. They whole-heartedly supported the striking employees of the N.Y. streetcars, and after the strike failed, boycotted the transportation system. They also participated in the struggle for an eight-hour day and in the efforts to obtain a pardon for the Chicago anarchists sentenced in the wake of the Haymarket riots. The liberal Henry George ran for mayor of N.Y., backed by Socialists and trade unions. On the East Side Jewish Workers committees organized for him. There are many photos of the East Side, a raid on vendors of spoiled fruit, etc. R wrote a poem "Di Letste Frucht" (last Fruits) about a fruit dealer who brings home spoiled fruit to his starving family (1886).

In the years 1885–1886 the Yiddish press on the East Side was "Yidische Folksaytung", "Yidishe Tageblat", "Yiddishe Gazetn", "Pesach Blat (part of Yidishe Gazetn), "Nuyorker Yidishe Tsaytung", (conservative), "Di Nuyorker Yidishe Folksaytung" (socialist), "Di Naye Tsayt" and "Di Farmer Tsaytung". In 1886 nine new Yiddish plays were presented on the East Side (from Marvin Leon Seiger's, "History of the Yidish Theatre in New York City to 1892).

The exhibit shows,among many documents, photos and artifacts, a call for the establishment of a Jewish workers' library, an enlargement of

R's poem on Dec 1886 calling on people not to remain aloof but to help "make an end to the gloomy night". An editorial in the N.Y.Folkstsaytung called upon the immigrants to "march onward under the banner of the socialist revolution".

III. YIDDISH SOCIAL POETRY IN AMERICA IN THE 1880's AND 1890'S

"The worker's song and the revolutionary song were a direct expression of the immigrant life of the 1880's and 1890's. It was therefore no fortuity that the social and proletarian motifs had their rise in America. Every rising poet collided daily with these exacerbated motifs. The first was misery and sympathy. The second motif was the song of conflict. The third was satire. In satire the poet unmasks the three foes of mankind: capital, the State, and the forces abetting them. The fourth is the social lyric and the fifth . . . is a highly romantic, pathetic motif, saturated with heroic tones and despair." This quote is from "Pioneers of Yiddish Poetry In America", 1956, (three vols.) by N.B. Minkoff. This section of the exhibit showed photos of the great poets Winchevsky and Edelstadt, Bovshover, David Goldstein, Isaac Ringold, Nokhem Babad, Hyman Strunsky and many other contemporaries of Rosenfeld. There were examples of their poetry, cartoons and caricatures. Oyzer Smolensky attacked not only capitalism but religious American Jewishness as being misleading, backward and reactionary. (We hear the same song today, 1n 1993, ed.). There were poems and photos and other data about Anna Rapport, Ephraim Leib Wolfson, Marmor, William Kaiser, Nathan Lamport and William Miller, among others. Joseph Joffe, writer of "Kontrastn", was the only one of the social poets whom Zisha Landau, of "Die Junge", acknowledged as a poet.

IV. ROSENFELD'S FIRST POEMS AND BOOKS

Toward the end of 1886 R. arrived again in New York where he worked in a clothing shop. His wife and two children arrived somewhat later. For a brief period he moved to Rochester, N.Y. In Dec. 1886 and Jan. 1887 the N.Y. Folkstsaytung published three of his poems. In 1888 appeared his first edition of poems followed in 1890-1897 by three more editions. In his autobiography (about 1897) R. speaks of a fifth edition entitled "Emigratsions Gedichte" (Poems of Emigration). From 1886–1890 he published 147 poems besides those that remained unknown to students because of the unidentified pen names he employed and the inaccessibility of periodicals from that period. From Nov. 1888 to June 1891 he published in the Folks-Advokat alone 75 poems, besides prose. In those years, and also somewhat later, there was hardly a Yiddish publication the world over that did not feature his poems. He rapidly gained fame with his national and social poems, becoming the favorite poet of the Jewish people. None-the-less, he could not eke out a living from his writing and, broken in health, he had to return to the shop.

"Dos 1886 Yor" (The Year 1886) was R's first published poem. M Starkman's analysis of R's early writings appears in his "Pinkes fun Amopteyl Yivo" in 1927. "Fur di Yidishe Folktsaytung" and "Dos Vign-lid" (Lullaby) were his second and third poems published in 1886–87. In 1887 R. received a letter from an editor stating that his poem is not acceptable. In 1888 R. published "Di Gloke", (The Bell), folk songs and revolutionary poems, with his friend I.A. Marison. There were 30 poems, one by Marison. Zalman Reisen, in his book "Leksikon fon der Yidisher Literatur", wrote, of Rosenfeld, "With all their tendentiousness, flaws in form, Germanisms, helpless rhymes these poems also manifest frequently a cordial mood and tone, truly poetic passages". One of those poems, "At Night On The Brooklyn Bridge", was regarded by critics as the best of his early poems.

"Di Blumenkette" (The Garland), his second collection of poems, in 1890, "a collection of divers folk songs and poetry", was published by Folksadvocat in N. Y. In the prefatory poem R. wrote, "Under trying circumstances/ this book I did write/ standing over the pressing iron/ and many a sleepless night." Reisen further states, "In this collection there is definite evidence of the later R. The advance of the poet in the course of two years is truly astonishing."

R.'s third collection of poems, "Poezyen und Lider was published in 1893. Seventeen poems of a national, religious and folk vein included "On the Sea's Bosom", "The Jewish May", and "By the Rivers of Babylon". In 1897 he published, "Lider Buch" (Book of Songs". In this volume was a picture of R. with flowing hair and a short beard, the first book of his with his photo. It was dedicated to Dr. Leo Wiener. At this time he lived in dire poverty. YIVO demonstrates letters to and from many friends and associates attesting to this condition. Leo Wiener, Abe Cahan (in his book "Bleter fon Mayn Lebn"), his friend Meyer Applebaum, all mention R's poverty. This did not stop him from writing poetry prolifically: "Rabbis and Machines:, "The Old System", etc.

V. THE POET OF THE SWEATSHOP

Infinite poems were written about the working conditions of the poor, such as, "The Voice of the Tailor's Tools", "A Tear On the Iron", "Frenkel Der Presser", and "Fayer" (Fire!) !), a poem about a tragic fire in Newark, N.J. in which 40 women lost their lives in a sweatshop blaze. The YIVO exhibit showed extensive photos, newspaper and magazine articles, books and individual poems enlarged demonstrating the ramifications of R's interests and impact on his immigrant workers. The ultimate tragedy was the Triangle Fire in which 154 women lost their lives in a clothing factory conflagration in 1911. R's poems on this fire were extensively published and did much to arouse the populace to action. There was shown R's poem "Der Svet Shop", Berthold Feivel's German translation, and music to the poem by Arieh Abrahamson, Bratislava, 1936, also a record of R's poem made by the Victor Company. Rosenfeld's poems included a wide range of laboring activities, from trolley car strikes, cigarette-factory employee problems, garment workers' tribulations and even the desperate situation of the miners in the Allegheny mountains. Many hundreds of poems and illustrations were available for viewing. Every aspect of immigrant and workers' lives was included, from scenes at the ferry slips, death of young working girls, love in the sweatshops, and "The First Wages" to polemics about "The Boss" and "What More Does He Want !". (The catalogue which we are here abbreviating makes mention of innumerable poems and articles about R.—too numerous for us to mention here. However many of the poems that are mentioned are includede in our section on Poetry. ed.) A sheet of Jacob Shaffer's music for R's poem, "I Am Driven Early To Work" is shown as well a William Gropper painting, "The Sweatshop".

VI. THE POET OF THE EAST SIDE

"There was a time when there were two musts, two marvels for visitors to New York: Chinatown and the Jewish section. outlandish excrescences. Today everyone knows that the Jewish section is a marvel of an entirely different kind. It is a marvel not of outlandishness but of a special kind of cultural flowering. It is a marvel of an unusual spiritual flowering in a soil of poverty . . . One of the first to attract the attention of the outside world to this marvel of our little world was Morris Rosenfeld". (Editorial in the "Forverts", March 8, 1913).

This section of the Rosenfeld exhibit shows numerous photos and other artifacts of the Lower East Side of New York, enlarged copies of R's poems about the area and the times, such as "Hester Street", "Jewish Bundles", "Organ grinders," "The Man with The Pushcart", "The Ghetto Tree" and "Castle Garden". This poem was sung to one of Goldfaden's many lovely melodies. (The constraints of space prevent us from including all the interesting quotations, articles, photos, paintings and poems by R. that the YIVO catalogue mentions. ed.)

VII. SONGS OF CLASS STRUGGLE AND REVOLUTION

"May his pen be both lyre and sword !" (M. Rosenfeld). Evidence is shown of Rosenfeld's activities in the revolutionary organizations: a receipt for a contribution of sixpence for the publication of the biographies of the 8 Chicago anarchists, also a receipt for a contribution to the anarchist group "Knights of Freedom", in which R. was active. He contributed

10 cents and a four-line poem; his wife 5 cents and their daughter, Dora, 5 cents. P. Lavrov, in "Lopatin's Biography", London 1888, contains R's poem "The Song Of Socialism", which is R's socialist credo, later reprinted in "Die Glocke". Also included are two of R.'s poems, "The Fighter's Grave" and "A Victory Song", as well as the "minutes of the First Convention of the Jewish Socialist Press Unions in America". (1897). A collection of socialist poems by R. including, "The Socialist Ticket", The "Worker", "Song of the Union Book", "The Beginning of the End" and a host of others.

Many symbolic revolutionary drawings are shown with Rosenfeld poems. R's poem, "The Revolution", on the French Revolution of 1789 was shown with an illustration of The Bastille. Also shown were title pages of many Yiddish publications with symbolic revolutionary cartoons. R. was a contributor to these publications. Shown here were R.'s poems "Shoot The Beast", "Lawrence's Children", and "The Miners' Joan of Arc" and his poems about the end of the Czar Alexander !!! and the revolutionary movement in Russia. There are R.'s poems on the striking tailors of Chicago, "Heroes of the Scissors". (1910), "The Tailors' Strike: a Battle Song), "To The Workers", "Desperate Cries", "On Strike!", "The Saved", and many others.

VIII. NATIONAL AND RELIGIOUS FOLK-MOTIFS IN ROSENFELD'S WORKS

"And those who claim that the social and revolutionary poems of the first Yiddish poets in America are not Jewish national, or that they are an outright foreign graft, are in error. Beneath all their wall-storming calls— Out of The Ghetto !—that exhuberantly and noisily went out to the four ends of the earth one feels the warmth of "let us not be ashamed of our own blood!" (B.Bialostotsky, 'Kholem un Vor', New York, 1956. "Rosenfeld is perhaps the most unique of Yiddish poets. The other Yiddish poets guided their Muse in one given direction. Rosenfeld's Muse has no single definite tendency. It is both conservative and revolutionary, religious and iconoclastic, international and national, all at once! (Alexander Harkavy, in his introduction to R.'s "Gezamelte Lider", 1904) The YIVO exhibit shows R's conflict with the leaders of the Jewish labor movement over his nationalist sentiments: an attack on R. in the "Arbayter Fraynd"for publishing a national poem on "Shulamith". "Among the Yiddish poets we have already our own reactionary . . . Rosenfeld. The ardent revolutionary has turned a mourner for Zion." (1889) In 1900 R. was a delegate to the 4th Zionist Congress, in London. In London he tried to secure funds to publish his poems in English. Available to view are tickets for various soirees in London and in Leeds, application to be a delegate to the next Zionist Congress (1903). A letter is shown where R. writes to K. Marmor describing his attitude toward proletarian and national problems.

On view were R's poems and satires on proletarian and national problems. In "Yid un Arbeiter" (Jew and Workman) he states, "I have searched in every book/ and found no contradiction/ between worker and Jew"; in "Dream and Reality" he wrote,"Time there was I mocked at the word Nation, I saw only one Mankind"; in "Comrade Greb" he wrote a satire on anti-Zionists. R's poem, "Golus March" (exile march), also known as "The Wanderer" is exhibited; a popular postcard of this poem is shown, with R's picture and music to the poem by M.D. Gotlieb, also with music by Herts Gershovits and, again the poem with music by Mark Silver. R's poem, "The Jewish May" is shown with a disc of music by Leon Blank, Columbia Records, also a copy of music to this poem by Arthur Wolf. There is a London edition of Prof. A. Garfinkel's music to the poem "By The Rivers of Babylon", as well as manuscripts for many of R's other poems .

There is a popular postcard with R's poetic text and music for "To A Bird" and "I Am A Jew" by the publishing house Kunst, in Warsaw, dated 1914. Seen is a copy of "Yehuda Halevi, greatest Jewish Poet", by Rosenfeld, 1907. On pp 61–64 is the translation of "Zion Wilt Thou Not Ask"; beside, a symbolic revolutionary drawing by Leon Barrett, showing Marx, Lassalle, Heine, Boerne, and Yehuda Halevi among the pillars in the fight against the "reactionary powers". Some of R's Zionist poems are shown against a background of Arthur Wolf's music. "A Prediction", composed on the occasion of the 10th Anniversary of the State of Israel. Also included writings such as "Where Shall I Go In Search of Peace and Happiness", "Theodore Herzl", "Summer And Exile", "From The Sacred Soil", "Far Eretz Yisroyl","A Song Of The Poale Zion" and "Jews Against A Nation".

R's poem "Chanukah Lights", a N.Y. postcard with the text of the poem, four musical versions to the poem: by L.Liow; by Henry Lefkowitz, as sung by Cantor Shlisky; by Samuel Lewin; by Zavel Zilberts; and much more of R's poetrry set to music, including Lefkowitz' music to "Awake!". (Postcards were very popular in those days, with poems, music, political messages. Many are shown at the exhibition. ed.) New Year's cards are shown with R's poems "Erev Yom Kippur" and "The Mocker Of Life Has Torn" as well as a New Years card from Tel Aviv with R's poem, "Comfort Ye, Comfort Ye My People". (Many more of R's poems were on exhibition but we cannot mention them all here. ed.)

IX. ROSENFELD'S NATURE AND LOVE POETRY

"In his love poems he employs the run-of-the-mill elements of the love poetry of his time, that is the general epithet which, in the taste of those years, was the "exalted word" and the expression of the "beautiful sentiment". He could not break with the instant and the near, that is, the cliches of his period. "(N.B.Minkoff, "Yidishe Klasiker Poetn", N.Y. 1937). "Late in life he began to write love poems which he had not dared to do in his younger years. A perusal of his better nature-poems shows their imagery is of Jewish origin. In "The Stream" one hears a Jewish wanderer reciting psalms on his journey, in "The Spring" a Jew meditating in solitude. "His Jewish experience leads him into the heart of nature". (B. Rivkin, Grunt Printsipn fun Der Yidisher Literatut in America", N.Y. 1948).

(Many, many poems by R. included, "The Arbutus", "Nature Poems", "The Bleeding Nightingale", "What Nature Comprises", "On The Eve of Spring", "September Motifs", "Autumn Reflections" (with two postcards illustrated by Lilien on the latter two poems), music to R's poem, "At Night In The Forest", by B.Trotwood Eberhardt, 1916; an allegorical drawing of "Poor People", in which summer refuses her flowers to the poor. There is an allegorical drawing of the struggle beteen love and "capital" and a revolutionary postcard with a drawing depicting the woman's suffering because of "conventional matrimony" and the role of the clergy. There is a newsclipping of part of R's "rhythmic translation" of the Song of Songs.

X. ROSENFELD THE SATIRIST

"It is easily conceivable, how in such a socialistically heated atmosphere, in which the workers were embittered, Rosenfeld lapsed into a satirical tone . . . and became one of the most bitter, mordant Jewish satirists . . . .beginning with individuals he gradually went on to criticise manners, mores and movements." (Joel Entin, Morgn Zhurnal, Dec. 19, 1943). "Because I sing constantly songs of grief, You think I know not how to laugh? / Make no mistake, Jews / I can also deride". R's poem on his writing satires is shown, "Tsvingt Mikh nit! Fray nokh Hayne's 'Wartet Nur' " (Do not constrain me! Free, after Heine's 'Wartet Nur'). In 1894 R, together with Sharkansky, published a journal, Der Ashmeday. No copies are extant. The motto of the journal was "Smite the Capitalists that their posts may shake!" with a humorous English translation, "Sock the mug, that the masticators make music !" The last issue of the journal appeared under the title "The Haman Noisemaker", (Der Homon Klaper). R's letter to a Moses Freeman describes Ashmeday, "He lacerates and cuts left, right and on all sides !"(This was my grandfather? EJG) He wrote a satire with the pen name, A German Of Kalwaria. R's satire, "Synagogues! Dedicated to the Comrades of the Philadelphia Lyseum" had an anti-clerical motif, "What capitalism leaves us/you synagogues take by fraud/ go, we do not need you/the bliss in the hereafter/ we leave to you rabbis", signed, Vesuvius.

R also prepared a book called "Kaas un Shmychel" (Ire and Smile),

"Satire, Humor, Sarcasm, Wit and Epigrams". (R. wrote many satires, of which only a few are mentioned here). "Der Reverend" (who was a European furrier who became a Reverend"; "The Pedler", who was a Rabbi and became a pedlar; "The Immigrant" who came to New York with a suitcase full of ideals and became a boss and a tenement owner; "Yom Kippur and High Prices"; "A Chap of Parts", etc. He even wrote satires of which he himself was the butt of his humor: "A Story About A Little Store", "A Merry Tale For Merry Readers", etc.

XI. POEMS ON JEWISH AND GENERAL EVENT

R. wrote poetry for almost every event, religious, national and local; Jewish or general. Just the titles should indicate by themselves the range of his interests. "To the Representatives of the Congregation of Israel", "A Good Heart", "Pity O Israel", "A Cry Of Anguish" (about the status of Jews in Europe during and after WW I), "Thanksgiving Day" (he scores the American capitalist system for the poverty and oppression that makes Thanksgiving Day a mockery), "The Golden Land", "The World Worships This God (The Dollar)." He expressed his indignation over the deportation of Jewish immigrants in "On The Bosom Of The Sea", "On The Death of McKinley", "George Washington", "The Fourth Of July", "To Our Heroes, on the Reception to the Returning 77th Division", and several poems about the terrible times Jews were having with the Czar and Russia. Included in his appraisal of the Russian brutality towards Jews were poems such as "The Yiddishe Soldat", "The Meeting Between The Czar and The Kaiser", "The Fall Of Babylon" expressing the hope that democracies will vanquish the Kaiser and also free Russia. "Bolshevism" is his poem attacking bolshevism, and there are "A Soldier, Dedicated to My New Home, America", and "To The Victims of the Pogroms".

XII. ROSENFELD AS READER OF HIS POETRY AND PUBLIC SPEAKER

"Rosenfeld's poems had reached the public by way of the platform and the literary soirees . . . long before he began to appear frequently in the press. He met his audience face to face reciting or even singing his poems from the literary-musical platform, which came into being simultaneously with the Jewish Socialist Press. For a while he even toyed with the idea of becoming a traveling poet-minstrel-declaimer, the calling that would rescue him from the tailor shop . . . Rosenfeld's poems were written deliberately to be recited publicly." (B. Rivkin) "Rosenfeld is the best Yiddish declaimer. He places the content of his reading in the minds and hearts of his audience." (J. Leibner,Yidishe Record, 1913). In a report on R's concert The Chicago Tribune wrote that the eyes of the people in the

hall "were full of tears, meeting face to face the poet who took their grind-
ing cares and wove them into beautiful poems" (Yidisher Record, 1914.

Folks Lide (Folk Songs) "by the famous Yiddish Folk singer and Poet
Morris Rosenfeld", price 1 cent (!) Grand Street, New York, 1891, contains three jokes and four advertisements. R. wrote, "I am launching a
whole series of folk songs and bright thoughts, calculated to please the
reader." He used to peddle his songs at cafes and meetings and in concert
halls where poetry was read. He appeared at soirees in many cities, including N.Y.,Chicago, Boston, Worcester,Mass., Radcliff College, Catskill
Mountain Resorts, Philadelphia, Montreal, and, of course, in many European cities. People such as Mrs. Cyrus Sulzberger and other wealthy devotees of culture invited him and helped support those soirees.

XIII. ROSENFELD THE DRAMATIST

From declaiming his poetry to the Yiddish theatre the distance was
not great. One source has it that in 1889 R. played the role of a Rabbi in
Shomer's play, "Rifke, or a Spark Of Jewishness". In 1890 R. wrote theatre reviews in the "Folks-Advokat". He also wrote several plays and one-
act dramas. His historical drama, "The Last High Priest" was played in
New York in the Windsor theatre, but with little success. He also participated in the "Grosses Sakred Kontsert" in May of 1891. He also wrote
musical plays, one of which (never published) had eleven songs of his own.
A play, "Life In New York" was performed for his benefit in March 1891.
R. wrote a satirical poem, "Kuni Leml un der Yidisher King Lear" in
1897. "This satirical poem is of value to culture history and can serve as a
piquant illustration of the fight among the New York dramatists at that
time and of the role of Morris Rosenfeld in that contest." (Dr. J. Shatsky,
in Archive far di Geschichte fun Yidishe Teater un Drame", 1930. YIVO
has copies of R.s one-act plays written in 1891 and 1908. Rosenfeld's
poetry was included in many popular collections of songs.

XIV. THE MUSIC TO ROSENFELD'S WORKS

"In those days a poem was only a poem if it was sung" (Leon Kobrin,
"TOG", 1923. "Quite frequently one hears a Jewish woman singing Rosenfeld's poems while doing her chores", (Hans Pospisel, Der Yidishe
Kunst-Fraynd, Chicago, 1916). Rosenfeld's poems were set to music by
the great Goldfaden, Jacob Rumshinsky, Prof. Artur Wolf, A. Abrahamson, (Bratislava) I. Shafer. His poem, "A Langer Oygen-blick" was set to
music by the Catholic organist in Chicago, August Halter. Music was also
written by N.L.Miller, Jacob Dymont, (Berlin), Henry Lefkowitz, Jassi-
nowsky, M. Kipnis, Jacob Davidson, Meyer Posner, Paul Held, M. Rauch,
Max Helfman, Joseph Shrogin and Elijah Zaludkowsky, among others.

XV. ROSENFELD'S JOURNALISTIC ACTIVITY

"In the first years of his poetic activity it never occurred to Rosenfeld to switch to prose. He lacked confidence in himself. He finally took this step as a result of his struggle for a livelihood. Realizing that journalistic prose is better paid than poetry he began writing prose." (Alexander Harkavy, Forverts, 1923) R. as an editor : in 1892 he edited several issues of the periodical "Di Zun" and in 1894, with A.M. Sharkansky, the "Ashmeday", "Der Pinkes", "A quarterly for Literature, History, and Contemporary Problems". These were listed in "Editors of Socialist and Radical Newspapers and magazines in America." (YIVO displayed hundreds of R.'s prose writings with many poems interspersed among them). Several of his poems were dedicated to the Jewish workmen's press. Included is a satirical poem, "The fight between the Abend Blat and the Forverts.", "a splendid poem, a biting satire, a criticism of the New York Comrades Socialists . . . by 'Klaynmichel Yokton' (another of his pseudonyms). In "The Eagle" he compares his journalistic activity to the eagle aloft, "who descends only when forced by hunger" ; "The Patcher" is a mordant satire, published in Ashmeday", on his detractors who claimed he was a tailor and no poet.

An unpublished volume was created by R. of satires on "yellow publications, trashy editors and trashy editorial staffs" Only a few of those articles were published, but they are still in existence at the YIVO. R. chose as his motto for those satires a Biblical passage, "There is no peace, saith my God, concerning the wicked". One satire was directed against his own poems, "Bad Rhymes". He wrote about the scrambling amongst the various journals for a "piece of the action" and even about Karl Marx who happened to come into a celebration in honor of Abe Cahan. There are many letters to and from R., and many more about him, on the circumstances of his leaving the staff of the Forverts after so many years. After he left the Forverts he joined the staff of the Tageblat. On March 4, 1921, he received a curt note from the Tageblat (for whom he had written, on and off for many years) informing him that his writings were no longer wanted for they are "inadequate in quality as well as quantity."

XVI. ROSENFELD IN OTHER LANGUAGES

a. English translations

"Rosenfeld was the first Yiddish poet to introduce Yiddish poetry into world literature, to reveal to the world at large the social and national suffering of the Jewish person and there, too, he aided indirectly in spreading the name of the Yiddish language and its literature" (Zalman Reisen, Lexicon of Yiddish Literature, Vilna). "Songs From The Ghetto", was the first collection of R.'s poetry translated into English. Prof. Leo Wiener of Harvard. Wiener truly introduced Rosenfeld to the non-Yiddish speaking world by this little work, published in 1898. A second edition of this book was a huge success. The publisher wrote to R. "the first edition of your book is completely exhausted". This was followed by "Songs From The Ghetto", "Songs of Labor and Other Poems", translated into English by Rose Pastor Stokes and Helena Frank, in 1914. "Songs of Russia" was translated by Alice Stone Blackwell in 1902. Aaron Kramer published a fine little volume, "The Teardrop Millionaire", with excellent English translations in 1957.

Shortly after the publication of Wiener's translation of R's poems a number of articles appeared in the non-Jewish press, some of them of a sensational character. R deprecated the sensationalism that the press created. S. Niger, in "Tog", in July 1933, wrote, "several critics are of the opinion that R. was corrupted by sudden fame . . . he wanted to impress, to strike a pose before the world—but his strength departed from him". The YIVO shows eighteen newsclippings from the non-Jewish press extolling R: the Boston Transcript, The Chicago Herald, The London Daily Express, The Chicago Dial, The Modern View, The New York Times, The Saturday Review, The Survey and the Chicago Reform Advocate.

ROSENFELD IN OTHER LANGUAGES
b. Original English Writings

"Morris Rosenfeld resolved to become an English poet after Leo Wiener had begun translating his poems into English. In an English letter to Wiener dated March 4, 1898, Rosenfeld adds a Yiddish postscript: "Do not laugh at my English. Next year I shall write English poems." (E. Lifschutz, "Morris Rosenfeld's English Poems".) "The contemptuous attitude of the younger Yiddish poets towards Rosenfeld, who was proud and confident of his talent, spurred him on to write in English and to seek recognition as an English poet." (Zalman Reisen) All efforts to find a publisher for his poems originally written in English proved unsuccessful. "I Know Not Why", shown at the exhibit, was R's well-known English poem written in 1898, music by Helena Bingham. First published in the "Commercial Advertiser" and frequently reprinted, among others, in Stedman's "An American Anthology" 1797–1900. YIVO has three copies of a collection of typewritten poems written in English called, "Songs of a Pilgrim", which have never been published as a collection. They were prepared at various times and comprise 139, 226 and 220 pages respectively. A letter exists of Elias Tobenkin to B. Zevin with reference to a report of a reader of the F.A.Stokes publishing house on R's "Songs of a Pilgrim." (A copy of that letter is included in this volume under English Poems" (ed.) These documents were laudatory but because of the war the book did not appear. R. tried manfully to get his book published as did his widow after he died: all without success. Israel Zangwill, who had been sent the unpublished document claimed he had returned the document; his letter to that effect exists. "Tailor's Tales", a volume of stories in English, was published in 1913, from Austerlitz, N.Y.

XVI. ROSENFELD IN OTHER LANGUAGES
a-languages-European
Professor Wiener's English translations of R's poems brought the poet fame in Europe too. Beginning in 1998 he was frequently mentioned in the European press.. Collections of his poems appeared in German, Rumanian, Czech, Croatian, Hungarian and Polish. Some of his poems also appeared in French and Russian periodicals.

b-German translations "Lieder Des Ghetto", Berlin, 1902. Thirty nine poems translated by Berthold Feivel, illustrated by Ephraim Lilien. Greatly instrumental in the success of R's poems was E.M. Lilien, at that time the most popular Jewish illustrator. Lilien illustrated several of R.'s poems, postcards with R's poetry and even newspaper articles with R's works. Numerous pictures of R. at the time testify to his popularity. One of the most effective portraits was done by Herman Struck. "Gedichte fon Rosenfeld", Prague, 1909 was a translation into German by the poet Friedrich Thieberger, with an introduction by Friedrich Adler, the editor of "Bohemia".

c-Rumanian, Czech, Croation and Hungarian Translations
"Cintece Din Ghetto," Iasi, 1904, a collection of R's poems trans-lated into Rumanian by M. Rusu, with Liliens' illustrations and a picture of the poet. "Zpevy Z Ghetta," Prague, 1905, a Czech transl. by the poet Jaroslav Vrchlicky, who also wrote a poem "Morris Rosenfeld" published in the Chicago Yidisher Record,1913. "Pjesme iz Geta," Zagreb, 1906, transl. into Croat by Aleksander Licht. "Koltemenyei", Budapest 1908, collection of R's poems into Hungarian by Dr. Arnold Kiss.

d-Rosenfeld's poems in Polish and Russian
"Piesni Pracy", Warsaw, 1906, transl. into Polish by Alfred Tom and S. Hirschhorn, copy now at Harvard University (wiener Collection). "Piesni z Ghetta", Warsaw, 1908, further translations into Polishby Tom and Hirschhorn. In Russian R's poems only appeared in periodicals. Jacob Rombro's article in Voskhod on "The Zhargon Literature in America"; Wiener's letter to R. in which he states that he sent R's poems to Tolstoy and that Gorky was said to have translated his poems. A letter from S.B. Komaiko to R. saying, "Here is one of your precious stones set in the Russian language."

e-Rosenfeld's Poems in French

Shortly after Wiener's translations were published (1898) R. became known in France. Alexander Harkavy's article "Rosenfeld's Poetry in French" in the Yidish-American Folks Kalendar, 1899–1900; an article by the Jewish labor leader, Elie Eberlin, in "Mercure de France", 1906; Edmond Fleg's "Anthologie Juive", Paris, with R's poem, all these were on display at the YIVO exhibition.

XVII. ROSENFELD'S ATTITUDE TO ENGLISH, HEBREW, YIDDISH

"In the 1880's Jewish labor-and-folk-life came into being in America. The Old World poor man was virtually reduced to a slave in the sweatshops of those years. The Yiddish language was facing a crucial test: how will it ring out in the roll of peoples and tongues? How will it be able to take on the new mode of life? And again Yiddish withstood the test" (B.Bialostotsky, "Kholem Vor", N.Y., 1856. "Before him Yiddish was afraid to lift its voice in the realm of literature. In life it was wild, powerful, virile. In the hands of writers it became women's orison language . . . Rosenfeld was the first to point out that there are thundering tones in the Yiddish language (S.Niger, "Tog", 1923. "He began writing at a time when the Yiddish language had no cultural physiognomy as yet, when the writers in America were still uncertain whether it is permissible to write pure Yiddish" (Forverts, 1923).

"Rosenfeld was an impulsively inconsistent man, and this was noticeable in his attitude to the Yiddish language. His mood was a good barometer: when his literary fortunes rose, Yiddish fell in his esteem. Conversely, when his literary fortunes fell, Yiddish rose in his esteem." (Lifschutz, "Rosenfeld's letters", Buenos Aires, 1955." In a letter to Prof. Wiener in 1897 R. predicted that "the Zhargon has no future in this country anyway; within 25 years even the best works written ion this language will remain mere literary curiosities." In his letter to the journalist and biographer, L. Trommer, R. said, "Always write to me in Yiddish. I am not Jacob Schiff. To me Yiddish is a language like all other languages. I am also of the belief that one can write and speak Yiddish and still be a good and loyal American."

R. wrote many poems about Yiddish, such as : "Eedish",: (written especially for the reception in honor of Sholem Asch); "Yidish un Zhargon", "Tsu Unser Mame-loshn", "Language, on the Yiddish Language Hysteria", "The Folk Language", "Unable To Rise", "A Bad Ending" "Hebrew and Yiddish: Polemic", "Yiddish and Hebrew: The Hysteria of Language Idolators", "Immortalized" (in which he expresses his joy that 'in the language of Scripture I saw a splendid translation'). He even carried on a polemic with his friend Reuben Brainin because of the latter's negative attitude toward Yiddish.

XVIII. ROSENFELD AND ENGLISH-SPEAKING JEWRY

English-speaking Jews attempted to help Rosenfeld by opening for him a cigar and candy store, which quickly closed. Later on R. wrote a humorous poem deriding his own inability to maintain a practical relationship with the busines world, saying that "You will not remain a tradesman . . . you will suffer and you will write." English-speaking Jews arranged soirees for him, to offer him extended aid. Prof. Seligman (brother of a banker) and Rabbi Wise helped in a movement to sustain the poet. R. had a low opinion of the famed banker, Jacob Schiff, who had a low opinion of Eastern European Jews and their Yiddish language, and made an address to that effect, which was written up in the New York press.

XIX. COLLECTED WORKS OF ROSENFELD

"Gezamelte Lider Fun Morris Rosenfeld," (Collected Works of M.R.) New York,1904; Preface by Harkavy, illustr. by Lilien, 122 poems, songs of freedom, of workers, lyrical and satirical poems, etc."Geklibene Lider fun M.R.", (Selected works of M.R.) Warsaw, 1905, "Schriften fun M.R.", 1908, (Works of M.R.) New York, R. and Harkavy prefaces, 3 volumes "Schriften fun M.R.", New York, 1910, several printings, Later there was an edition of 9 volumes (Kalman Marmor) "Shriften", Star Publ."Gevaylte Schriften fun M.R.", 1912, 3 vols., the second two contain prose."Dos Buch fun Libe", (the Book of Love), 1914, two parts in one volume, this collection has 129 poems and a translation into Yiddish of the Song of Songs, dedicated to his three daughters "Grine Tsores un Andere Shriften", ('Green' tribulations and other works), a humorous, satirical book in 3 parts; There was also an edition of poetry for children, 1924. In addition there is a manuscript of a book (never published) called "Book of two wars: The war in Europe and the war between Capital and Labor". It was originally called "Blood and Fire". It was to include mainly published poems.

R. also planned to issue a book as a collection of his prose writings from various publications, called "From the Mute World. Half-philosophical Discourses and Arguments". R. also planned two volumes, the material already bound, called "The Poetic Treasury of Morris Rosenfeld" and "World and Life". There is also an unpublished book R. wrote about himself, including critical opinions on his works, reports of his European tour in 1908, introductions written by himself in the third person. Kalman Marmor also left a manuscript of a work on Rosenfeld. There is a fine book of Rosenfeld's letters, "Morris Rosenfeld's Briv" by E. Lifschutz, Buenos Aires, 1955.

XX. ROSENFELD'S POEMS IN SONGSTERS, TEXTBOOKS AND ANTHOLOGIES

Workmen's reciters were published (before 1923) by "Freedom Revolutionary Poems", 1901, also in 1905, published by the Jewish Labor

Bund; There are two editions, one written on cigarette paper, designed to be easily smuggled into Russis. (!!) Two anthologies of his poems by Di Velt, Vilna, 1906. "Arbyter Lider", publ. by "Progress". Warsaw,1906, "Di Fraye Harfe", compiled by Glatshtein, Warsaw, 1918, who also published "Frayheits Lider" by R. in 1919. Workmen's reciters were published after 1923 also: "Arbeter Deklamator", Warsaw 1935, a Communist publication (This publisher, Lemaan Hasefer, was refused permission by Dr. Leon Goldenthal, the custodian of Rosenfeld's effects, to use Rosenfeld's writings in any way. Apparently it did not stop them. ed.); "Lider Buch. Gezamelte Repertoir fun Freyheit Gezangs Fareyn", Chicago, 1923; "Zamlung fun Yidishe Arbeter un Folks Lide", N.Y., 1937; "Song Book, songs of Revolution", Publ. by IWW, (who were asked not to publish Rosenfeld's works by Dr. Leon Goldenthal, ed.); "Oyservelte Arbayter un Folks Lider", publ. by N.Y. Socialist party; "Courage. A Collection of Poems", Yiddish Communist Library, Moscow, 1920. (This publication was done without the permission of Rosenfeld. ed.) Other reciters with R.'s poems: "Shire Tsion. Yiddish-Polish-Hebraish, German Songbook"-,Drohobycz, 1906; "Di Yidishe Muze" Jacob Fichman, Warsaw, 1911; "Kitve MiBaShan", Menahem Bronstein, 1913, Hebrew Translations of several of R's poems;"Tsions Harfe", nationalist poems, Warsaw, 1917; "Lider fun Folk", L. Yofe, Odessa. R.'s poems were also in anthologies of Yiddish literature: "Dos Yidishe Vort", Olgin, Vilna, 1912; "Ameriacan Yiddish Poetry", Bassin, N.Y., 11940; "Hebraische Melodien", Dr. Julius Mones, Berlin, 1907. Reciters for children and textbooks with R's poems were: "ZamlBuch fun Kinderlider", Gomel, Russia, 1921; "Arbayts-Kinder", Ukrainian Ed., 1922; "Lider", Kulter Liga, Warsaw, 1924; "Kinder Deklamator far Shul un Haym", Halevi, N.Y. 1929; Morris Rosenfeld", Workmens Circle, 1941; "Gezang fun Kampf", Warsaw 1951.

XXI. ROSENFELD'S PLACE IN CONTEMPORARY YIDDISH HISTORY

"The new turn in Jewish life gave rise to a new conception, which Rosenfeld utilized. However, no new form was created for this material. He relied on casualness of mood. Rosenfeld's dynamism was unbridled, uncontrolled, hence it became exhausted in his last years. In those poems in which his impetus has not inundated the content Rosenfeld is revealed as a rare classical manifestation in Yiddish poetry. His innovation in Yiddish poetry consisted of a dynamic soar that occasionally lifted his song to pathos and ecstasy, a sudden sublimated poetic transition from one mood to another and a substantive multitonal lyricism. Neither the sweat-shop nor the cultural level of immigrant nor his impetuous soar provided for Rosenfeld an opportunity for the cultivation of his artistic consciousness." (N.B. Minkoff, "Classical Yiddish Poets", N.Y., 1959) Poems expressing R's literary credo: "To Myself", in Di Gloke, 1888, "I would have like to sing also beautiful songs/ had it not been for your royal voice that I heard/ . . . Of what shall I write them and speak?"; "The Teardrop Millionaire", It is not a golden tuning fork/ that sets my singing voice"; "'On the Poets", "Poets, enough of fantasy/ Cease floating in the clouds/ Break off the gentle tunes/ Sing cannon songs/ speak songs !"

"Di Muze" (The Muse), "Take back your harp, O Muse/ Little did I use it/ Only my tears at times/ moistened it." From "To My Verse", "I am not to blame for my song/ I am doubly oppressed: a slave and a Jew !" From "Der Kuku", "Sing, for the winter will pass/ and gentle May will come"; From "Mayn Harf" (My Harp), "I have found my harp in the gloomy shop/among the machines, splattered with the blood of slaves." From "Why I am I, As a Workman's Poet", "Arise, O Muse, sing my rank, my dignity amond Jews and among slaves." From "My Themes", "I am a Jewish poet/ Love has given me a bill of divorce"; From "To a Bird", On tears I was nursed/ brought up on sighs/ A Jew am I, a Jew."; From "Die Arbayter" (The Workmen), I have made the graves speak/ have torn the heavens wide open." and from his satire, "To My Critics", and in "Bad Rhymes" he criticises himself.

ROSENFELD'S BATTLE WITH "THE YOUNG"

"Morris Rosenfeld accepted the realities of this country and wished to be absorbed in them. To all appearances the match was suitable, and great results were anticipated. But they failed to come. Instead came strife, ridicule, derision, confusion. It was not an encounter of light with light but hate with hate and mockery with mockery. The mean wormy reality beat the poet over the head, cast him down the stairs and he returned blow for blow. I see him as the tragic symbol of a twenty-five year immigration period; its true expression. All its characteristics, all its drollness and disorder, its view of commonality, the press, its attitude to Yiddish this epoch poured into him" (Excerpts of H. Leivick's article in "Die Freiheit, May 1924)) (All poems mentioned in this connection will be in English translation. ed.) R.'s satitical poems about the "Young":"The young. Scribblers of the Latest Vintage";"As Long as The Lines Are Short"; "The Yiddish Language on The Young"; "The Arguments of a Young One"; "A Scribbler of the New School Declares Why He Scribbles" and many more of the same temper and tone are included in the exhibition.

XXII. ROSENFELD'S CONTACT WITH READERS

(There are many letters, and correspondence to various journals and newspapers about Rosenfeld, mostly from admiring readers. In 1915, L. Gorelik wrote a story, "A New Talent" in the "Yidisher Record"in which the heroine, Sonia, reads a poem by R. to her father. There are also many pictures and notices about R's performances in this part of the exhibit, ed.)

XXIII. THE POET'S INCIPIENT BLINDNESS

In the beginning of 1906 Rosenfeld took ill and was confined to bed for several months. He was in danger of paralysis. No sooner than he had slightly recovered from his illness than he was threatened anew in 1907 by incipient blindness. During these prolonged periods of illness Rosenfeld's readers both here and in Europe came to the aid of their beloved poet and collected funds for him. In some literary quarters Rosenfeld was criticised for inspiring or even permitting such collections. Of interest is the appeal issued by the interparty workmen's committee to aid Rosenfeld, in Paris. It reads, "The finest poet of Jewish Labor, Morris Rosenfeld, is sick, suffering from paralysis in New York. Brother workers, to you Morris Rosenfeld has dedicated his gifts and his strength! In your life and suffering, your despair and hopes his great spirit found the material for his remarkable songs of affliction and want. In the sweat of his own toil he, the worker-poet, dipped his pen and created the powerful pictures, the frightful description of an enslaved existence. In your mind he sowed awareness, in your hearts he roused freedom. Out of your midst he came and to you he belongs! Brother workers, you are in duty bound to come to the aid of the stricken poet . . . Morris Rosenfeld belongs to all of the Jewish working masses and all must help him!" (Many letters went to and from the ill poet, which would overburden this volume even to list them. There were soirees and dances, lectures and collections to aid the ill poet. Leivick wrote a play, "The Blind Poet" in his honor. It was even performed in Yiddish in Buenos Aires, as recently as 1936. ed.)

Rumors of his death swept Europe in 1907. When R recovered he wrote a humorous satire on the whole situation, and wrote a "declaration" in the Forverts. Joseph Bank, publisher of the "Shtot Bok", wrote, in 1961, "R and I were close friends in the last five years of his life. Had we been that close earlier on, charges and mock poems would probably not have appeared in that publication". In "Jewish Needs", a humorous account of charities distributed by a philanthropist include one ruble for R., "as he was about to die", one ruble "when he was resurrected" and another ruble "for spectacles". "Baytch", 1908.

XXIV. THE TRIUMPHAL TOUR OF EUROPE IN 1908

In 1908 R. visited Europe, where he gave readings in Germany, Austria-Hungary and Rumania. Everywhere he was received with great acclaim. Typical of such a reaction: "Tomorrow we shall see him and hear him. Many Jewish hearts will rejoice. Six years ago a Rosenfeld soiree was arranged in Vienna by the Vienna Association for the Preservation of Jewish Antiquities. Vienna Jewish society gathered in the large Ronacker Hall. The greatest actor, Adolph Sonnenthal appeared on the platform and declaimed Morris Rosenfeld's poems. The first seat was occupied by Baron Rothschild, who applauded heartily. The millionaire in money congratulated the "millionaire in tears". Those who arranged the evening were greatly surprised. They wanted to "preserve Jewish antiquities" and actually came to sense the present, perceived the future . . . This unforgettable spectacle shows us most effectively the place and significance of Rosenfeld" (Togblat, Lvov, Sept. 13, 1908) Among the artifacts from this tour were a collection of calling cards, a bandarole from a large floral bouquet,- reports of soirees in R.'s honor in Galicia, in Cracow, in Lvov, interviews in all of Eastern Europe, a soiree in Prague, a silver laurel wreath with a reproduction of Herman Struck's portrait of R. in the center, with the inscription, "The Jewish People's Association to The Jewish Poet." (This framed wreath has always been in our home, which wouldn't be home without it. ed.). There are "banderoles" from wreaths presented in Pilsen, Drohobycz, Galicia, and newsclippings from all over Europe extolling the poet.

During his visit to Vienna, R. dedicated a verse to the well-known cantor, Don Fuchs, "To the celebrated cantor, Don Fuchs, I have listened to your sweet prayers, your chanting of devout hymns, and for the first time I understood the magic force imbedded in the prayer book. I am a man of little faith, no longer familiar with the prayers, but you won me back. I believed and I prayed." Not impractically, R. wrote to Samuel Lifschutz, who was arranging a soiree in Berlin, "Those who are interested must be my friends, but not people who through me derive benefits for their organizations, no matter how sacred." There are articles in the American Jewish press, especially the Forverts, occasionally satirizing R.'s tour and his huge success; but the satire was truly not mean.

XXV. ROSENFELD'S FAMILY

Morris Rosenfeld was the son of Ephraim Leyb Rosenfeld and Rachel Chmelevsky. His father died in New York on Jan. 14, 1916, reputedly at the age of 106. In an epidemic that raged in Europe six of R.'s siblings died and for a considerable period he was an only child. Later on his brother Joseph (Zundel Peretz) was born. In 1880 R. married a relative but divorced her six months later. In 1882 he married Rifke Asne Beyle (Bessie) the daughter of a Suwalki merchant, Avom-Itche Yavorovsky. (In America the Yavorovsky family changed its name to Guttenberg). The Rosenfelds had seven children. Three of them, Sarah, Abe and Lilly, died in their infancy and his son Joseph (Mayn Ingele) died at the age of 15 on Apr. 24, 1905. Three daughters survived: Doba (Dora), Fraydl(Frieda Iona) and Reyzl (Rose).(The author's mother, ed.)

This portion of the Rosenfeld exhibit contains letters and photos of the family, copies of R's poem of "Mayn Ingele" and obituary notices of Joseph. Apparently Joseph was talented at poetry and three of his poems, translated into Yiddish by his father, are available.

XXVI. ROSENFELD IN PICTURES AND CARICATURE

This portion of the exhibit had a multitude of photos and drawings of R. at every age and circumstance. There was a photo of R. in a calendar in Berlin, postcards with his photo, some of the photos were with other notable writers, such as Reisen, Frug, Asch, Pinski. Articles in the non-Jewish press appeared (with photos or drawings, frequently) in Berlin, Warsaw, New York, Manchester, Montreal, London, and there were many caricatures of R., not all of them generous or pleasant. Some claimed he thought he was like Shakespeare, or Heine, Milton and other greats. In a satire on a group of poets, R. was included as "the much-crowned poet". In London he was drawn as a "great Cantor" officiating at the silver wedding of trade unionism. And there is "Old Things donated by our notables . . . to the immigrants of London", where R. is shown offering his last shirt.

XXVII. ROSENFELD IN OLD AGE MISERY

"As a child of caprice, like the usual run of artists and poets, Rosenfeld's relation to his fellow writers and to the Yiddish press was not normal. His excited nature impelled him to attack them, justly at times and unjustly at others. The offended . . . . retaliated by ignoring him." (A. Harkavy, Forverts, 1923). "Of all his great gifts there remained only acrimony, hatred, mordacity—not a trace of the true poetic splendor" (Reuben Brainin, TOG, 1923), Rosenfeld had the ability to hate, scold and bite greatly and thus he found an outlet for the loneliness of his heart." (Joel Entin, Morgn Journal, 1943), "Joel, my life is like a shard/ I look at the leaves/ I sense death, I feel I shall soon die/ Joel, right you are/I shall yet set aflame/the world. I still have glorious desires/ Not only will I attain the heavens/ I want. I will reach God himself!" (From Joel Slonim's poem, "Morris Rosenfeld in Crotona Park".)

In 1912 a fiftieth birthday celebration for Rosenfeld was held at Carnegie Hall in N.Y. Many major figures in Jewish life were present to to offer their respects to Rosenfeld. Addresses by B. Feigenbaum, A. Reisen, Leo Wiener, Rabbi Stephen Wise, among others were heard. R. wrote a poem, "Fifty Years" especially for the occasion. It was a dialogue between an optimist and a pessimist. Similar celebrations were held in Worcester, Mass, Chicago, Ill., (where Jane Addams and Kalman Marmor spoke).

Rosenfeld had begun to write poetry complaining that his friends had deserted him: "Fargessen" (Forgotten), "Gute Fraynd", "Zay Viln Mich

Nit" (They don't want me), "Farvos Ich Layud" (Why I Suffer). The "Yunge" attacked him mercilessly, accusing him of loving money (!) when he was at the brink of starvation, and the young writers of the Jewish press took up the attacks with cartoons and occasional articles. One such cartoon showed R. against a background of tenement houses, saying, "On a bed of money, full of dollars . . . many houses, houses without end he sees." (One has to realize that some of the socialists in the press and among the poets were off the deep end, holding in contempt anyone without their extreme convictions. Incidentally, none of them preferred starvation to success either. ed.) It was not only R. who was thus castigated. Leon Kobrin and other were accused of mounting a war (A Jewish War) against "an invasion" of other European Jewish writers, such as Sholom Aleichem, Peretz, Asch and others. They accused Sholem Asch of coming to America with his deep pockets to get rich. Rosenfeld did not take this lying down. He rose to his defense with many poems, some of which were rude and crude, trying to put down his detractors as immature, ungrateful, talentless and anti-everything. In addition he wrote at least one poem that was sad and moving, revealing his true misery: "Ich zing far zich" (I sing for myself), "Now I am not so easily moved/ I am cautious ere I sing/ The stone alone is my companion here, none else/ For like he I am lonely and friendless."

About a month before R.'s death The Y.L. Peretz Assoc. celebrated his 60th birthday with a banquet. On the tribute of the association, here exhibited, are signed not only his friends but also some of "Di Yunge". The signatures are J.B.Beilin, A. Glanz, M.L.Halpern (one of his worst tormentors),Leon Kobrin,A Kritschmar-Israeli, H. Leivick, A Liessin, Rachel Luria, J. Magidoff, K. Marmor (One of his dearest friends and supporters), Menachem, Jacob Milch, C.J. Minikes, S. Niger (noted critic and writer), A. Reisen, Hillel Rogoff, A.S. Sachs, M. Spector, Taschrak, Morris Vinchevsky and Nochum Yud. (There are some great names in there. Kritschmar-Israeli alone ate more of my mother's blintzes than anyone in the family! Kids can remember anything. ed.)

XXVIII. ROSENFELD'S DEATH

On the night of the 21 to 22 of June, 1923 R. died in loneliness. He died and was buried as he had predicted in one of his poems: "Forsaken in my sickroom/ Alone I lie sad/ Only the mute walls hear/ My groans, my cries./When I shall die wretchedly/ quietly forgotten before my time/ Notable people/ will follow my bier./ It will be an honor then/ To drive the funeral carriage/ and then to cast/ On the grave a shovelful of earth." "Der Tog" wrote: "Death has snatched from our midst the first significant poet that Yiddish produced in America." The "Yidishe Arbeiiter" wrote; "The Workers' poet, but the workers, who sang his poems, did not come to his funeral. No Jewish union official was officially represented there. The singer of the ghetto—but the Ghetto was merely an indifferent spectator at the funeral, "arranged by his fellow writers from a sheer sense of duty. The national poet —but we have read nowhere that at the Young Judeans (a Zionist group, EJG) convention there was as much as a mention of him . . . and yet he was one of the greatest."

At the YIVO exhibition there is a montage of newspaper articles from journals all over the world: Winnepeg, New York, Chicago, Philadelphia, Montreal, Cincinnati, London, San Francisco, Boston, Detroit, Cleveland, New Orleans, Milwaukee, Baltimore, Buffalo, Amsterdam, Paris, Prague, and elsewhere. Not only were there news articles and death notices, there were also personal expressions by most of the notable Jewish writers of the time, some of whom had been his cruelest detractors but who, on this occasion, demonstrated some warmth and humanity towards the poet. Numerous photos are exhibited as well as notices of memorial meetings in Paris, Kopenhagen and Czestochowa, Poland.

XXIX. MISCELLANEOUS ROSENFELDIA

Shown is a page of R.'s "Lider Buch" (Book of Poems) with the poet's presentation, "To my dear friend, the celebrated poet and novelist, N.M. Shaikevitch (Shomer), 1897. R's calling cards. "Receipts indicating that I paid income tax to the government". An item (in the N.Y. Times) that Rosenfeld reduced the rent of his tenants by one dollar a month. A copy of Kipling's poem, "Hymn Before Action", copies of R', poems in "The Open Road", Indiana. Also included are many notices, invitations, photograps of family, friends and opponents from "Di Yunge" as well as manuscripts, single poems, scripts of plays and proposed books.

(A whole universe of items about this one immigrant and his times is on display. With the end of the exhibition the Rosenfeld "universe" es into temporary eclipse, to be partially illuminated here in this volume and whenever someone writes about the immigrant experience and Yiddish history in America. ed.)

(When you have read the following little piece see if you can figure out who the little boy is whom Miss Trommer mentions in this story.)

RECOLLECTIONS OF AN ADMIRER
MY RECOLLECTIONS OF MORRIS ROSENFELD
By Marie Trommer

We invited Morris Rosenfeld, the famous Jewish poet and his wife to visit us on a Sunday afternoon during the Passover holidays of 1922. As we expected our guests in the afternoon, mother and I felt there was still time to go out and do some additional marketing in the morning.

Emerging from the front lawn of our house, we saw a man and a woman, apparently strangers in the neighborhood, peering at the house numbers. We stopped and watched them approach. As they came closer I recognized Morris Rosenfeld and his wife. I had met them previously in the home of their youngest daughter. Of course we gave up our marketing trip and welcomed the Rosenfelds into our house. Mr. Rosenfeld was not very well at the time. The illness, which proved fatal, was already visible in his demeanor. He spoke little.

It was the hour for luncheon. Mother and I served baked carp with horseradish, matzo cheese pie, coffee, cakes and fresh fruit. Rosenfeld seemed to enjoy his food silently, while Mrs. Rosenfeld remarked upon the excellence of our home-made horseradish. She felt that, although she was forbidden spicy foods, our horseradish made her want more. She also admire the baked fish and asked for the recipe.

When Rosenfeld was given coffee he broke his cake into bits and dropped them into his cup. Mrs. Rosenfeld, seeing this action, admonished him, "Don't do that, Morris!" Through with his meal Mr. Rosenfeld became more talkative. He began to tell about the cleverness of his five-year-old grandson, the son of his youngest daughter, married to a dentist. "You wouldn't think that a tiny tot like him would be so smart! Listen to what happened. The father of my son-in-law had recently died. About five weeks after his death we all gathered at my daughter's home. Someone passed a funny remark and my son-in-law laughed. Here my little grandson interrupted, "Papa, how can you laugh after your father has died?" Rosenfeld finished his story and his love for this child emanated from his being.

"Your grandson," my mother remarked, "takes after you. He is evidently capable of deep feeling and affection." Rosenfeld chuckled, pleased. The sympathetic and understanding atmosphere of our home made both Mr. and Mrs. Rosenfeld feel quite at ease. "You remember, Mrs. Trommer," confided Mrs. Rosenfeld to my mother, "the time when your son was staying with us at our country place in the Berkshires? Well, I was telling Morris then that it would have been a fine plan to have your son marry our daughter. But Fate decreed otherwise and she married the dentist."

Rosenfeld looked up from his pear, which he was cutting into small pieces. "Let me tell you about my son-in-law, the dentist. Ever since he learned his Yiddish in Rumania, where he was brought up, he dreamed of coming to America and meeting me! His dream came true!" Rosenfeld resumed eating his pear. "That was a fine dream come true!" replied mother. Rosenfeld then inquired about my writiings and praised my translations of his prose sketches into English. As we conversed, the afternoon drew to a close and mother suggested that our guests stay for dinner. "You hear. Morris! We are asked to stay for dinner!" Mrs Rosenfeld beamed. After the dinner, consisting of chicken and borscht and all other delicacies associated with a Passover meal, we escorted the Rosenfelds to the subway. This was the last time I saw Rosenfeld. His ill-health worsened and his death came in less than two years.

Bibliography

Adams, Hazard. The Interests of Criticism. New York: Harcourt, Brace and World. 1969

Aleichem, Sholom. (by Halkin, Hillel.) Tevye and the Railroad Stories. New York: Library of Yiddish Classics. 1987

Bialostotski, B. M. Rosenfeld. New York: Farlag Kinder Ring, Educational Committee, Workmen's Circle. 1941

Cohen, Mortimer T. Poems of Morris Rosenfeld Transliterated with English Word Meanings. New York: Retriever Books. 1979

Connolly, Francis X. Poetry, Its Power and Wisdom. New York: Charles Scribners. 1960.

Elbogen, Ismar. A Century of Jewish Life. Philadelphia: The Jewish Publication Society of America. 1945

Fine, Morris; Himmelfarb, Milton. American Jewish Yearbook. Philadelphia: The Jewish Publication Society of America. 1961

Galvin, Herman; Tamarkin, Stanley. The Yiddish Dictionary Sourcebook. Hoboken: Ktav Publication Co. 1986.

George, H.J. Wordsworth's Preface and Essays on Poetry. New York: 1892

Goldberg, Itche; Rosenfeld, Max. Morris Rosenfeld: Selections From His Poetry and Prose. New York: Yiddisher Kultur Farband. 1964

Goldberg, Itche. Let's Sing a Yiddish Song. New York: Kinderbook Publication. 1985

Goldenthal, Dr. Leon. Toil And Triumph. New York: Pageant Press. 1960.

Gordon, Albert. Jews in Suburbia. Boston: Beacon Press. 1959

Grayzel, Solomon. A History of the Jews. Philadelphia: The Jewish Publication Society of America, 1965

Greenstone, Julius R. The Messiah Idea In Jewish History. Philadelphia: The Jewish Publication Society of America. 1906.

Gutin, Jo Ann C., That Fine Madness, New York: Discover Magazine, October 1996

Gwynn, Frederick L., Condee, R.W., Lewis, A.O. Jr. The Case For Poetry. Englewood Cliffs: Prentice Hall. 1954

Hapgood, Hutchins. The Spirit of the Ghetto. New York: Schocken Books. 1902, 1966

Harshav, Benjamin and Barbara. American Yiddish Poetry. Berkeley: U. of California Press, 1986

Harshav, Benjamin. The Meaning of Yiddish. Berkeley: University of California Press. 1990.

Hautzig, Esther. I.L. Peretz: The Seven Good Years, etc. Philadelphia: The Jewish Publication Society of America. 1984.

Howe,I.; Wisse, Ruth R. The Best Of Sholom Aleichem. Northvale, New Jersey: Jason Aronson, Inc.1989

Howe, Irving; Wisse, Ruth; Shmeruk, Khone. The Penguin Book Of Modern Yiddish Verse. New York: Viking Penguin, Inc. 1987

Howe, Irving. The World of Our Fathers. New York: Simon and Shuster. 1976

Howe. Irving, Greenberg, Eliezer. A Treasury of Yiddish Poetry. New York: Schocken Books. 1976

Karp, Abraham J. Haven And Home. New York: Schocken Books. 1985.

Kogos, Frederick. Dictionary of Yiddish Slang and Idioms. New York; Paperback Library. 1969.

Kramer, Aaron. The Teardrop Millionaire. New York: Emma Lazarus Clubs of Manhattan. 1955.

Liptzin, Sol. A History of Yiddish Literature. Jonathan David Publ. Middle Village, New York. 1985

Madison, Charles. Yiddish Liter., Its Scope and Major Writers. New York; Schocken Books. 1971.

Meltzer, Milton. The Jewish Americans. New York: Harper Collins. 1982.

Mlotek, Eleanor Gordon. Mir Trogn A Gezang. New York: Workmen's Circle. 1987

Morris, Walker, Bradshaw. Imaginative Literature. New York: Harcourt, Brace. 1968.

Moses, Dr. Julius. Hebraische Melodien, Eine Anthologie. Berlin: Curt Wigand. 1907.

N.Y. Cooperative Society. Addresses on 250th Anniversary of Jewish Settlement in the United States. New York: New York Coop Soc. 1905

Ober, Warren U.; Seat, William R. The Enigma of Poe. Boston: D.C. Heath and Co. 1960

Perrine, Laurence. Sound and Sense. New York: Harcourt, Brace, Jovanovich. 1973.

Preminger, Alex. Princeton Encyclopedia of Poetry and Poetics. Princeton: Princeton University Press. 1974

Raskin, Philip M. An Anthology of Modern Jewish Poetry. New York: Behrman's Jewish Book Shop. 1927

Reiss, Edmund. Elements of Literary Analysis. Cleveland: The World Publishing Co. 1967

Richards, I.A. Practical Criticism, New York, Harcourt, Brace and World, 1929

Richardson, H. Edward; Shroyer, Frederick B. Muse of Fire. New York: Knopf. 1971.

Rogoff, Harry. Nine Yiddish Writers. East and West. 1913–1915

Rosenfeld, Morris. Historische Schrifter. New York: Workmen's Circle. 1941

Rosenfeld, Morris. "Lieder" New York: Star Hebrew Book Co. 1910

Rosenfeld, Morris. Gezamelte Lieder (Collected Poems). New York: International Library Publishing Co. 1906

Rosenfeld, Morris. Schriften Fon Moris Rosenfeld. New York: The International Library Publishing Co. 1910.(Six Volumes)

Rosenfeld, Morris. Lieder Des Ghetto. Feivel and Lilien. Berlin: Marquardt & Co. 1910.

Rosenfeld, Morris. Songs From the Ghetto. Boston: Copeland and Day. 1898.

Rosenfeld, Morris. Dem Buch fon Libe. New York: M. Guravitch.1914

Rosenfeld, Morris. Grine Tsoris. New York: Literature Publ. Co. 1919

Rosenfeld, Morris. Gevelte Schriften. New York: Forverts. 1912

Rosenfeld, Morris. Oysgeklibene Schriften. Buenos Aires: Shmuel Rozshanski. 1962

Rosenfeld, Morris. Morris Rosenfeld's Briv. Lifschutz, E. Buenos Aires: Yiddishe Visenshaftlekher Inst. YIVO. 1955

Rosten, Leo. The Joys of Yiddish. New York: Pocket Books. 1968.

Rubin, Ruth. Jewish Folk Songs. New York: Oak Publications. 1980.

Rubin, Ruth. Voices of a People. Philadelphia: The Jewish Publication Society of America, 1979.

Sachar, Howard M. The Course of Modern Jewish History. Cleveland and New York: The World Publishing Co. 1958

Shepard, Richard F.; Levi, Vicki Gold. Live and Be Well. New York: Ballantine Books. 1982

Simonhoff, Harry, Saga Of American Jewry. New York: Arco Publishing. Co., 1959

Sklare, Marshall. The Jews. Social Patterns. Toronto: Collier, Macmillan. 1958

Stein, Leon. The Triangle Fire. New York: Carroll and Graf, Quicksilver Edition. 1962

Stone, Allan A.,Stone, Sue Smart, The Abnormal Personality Through Literature: Englewood Cliffs, New Jersey: Prentice Hall, 1966

Takaki, Ronald. A Different Mirror. New York: Little, Brown. 1993

Van Dorn, Mark. An Anthology of World Poetry. New York: Blue Ribbon Books. 1941.

Wallechinsky, David; Wallace, Irving. New York: Doubleday. 1975

Warren, Robert Penn; Brooks, Cleanth. Understanding Poetry. New York: Holt, Rinehart. 1976

Wisse, Ruth. I.L. Peretz and the Making of Jewish Culture, Seattle: University of Washington Press,1991.

YIVO. Szajkowski, Z. Catalogue of the Exhibition: Morris Rosenfeld and His Time. New York: YIVO. 1962